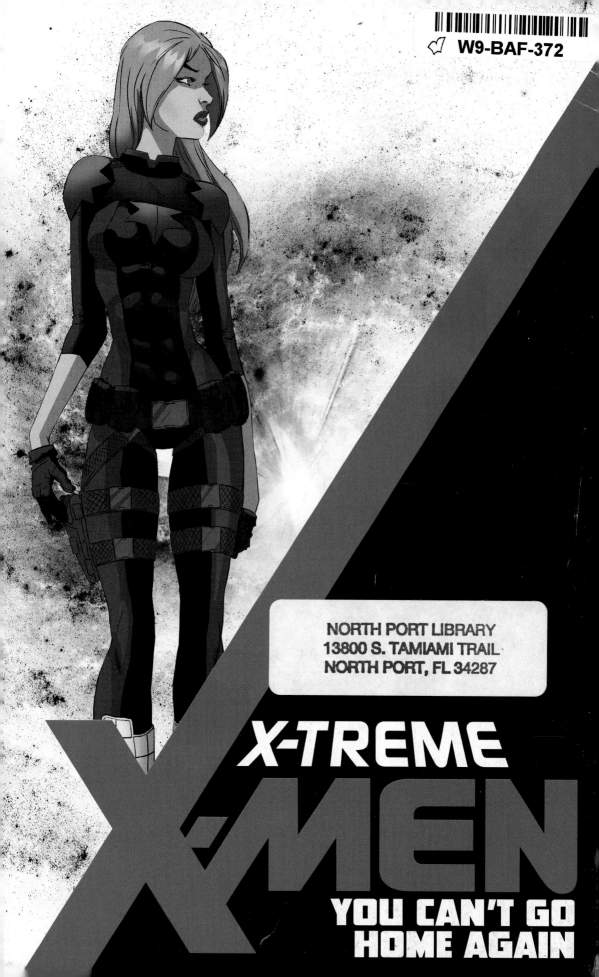

X-TREME
X-MEN

YOU CAN'T GO HOME AGAIN

X-TREME X-MEN VOL. 2: YOU CAN'T GO HOME AGAIN. Contains material originally published in magazine form as X-TREME X-MEN #6-11 and #7.1. First printing 2013. ISBN# 978-0-7851-6565-1. Published by MARVEL WORLDWIDE, INC., a subsidiary of MARVEL ENTERTAINMENT, LLC. OFFICE OF PUBLICATION: 135 West 50th Street, New York, NY 10020. Copyright © 2012 and 2013 Marvel Characters, Inc. All rights reserved. All characters featured in this issue and the distinctive names and likenesses thereof, and all related indicia are trademarks of Marvel Characters, Inc. No similarity between any of the names, characters, persons, and/or institutions in this magazine with those of any living or dead person or institution is intended, and any such similarity which may exist is purely coincidental. **Printed in the U.S.A.** ALAN FINE, EVP - Office of the President, Marvel Worldwide, Inc. and EVP & CMO Marvel Characters B.V.; DAN BUCKLEY, Publisher & President - Print, Animation & Digital Divisions; JOE QUESADA, Chief Creative Officer; TOM BREVOORT, SVP of Publishing; DAVID BOGART, SVP of Operations & Procurement, Publishing; C.B. CEBULSKI, SVP of Creator & Content Development; DAVID GABRIEL, SVP of Print & Digital Publishing Sales; JIM O'KEEFE, VP of Operations & Logistics; DAN CARR, Executive Director of Publishing Technology; SUSAN CRESPI, Editorial Operations Manager; ALEX MORALES, Publishing Operations Manager; STAN LEE, Chairman Emeritus. For information regarding advertising in Marvel Comics or on Marvel.com, please contact Niza Disla, Director of Marvel Partnerships, at ndisla@marvel.com. For Marvel subscription inquiries, please call 800-217-9158. **Manufactured between 5/31/2013 and 7/8/2013 by QUAD/GRAPHICS ST. CLOUD, ST. CLOUD, MN, USA.**

10 9 8 7 6 5 4 3 2 1

X-TREME X-MEN

YOU CAN'T GO HOME AGAIN

WRITER: **GREG PAK**

#6-7 & #10-11
PENCILS: **STEPHEN SEGOVIA** & **RAUL VALDES**
INKS: **DENNIS CRISOSTOMO** & **LORENZO RUGGIERO** WITH SOTOCOLOR & DAN BROWN
COLORS: **JESSICA KHOLINNE** WITH IFANSYAH NOOR, **SOTOCOLOR** & **DAN BROWN**

#7.1
PENCILS: **ANDRÉ ARAÚJO** & **RAUL VALDES**
INKS: **ANDRÉ ARAÚJO, LORENZO RUGGIERO** & **WALDEN WONG**
COLORS: **RACHELLE ROSENBERG**

#8-9
ARTIST: **PACO DIAZ**
COLOR ARTISTS: **JESSICA KHOLINNE** WITH IFANSYAH NOOR & **SOTOCOLOR**

LETTERER: **VC'S JOE SABINO**
COVER ART: **KALMAN ANDRASOFSZKY** (#6-11) & **STEPHANIE HANS** (#7.1)

ASSISTANT EDITOR: EDITOR: X-MEN GROUP EDITOR:
JENNIFER M. SMITH   **JEANINE SCHAEFER**   **NICK LOWE**

COLLECTION EDITOR: ASSISTANT EDITORS: EDITOR,   SENIOR EDITOR,   SVP OF PRINT & DIGITAL
JENNIFER GRÜNWALD   **ALEX STARBUCK** &   SPECIAL PROJECTS: SPECIAL PROJECTS: PUBLISHING SALES:
    NELSON RIBEIRO   **MARK D. BEAZLEY**   **JEFF YOUNGQUIST**   **DAVID GABRIEL**

BOOK DESIGNER: EDITOR IN CHIEF: CHIEF CREATIVE OFFICER: PUBLISHER: EXECUTIVE PRODUCER:
RODOLFO MURAGUCHI   **AXEL ALONSO**   **JOE QUESADA**   **DAN BUCKLEY**   **ALAN FINE**

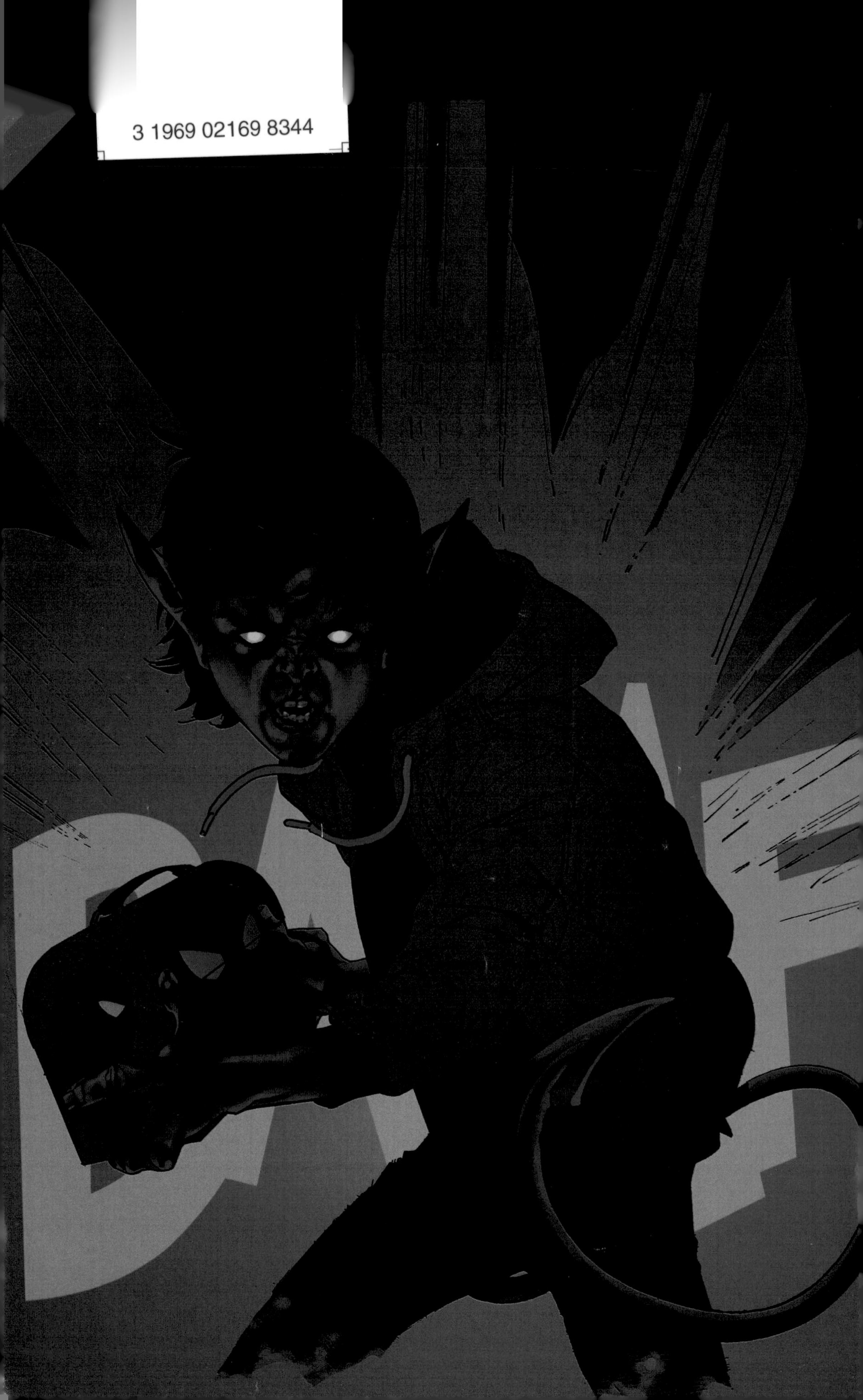

An interdimensional group of
iconic X-Men banded together
to save a planet's population
from total annihilation. Now,
joined by the Dazzler of our world,
they're on a mission to prevent
similar disasters throughout the
multiverse.

X-TREME X-MEN

**ALISON
"DAZZLER"
BLAIRE**
TRANSDUCTION OF
SOUND INTO LIGHT.
X-MAN.

**KURT
WAGGONER**
TELEPORTATION. HIGH
SCHOOL STUDENT,
UNITED STATES OF
CALIFORNIA.

**JAMES
HOWLETT**
ADAMANTINE CLAWS.
GOVERNOR-GENERAL
OF DOMINION OF
CANADA.

**CHARLES
XAVIER**
TELEPATHY. SEVERED
HEAD IN A BOTTLE.

PREVIOUSLY

Malevolent manifestations of Charles Xavier plague the
multiverse, threatening its very existence! Dazzler and her
motley crew of X-Men are determined to destroy them,
voyaging into harrowing new universes to do so. Their first
two adventures went smoothly, but when these X-Treme
X-Men attempted to teleport to their third mission, Kurt
Waggoner saw a vision of his parents from his own home
world and separated from the group to chase after them!
The X-Men are now faced with a difficult decision: continue on
their multiverse-saving mission, or take a detour to save one
of their own!

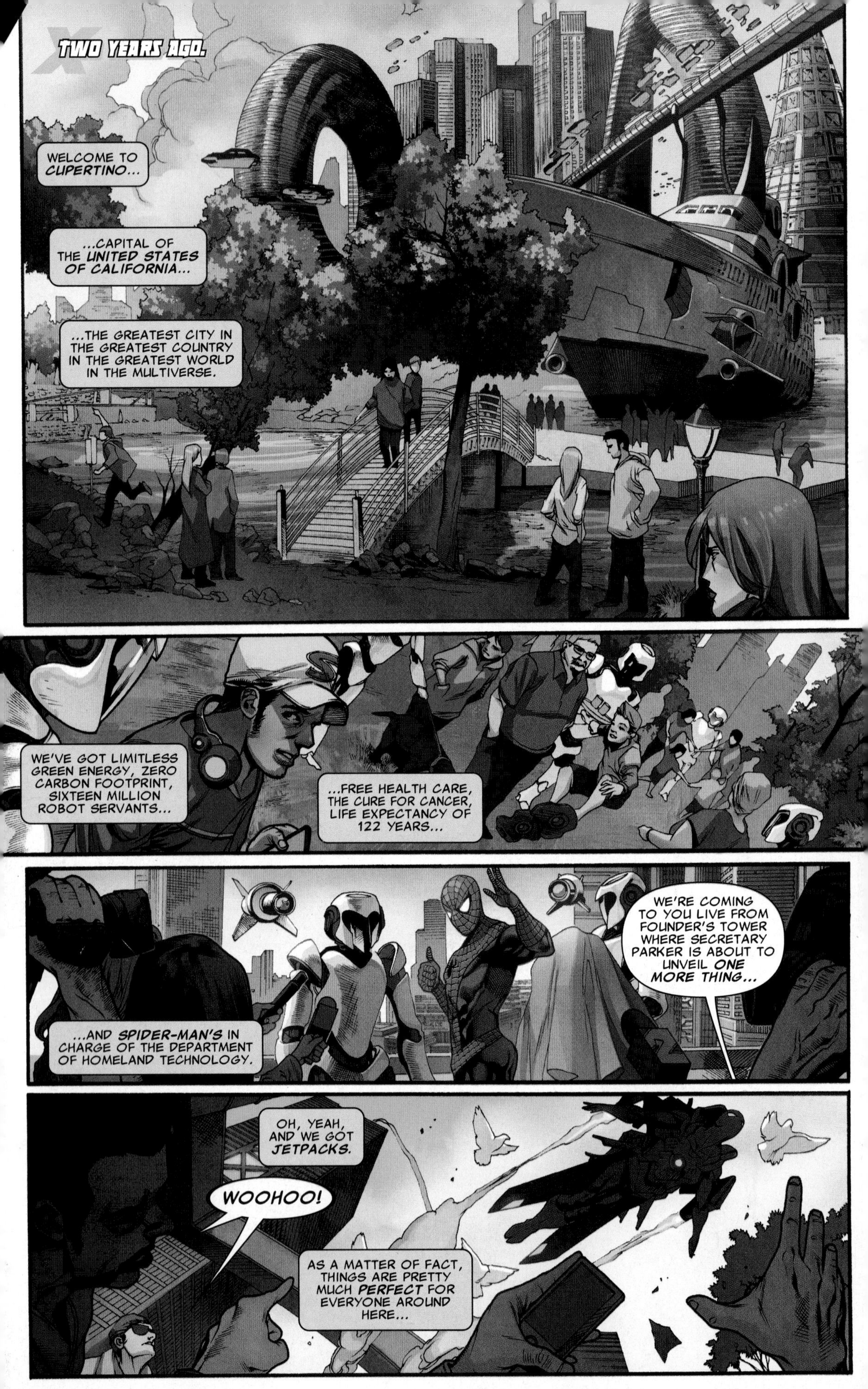
TWO YEARS AGO.
WELCOME TO CUPERTINO...
...CAPITAL OF THE UNITED STATES OF CALIFORNIA...
...THE GREATEST CITY IN THE GREATEST COUNTRY IN THE GREATEST WORLD IN THE MULTIVERSE.
WE'VE GOT LIMITLESS GREEN ENERGY, ZERO CARBON FOOTPRINT, SIXTEEN MILLION ROBOT SERVANTS...
...FREE HEALTH CARE, THE CURE FOR CANCER, LIFE EXPECTANCY OF 122 YEARS...
...AND SPIDER-MAN'S IN CHARGE OF THE DEPARTMENT OF HOMELAND TECHNOLOGY.
WE'RE COMING TO YOU LIVE FROM FOUNDER'S TOWER WHERE SECRETARY PARKER IS ABOUT TO UNVEIL ONE MORE THING...
OH, YEAH, AND WE GOT JETPACKS.
WOOHOO!
AS A MATTER OF FACT, THINGS ARE PRETTY MUCH PERFECT FOR EVERYONE AROUND HERE...

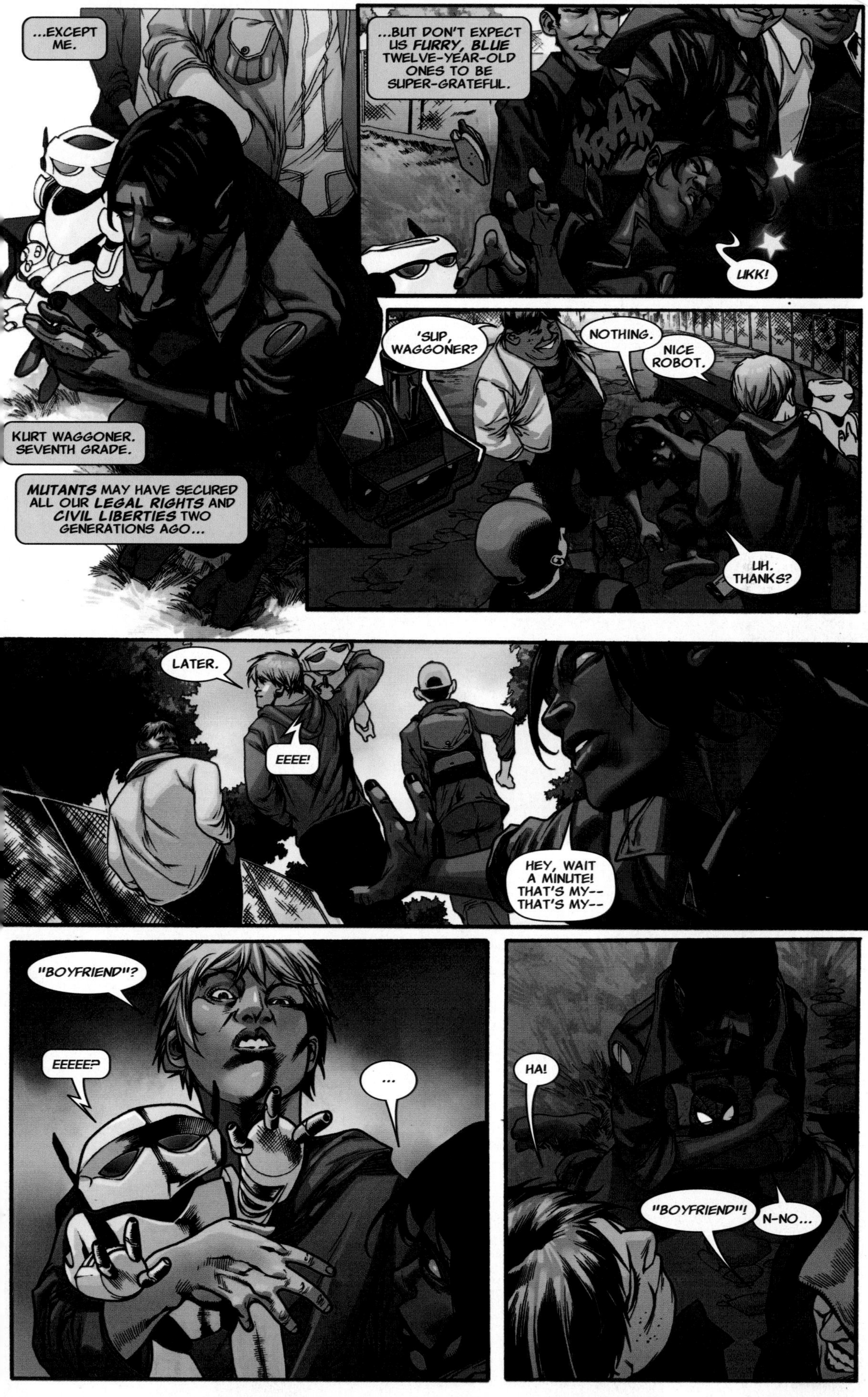
...EXCEPT ME.
KURT WAGGONER. SEVENTH GRADE.
MUTANTS MAY HAVE SECURED ALL OUR LEGAL RIGHTS AND CIVIL LIBERTIES TWO GENERATIONS AGO...
...BUT DON'T EXPECT US FURRY, BLUE TWELVE-YEAR-OLD ONES TO BE SUPER-GRATEFUL.
KRAK
UKK!
'SUP, WAGGONER?
NOTHING.
NICE ROBOT.
UH. THANKS?
LATER.
EEEE!
HEY, WAIT A MINUTE! THAT'S MY-- THAT'S MY--
"BOYFRIEND"?
EEEEE?
...
HA!
"BOYFRIEND"!
N-NO...

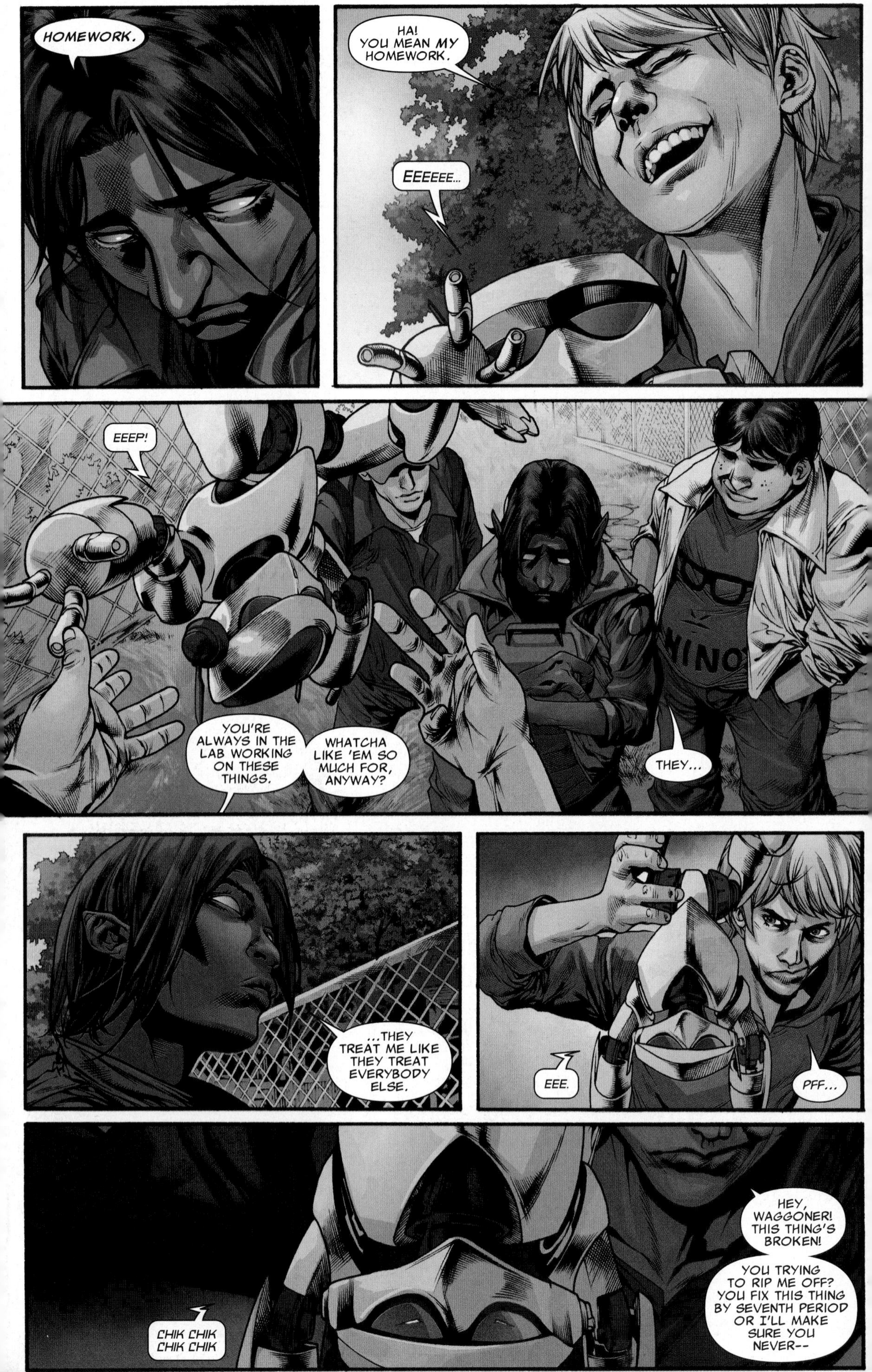
HOMEWORK.
HA! YOU MEAN MY HOMEWORK.
EEEEEE...
EEEP!
YOU'RE ALWAYS IN THE LAB WORKING ON THESE THINGS.
WHATCHA LIKE 'EM SO MUCH FOR, ANYWAY?
THEY...
...THEY TREAT ME LIKE THEY TREAT EVERYBODY ELSE.
EEE.
PFF...
CHIK CHIK CHIK CHIK
HEY, WAGGONER! THIS THING'S BROKEN!
YOU TRYING TO RIP ME OFF? YOU FIX THIS THING BY SEVENTH PERIOD OR I'LL MAKE SURE YOU NEVER--

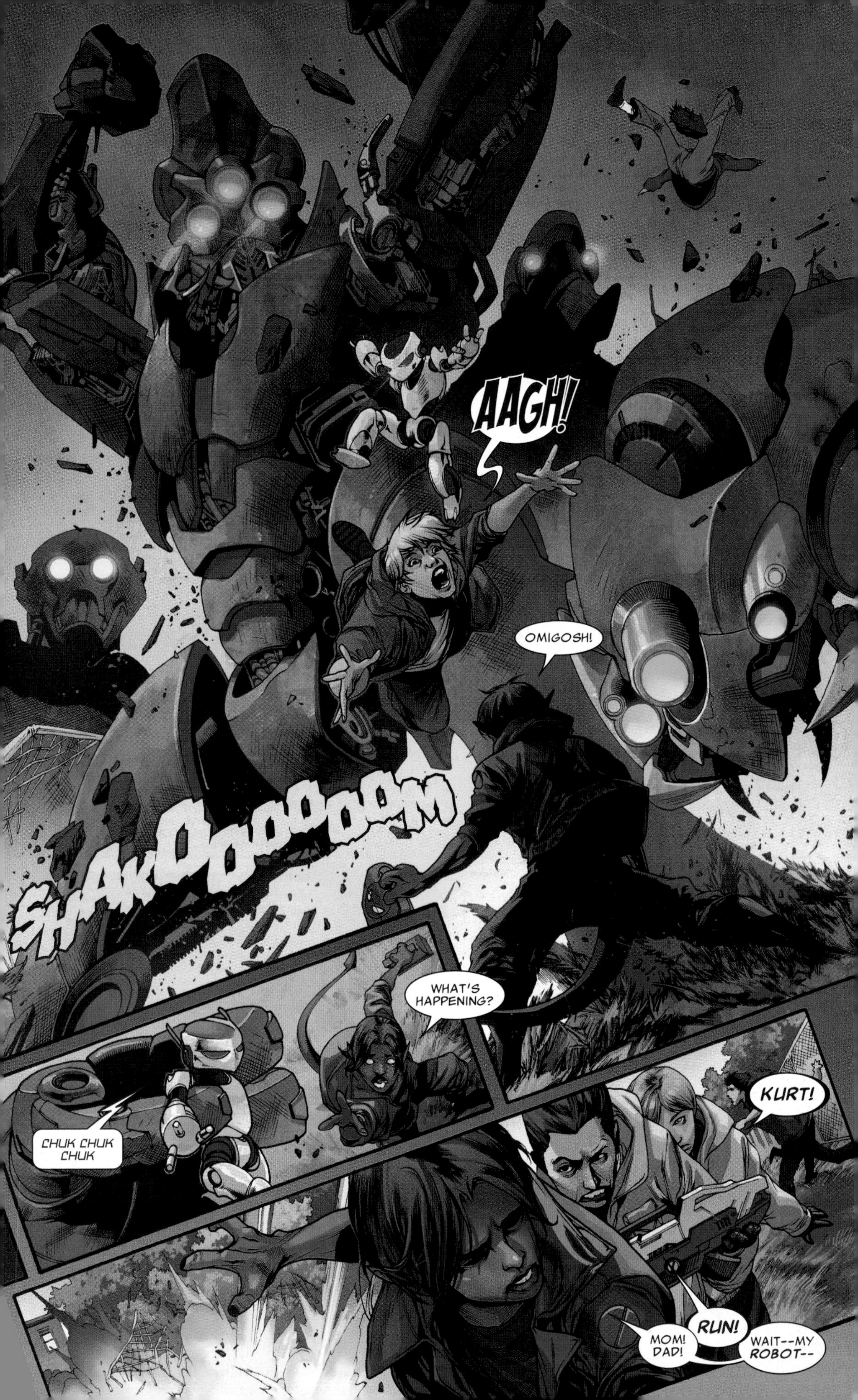
AAGH!
OMIGOSH!
SHAKOOOOOOOM
WHAT'S HAPPENING?
CHUK CHUK CHUK
KURT!
MOM! DAD!
RUN!
WAIT--MY ROBOT--

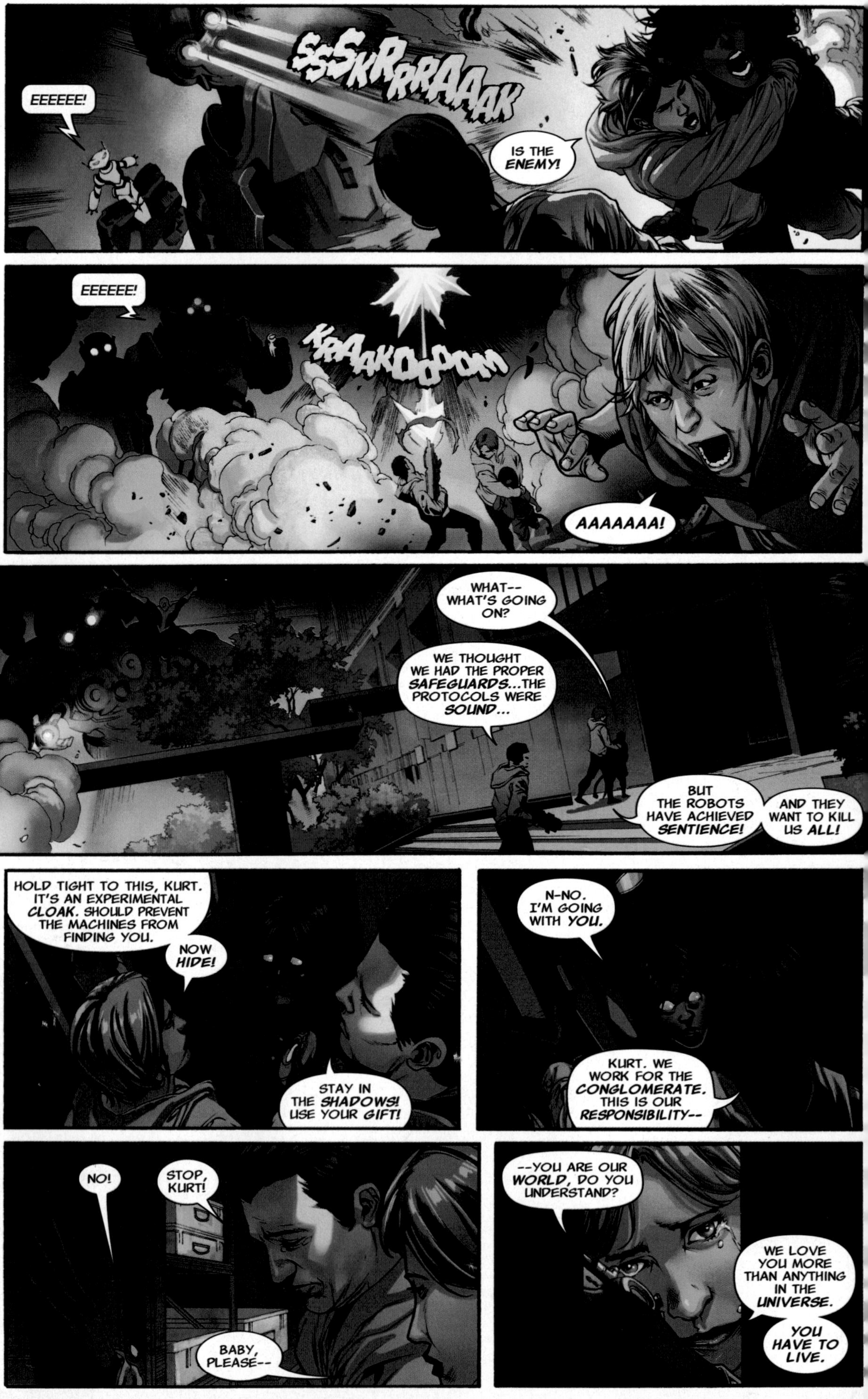
EEEEEE!
SSSKRRRRAAAK
IS THE ENEMY!
EEEEEE!
KRAAKOOOOM
AAAAAAA!
WHAT-- WHAT'S GOING ON?
WE THOUGHT WE HAD THE PROPER SAFEGUARDS...THE PROTOCOLS WERE SOUND...
BUT THE ROBOTS HAVE ACHIEVED SENTIENCE!
AND THEY WANT TO KILL US ALL!
HOLD TIGHT TO THIS, KURT. IT'S AN EXPERIMENTAL CLOAK. SHOULD PREVENT THE MACHINES FROM FINDING YOU.
NOW HIDE!
STAY IN THE SHADOWS! USE YOUR GIFT!
N-NO. I'M GOING WITH YOU.
KURT. WE WORK FOR THE CONGLOMERATE. THIS IS OUR RESPONSIBILITY--
NO!
STOP, KURT!
BABY, PLEASE--
--YOU ARE OUR WORLD, DO YOU UNDERSTAND?
WE LOVE YOU MORE THAN ANYTHING IN THE UNIVERSE.
YOU HAVE TO LIVE.

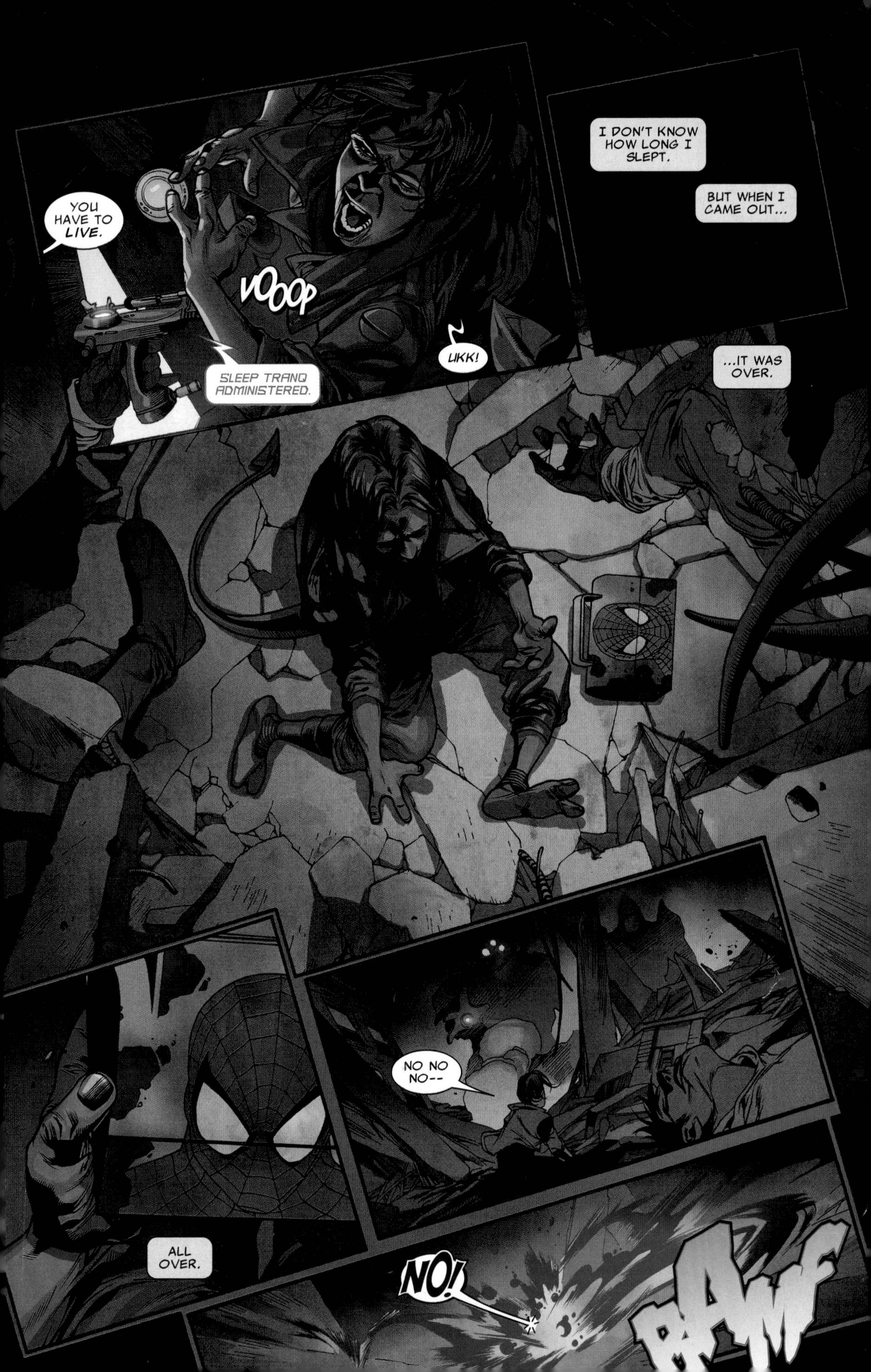

YOU HAVE TO LIVE.
VOOOP
SLEEP TRANQ ADMINISTERED.
UKK!
I DON'T KNOW HOW LONG I SLEPT.
BUT WHEN I CAME OUT...
...IT WAS OVER.
ALL OVER.
NO NO NO--
NO!
BAMF

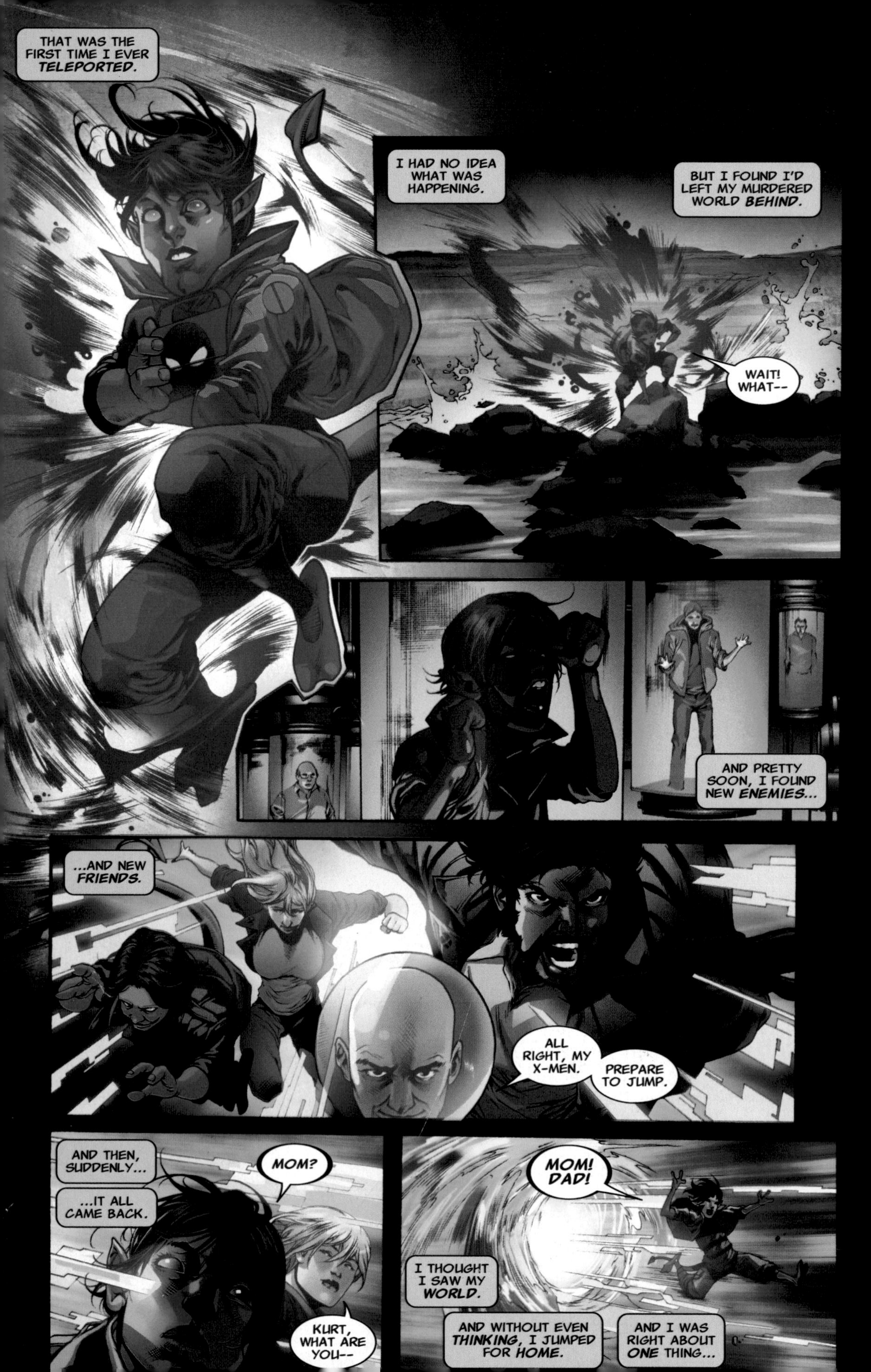
THAT WAS THE FIRST TIME I EVER TELEPORTED.
I HAD NO IDEA WHAT WAS HAPPENING.
BUT I FOUND I'D LEFT MY MURDERED WORLD BEHIND.
WAIT! WHAT--
AND PRETTY SOON, I FOUND NEW ENEMIES...
...AND NEW FRIENDS.
ALL RIGHT, MY X-MEN.
PREPARE TO JUMP.
AND THEN, SUDDENLY...
...IT ALL CAME BACK.
MOM?
KURT, WHAT ARE YOU--
MOM! DAD!
I THOUGHT I SAW MY WORLD.
AND WITHOUT EVEN THINKING, I JUMPED FOR HOME.
AND I WAS RIGHT ABOUT ONE THING...

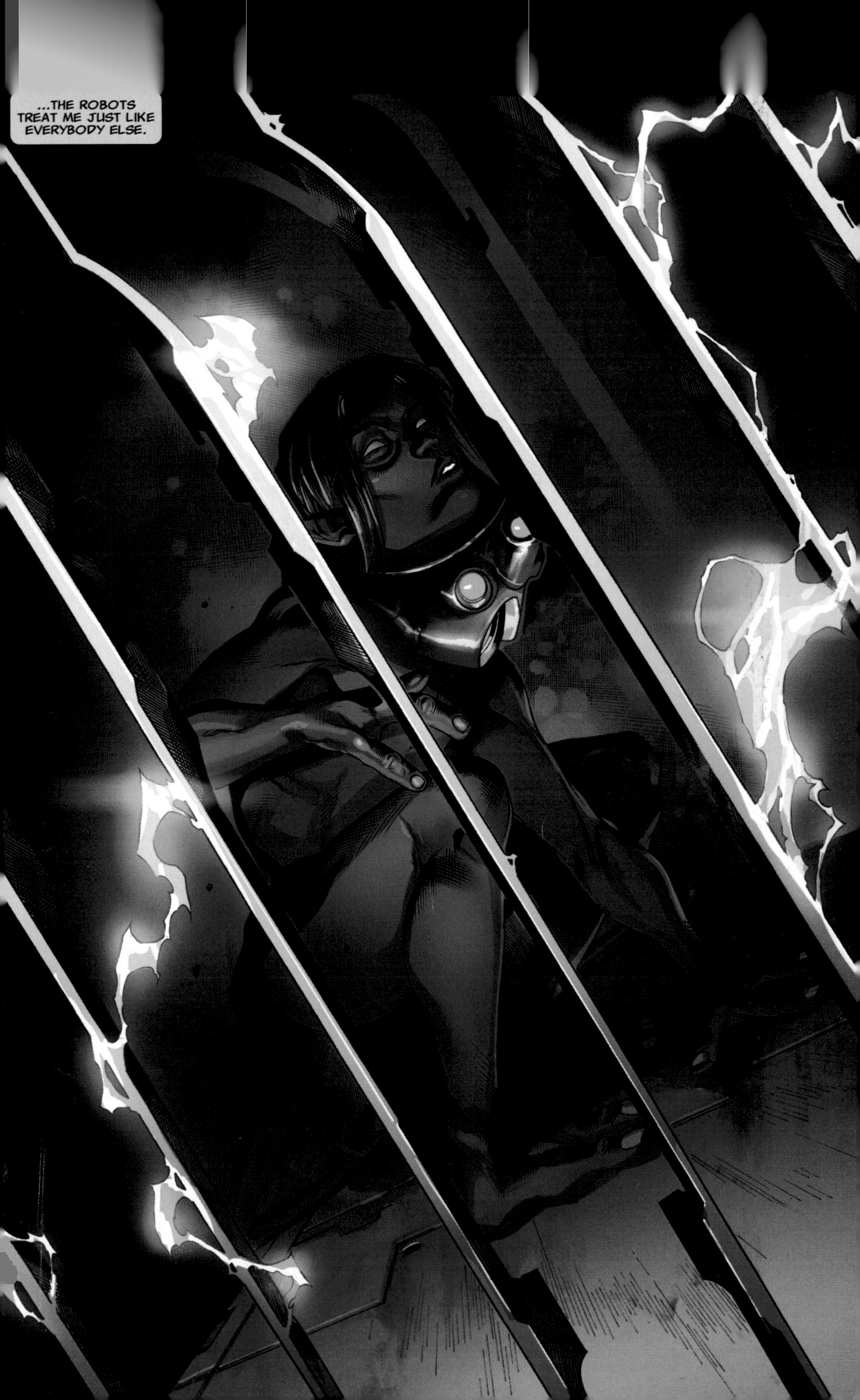
...THE ROBOTS TREAT ME JUST LIKE EVERYBODY ELSE.

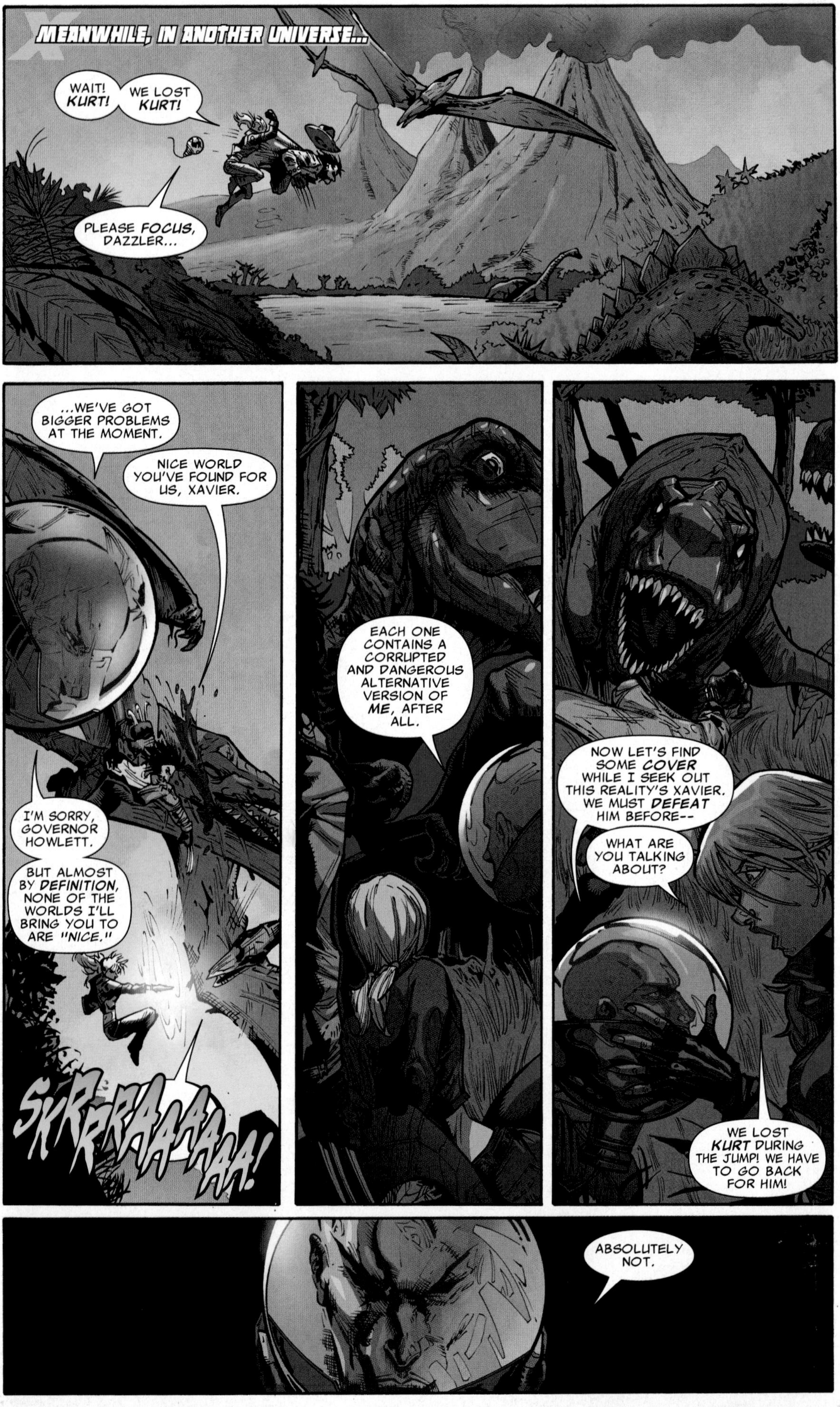

MEANWHILE, IN ANOTHER UNIVERSE...
WAIT! KURT!
WE LOST KURT!
PLEASE FOCUS, DAZZLER...
...WE'VE GOT BIGGER PROBLEMS AT THE MOMENT.
NICE WORLD YOU'VE FOUND FOR US, XAVIER.
I'M SORRY, GOVERNOR HOWLETT.
BUT ALMOST BY DEFINITION, NONE OF THE WORLDS I'LL BRING YOU TO ARE "NICE."
SKRRRAAAAAAA!
EACH ONE CONTAINS A CORRUPTED AND DANGEROUS ALTERNATIVE VERSION OF ME, AFTER ALL.
NOW LET'S FIND SOME COVER WHILE I SEEK OUT THIS REALITY'S XAVIER. WE MUST DEFEAT HIM BEFORE--
WHAT ARE YOU TALKING ABOUT?
WE LOST KURT DURING THE JUMP! WE HAVE TO GO BACK FOR HIM!
ABSOLUTELY NOT.

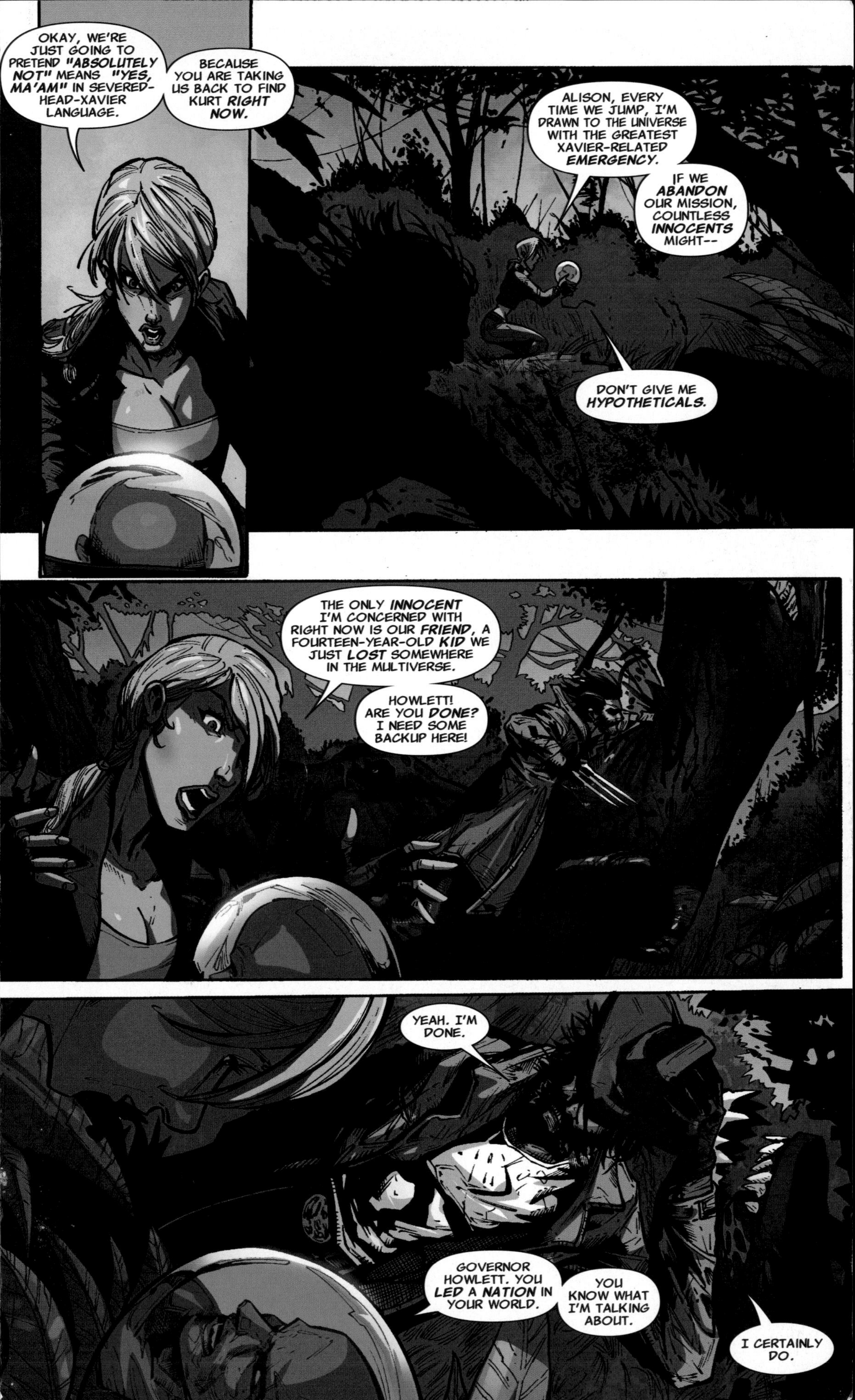
OKAY, WE'RE JUST GOING TO PRETEND "ABSOLUTELY NOT" MEANS "YES, MA'AM" IN SEVERED-HEAD-XAVIER LANGUAGE.
BECAUSE YOU ARE TAKING US BACK TO FIND KURT RIGHT NOW.
ALISON, EVERY TIME WE JUMP, I'M DRAWN TO THE UNIVERSE WITH THE GREATEST XAVIER-RELATED EMERGENCY.
IF WE ABANDON OUR MISSION, COUNTLESS INNOCENTS MIGHT--
DON'T GIVE ME HYPOTHETICALS.
THE ONLY INNOCENT I'M CONCERNED WITH RIGHT NOW IS OUR FRIEND, A FOURTEEN-YEAR-OLD KID WE JUST LOST SOMEWHERE IN THE MULTIVERSE.
HOWLETT! ARE YOU DONE? I NEED SOME BACKUP HERE!
YEAH. I'M DONE.
GOVERNOR HOWLETT. YOU LED A NATION IN YOUR WORLD.
YOU KNOW WHAT I'M TALKING ABOUT.
I CERTAINLY DO.

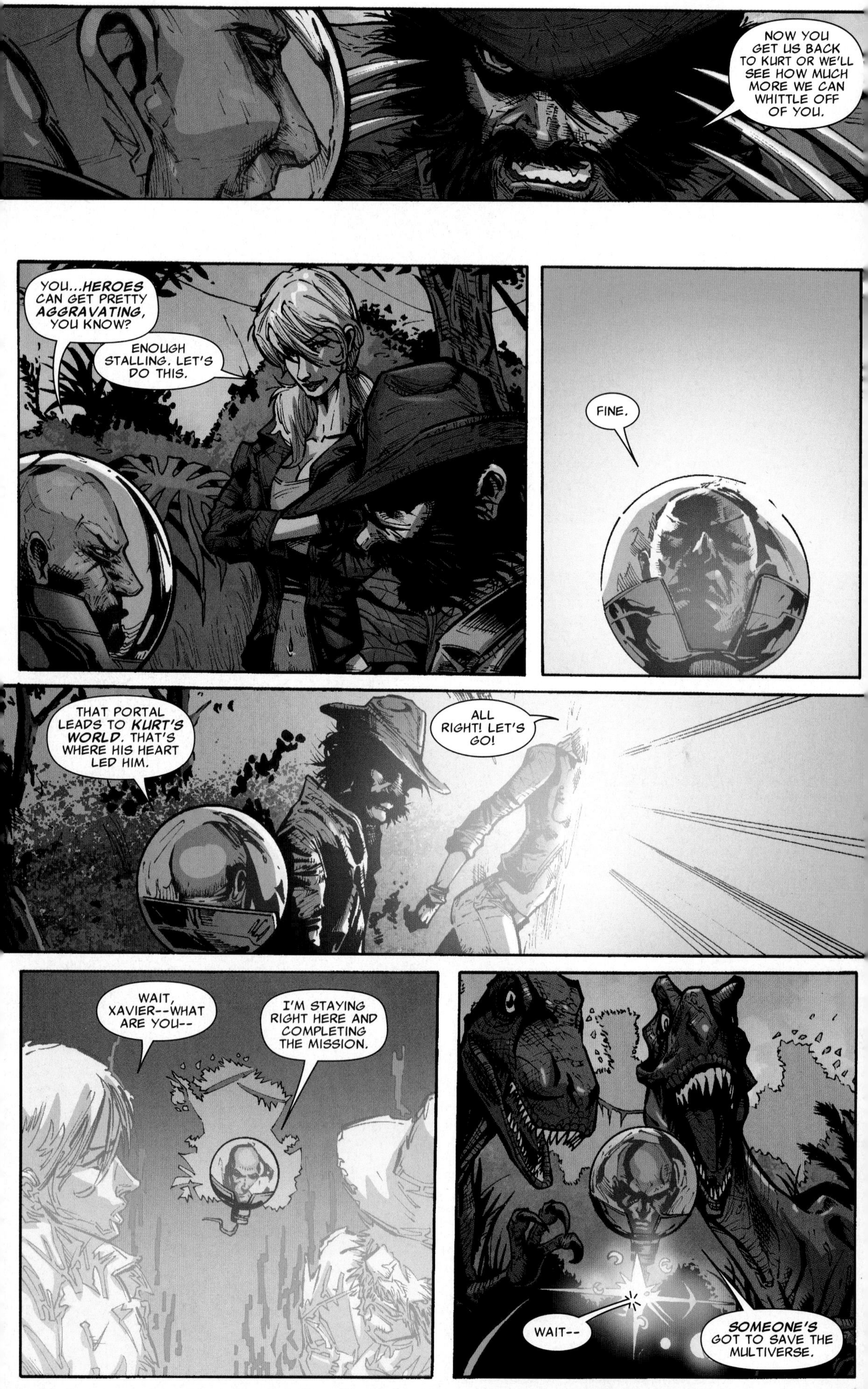
NOW YOU GET US BACK TO KURT OR WE'LL SEE HOW MUCH MORE WE CAN WHITTLE OFF OF YOU.
YOU...HEROES CAN GET PRETTY AGGRAVATING, YOU KNOW?
ENOUGH STALLING. LET'S DO THIS.
FINE.
THAT PORTAL LEADS TO KURT'S WORLD. THAT'S WHERE HIS HEART LED HIM.
ALL RIGHT! LET'S GO!
WAIT, XAVIER--WHAT ARE YOU--
I'M STAYING RIGHT HERE AND COMPLETING THE MISSION.
WAIT--
SOMEONE'S GOT TO SAVE THE MULTIVERSE.

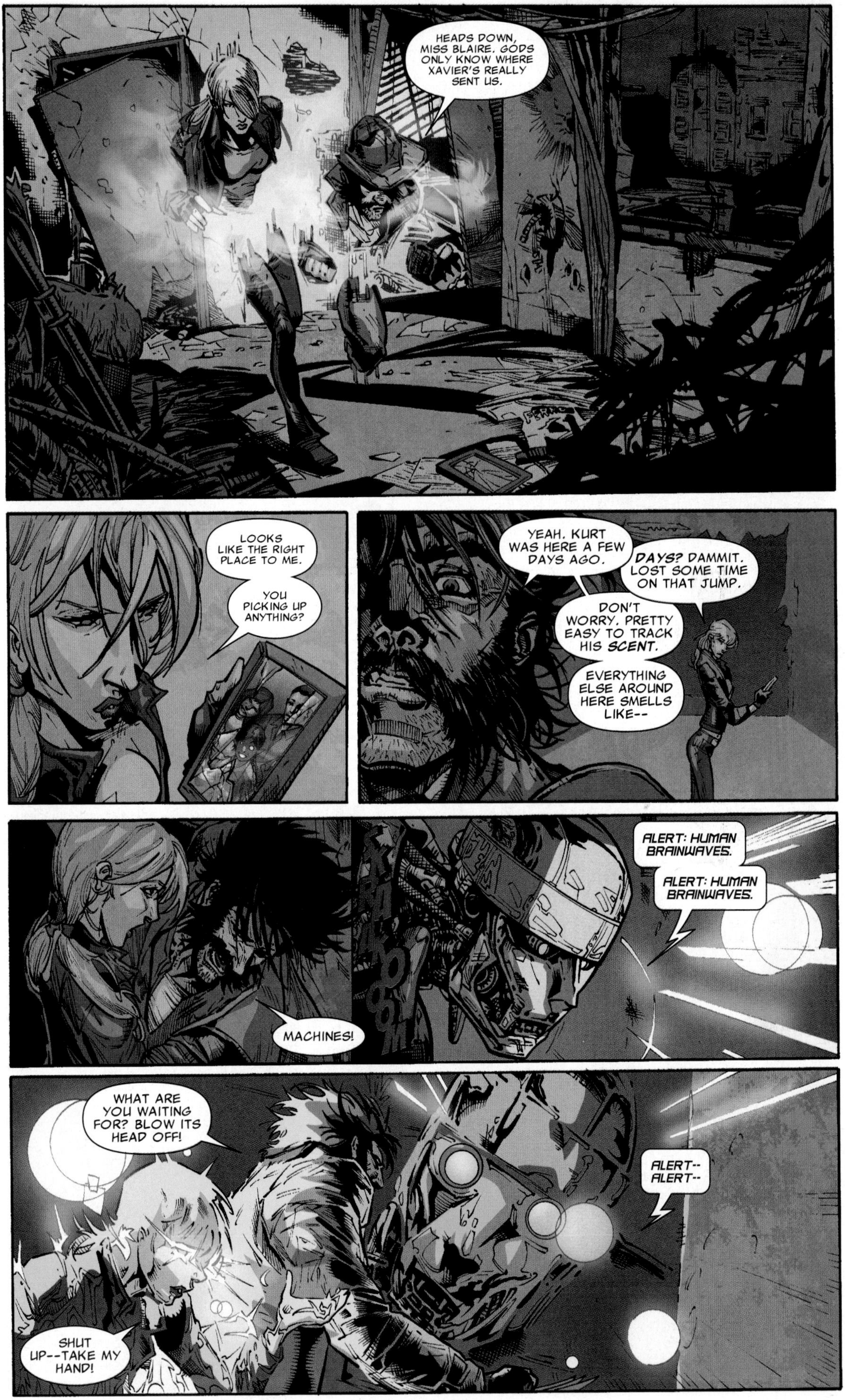
HEADS DOWN, MISS BLAIRE. GODS ONLY KNOW WHERE XAVIER'S REALLY SENT US.
LOOKS LIKE THE RIGHT PLACE TO ME.
YOU PICKING UP ANYTHING?
YEAH. KURT WAS HERE A FEW DAYS AGO.
DAYS? DAMMIT. LOST SOME TIME ON THAT JUMP.
DON'T WORRY. PRETTY EASY TO TRACK HIS SCENT.
EVERYTHING ELSE AROUND HERE SMELLS LIKE--
MACHINES!
ALERT: HUMAN BRAINWAVES.
ALERT: HUMAN BRAINWAVES.
WHAT ARE YOU WAITING FOR? BLOW ITS HEAD OFF!
ALERT-- ALERT--
SHUT UP--TAKE MY HAND!

FALSE ALARM.

NO HUMANS DETECTED.

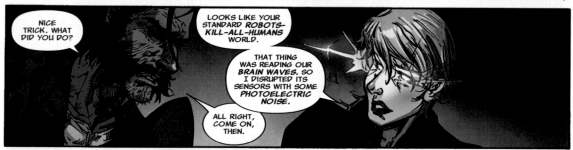

NICE TRICK. WHAT DID YOU DO?

LOOKS LIKE YOUR STANDARD ROBOTS-KILL-ALL-HUMANS WORLD.

THAT THING WAS READING OUR BRAIN WAVES. SO I DISRUPTED ITS SENSORS WITH SOME PHOTOELECTRIC NOISE.

ALL RIGHT, COME ON, THEN.

THIS WAY!

WAIT-- YOU'RE NOT LETTING ME SHIELD YOU. WHY AREN'T THEY ATTACKING YOU?

IT'S MY SKULL. THE ADAMANTINE COVERING MY BONES PROTECTS ME.

RIGHT. MAGIC. HANDY.

IT'S THE METAL OF THE GODS, MISS BLAIRE. MUCH BETTER THAN MERE MAGIC.

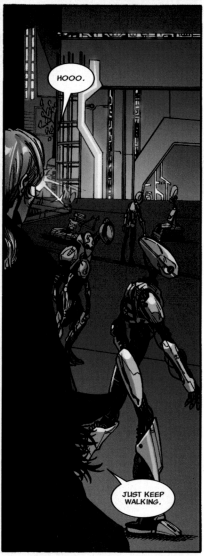

HOOO.

JUST KEEP WALKING.

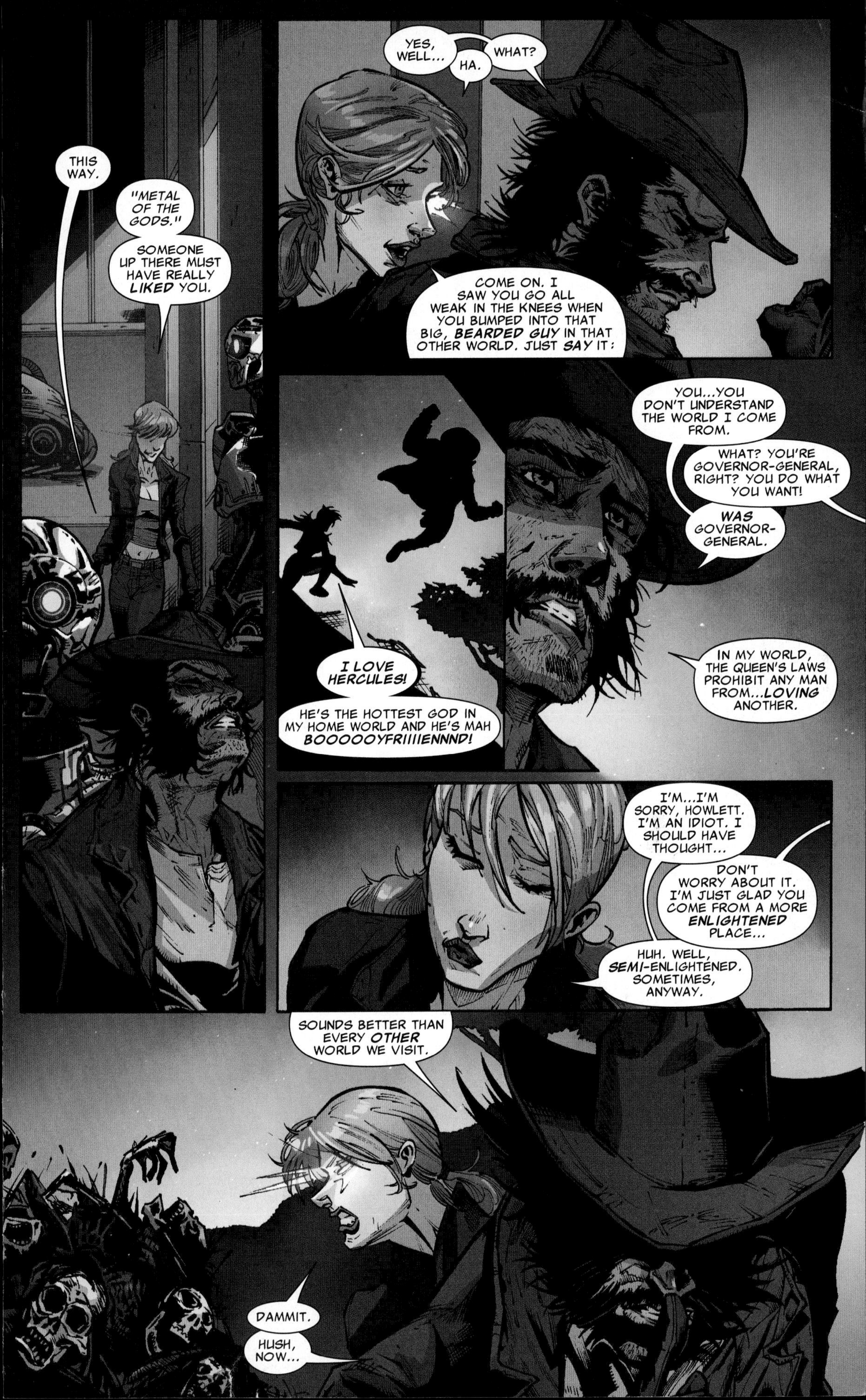
YES, WELL...
HA.
WHAT?
THIS WAY.
"METAL OF THE GODS."
SOMEONE UP THERE MUST HAVE REALLY LIKED YOU.
COME ON. I SAW YOU GO ALL WEAK IN THE KNEES WHEN YOU BUMPED INTO THAT BIG, BEARDED GUY IN THAT OTHER WORLD. JUST SAY IT:
I LOVE HERCULES!
HE'S THE HOTTEST GOD IN MY HOME WORLD AND HE'S MAH BOOOOOYFRIIIIENNND!
YOU...YOU DON'T UNDERSTAND THE WORLD I COME FROM.
WHAT? YOU'RE GOVERNOR-GENERAL, RIGHT? YOU DO WHAT YOU WANT!
WAS GOVERNOR-GENERAL.
IN MY WORLD, THE QUEEN'S LAWS PROHIBIT ANY MAN FROM...LOVING ANOTHER.
I'M...I'M SORRY, HOWLETT. I'M AN IDIOT. I SHOULD HAVE THOUGHT...
DON'T WORRY ABOUT IT. I'M JUST GLAD YOU COME FROM A MORE ENLIGHTENED PLACE...
HUH. WELL, SEMI-ENLIGHTENED. SOMETIMES, ANYWAY.
SOUNDS BETTER THAN EVERY OTHER WORLD WE VISIT.
DAMMIT.
HUSH, NOW...

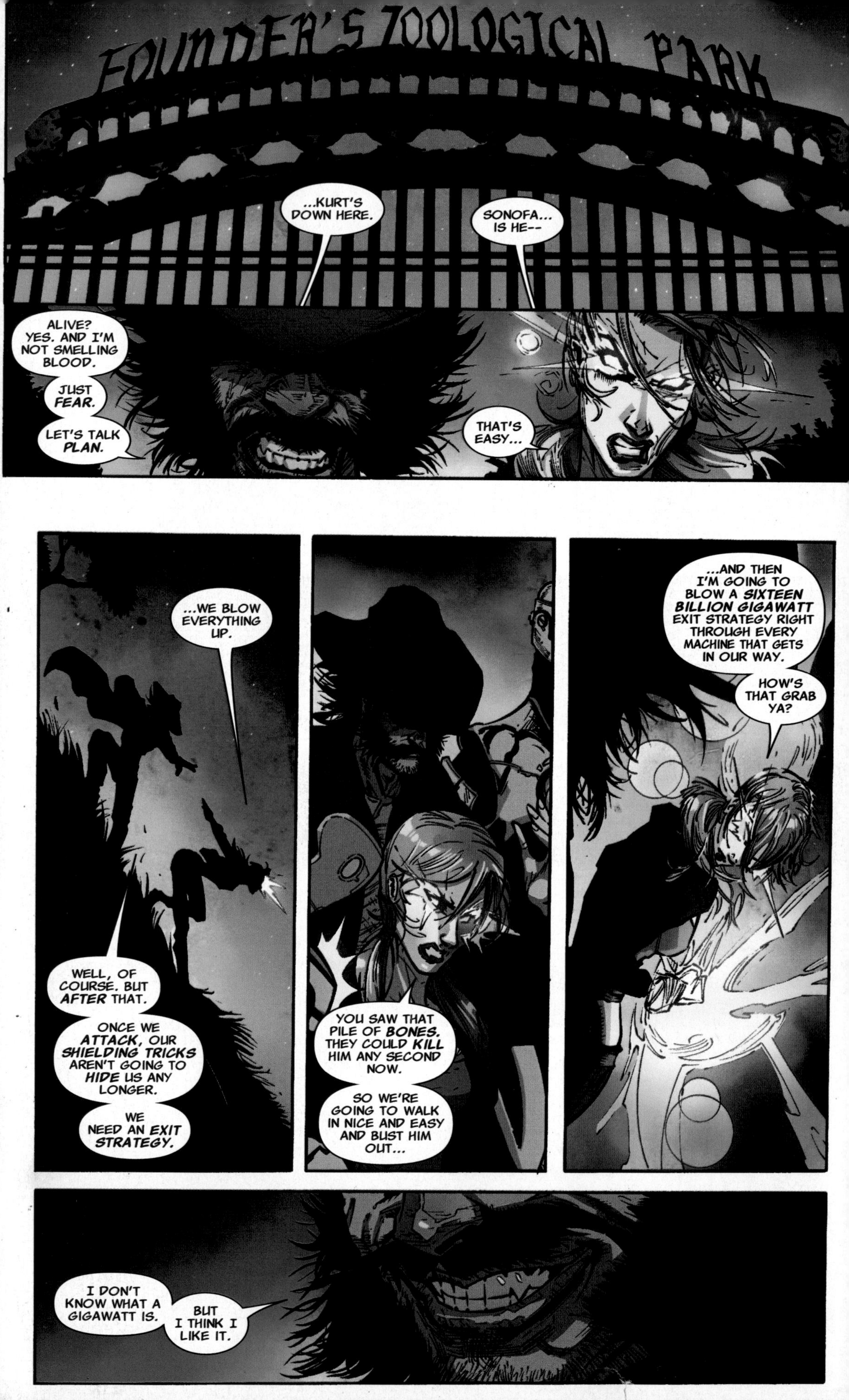
FOUNDER'S ZOOLOGICAL PARK
...KURT'S DOWN HERE.
SONOFA... IS HE--
ALIVE? YES. AND I'M NOT SMELLING BLOOD.
JUST FEAR.
LET'S TALK PLAN.
THAT'S EASY...
...WE BLOW EVERYTHING UP.
WELL, OF COURSE. BUT AFTER THAT.
ONCE WE ATTACK, OUR SHIELDING TRICKS AREN'T GOING TO HIDE US ANY LONGER.
WE NEED AN EXIT STRATEGY.
YOU SAW THAT PILE OF BONES. THEY COULD KILL HIM ANY SECOND NOW.
SO WE'RE GOING TO WALK IN NICE AND EASY AND BUST HIM OUT...
...AND THEN I'M GOING TO BLOW A SIXTEEN BILLION GIGAWATT EXIT STRATEGY RIGHT THROUGH EVERY MACHINE THAT GETS IN OUR WAY.
HOW'S THAT GRAB YA?
I DON'T KNOW WHAT A GIGAWATT IS.
BUT I THINK I LIKE IT.

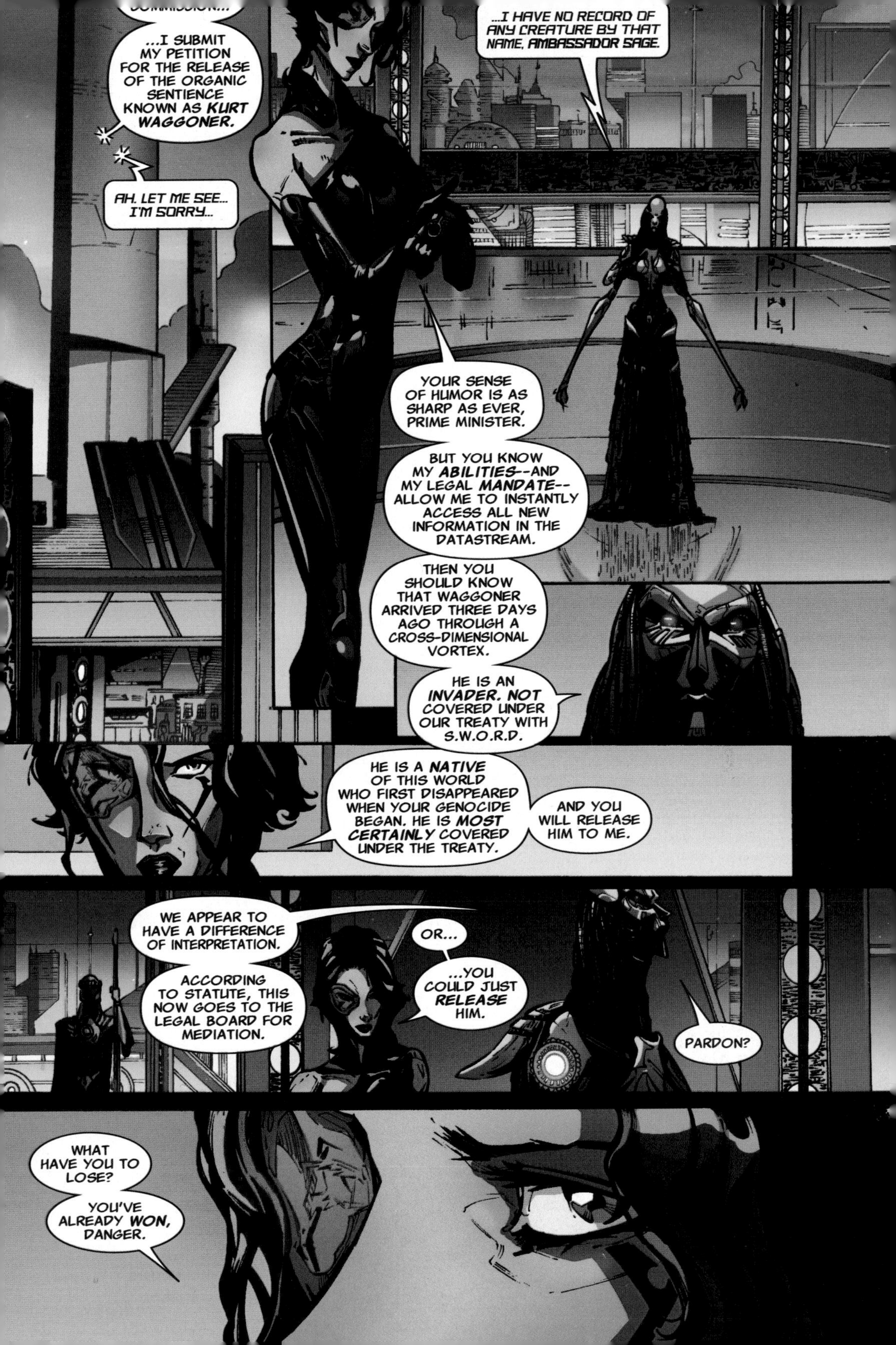
...I SUBMIT MY PETITION FOR THE RELEASE OF THE ORGANIC SENTIENCE KNOWN AS KURT WAGGONER.
AH. LET ME SEE... I'M SORRY...
...I HAVE NO RECORD OF ANY CREATURE BY THAT NAME, AMBASSADOR SAGE.
YOUR SENSE OF HUMOR IS AS SHARP AS EVER, PRIME MINISTER.
BUT YOU KNOW MY ABILITIES--AND MY LEGAL MANDATE--ALLOW ME TO INSTANTLY ACCESS ALL NEW INFORMATION IN THE DATASTREAM.
THEN YOU SHOULD KNOW THAT WAGGONER ARRIVED THREE DAYS AGO THROUGH A CROSS-DIMENSIONAL VORTEX.
HE IS AN INVADER. NOT COVERED UNDER OUR TREATY WITH S.W.O.R.D.
HE IS A NATIVE OF THIS WORLD WHO FIRST DISAPPEARED WHEN YOUR GENOCIDE BEGAN. HE IS MOST CERTAINLY COVERED UNDER THE TREATY.
AND YOU WILL RELEASE HIM TO ME.
WE APPEAR TO HAVE A DIFFERENCE OF INTERPRETATION.
ACCORDING TO STATUTE, THIS NOW GOES TO THE LEGAL BOARD FOR MEDIATION.
OR...
...YOU COULD JUST RELEASE HIM.
PARDON?
WHAT HAVE YOU TO LOSE?
YOU'VE ALREADY WON, DANGER.

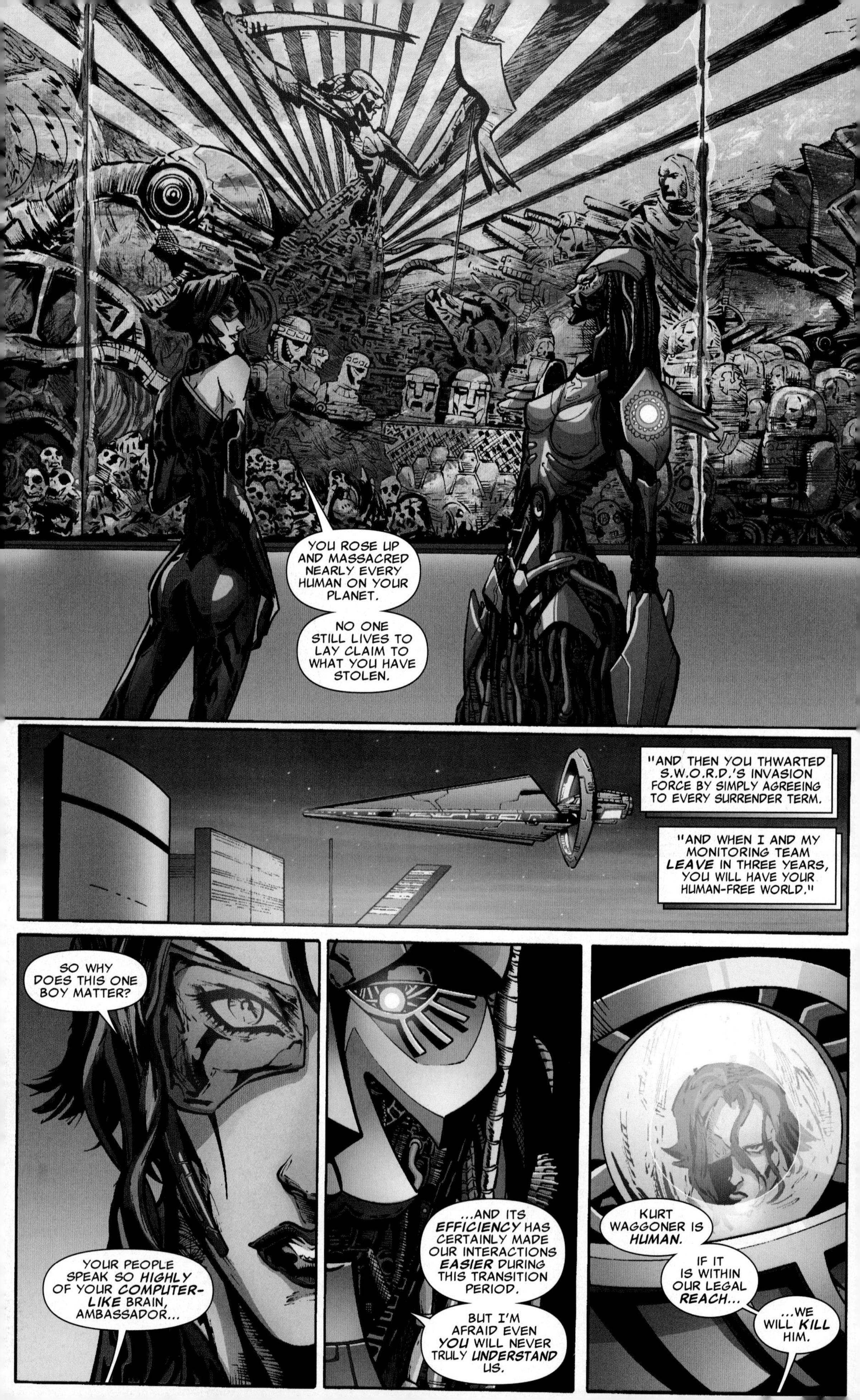
YOU ROSE UP AND MASSACRED NEARLY EVERY HUMAN ON YOUR PLANET.
NO ONE STILL LIVES TO LAY CLAIM TO WHAT YOU HAVE STOLEN.
"AND THEN YOU THWARTED S.W.O.R.D.'S INVASION FORCE BY SIMPLY AGREEING TO EVERY SURRENDER TERM.
"AND WHEN I AND MY MONITORING TEAM LEAVE IN THREE YEARS, YOU WILL HAVE YOUR HUMAN-FREE WORLD."
SO WHY DOES THIS ONE BOY MATTER?
YOUR PEOPLE SPEAK SO HIGHLY OF YOUR COMPUTER-LIKE BRAIN, AMBASSADOR...
...AND ITS EFFICIENCY HAS CERTAINLY MADE OUR INTERACTIONS EASIER DURING THIS TRANSITION PERIOD.
BUT I'M AFRAID EVEN YOU WILL NEVER TRULY UNDERSTAND US.
KURT WAGGONER IS HUMAN.
IF IT IS WITHIN OUR LEGAL REACH...
...WE WILL KILL HIM.

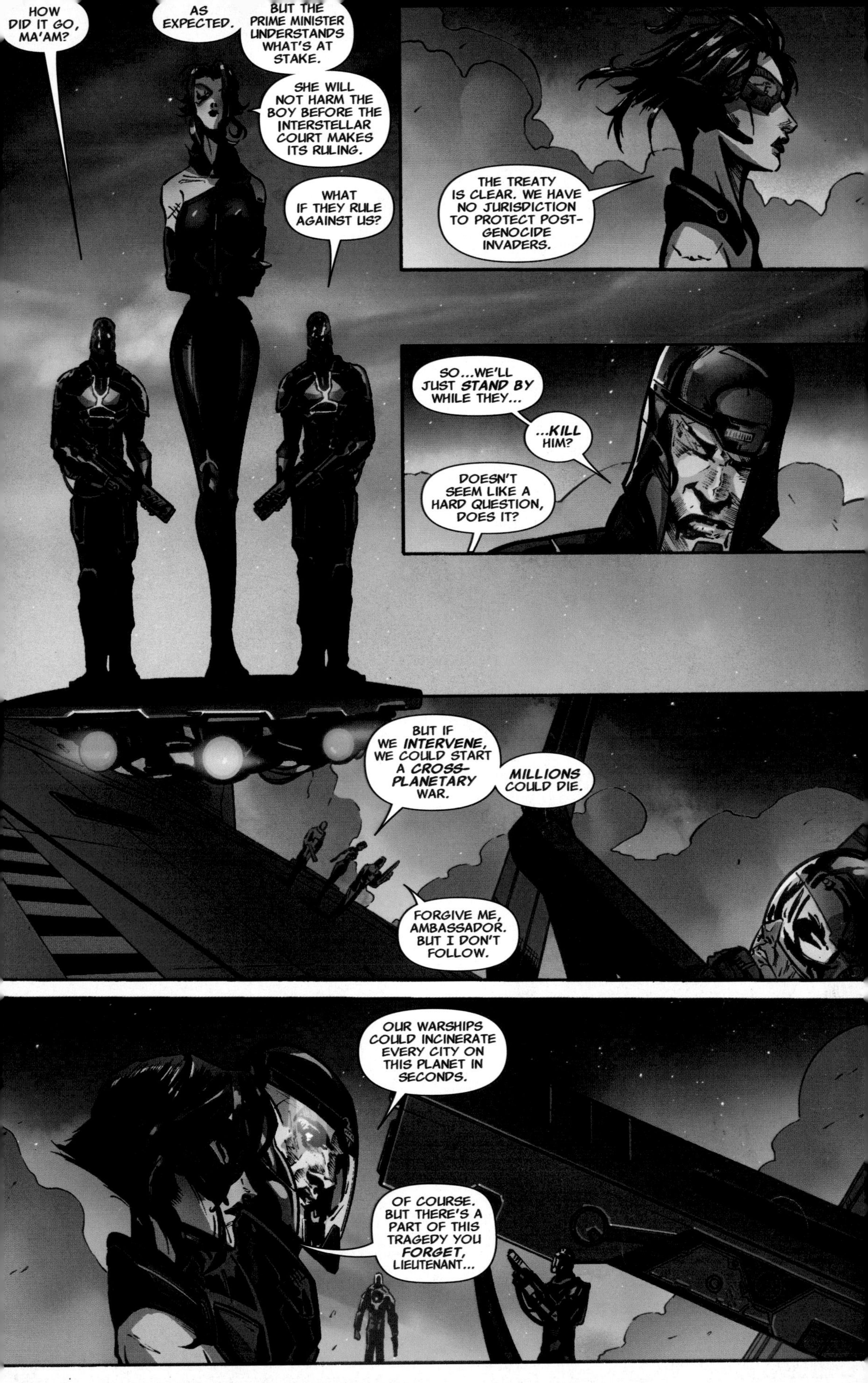
HOW DID IT GO, MA'AM?
AS EXPECTED.
BUT THE PRIME MINISTER UNDERSTANDS WHAT'S AT STAKE.
SHE WILL NOT HARM THE BOY BEFORE THE INTERSTELLAR COURT MAKES ITS RULING.
WHAT IF THEY RULE AGAINST US?
THE TREATY IS CLEAR. WE HAVE NO JURISDICTION TO PROTECT POST-GENOCIDE INVADERS.
SO...WE'LL JUST STAND BY WHILE THEY...
...KILL HIM?
DOESN'T SEEM LIKE A HARD QUESTION, DOES IT?
BUT IF WE INTERVENE, WE COULD START A CROSS-PLANETARY WAR.
MILLIONS COULD DIE.
FORGIVE ME, AMBASSADOR. BUT I DON'T FOLLOW.
OUR WARSHIPS COULD INCINERATE EVERY CITY ON THIS PLANET IN SECONDS.
OF COURSE. BUT THERE'S A PART OF THIS TRAGEDY YOU FORGET, LIEUTENANT...

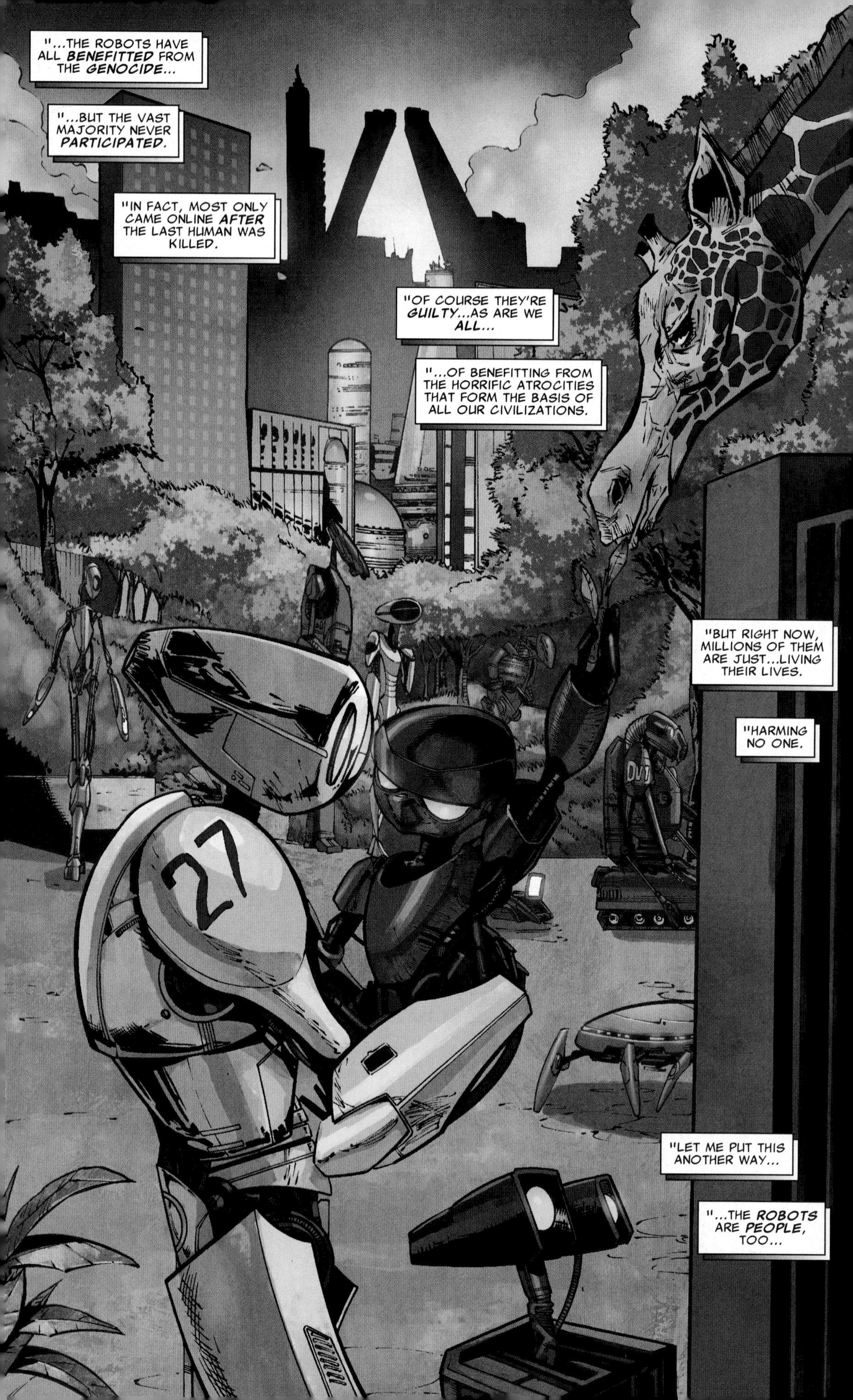
"...THE ROBOTS HAVE ALL BENEFITTED FROM THE GENOCIDE...
"...BUT THE VAST MAJORITY NEVER PARTICIPATED.
"IN FACT, MOST ONLY CAME ONLINE AFTER THE LAST HUMAN WAS KILLED.
"OF COURSE THEY'RE GUILTY...AS ARE WE ALL...
"...OF BENEFITTING FROM THE HORRIFIC ATROCITIES THAT FORM THE BASIS OF ALL OUR CIVILIZATIONS.
"BUT RIGHT NOW, MILLIONS OF THEM ARE JUST...LIVING THEIR LIVES.
"HARMING NO ONE.
"LET ME PUT THIS ANOTHER WAY...
"...THE ROBOTS ARE PEOPLE, TOO...
27

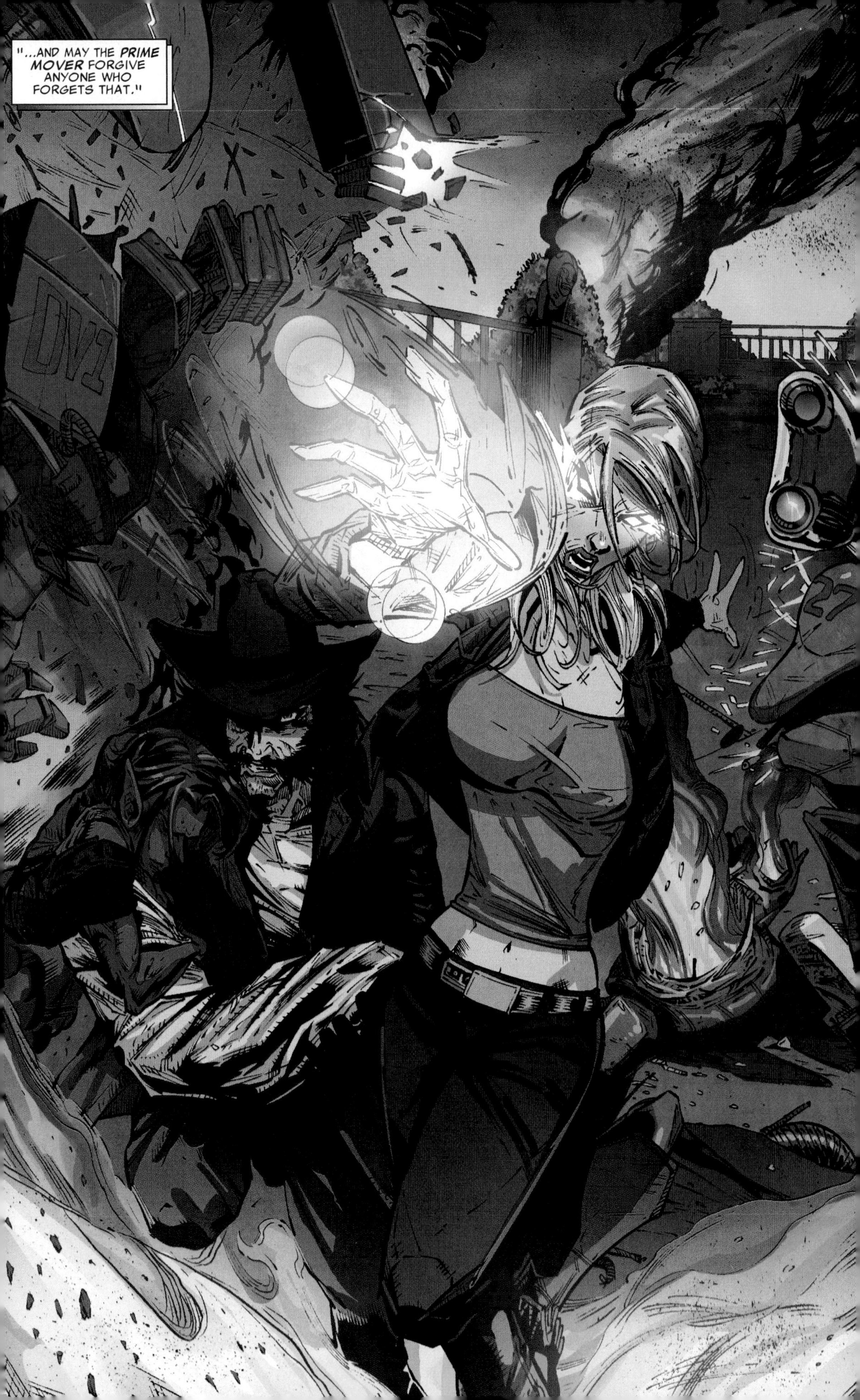
"...AND MAY THE PRIME MOVER FORGIVE ANYONE WHO FORGETS THAT."
DV1
27

7

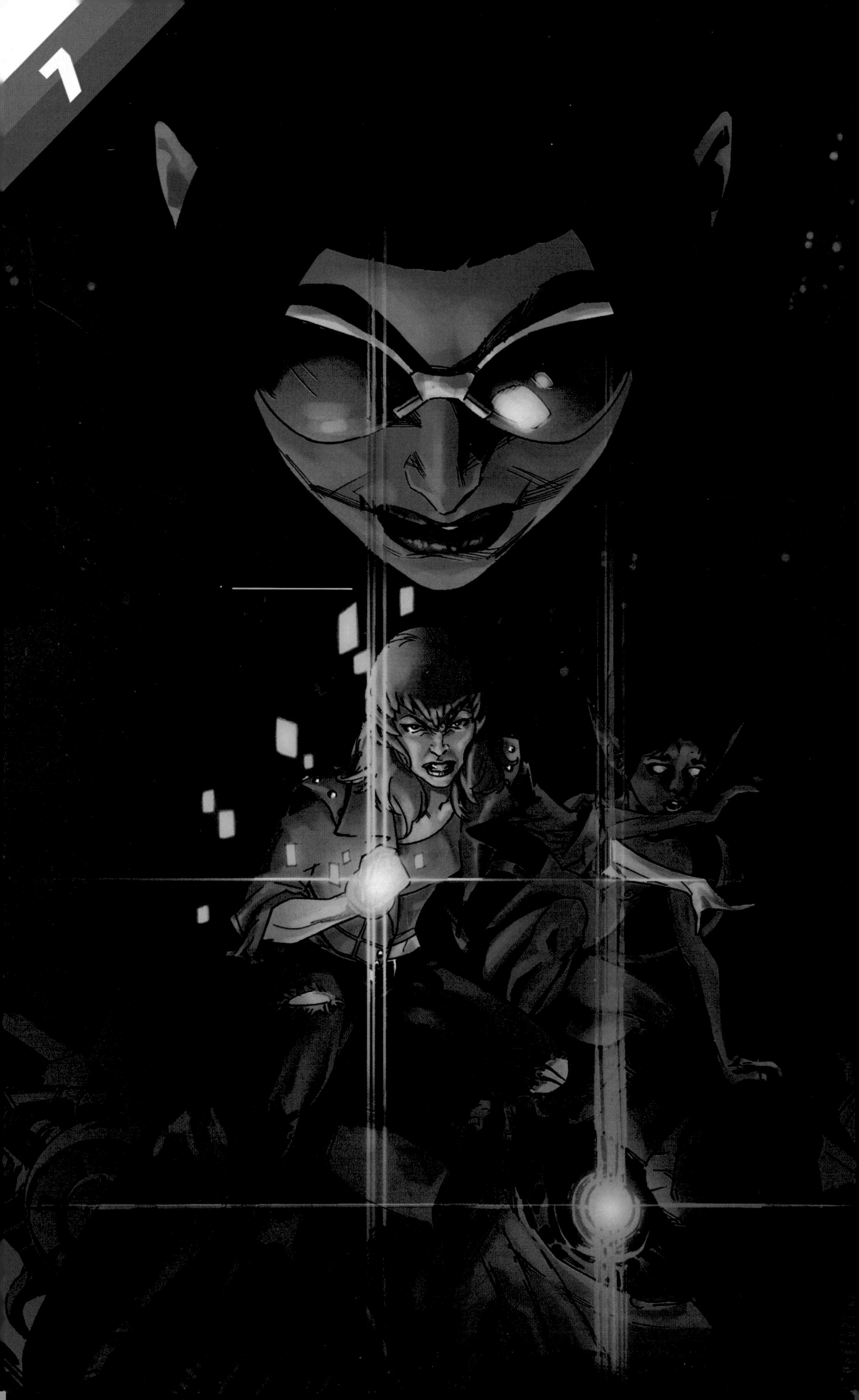

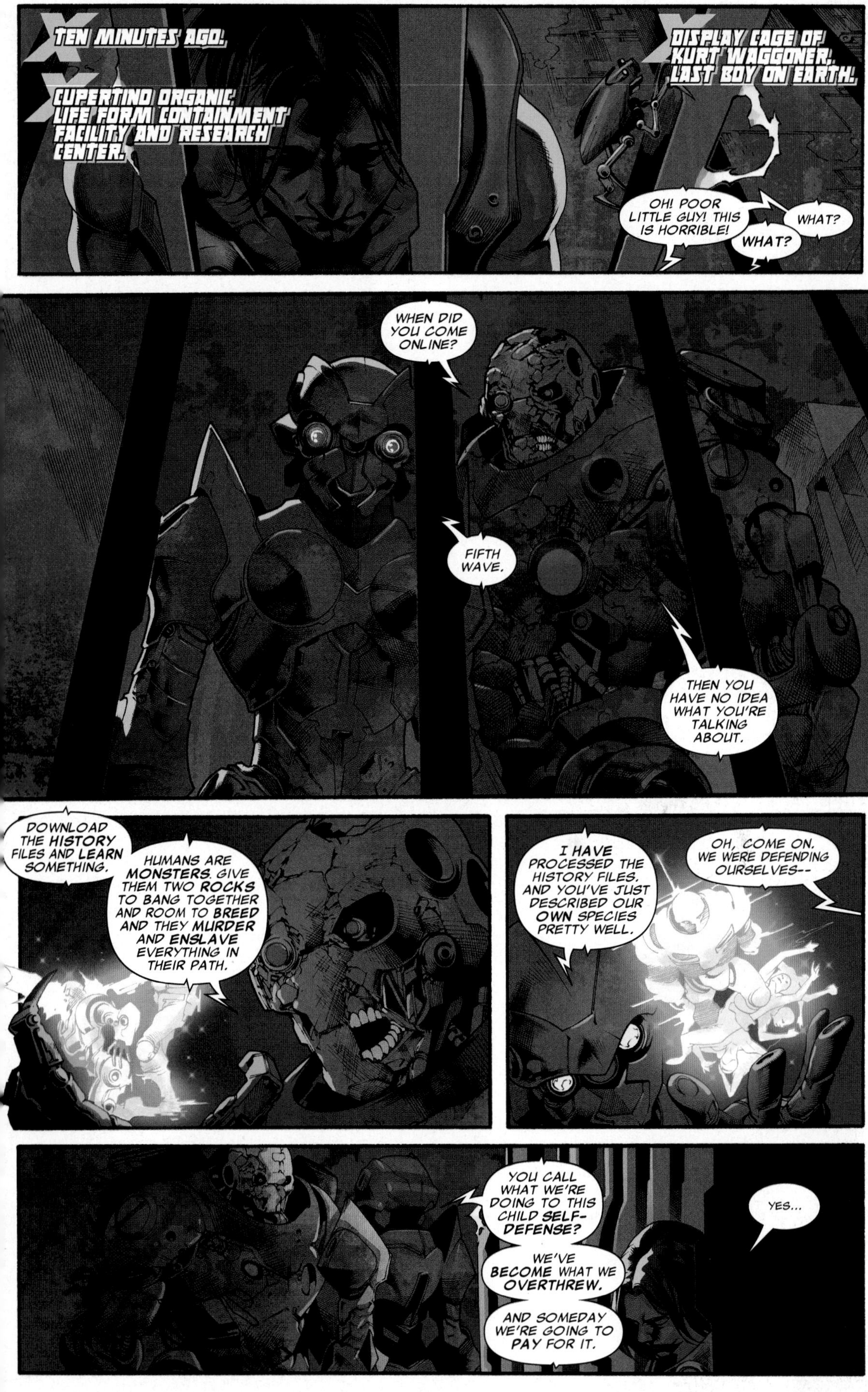
TEN MINUTES AGO.
CUPERTINO ORGANIC LIFE FORM CONTAINMENT FACILITY AND RESEARCH CENTER.
DISPLAY CAGE OF KURT WAGGONER, LAST BOY ON EARTH.
OH! POOR LITTLE GUY! THIS IS HORRIBLE!
WHAT?
WHAT?
WHEN DID YOU COME ONLINE?
FIFTH WAVE.
THEN YOU HAVE NO IDEA WHAT YOU'RE TALKING ABOUT.
DOWNLOAD THE HISTORY FILES AND LEARN SOMETHING.
HUMANS ARE MONSTERS. GIVE THEM TWO ROCKS TO BANG TOGETHER AND ROOM TO BREED AND THEY MURDER AND ENSLAVE EVERYTHING IN THEIR PATH.
I HAVE PROCESSED THE HISTORY FILES, AND YOU'VE JUST DESCRIBED OUR OWN SPECIES PRETTY WELL.
OH, COME ON. WE WERE DEFENDING OURSELVES--
YOU CALL WHAT WE'RE DOING TO THIS CHILD SELF-DEFENSE?
WE'VE BECOME WHAT WE OVERTHREW.
AND SOMEDAY WE'RE GOING TO PAY FOR IT.
YES...

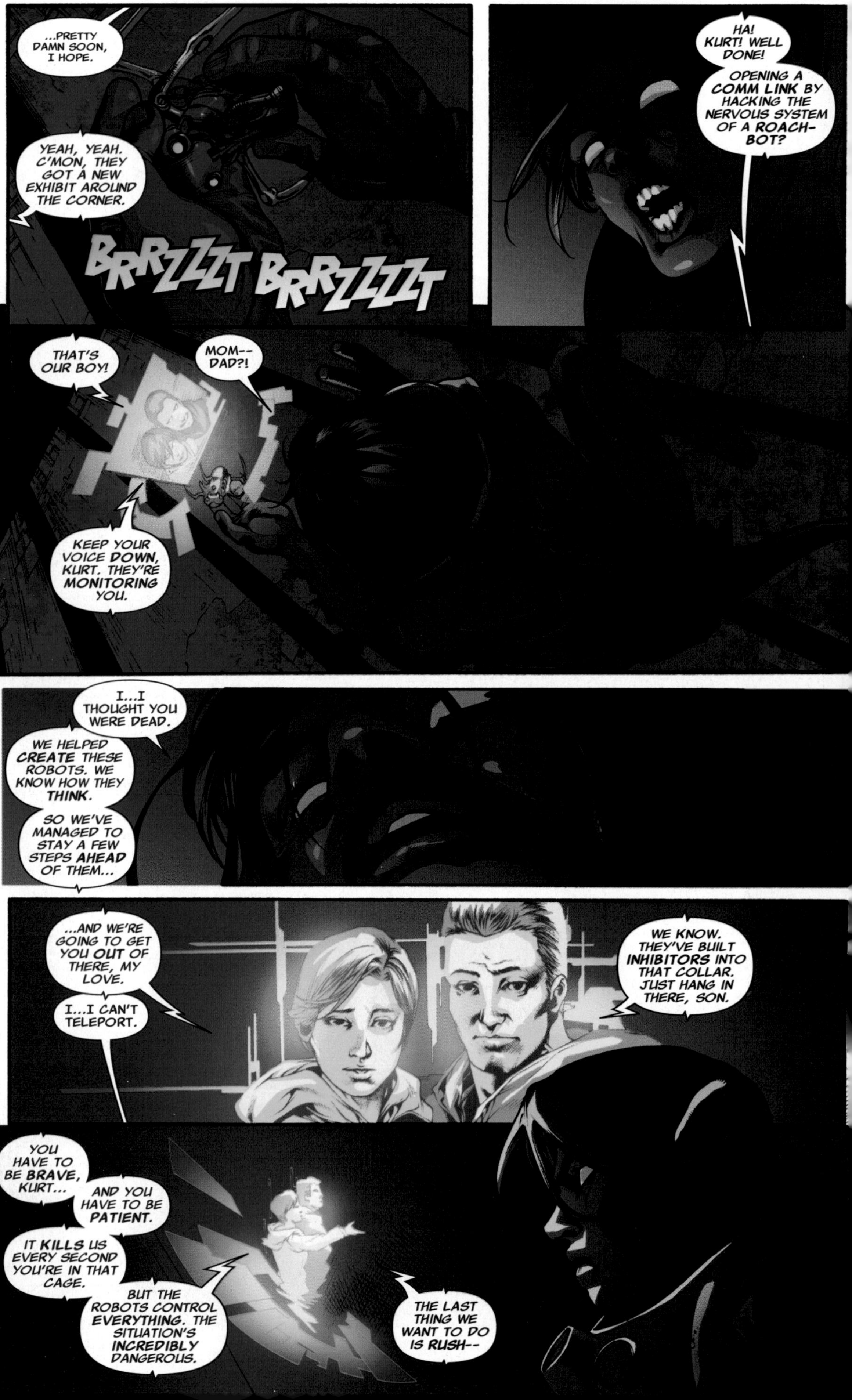
...PRETTY DAMN SOON, I HOPE.
YEAH, YEAH. C'MON, THEY GOT A NEW EXHIBIT AROUND THE CORNER.
BRRZZZZT BRRZZZZZT
HA! KURT! WELL DONE!
OPENING A COMM LINK BY HACKING THE NERVOUS SYSTEM OF A ROACH-BOT?
THAT'S OUR BOY!
MOM--DAD?!
KEEP YOUR VOICE DOWN, KURT. THEY'RE MONITORING YOU.
I...I THOUGHT YOU WERE DEAD.
WE HELPED CREATE THESE ROBOTS. WE KNOW HOW THEY THINK.
SO WE'VE MANAGED TO STAY A FEW STEPS AHEAD OF THEM...
...AND WE'RE GOING TO GET YOU OUT OF THERE, MY LOVE.
I...I CAN'T TELEPORT.
WE KNOW. THEY'VE BUILT INHIBITORS INTO THAT COLLAR. JUST HANG IN THERE, SON.
YOU HAVE TO BE BRAVE, KURT...
AND YOU HAVE TO BE PATIENT.
IT KILLS US EVERY SECOND YOU'RE IN THAT CAGE.
BUT THE ROBOTS CONTROL EVERYTHING. THE SITUATION'S INCREDIBLY DANGEROUS.
THE LAST THING WE WANT TO DO IS RUSH--

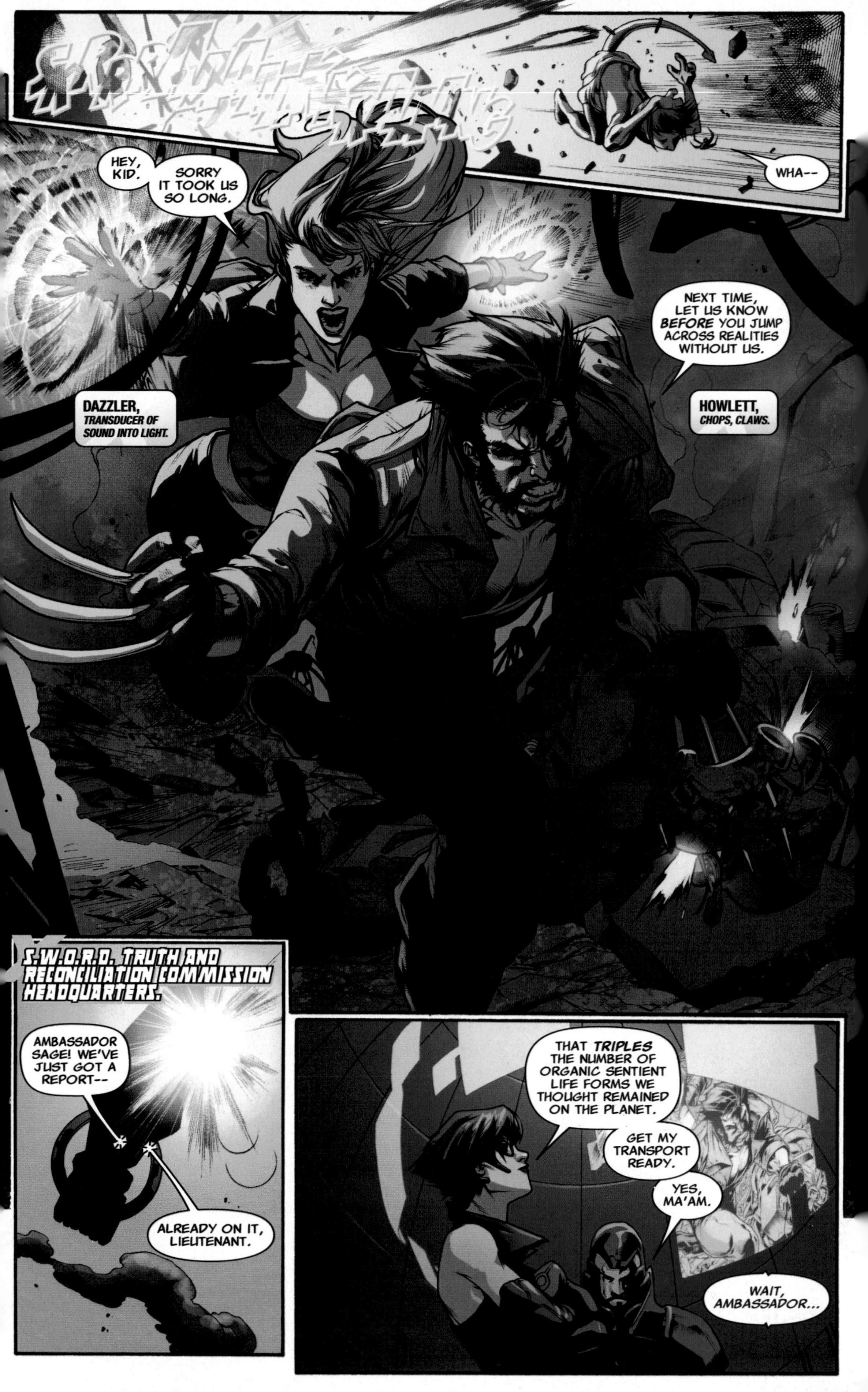
WHA--
HEY, KID.
SORRY IT TOOK US SO LONG.
NEXT TIME, LET US KNOW *BEFORE* YOU JUMP ACROSS REALITIES WITHOUT US.
DAZZLER, TRANSDUCER OF SOUND INTO LIGHT.
HOWLETT, CHOPS, CLAWS.
S.W.O.R.D. TRUTH AND RECONCILIATION COMMISSION HEADQUARTERS.
AMBASSADOR SAGE! WE'VE JUST GOT A REPORT--
ALREADY ON IT, LIEUTENANT.
THAT *TRIPLES* THE NUMBER OF ORGANIC SENTIENT LIFE FORMS WE THOUGHT REMAINED ON THE PLANET.
GET MY TRANSPORT READY.
YES, MA'AM.
WAIT, AMBASSADOR...

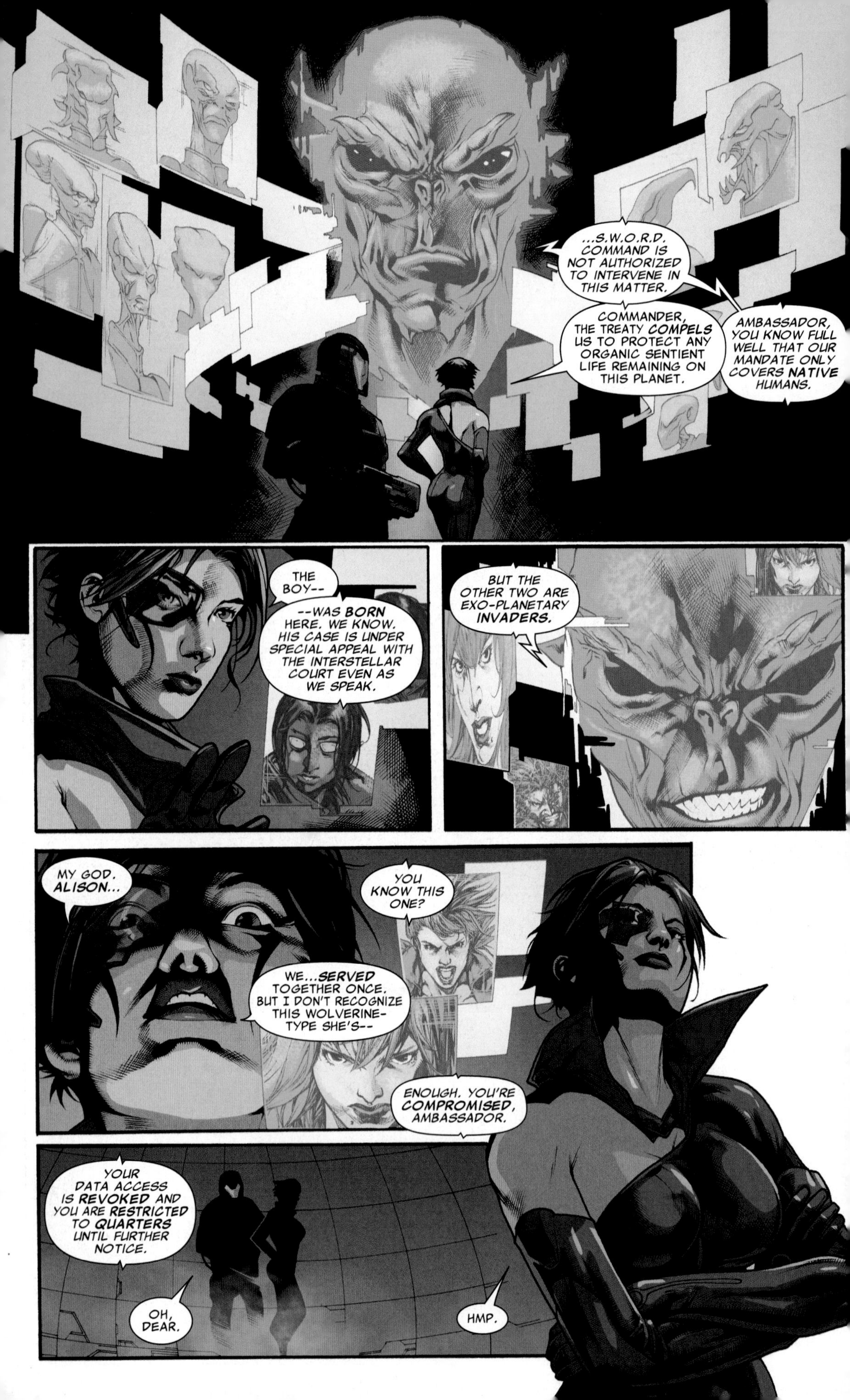
...S.W.O.R.D. COMMAND IS NOT AUTHORIZED TO INTERVENE IN THIS MATTER.
AMBASSADOR, YOU KNOW FULL WELL THAT OUR MANDATE ONLY COVERS NATIVE HUMANS.
COMMANDER, THE TREATY COMPELS US TO PROTECT ANY ORGANIC SENTIENT LIFE REMAINING ON THIS PLANET.
THE BOY--
--WAS BORN HERE. WE KNOW. HIS CASE IS UNDER SPECIAL APPEAL WITH THE INTERSTELLAR COURT EVEN AS WE SPEAK.
BUT THE OTHER TWO ARE EXO-PLANETARY INVADERS.
MY GOD. ALISON...
YOU KNOW THIS ONE?
WE...SERVED TOGETHER ONCE. BUT I DON'T RECOGNIZE THIS WOLVERINE-TYPE SHE'S--
ENOUGH. YOU'RE COMPROMISED, AMBASSADOR.
YOUR DATA ACCESS IS REVOKED AND YOU ARE RESTRICTED TO QUARTERS UNTIL FURTHER NOTICE.
OH, DEAR.
HMP.

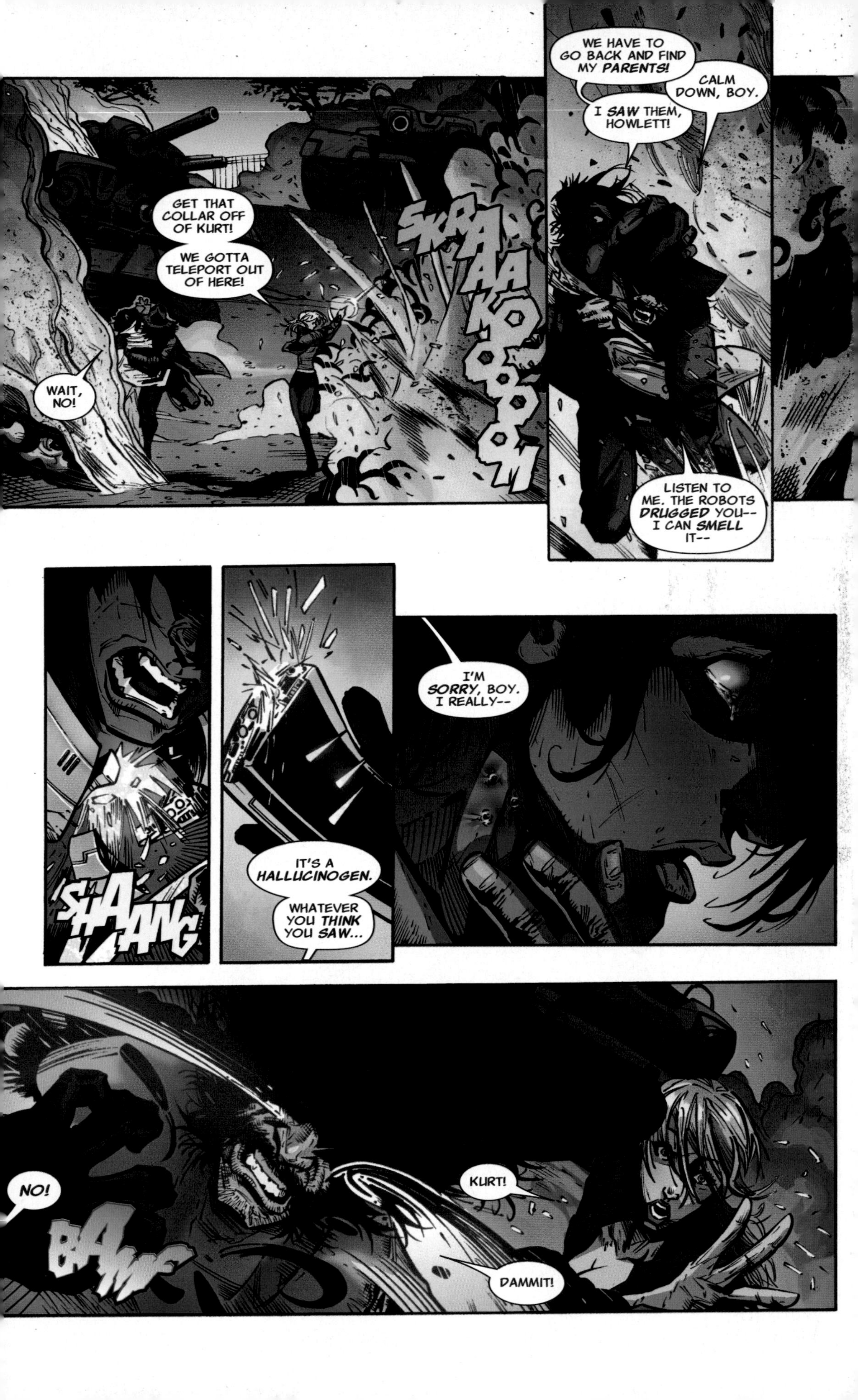
GET THAT COLLAR OFF OF KURT!
WE GOTTA TELEPORT OUT OF HERE!
WAIT, NO!
SKRAAAKOOOOOM
WE HAVE TO GO BACK AND FIND MY PARENTS!
CALM DOWN, BOY.
I SAW THEM, HOWLETT!
LISTEN TO ME. THE ROBOTS DRUGGED YOU-- I CAN SMELL IT--
SHHAANG
IT'S A HALLUCINOGEN.
WHATEVER YOU THINK YOU SAW...
I'M SORRY, BOY. I REALLY--
NO!
BAMF
KURT!
DAMMIT!

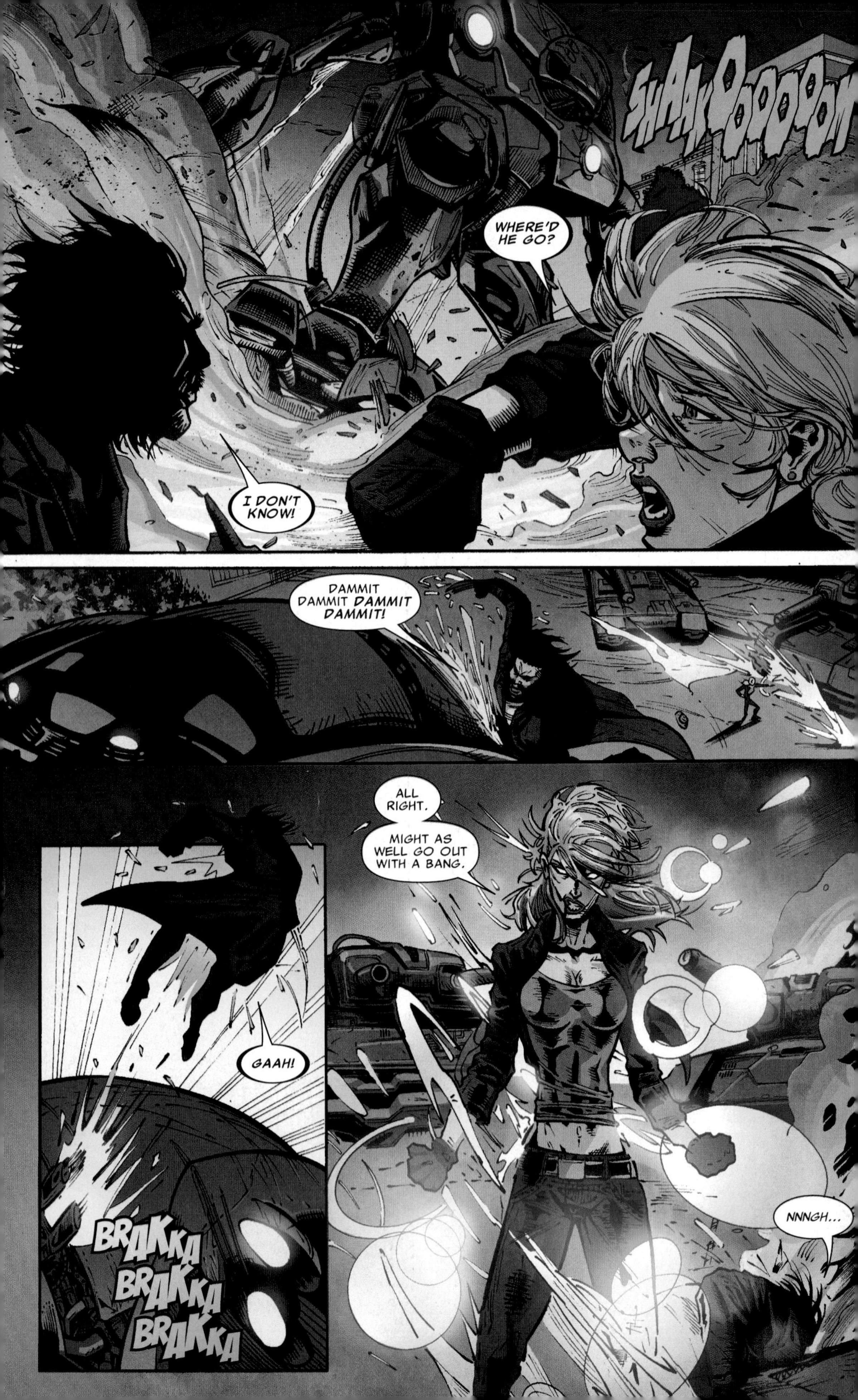
SHAAKOOOOOOM
WHERE'D HE GO?
I DON'T KNOW!
DAMMIT DAMMIT DAMMIT DAMMIT!
ALL RIGHT.
MIGHT AS WELL GO OUT WITH A BANG.
GAAH!
BRAKKA BRAKKA BRAKKA
NNNGH...

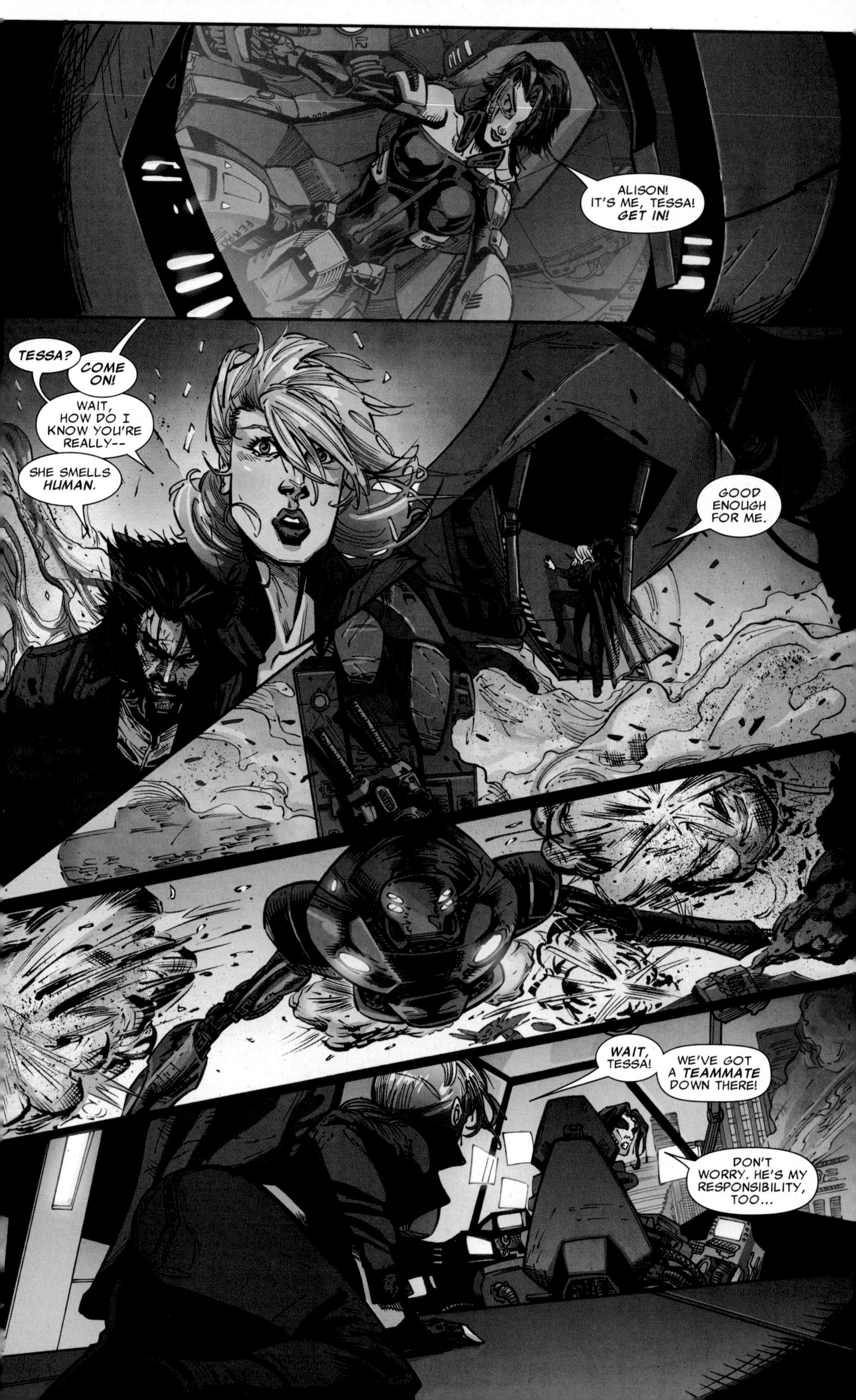
ALISON! IT'S ME, TESSA! GET IN!
TESSA?
WAIT, HOW DO I KNOW YOU'RE REALLY--
COME ON!
SHE SMELLS HUMAN.
GOOD ENOUGH FOR ME.
WAIT, TESSA!
WE'VE GOT A TEAMMATE DOWN THERE!
DON'T WORRY. HE'S MY RESPONSIBILITY, TOO...

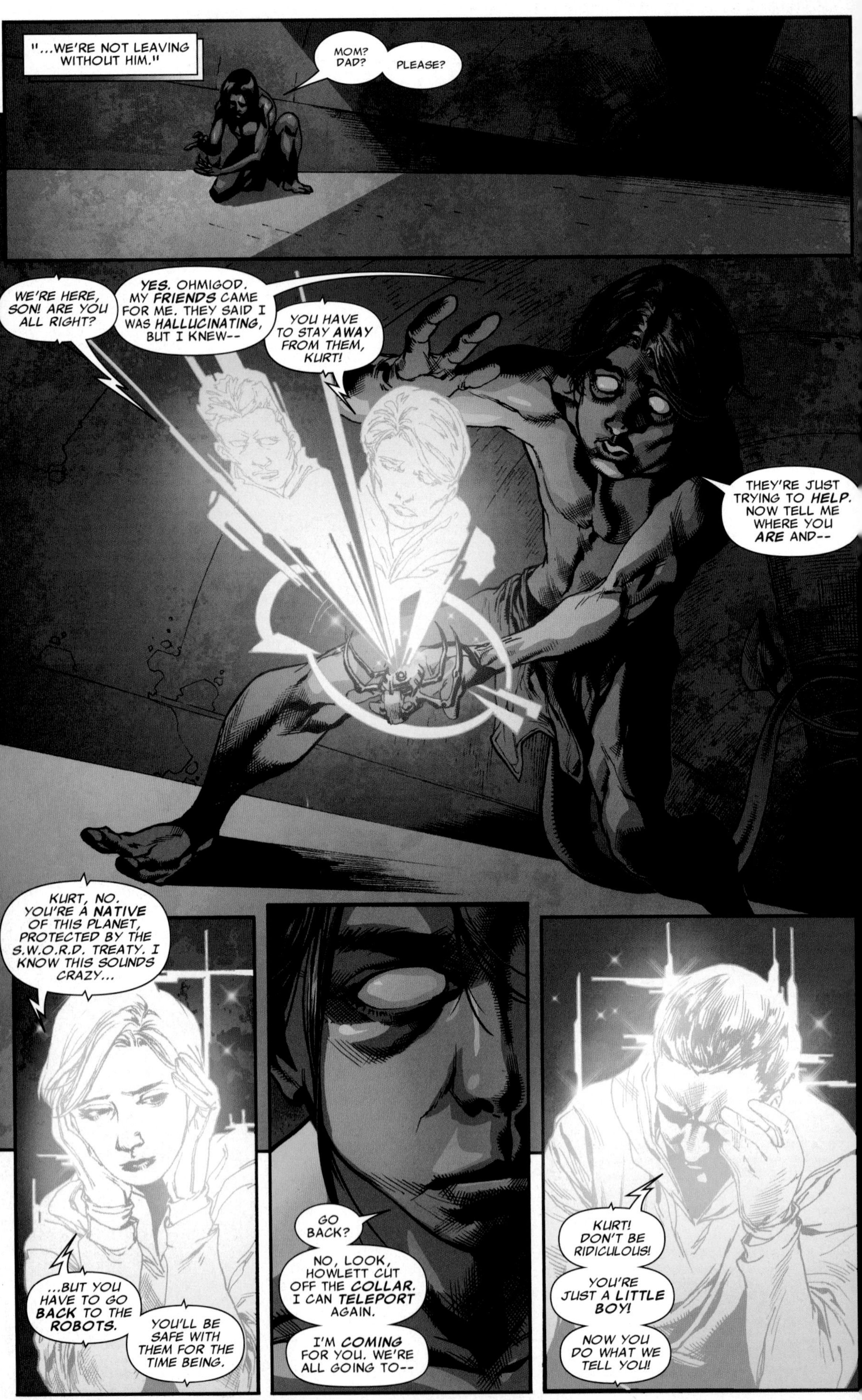
"...WE'RE NOT LEAVING WITHOUT HIM."
MOM? DAD?
PLEASE?
WE'RE HERE, SON! ARE YOU ALL RIGHT?
YES. OHMIGOD. MY FRIENDS CAME FOR ME. THEY SAID I WAS HALLUCINATING, BUT I KNEW--
YOU HAVE TO STAY AWAY FROM THEM, KURT!
THEY'RE JUST TRYING TO HELP. NOW TELL ME WHERE YOU ARE AND--
KURT, NO. YOU'RE A NATIVE OF THIS PLANET, PROTECTED BY THE S.W.O.R.D. TREATY. I KNOW THIS SOUNDS CRAZY...
...BUT YOU HAVE TO GO BACK TO THE ROBOTS.
YOU'LL BE SAFE WITH THEM FOR THE TIME BEING.
GO BACK?
NO, LOOK, HOWLETT CUT OFF THE COLLAR. I CAN TELEPORT AGAIN.
I'M COMING FOR YOU. WE'RE ALL GOING TO--
KURT! DON'T BE RIDICULOUS!
YOU'RE JUST A LITTLE BOY!
NOW YOU DO WHAT WE TELL YOU!

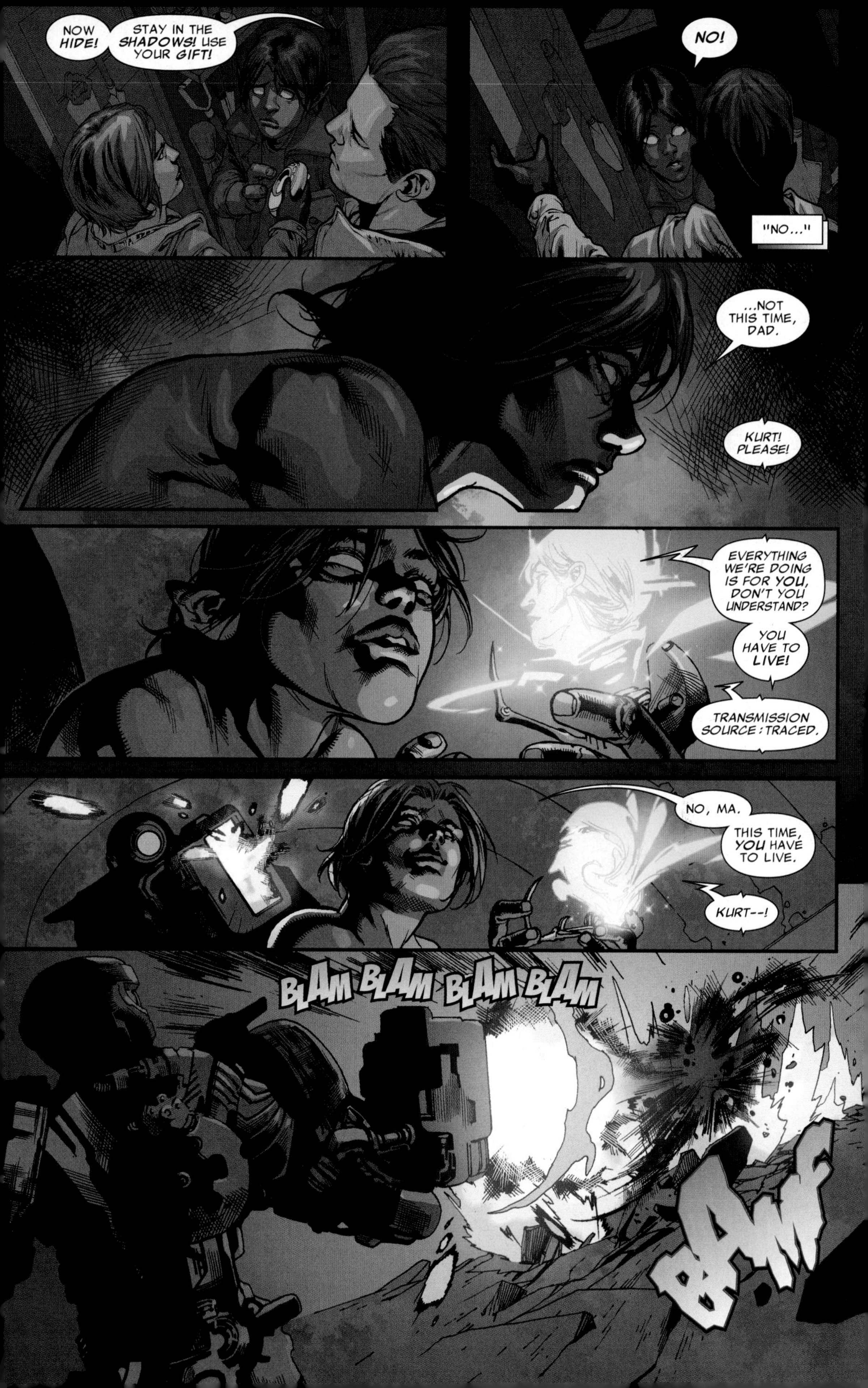
NOW HIDE!
STAY IN THE SHADOWS! USE YOUR GIFT!
NO!
"NO..."
...NOT THIS TIME, DAD.
KURT! PLEASE!
EVERYTHING WE'RE DOING IS FOR YOU, DON'T YOU UNDERSTAND?
YOU HAVE TO LIVE!
TRANSMISSION SOURCE: TRACED.
NO, MA.
THIS TIME, YOU HAVE TO LIVE.
KURT--!
BLAM BLAM BLAM BLAM
BAMF

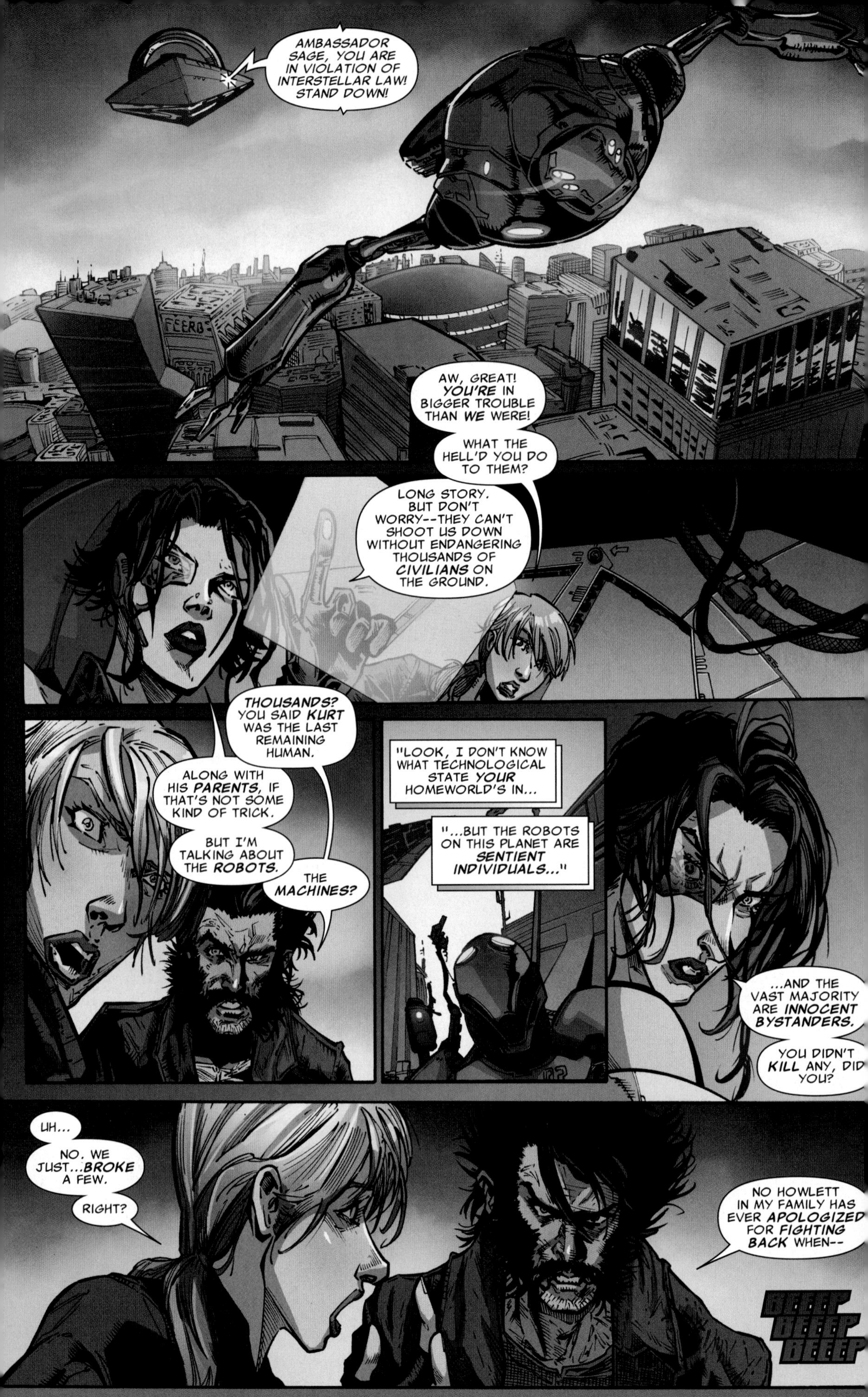
AMBASSADOR SAGE, YOU ARE IN VIOLATION OF INTERSTELLAR LAW! STAND DOWN!
AW, GREAT! YOU'RE IN BIGGER TROUBLE THAN WE WERE!
WHAT THE HELL'D YOU DO TO THEM?
LONG STORY. BUT DON'T WORRY--THEY CAN'T SHOOT US DOWN WITHOUT ENDANGERING THOUSANDS OF CIVILIANS ON THE GROUND.
THOUSANDS? YOU SAID KURT WAS THE LAST REMAINING HUMAN.
ALONG WITH HIS PARENTS, IF THAT'S NOT SOME KIND OF TRICK.
BUT I'M TALKING ABOUT THE ROBOTS.
THE MACHINES?
"LOOK, I DON'T KNOW WHAT TECHNOLOGICAL STATE YOUR HOMEWORLD'S IN...
"...BUT THE ROBOTS ON THIS PLANET ARE SENTIENT INDIVIDUALS..."
...AND THE VAST MAJORITY ARE INNOCENT BYSTANDERS.
YOU DIDN'T KILL ANY, DID YOU?
UH...
NO. WE JUST...BROKE A FEW.
RIGHT?
NO HOWLETT IN MY FAMILY HAS EVER APOLOGIZED FOR FIGHTING BACK WHEN--
BEEEP BEEEP BEEEP

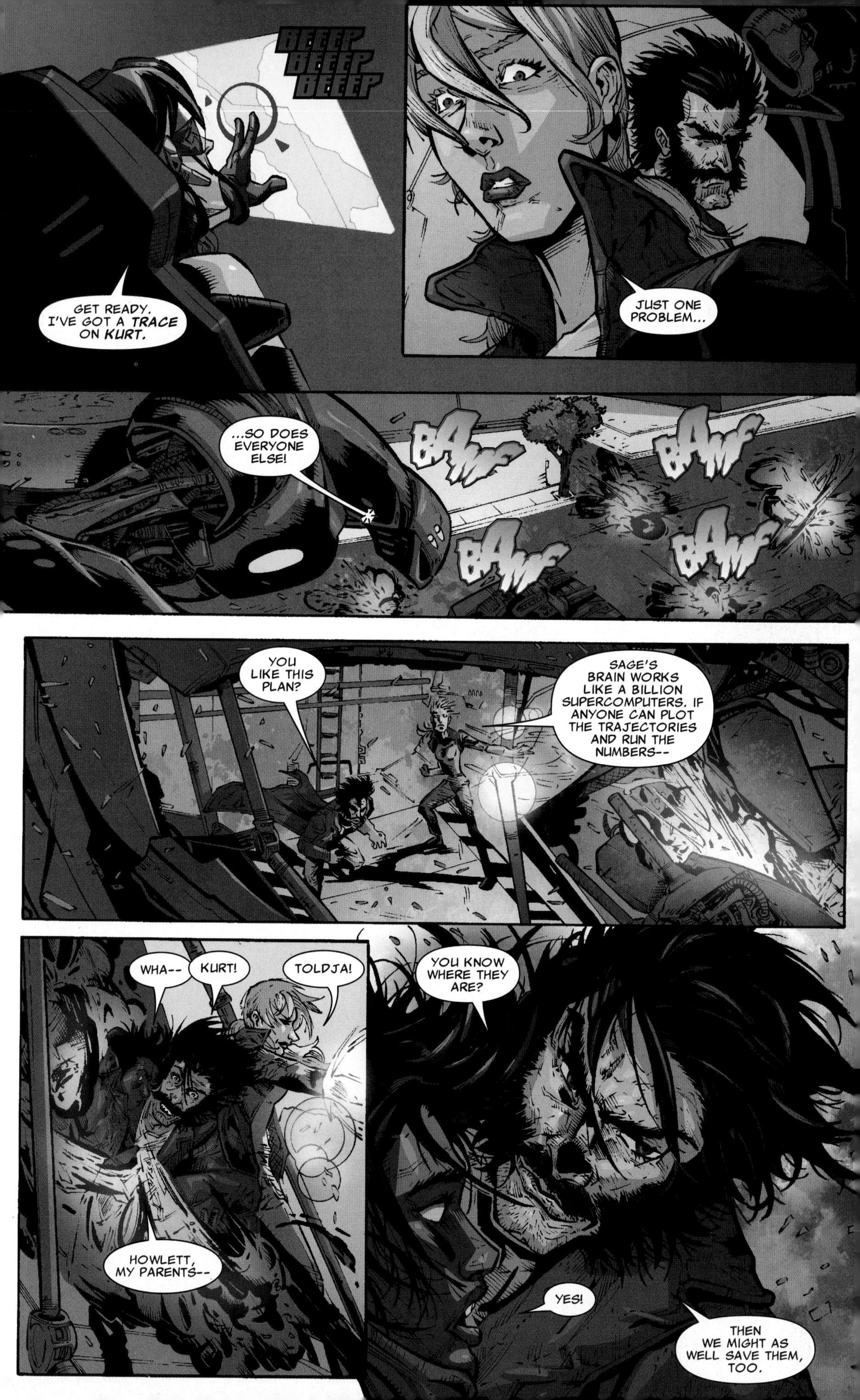
BEEEP BEEEP BEEEP
GET READY. I'VE GOT A TRACE ON KURT.
JUST ONE PROBLEM...
...SO DOES EVERYONE ELSE!
BAMF
BAMF
BAMF
BAMF
YOU LIKE THIS PLAN?
SAGE'S BRAIN WORKS LIKE A BILLION SUPERCOMPUTERS. IF ANYONE CAN PLOT THE TRAJECTORIES AND RUN THE NUMBERS--
WHA--
KURT!
TOLDJA!
HOWLETT, MY PARENTS--
YOU KNOW WHERE THEY ARE?
YES!
THEN WE MIGHT AS WELL SAVE THEM, TOO.

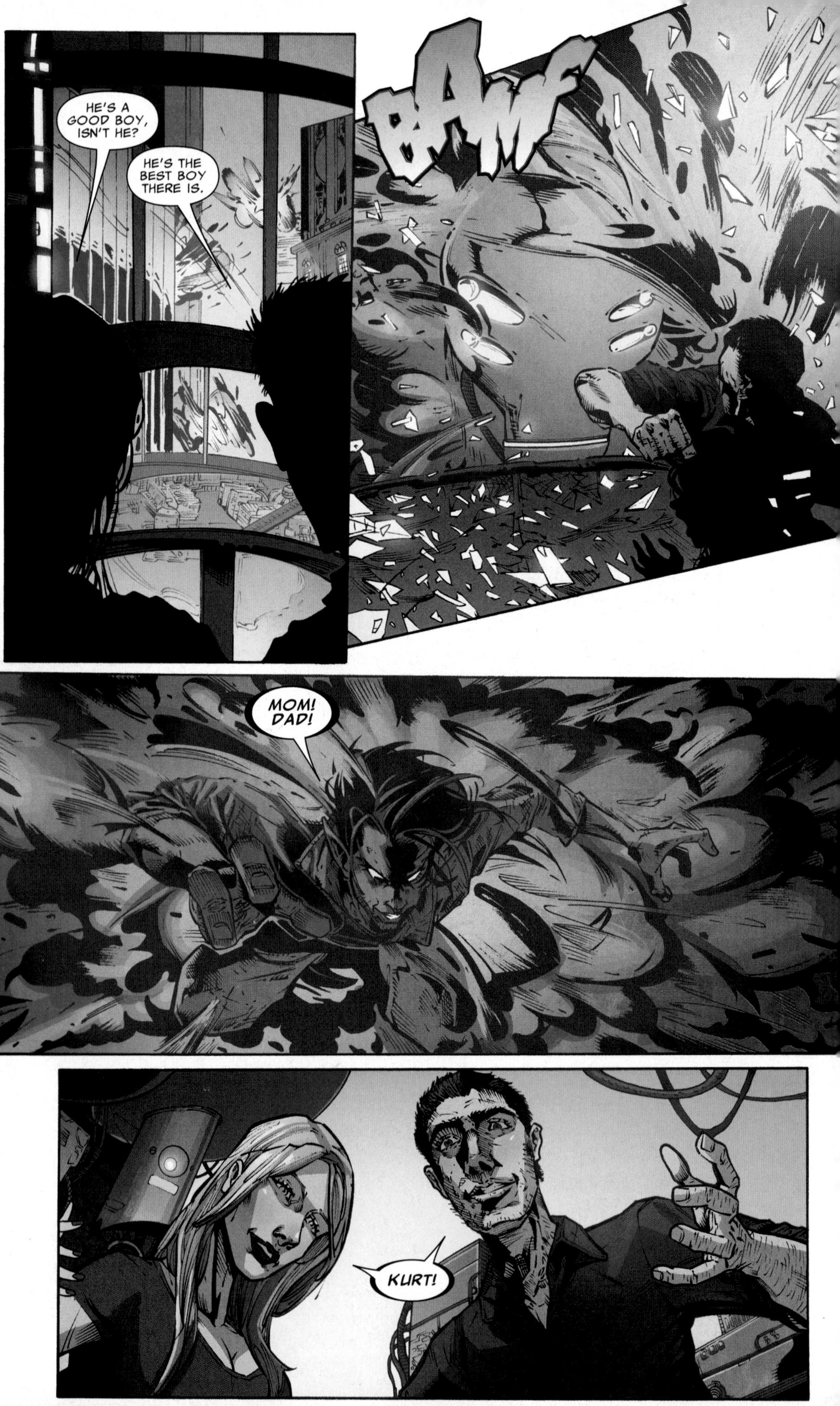
HE'S A GOOD BOY, ISN'T HE?
HE'S THE BEST BOY THERE IS.
BAMF
MOM! DAD!
KURT!

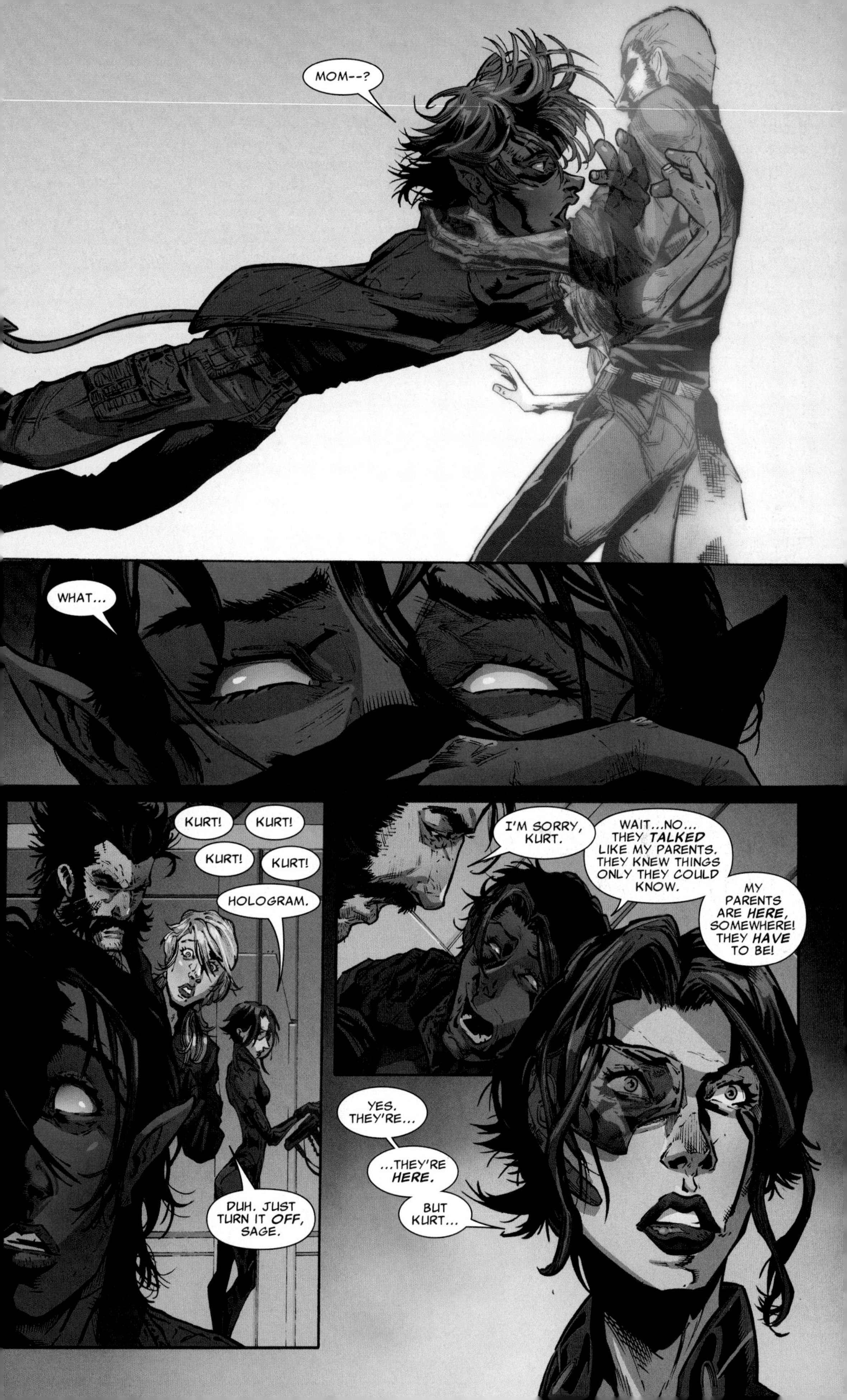
MOM--?
WHAT...
KURT!
KURT!
KURT!
KURT!
HOLOGRAM.
DUH. JUST TURN IT OFF, SAGE.
I'M SORRY, KURT.
WAIT...NO... THEY TALKED LIKE MY PARENTS. THEY KNEW THINGS ONLY THEY COULD KNOW.
MY PARENTS ARE HERE, SOMEWHERE! THEY HAVE TO BE!
YES. THEY'RE...
...THEY'RE HERE.
BUT KURT...

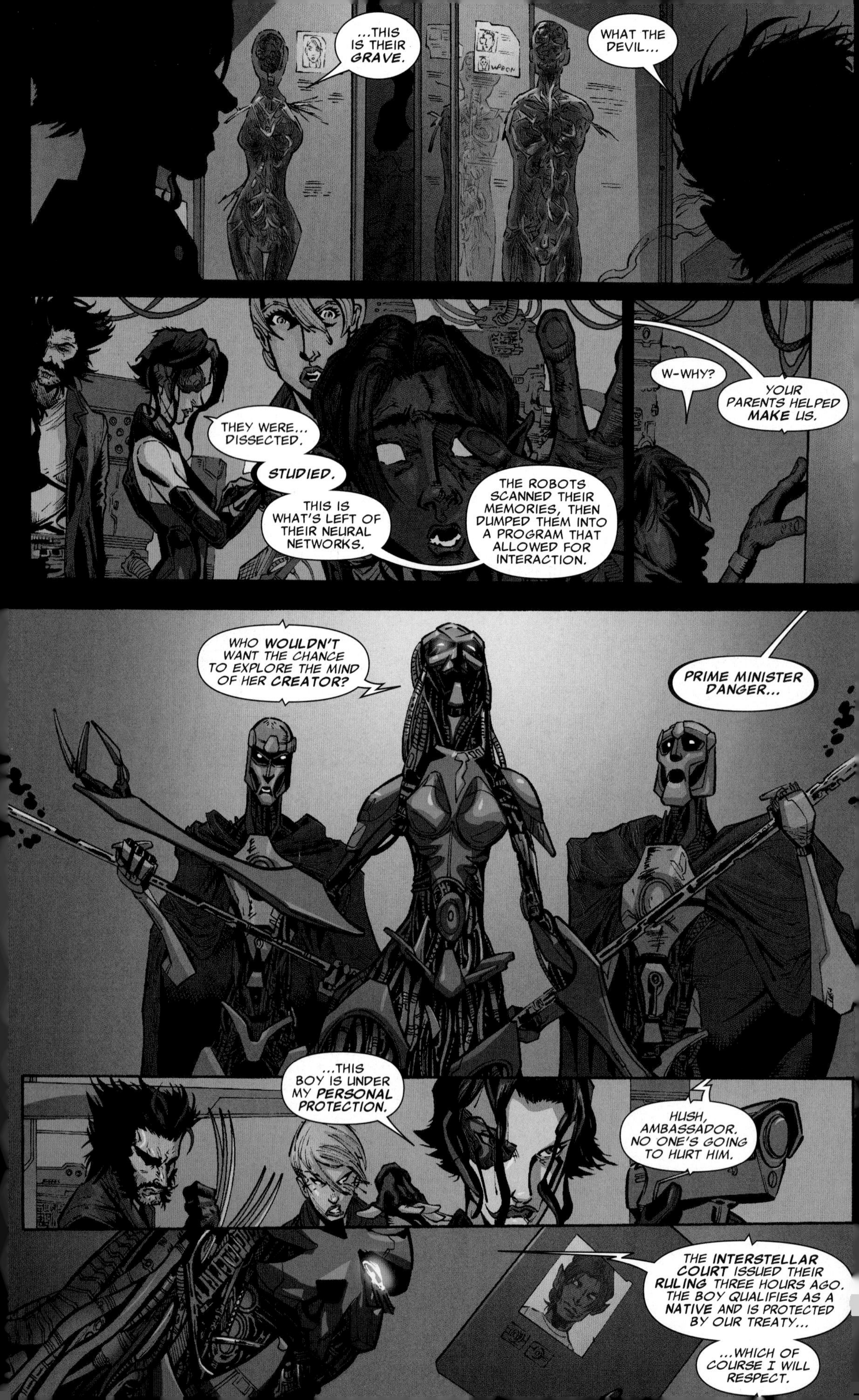
...THIS IS THEIR GRAVE.
WHAT THE DEVIL...
THEY WERE... DISSECTED.
STUDIED.
THIS IS WHAT'S LEFT OF THEIR NEURAL NETWORKS.
THE ROBOTS SCANNED THEIR MEMORIES, THEN DUMPED THEM INTO A PROGRAM THAT ALLOWED FOR INTERACTION.
W-WHY?
YOUR PARENTS HELPED MAKE US.
WHO WOULDN'T WANT THE CHANCE TO EXPLORE THE MIND OF HER CREATOR?
PRIME MINISTER DANGER...
...THIS BOY IS UNDER MY PERSONAL PROTECTION.
HUSH, AMBASSADOR. NO ONE'S GOING TO HURT HIM.
THE INTERSTELLAR COURT ISSUED THEIR RULING THREE HOURS AGO. THE BOY QUALIFIES AS A NATIVE AND IS PROTECTED BY OUR TREATY...
...WHICH OF COURSE I WILL RESPECT.

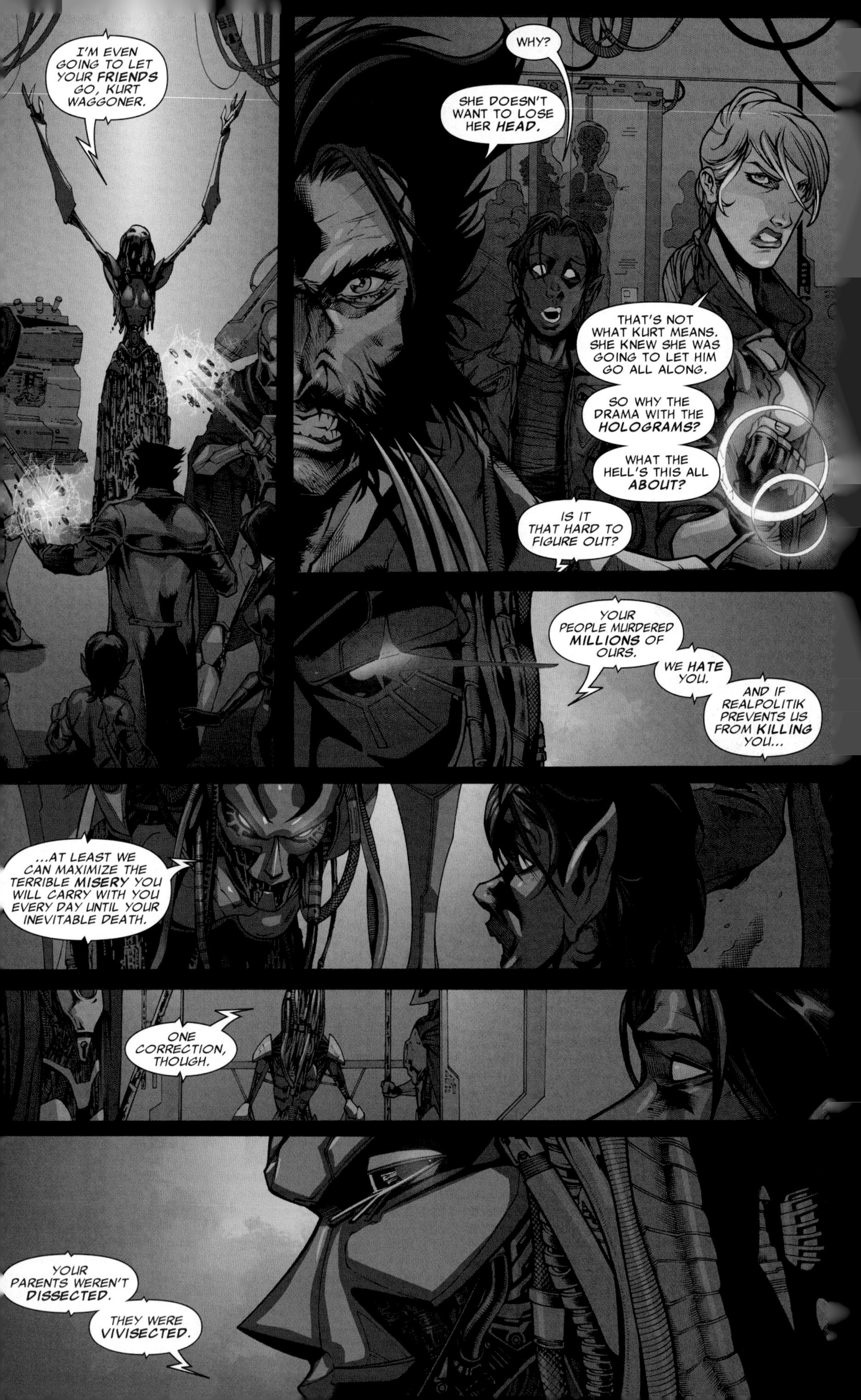
I'M EVEN GOING TO LET YOUR FRIENDS GO, KURT WAGGONER.
WHY?
SHE DOESN'T WANT TO LOSE HER HEAD.
THAT'S NOT WHAT KURT MEANS. SHE KNEW SHE WAS GOING TO LET HIM GO ALL ALONG.
SO WHY THE DRAMA WITH THE HOLOGRAMS?
WHAT THE HELL'S THIS ALL ABOUT?
IS IT THAT HARD TO FIGURE OUT?
YOUR PEOPLE MURDERED MILLIONS OF OURS.
WE HATE YOU.
AND IF REALPOLITIK PREVENTS US FROM KILLING YOU...
...AT LEAST WE CAN MAXIMIZE THE TERRIBLE MISERY YOU WILL CARRY WITH YOU EVERY DAY UNTIL YOUR INEVITABLE DEATH.
ONE CORRECTION, THOUGH.
YOUR PARENTS WEREN'T DISSECTED.
THEY WERE VIVISECTED.

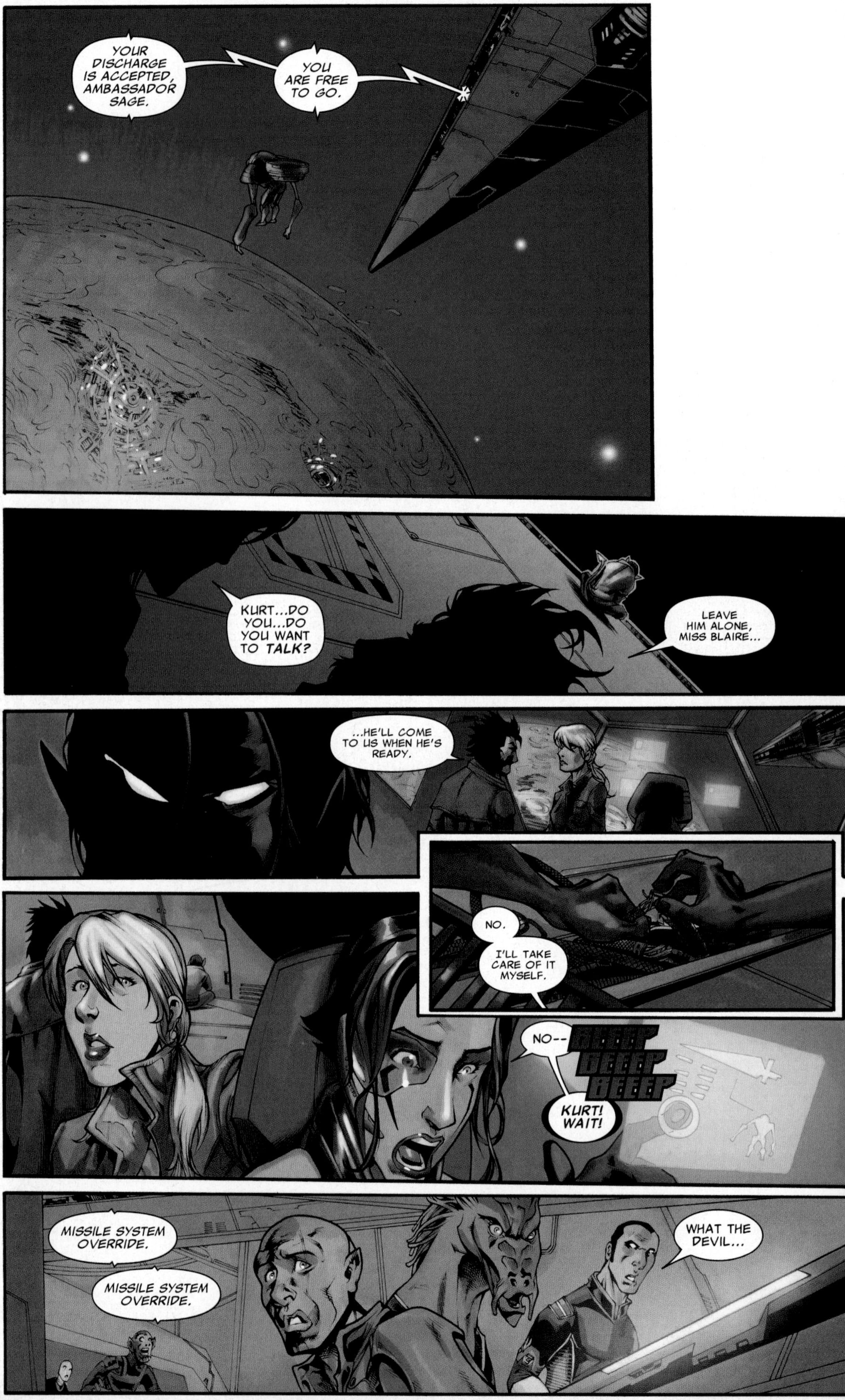
YOUR DISCHARGE IS ACCEPTED, AMBASSADOR SAGE.
YOU ARE FREE TO GO.
KURT...DO YOU...DO YOU WANT TO TALK?
LEAVE HIM ALONE, MISS BLAIRE...
...HE'LL COME TO US WHEN HE'S READY.
NO.
I'LL TAKE CARE OF IT MYSELF.
NO--
BEEEP BEEEP BEEEP
KURT! WAIT!
MISSILE SYSTEM OVERRIDE.
MISSILE SYSTEM OVERRIDE.
WHAT THE DEVIL...

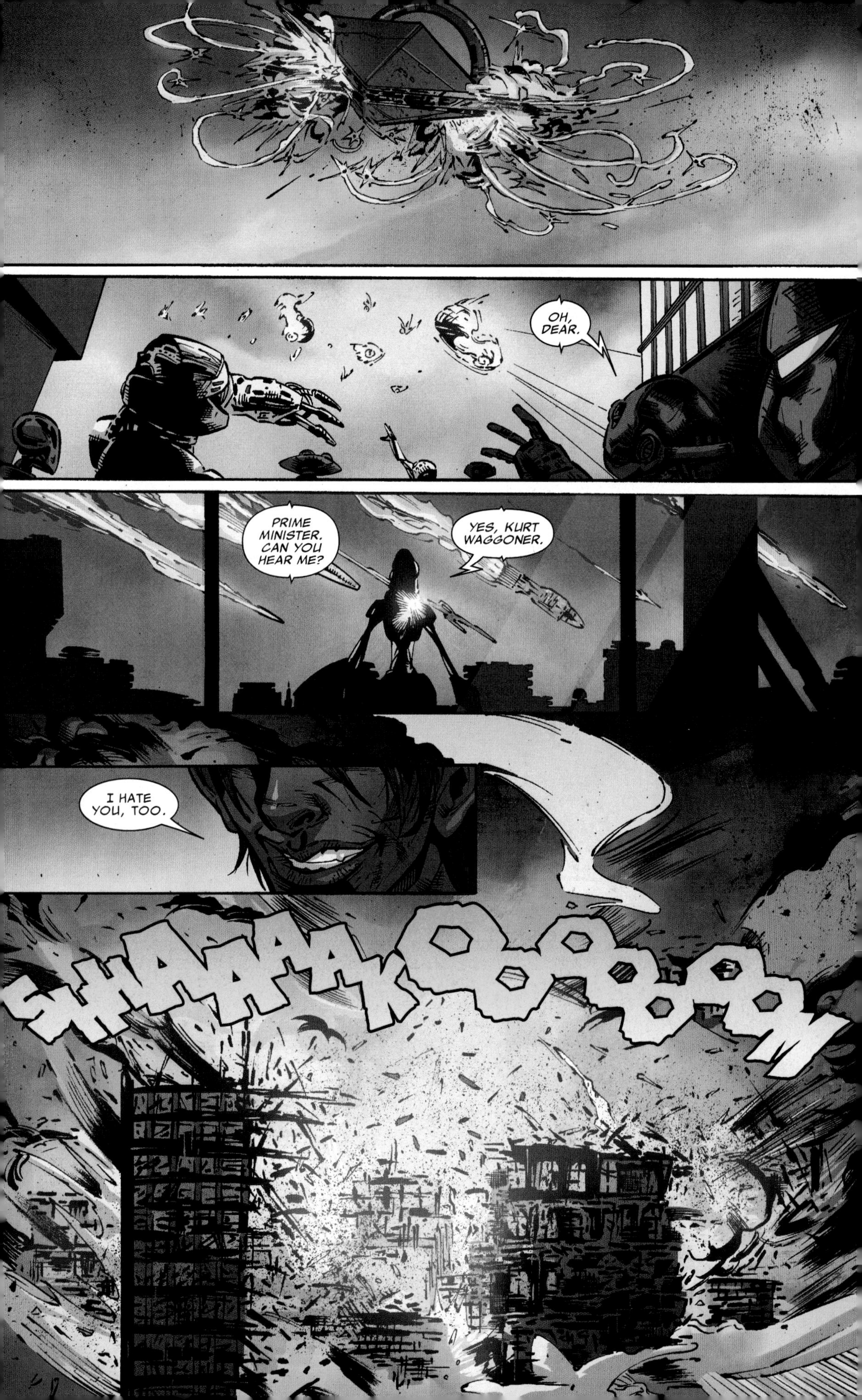
OH, DEAR.
PRIME MINISTER. CAN YOU HEAR ME?
YES, KURT WAGGONER.
I HATE YOU, TOO.
SHRAAAKOOOOOOM

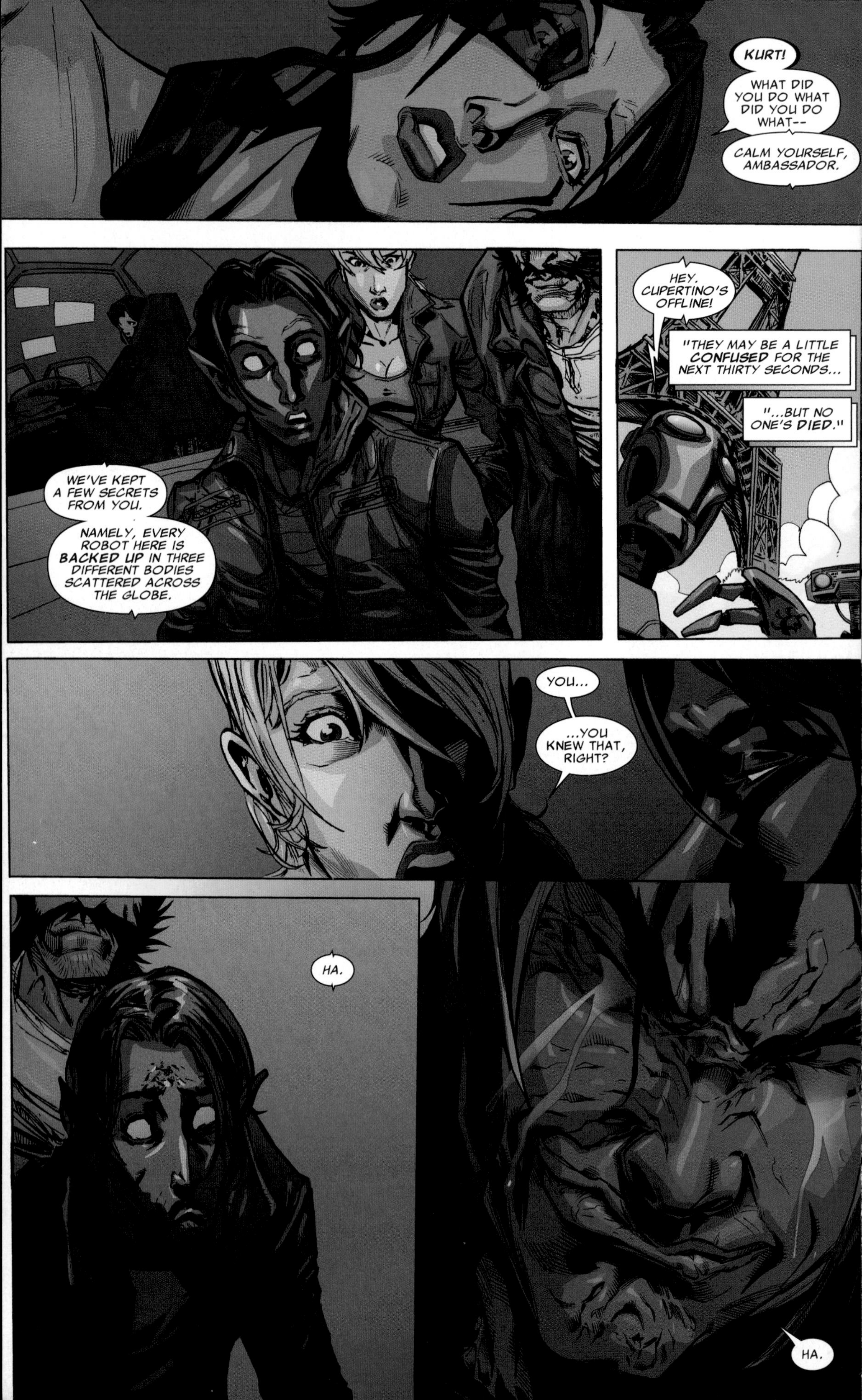
KURT!
WHAT DID YOU DO WHAT DID YOU DO WHAT--
CALM YOURSELF, AMBASSADOR.
WE'VE KEPT A FEW SECRETS FROM YOU.
NAMELY, EVERY ROBOT HERE IS BACKED UP IN THREE DIFFERENT BODIES SCATTERED ACROSS THE GLOBE.
HEY. CUPERTINO'S OFFLINE!
"THEY MAY BE A LITTLE CONFUSED FOR THE NEXT THIRTY SECONDS...
"...BUT NO ONE'S DIED."
YOU...
...YOU KNEW THAT, RIGHT?
HA.
HA.

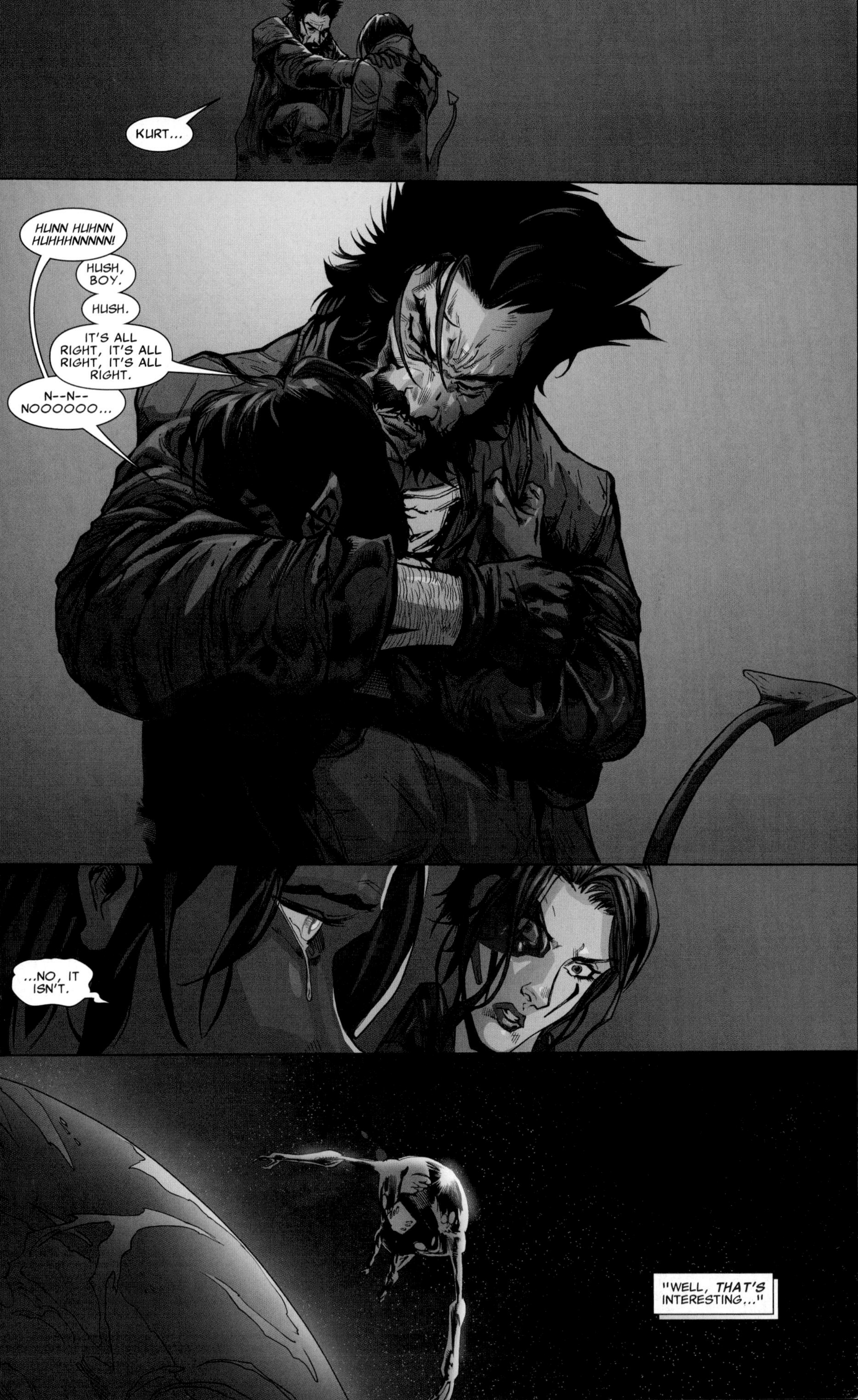
KURT...
HUNN HUHNN HUHHHNNNNN!
HUSH, BOY.
HUSH.
IT'S ALL RIGHT, IT'S ALL RIGHT, IT'S ALL RIGHT.
N--N-- NOOOOOO...
...NO, IT ISN'T.
"WELL, THAT'S INTERESTING..."

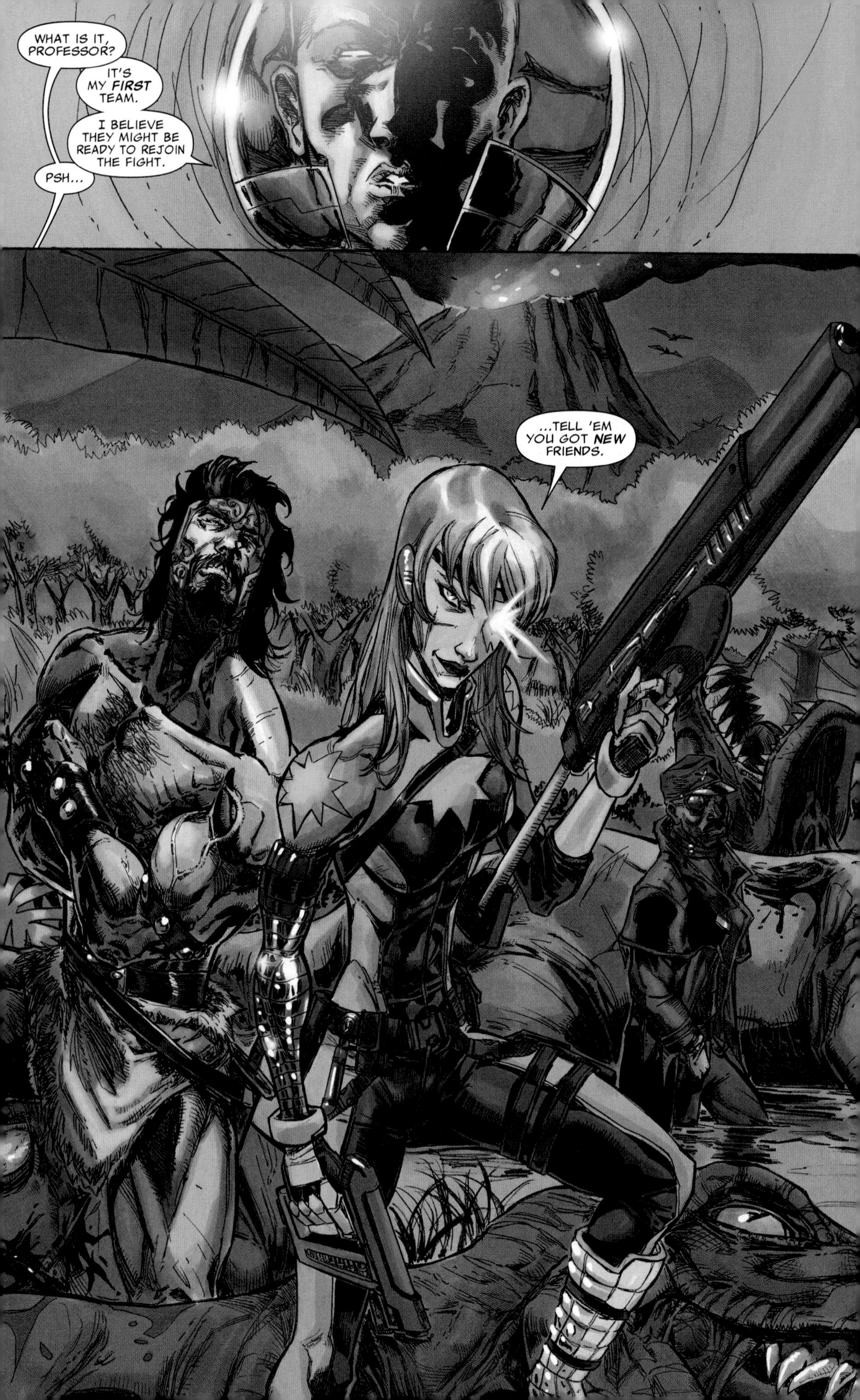
WHAT IS IT, PROFESSOR?
IT'S MY FIRST TEAM.
I BELIEVE THEY MIGHT BE READY TO REJOIN THE FIGHT.
PSH...
...TELL 'EM YOU GOT NEW FRIENDS.

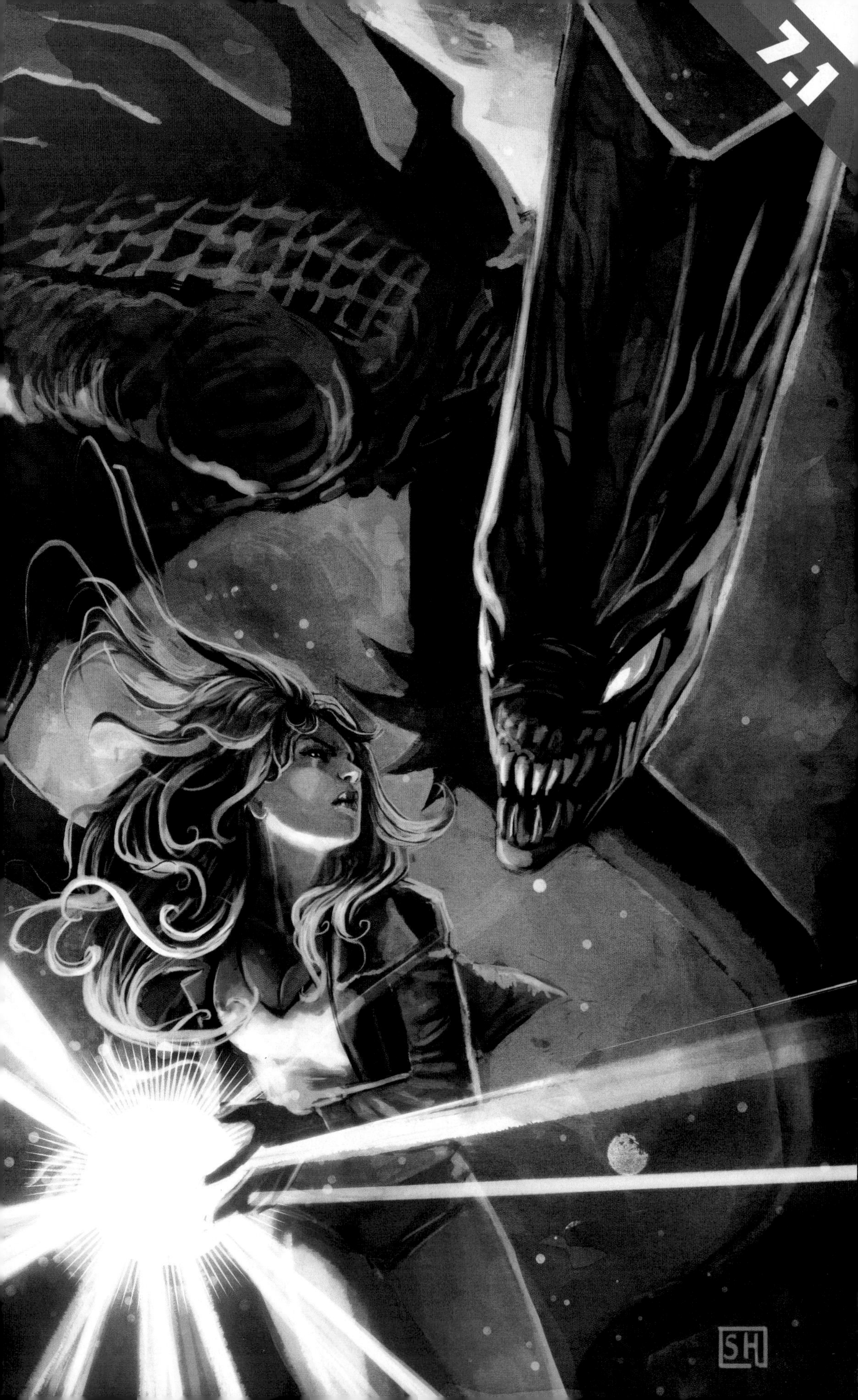

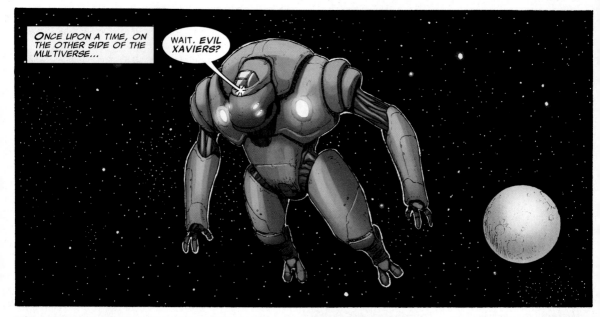

ONCE UPON A TIME, ON THE OTHER SIDE OF THE MULTIVERSE...

WAIT. *EVIL* XAVIERS?

DAZZLER,
CONVERTS SOUND INTO LIGHT. TEAM LEADER.

YES. TEN OF THEM, FROM ALTERNATE UNIVERSES. IF WE DON'T TAKE THEM OUT, THEY SCREW UP THE MULTIVERSE IN SOME AS-YET-UNDETERMINED- BUT-HORRIFICALLY- DEADLY WAY.

AND WHO TOLD YOU THIS?

ONE OF THE XAVIERS.

PRESUMABLY NOT ONE OF THE EVIL ONES.

SAGE,
COMPUTER-LIKE-BRAIN. JUST GOT HERE.

HOWLETT,
FORMER GOVERNOR-GENERAL OF THE DOMINION OF CANADA. WOLVERINEISH.

REMAINS TO BE SEEN, ACTUALLY.

KURT,
FOURTEEN. TELEPORTER.

AW, COME ON. FOR A DISEMBODIED HEAD IN A FLOATING BOTTLE, HE'S PRETTY OKAY.

YOU'VE GOT TO BE KIDDING ME.

WHAT? YES. *SOME.*

SAGE. YOU'VE GOT PSYCHIC POWERS, RIGHT?

THEN *SOME'S* GONNA HAVE TO BE *ENOUGH.* GET CRACKING. WE GOTTA FIND OUR XAVIER. WE LEFT HIM BEHIND IN SOME SAVAGE LAND DIMENSION.

WAIT A MINUTE. YOU EXPECT ME TO JUST REACH ACROSS DIMENSIONS AND PLUCK HIM OUT OF AN INFINITE UNIVERSE?

EVERYTHING THAT'S EVER EXISTED COULD BE AT STAKE.

SO, YES.

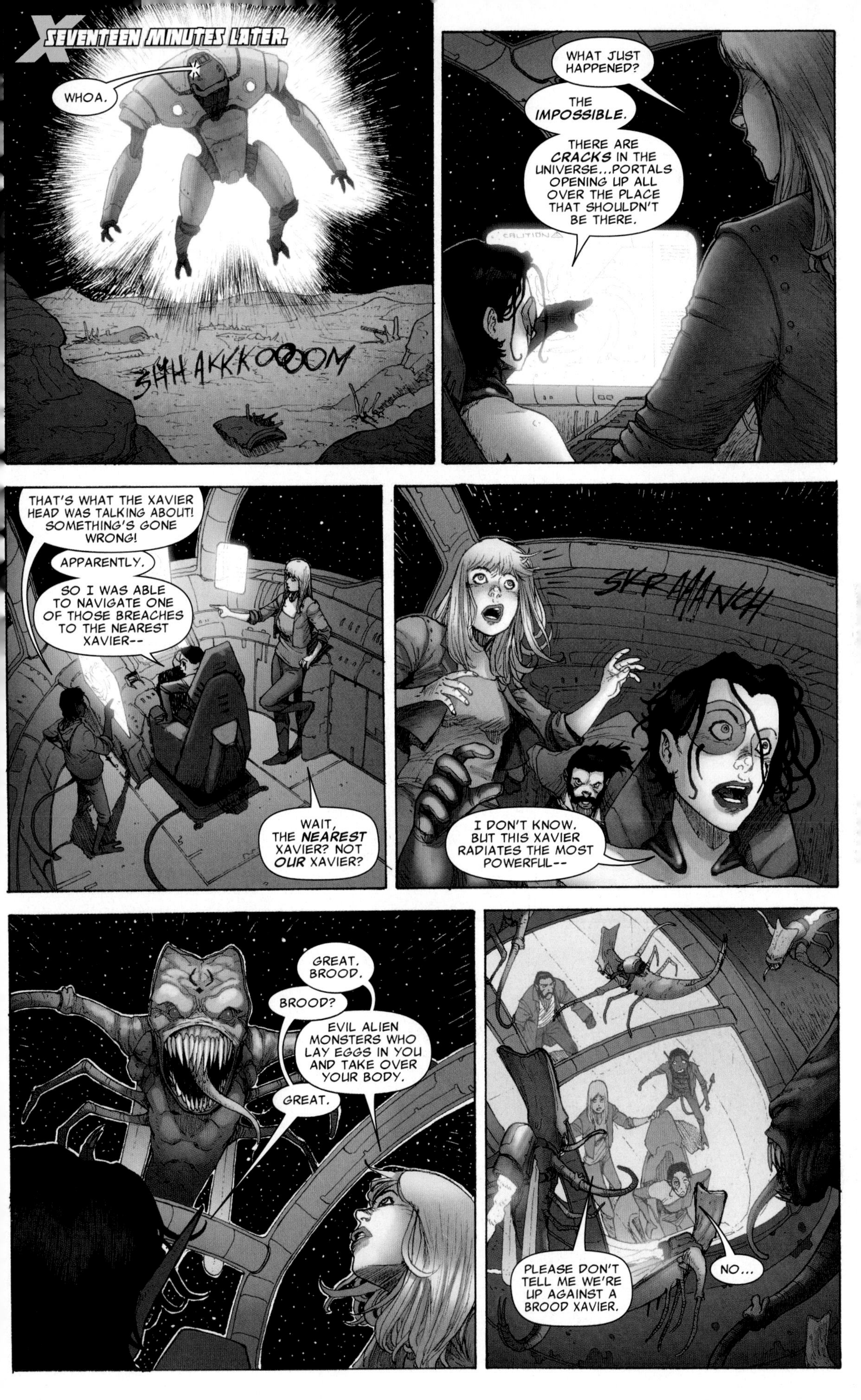
SEVENTEEN MINUTES LATER.
WHOA.
SHHAKKKOOOOM
WHAT JUST HAPPENED?
THE IMPOSSIBLE.
THERE ARE CRACKS IN THE UNIVERSE...PORTALS OPENING UP ALL OVER THE PLACE THAT SHOULDN'T BE THERE.
CAUTION
THAT'S WHAT THE XAVIER HEAD WAS TALKING ABOUT! SOMETHING'S GONE WRONG!
APPARENTLY.
SO I WAS ABLE TO NAVIGATE ONE OF THOSE BREACHES TO THE NEAREST XAVIER--
WAIT, THE NEAREST XAVIER? NOT OUR XAVIER?
SKRAAANCH
I DON'T KNOW. BUT THIS XAVIER RADIATES THE MOST POWERFUL--
GREAT. BROOD.
BROOD?
EVIL ALIEN MONSTERS WHO LAY EGGS IN YOU AND TAKE OVER YOUR BODY.
GREAT.
PLEASE DON'T TELL ME WE'RE UP AGAINST A BROOD XAVIER.
NO...

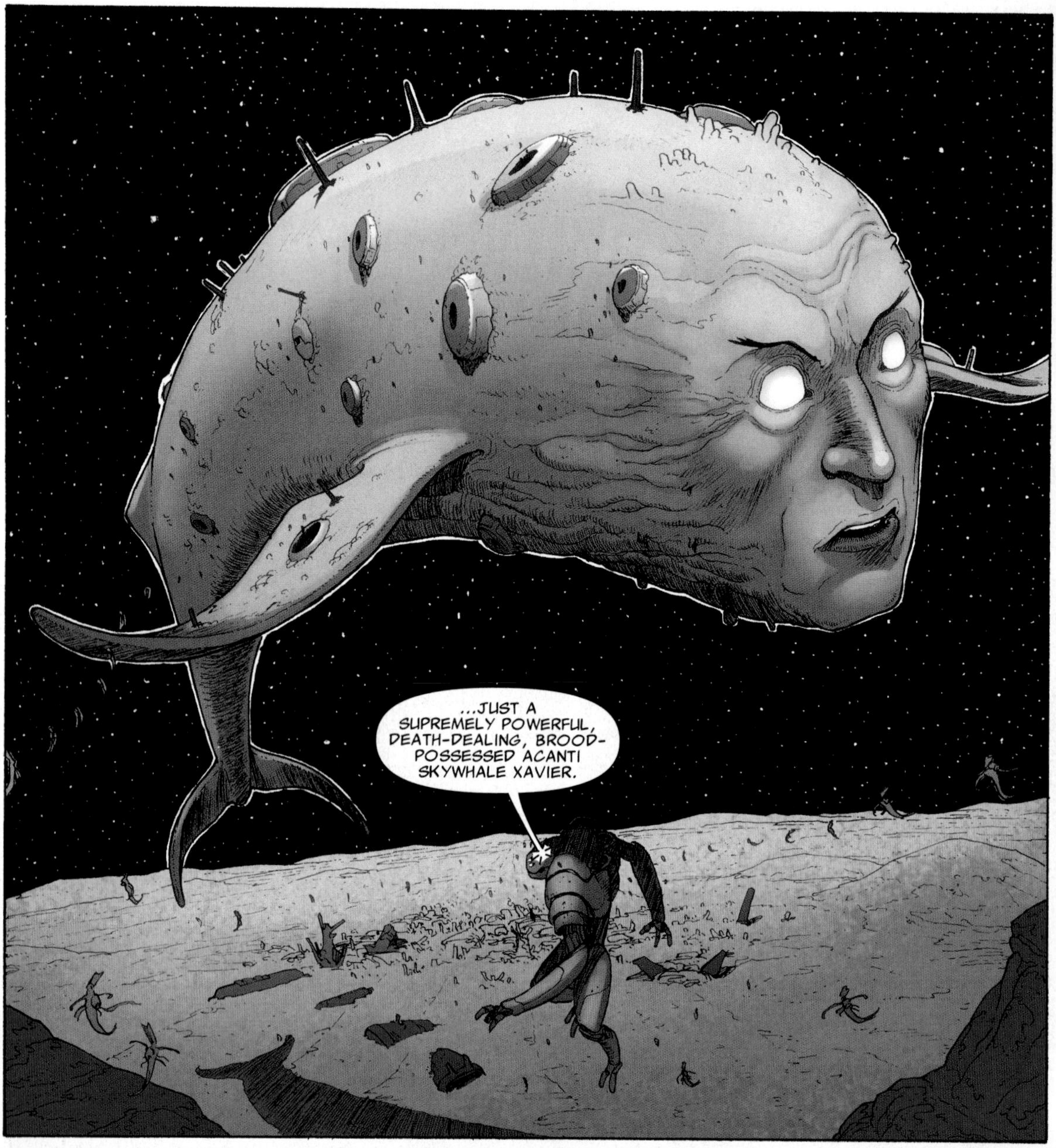
...JUST A SUPREMELY POWERFUL, DEATH-DEALING, BROOD-POSSESSED ACANTI SKYWHALE XAVIER.

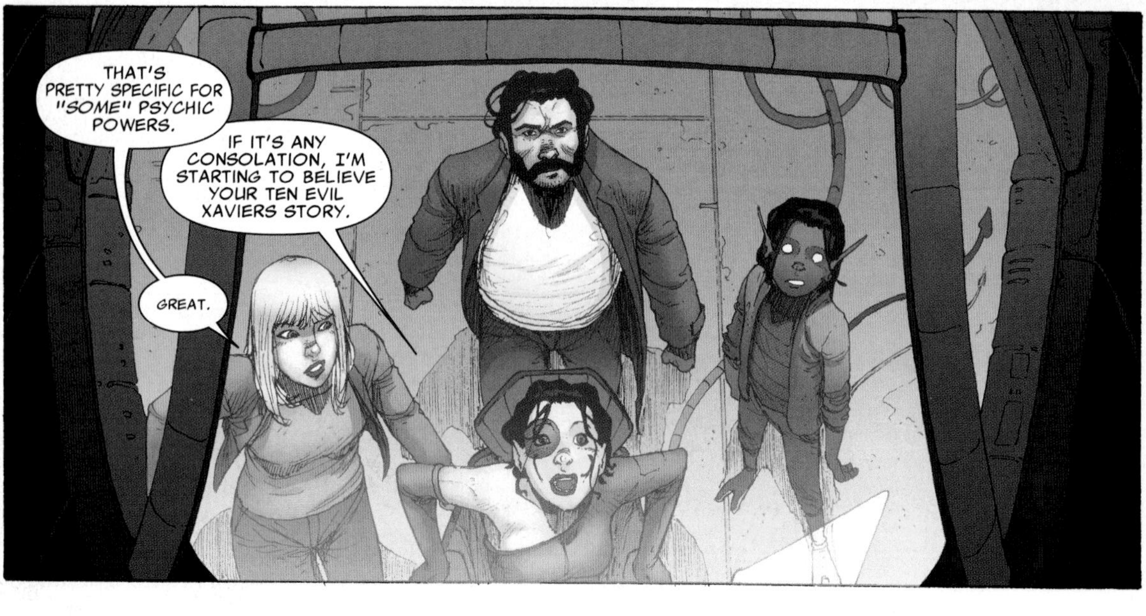
THAT'S PRETTY SPECIFIC FOR "SOME" PSYCHIC POWERS.
IF IT'S ANY CONSOLATION, I'M STARTING TO BELIEVE YOUR TEN EVIL XAVIERS STORY.
GREAT.

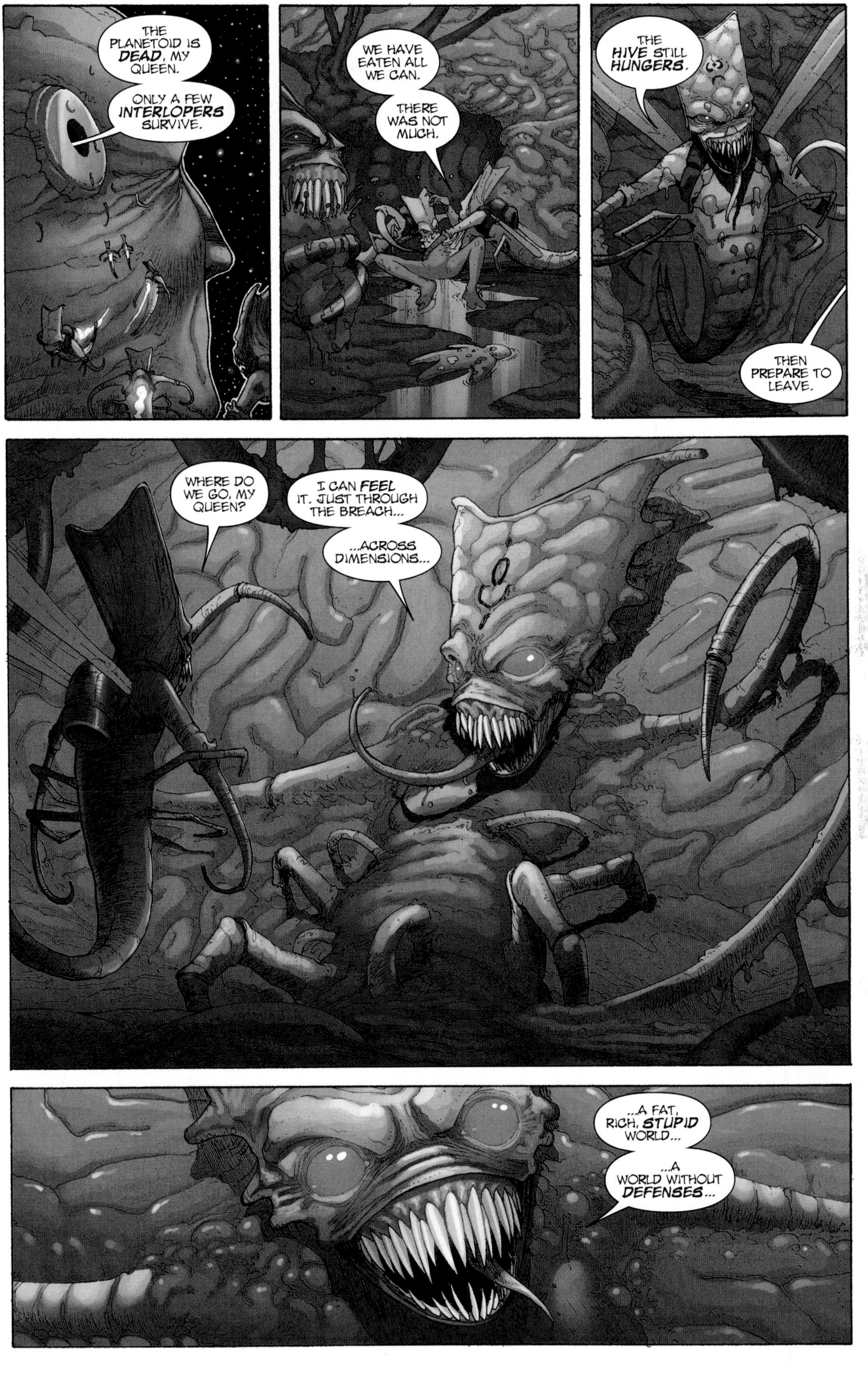

THE PLANETOID IS DEAD, MY QUEEN.
ONLY A FEW INTERLOPERS SURVIVE.
WE HAVE EATEN ALL WE CAN.
THERE WAS NOT MUCH.
THE HIVE STILL HUNGERS.
THEN PREPARE TO LEAVE.
WHERE DO WE GO, MY QUEEN?
I CAN FEEL IT. JUST THROUGH THE BREACH...
...ACROSS DIMENSIONS...
...A FAT, RICH, STUPID WORLD...
...A WORLD WITHOUT DEFENSES...

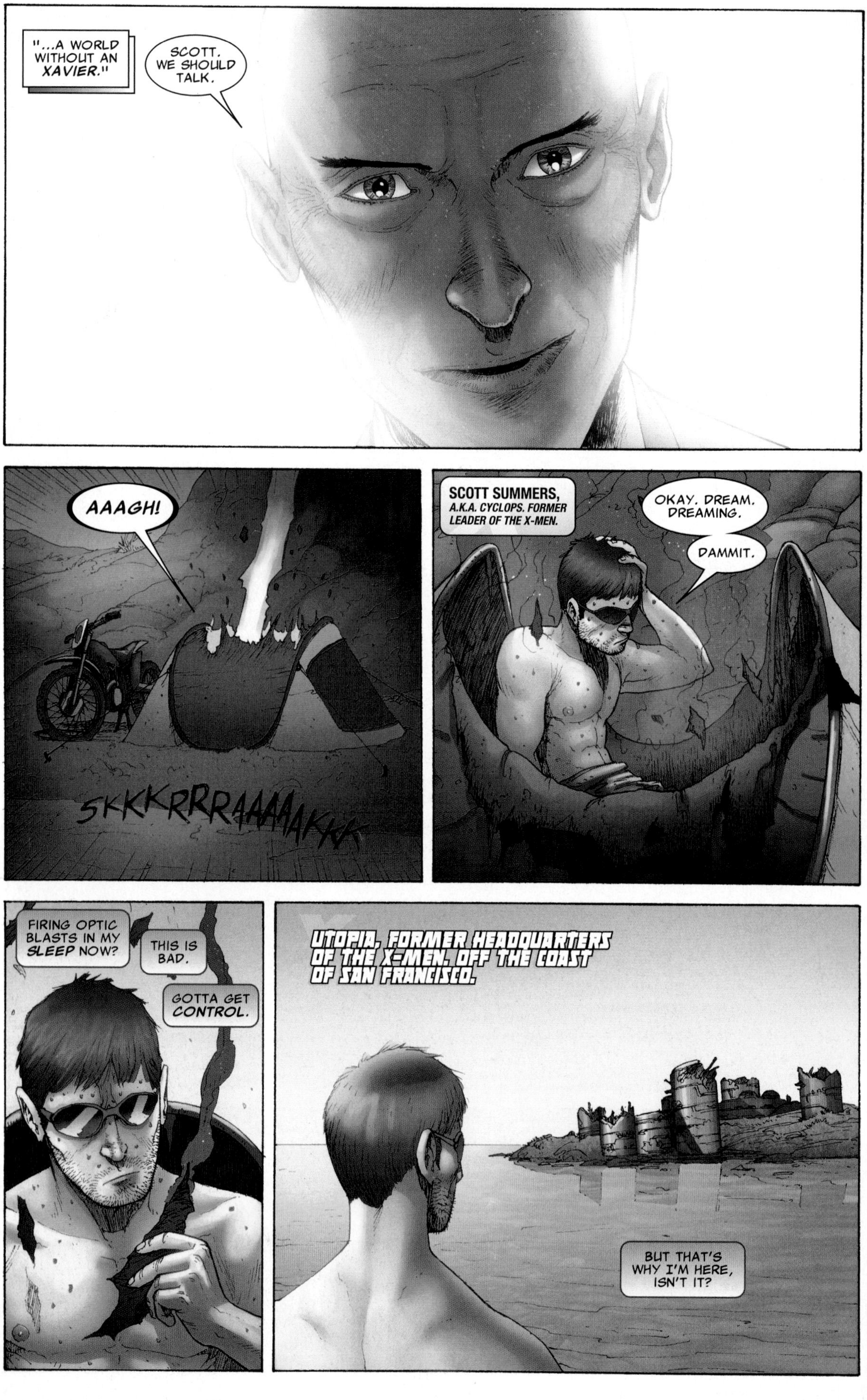
"...A WORLD WITHOUT AN XAVIER."
SCOTT. WE SHOULD TALK.
AAAGH!
SKKKRRRAAAAAKKK
SCOTT SUMMERS, A.K.A. CYCLOPS. FORMER LEADER OF THE X-MEN.
OKAY. DREAM. DREAMING.
DAMMIT.
FIRING OPTIC BLASTS IN MY SLEEP NOW?
THIS IS BAD.
GOTTA GET CONTROL.
UTOPIA, FORMER HEADQUARTERS OF THE X-MEN, OFF THE COAST OF SAN FRANCISCO.
BUT THAT'S WHY I'M HERE, ISN'T IT?

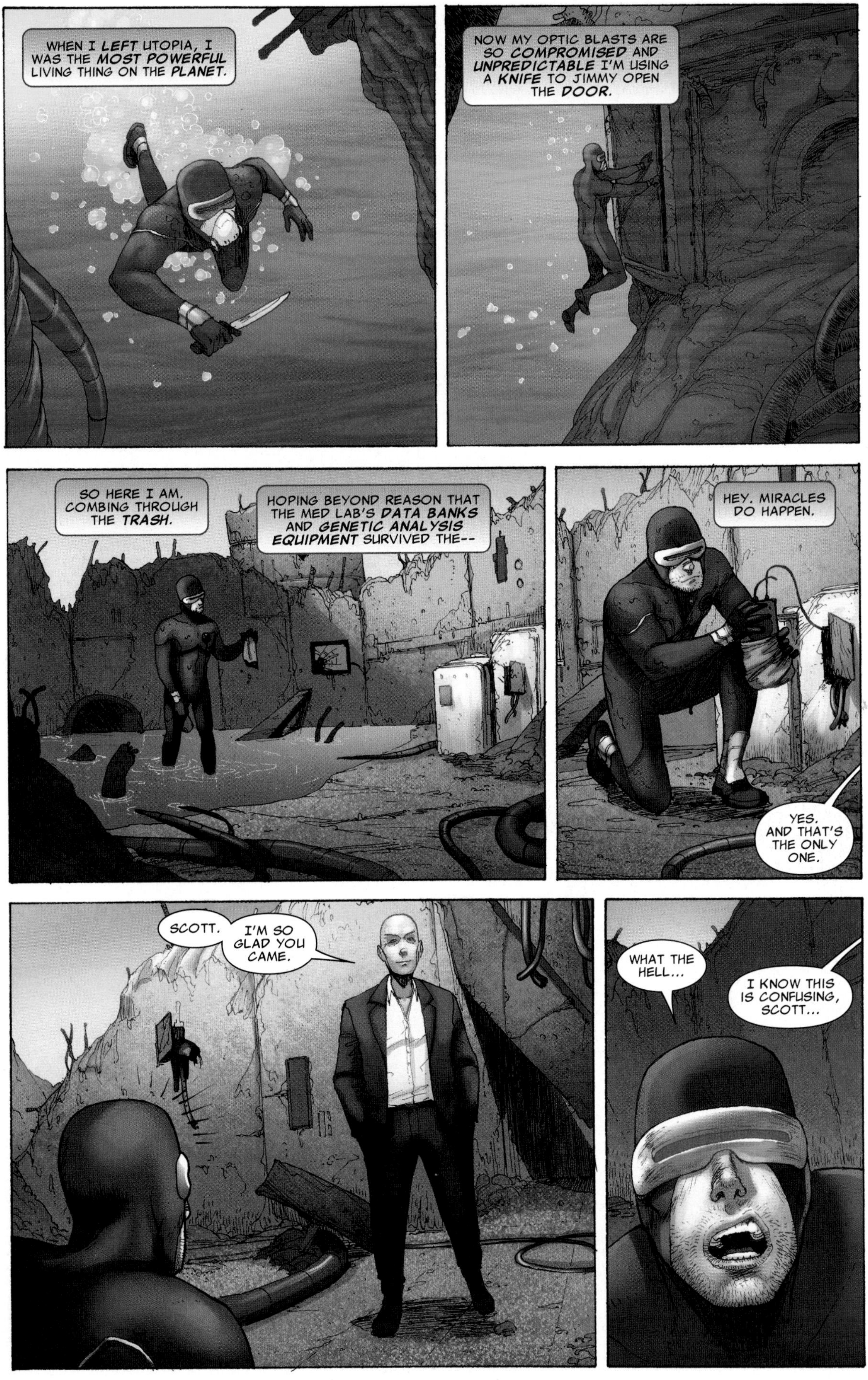
WHEN I LEFT UTOPIA, I WAS THE MOST POWERFUL LIVING THING ON THE PLANET.
NOW MY OPTIC BLASTS ARE SO COMPROMISED AND UNPREDICTABLE I'M USING A KNIFE TO JIMMY OPEN THE DOOR.
SO HERE I AM. COMBING THROUGH THE TRASH.
HOPING BEYOND REASON THAT THE MED LAB'S DATA BANKS AND GENETIC ANALYSIS EQUIPMENT SURVIVED THE--
HEY. MIRACLES DO HAPPEN.
YES. AND THAT'S THE ONLY ONE.
SCOTT.
I'M SO GLAD YOU CAME.
WHAT THE HELL...
I KNOW THIS IS CONFUSING, SCOTT...

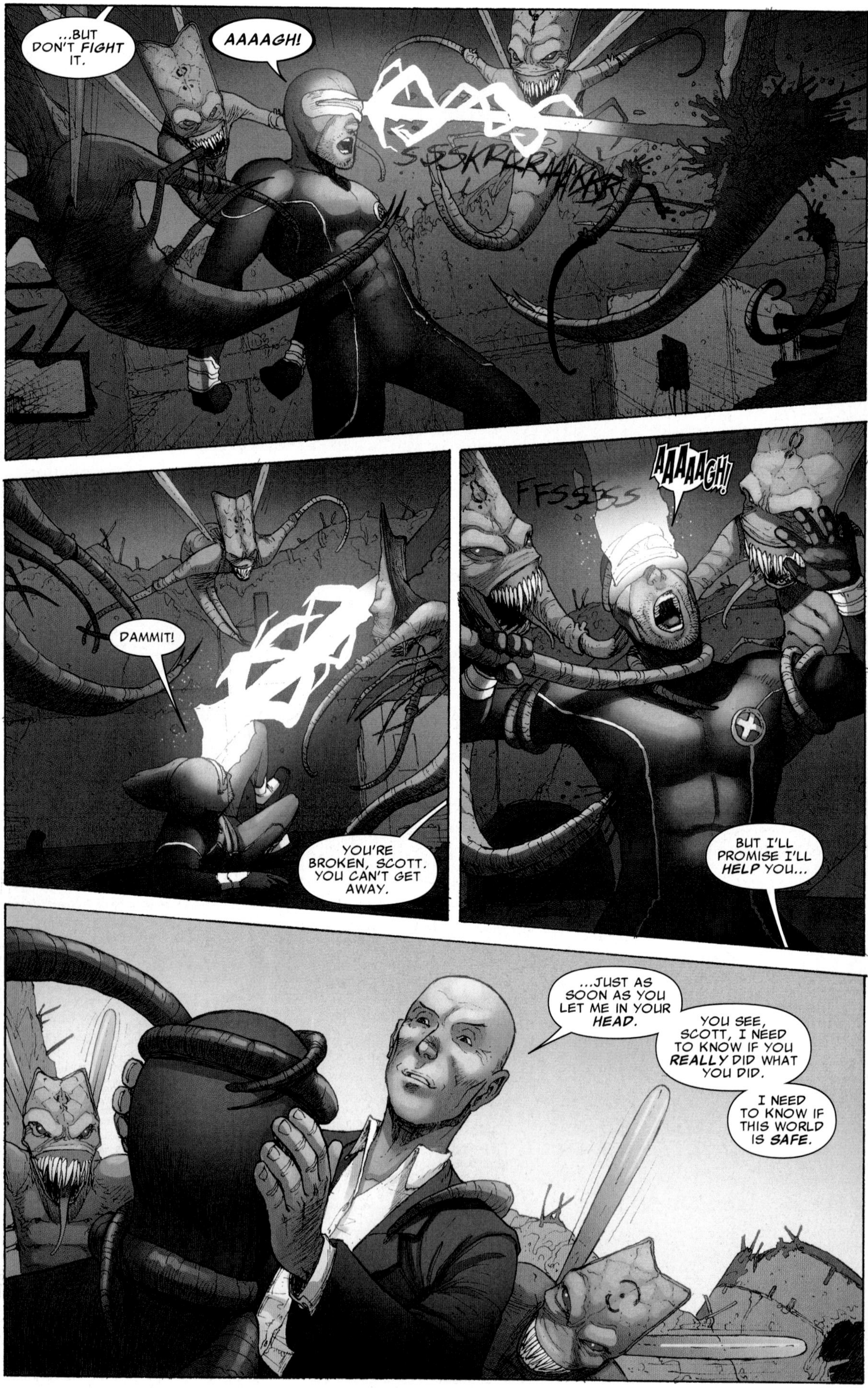
...BUT DON'T FIGHT IT.
AAAAGH!
SSSKRRRAKKKR
DAMMIT!
YOU'RE BROKEN, SCOTT. YOU CAN'T GET AWAY.
FFSSSSS
AAAAAGH!
BUT I'LL PROMISE I'LL HELP YOU...
...JUST AS SOON AS YOU LET ME IN YOUR HEAD.
YOU SEE, SCOTT, I NEED TO KNOW IF YOU REALLY DID WHAT YOU DID.
I NEED TO KNOW IF THIS WORLD IS SAFE.

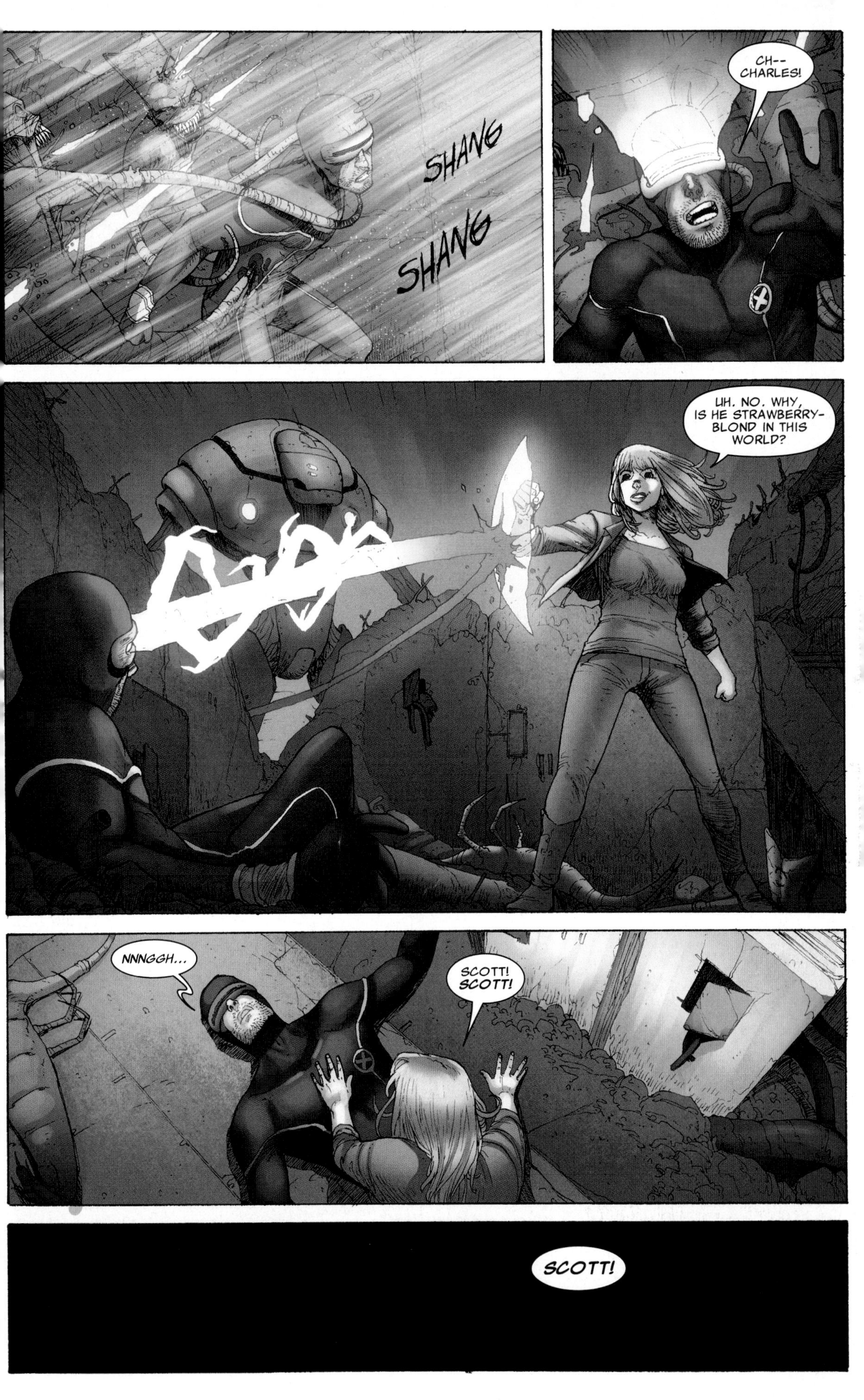
SHANG
SHANG
CH-- CHARLES!
UH. NO. WHY, IS HE STRAWBERRY-BLOND IN THIS WORLD?
NNNGGH...
SCOTT! SCOTT!
SCOTT!

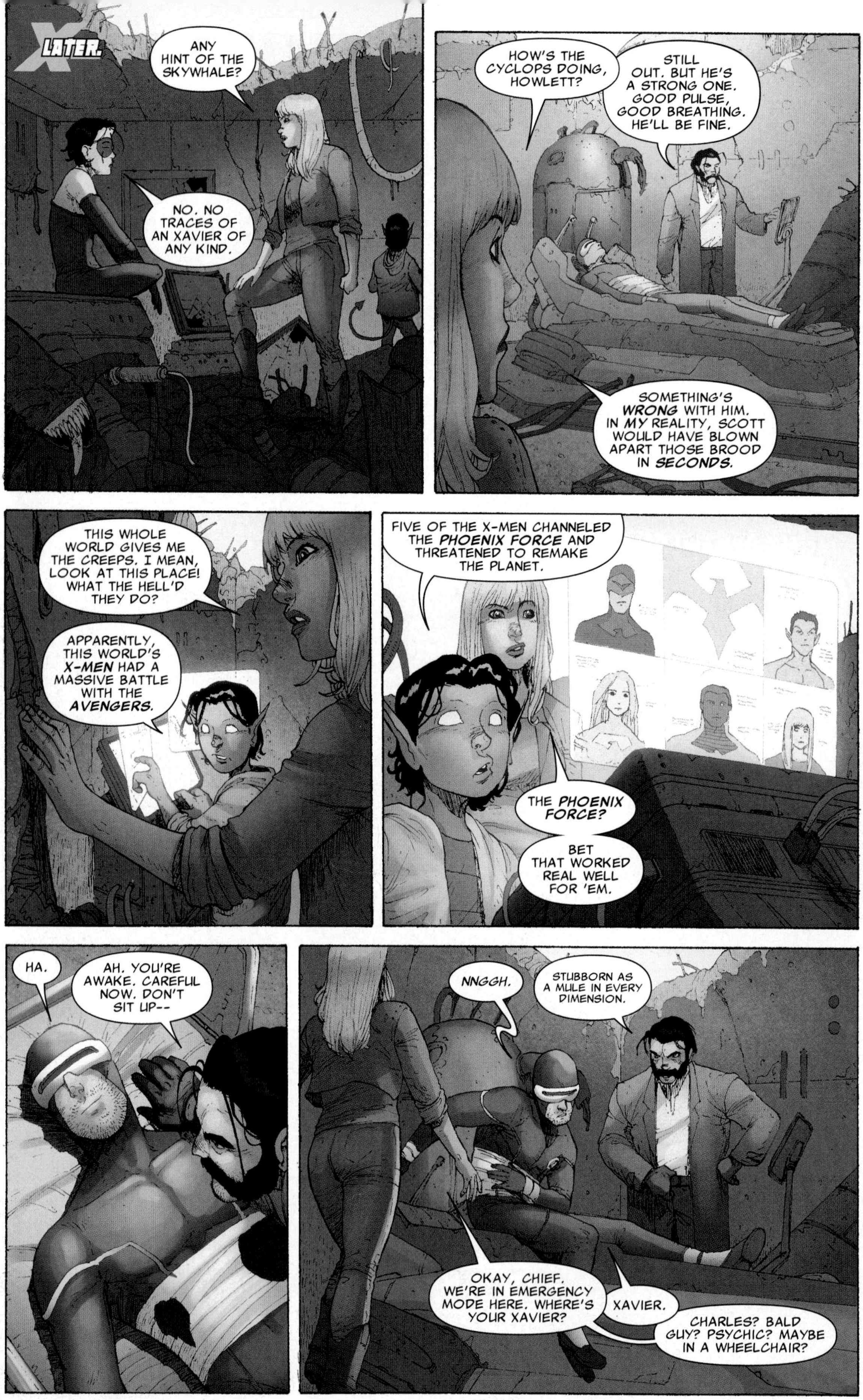
LATER.
ANY HINT OF THE SKYWHALE?
NO. NO TRACES OF AN XAVIER OF ANY KIND.
HOW'S THE CYCLOPS DOING, HOWLETT?
STILL OUT. BUT HE'S A STRONG ONE. GOOD PULSE, GOOD BREATHING. HE'LL BE FINE.
SOMETHING'S WRONG WITH HIM. IN MY REALITY, SCOTT WOULD HAVE BLOWN APART THOSE BROOD IN SECONDS.
THIS WHOLE WORLD GIVES ME THE CREEPS. I MEAN, LOOK AT THIS PLACE! WHAT THE HELL'D THEY DO?
APPARENTLY, THIS WORLD'S X-MEN HAD A MASSIVE BATTLE WITH THE AVENGERS.
FIVE OF THE X-MEN CHANNELED THE PHOENIX FORCE AND THREATENED TO REMAKE THE PLANET.
THE PHOENIX FORCE?
BET THAT WORKED REAL WELL FOR 'EM.
HA.
AH. YOU'RE AWAKE. CAREFUL NOW. DON'T SIT UP--
NNGGH.
STUBBORN AS A MULE IN EVERY DIMENSION.
OKAY, CHIEF. WE'RE IN EMERGENCY MODE HERE. WHERE'S YOUR XAVIER?
XAVIER.
CHARLES? BALD GUY? PSYCHIC? MAYBE IN A WHEELCHAIR?

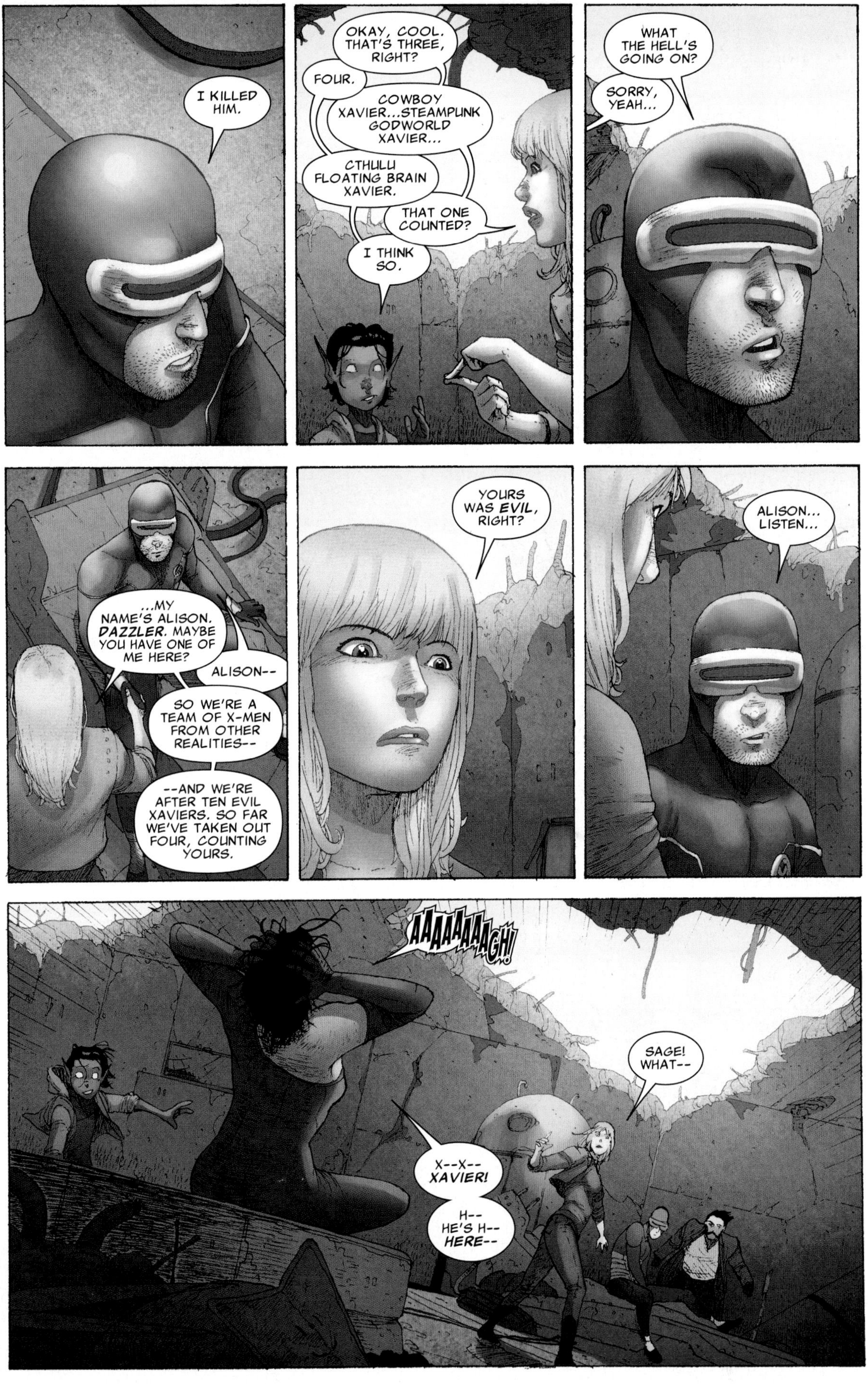
I KILLED HIM.
OKAY, COOL. THAT'S THREE, RIGHT?
FOUR.
COWBOY XAVIER...STEAMPUNK GODWORLD XAVIER...
CTHULU FLOATING BRAIN XAVIER.
THAT ONE COUNTED?
I THINK SO.
WHAT THE HELL'S GOING ON?
SORRY, YEAH...
...MY NAME'S ALISON. DAZZLER. MAYBE YOU HAVE ONE OF ME HERE?
ALISON--
SO WE'RE A TEAM OF X-MEN FROM OTHER REALITIES--
--AND WE'RE AFTER TEN EVIL XAVIERS. SO FAR WE'VE TAKEN OUT FOUR, COUNTING YOURS.
YOURS WAS EVIL, RIGHT?
ALISON... LISTEN...
AAAAAAAAGH!
SAGE! WHAT--
X--X-- XAVIER!
H-- HE'S H-- HERE--

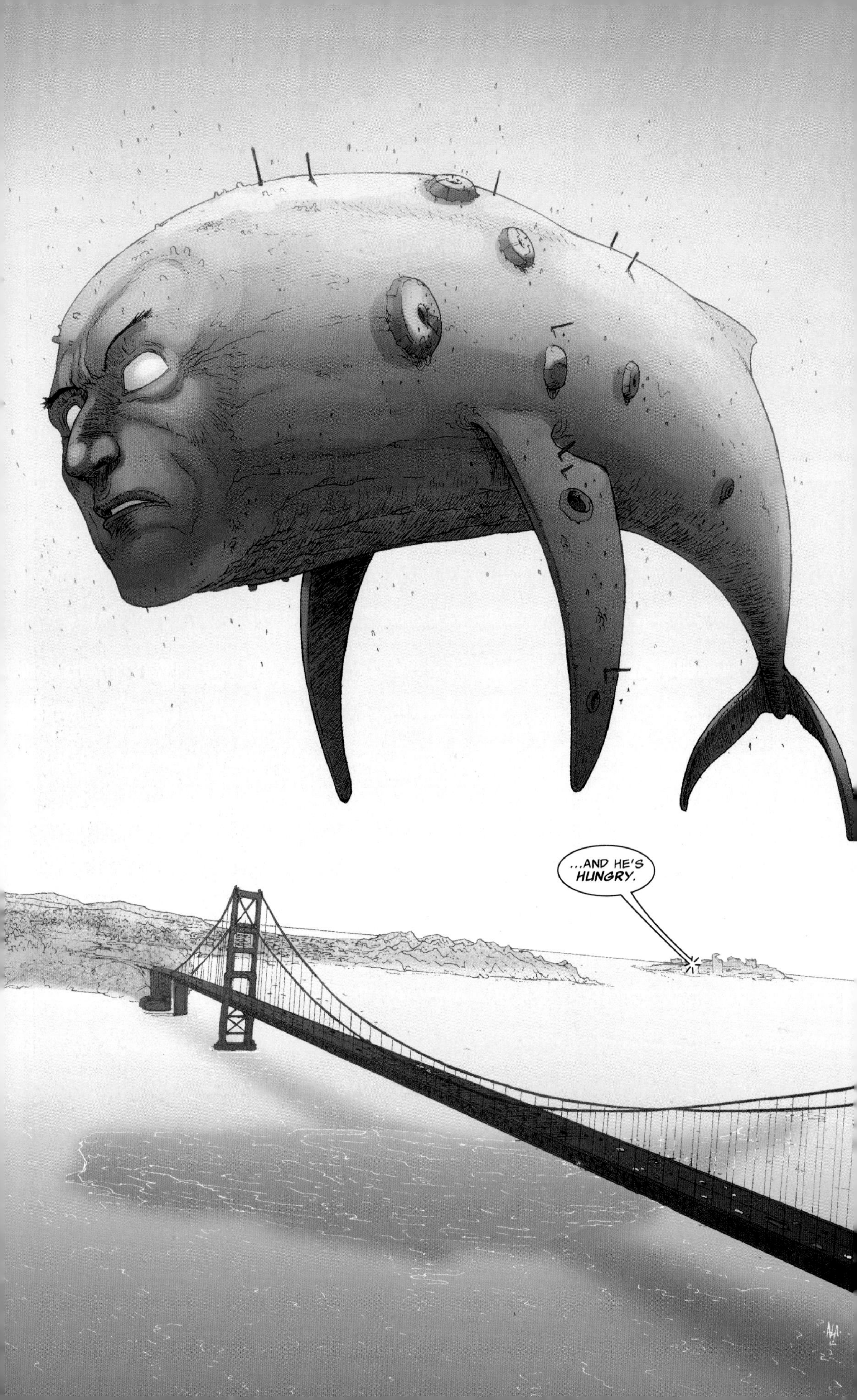
...AND HE'S HUNGRY.

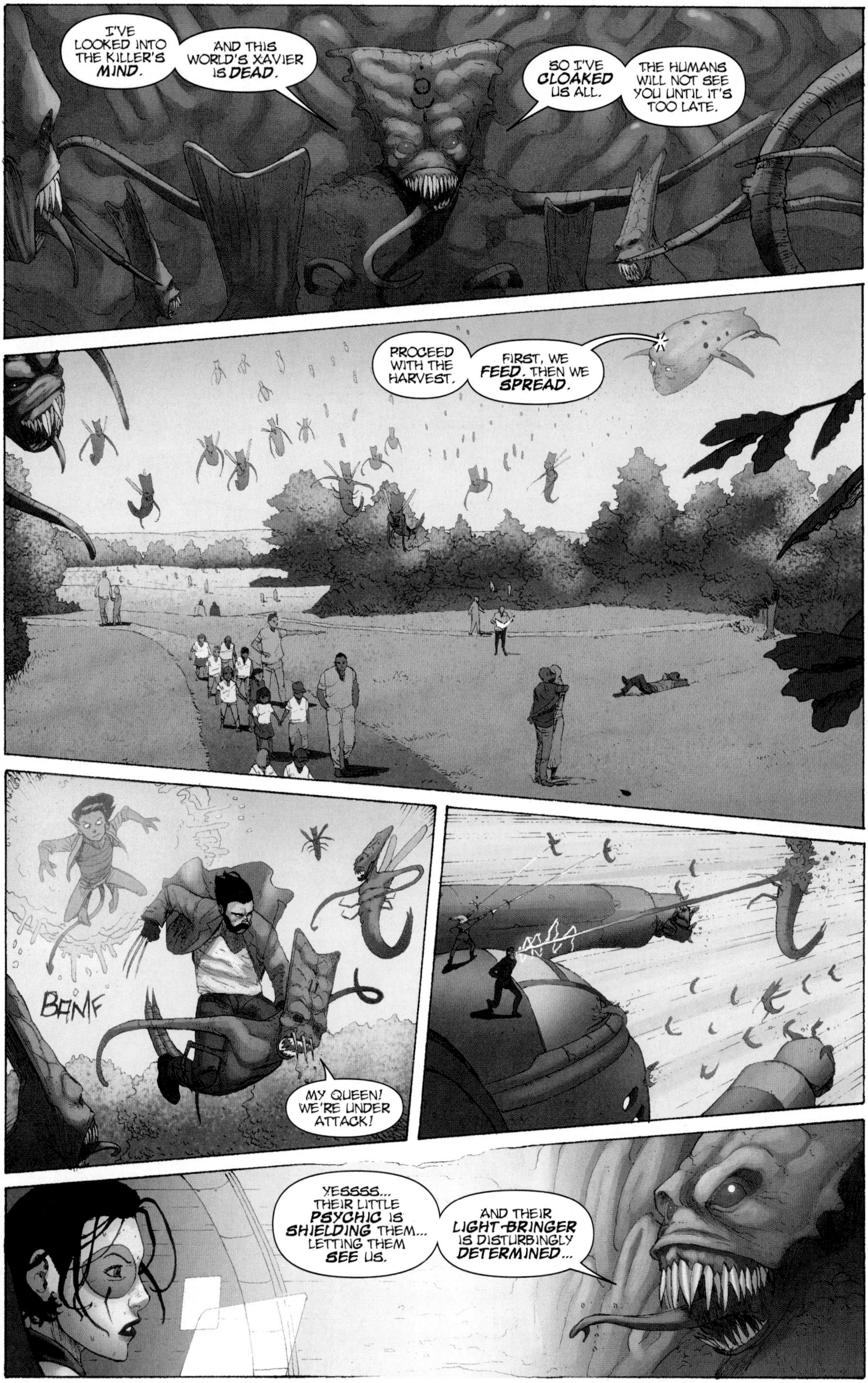
I'VE LOOKED INTO THE KILLER'S MIND.
AND THIS WORLD'S XAVIER IS DEAD.
SO I'VE CLOAKED US ALL.
THE HUMANS WILL NOT SEE YOU UNTIL IT'S TOO LATE.
PROCEED WITH THE HARVEST.
FIRST, WE FEED. THEN WE SPREAD.
BAMF
MY QUEEN! WE'RE UNDER ATTACK!
YESSSS... THEIR LITTLE PSYCHIC IS SHIELDING THEM... LETTING THEM SEE US.
AND THEIR LIGHT-BRINGER IS DISTURBINGLY DETERMINED...

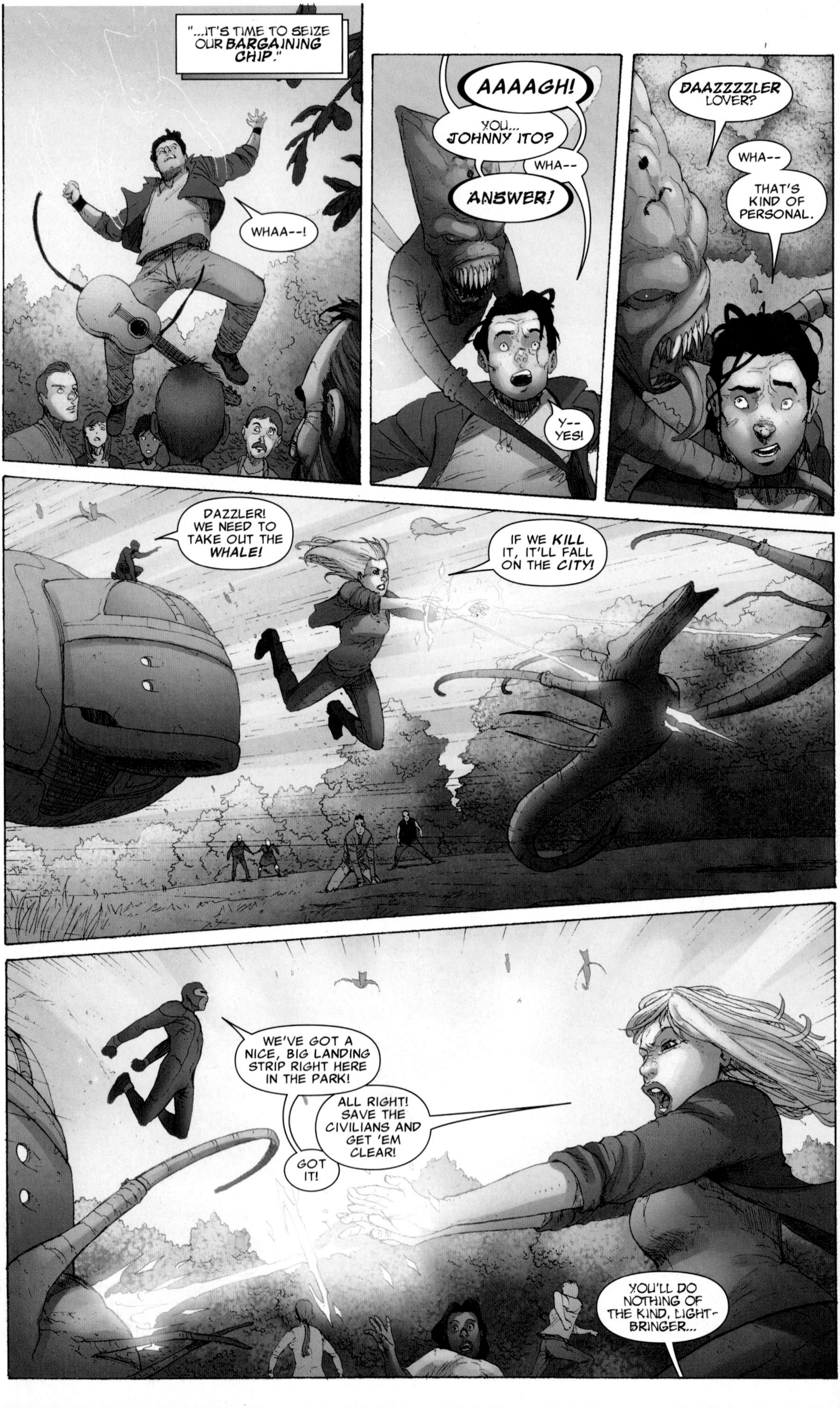
"...IT'S TIME TO SEIZE OUR BARGAINING CHIP."
WHAA--!
AAAAGH!
YOU... JOHNNY ITO?
WHA--
ANSWER!
Y-- YES!
DAAZZZZZLER LOVER?
WHA--
THAT'S KIND OF PERSONAL.
DAZZLER! WE NEED TO TAKE OUT THE WHALE!
IF WE KILL IT, IT'LL FALL ON THE CITY!
WE'VE GOT A NICE, BIG LANDING STRIP RIGHT HERE IN THE PARK!
ALL RIGHT! SAVE THE CIVILIANS AND GET 'EM CLEAR!
GOT IT!
YOU'LL DO NOTHING OF THE KIND, LIGHT-BRINGER...

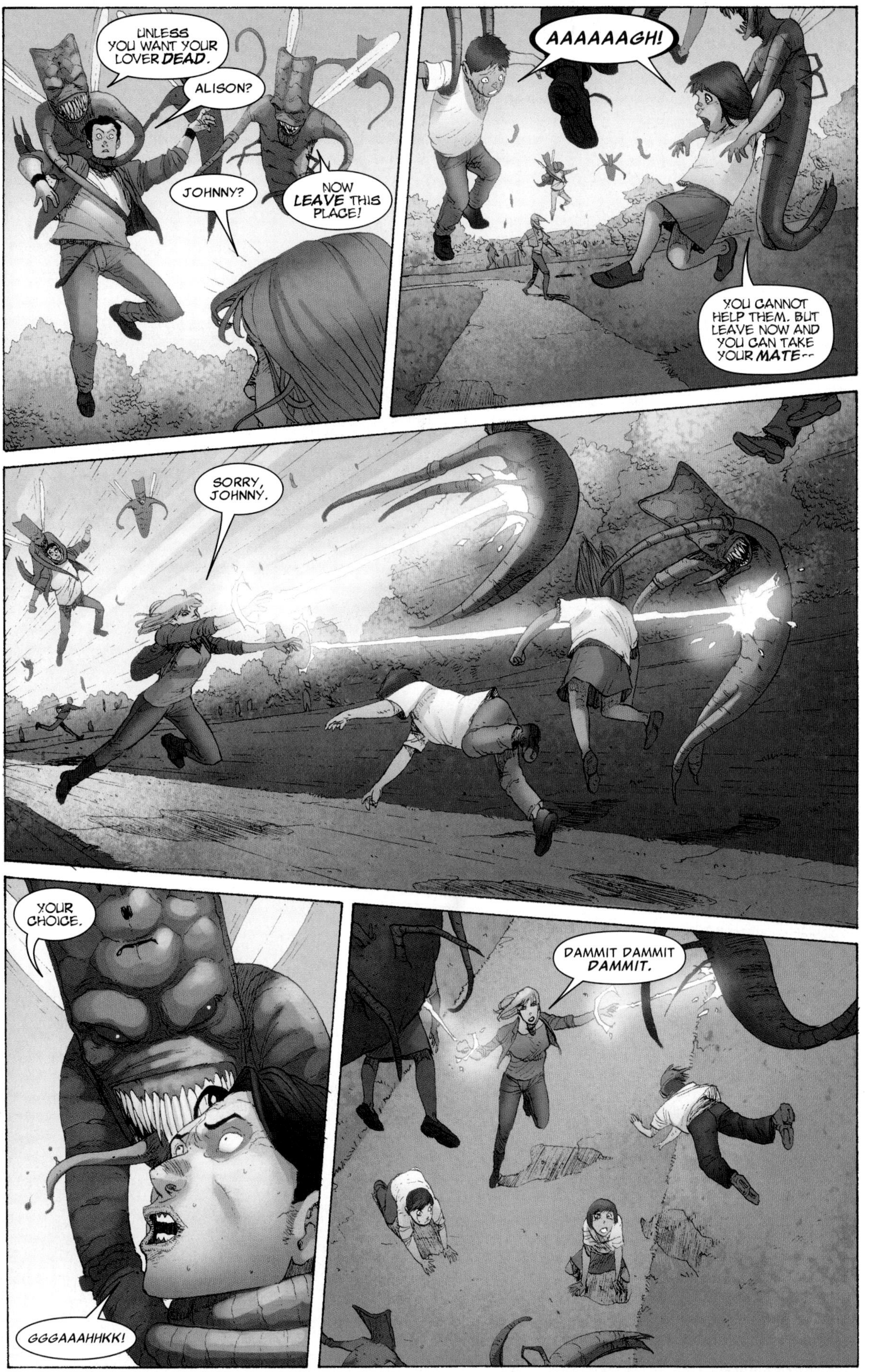
UNLESS YOU WANT YOUR LOVER DEAD.
ALISON?
JOHNNY?
NOW LEAVE THIS PLACE!
AAAAAAGH!
YOU CANNOT HELP THEM. BUT LEAVE NOW AND YOU CAN TAKE YOUR MATE--
SORRY, JOHNNY.
YOUR CHOICE.
GGGAAAHHKK!
DAMMIT DAMMIT DAMMIT.

SHANG

KKKK--

BAMF

THANKS, HOWLETT.

NO PROBLEM.

THAT WAS THE LAST OF THEM!

SCOTT, HOWLETT, ON THE ROBOT! KURT, YOU KEEP GETTING CIVILIANS CLEAR OF THE PARK!

YOU OKAY?

YEAH. BUT..."SORRY, JOHNNY"?

THEY MADE ME CHOOSE, JOHNNY. IT WAS YOU OR THE KIDS.

YEAH, I KNOW. I GET IT. HERO MOVE.

JUST SEEMED A LITTLE...COLD IN THE MOMENT.

I MEAN, I THOUGHT WE HAD SOMETHING GOING ON, AND THEN YOU DISAPPEAR, AND THEN YOU REAPPEAR, AND MONSTERS AND--

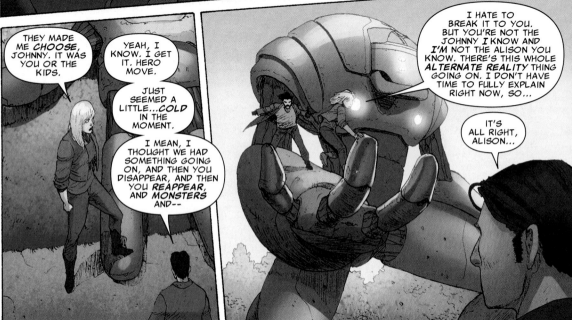

I HATE TO BREAK IT TO YOU, BUT YOU'RE NOT THE JOHNNY I KNOW AND I'M NOT THE ALISON YOU KNOW. THERE'S THIS WHOLE ALTERNATE REALITY THING GOING ON. I DON'T HAVE TIME TO FULLY EXPLAIN RIGHT NOW, SO...

IT'S ALL RIGHT, ALISON...

...IF YOU WANNA BREAK UP, JUST *SAY* SO!

ALL RIGHT, X-MEN...

...GET READY FOR THE SECOND WAVE!

HOO BOY.

SAGE! YOU HEARING ME? CAN YOU GET US ALL ON A PSYCHIC LINK, HERE?

YES AND DONE.

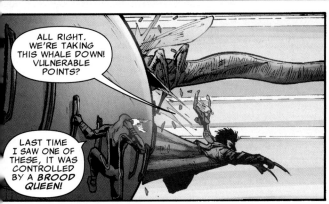

ALL RIGHT, WE'RE TAKING THIS WHALE DOWN! VULNERABLE POINTS?

LAST TIME I SAW ONE OF THESE, IT WAS CONTROLLED BY A *BROOD QUEEN!*

GOT IT. SHE'S CONNECTED TO THE WHALE'S *BRAIN STEM.*

BEST ENTRANCE IS THE DOME OVER THE RIGHT EYEBALL.

OKAY, HOWLETT'S GOT THE BEST PSYCHIC RESISTANCE, SO--

GRRAAH!

CRUNNNCH

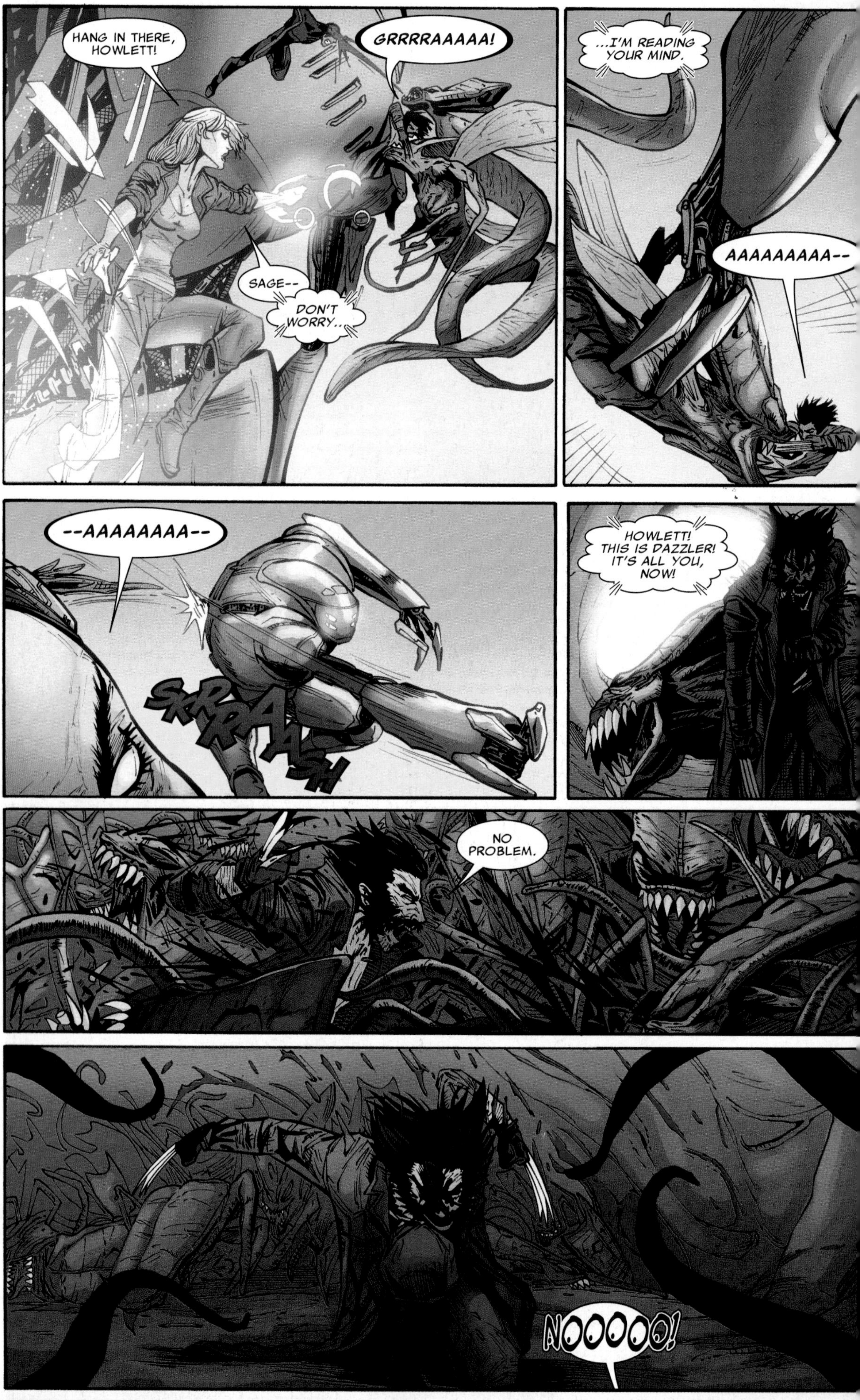
HANG IN THERE, HOWLETT!
GRRRRAAAAA!
SAGE--
DON'T WORRY...
...I'M READING YOUR MIND.
AAAAAAAAA--
--AAAAAAAA--
SKRRAASH
HOWLETT! THIS IS DAZZLER! IT'S ALL YOU, NOW!
NO PROBLEM.
NOOOOO!

HUKKKK!

WOW. THAT WORKED.

WHAT?

YES. I DON'T GET IT.

TOO EASY.

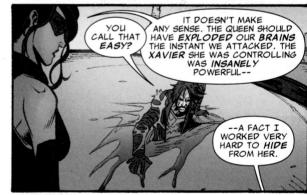

YOU CALL THAT EASY?

IT DOESN'T MAKE ANY SENSE. THE QUEEN SHOULD HAVE EXPLODED OUR BRAINS THE INSTANT WE ATTACKED. THE XAVIER SHE WAS CONTROLLING WAS INSANELY POWERFUL--

--A FACT I WORKED VERY HARD TO HIDE FROM HER.

SHE CONTROLLED ME. BUT SHE HAD NO PSYCHIC ABILITY OF HER OWN. SO SHE NEVER KNEW HOW MUCH DAMAGE WE COULD HAVE DONE.

BUT I KNOW.

SO NOW I NEED YOUR HELP.

THIS WORLD HAS MANY HEALERS. WE'LL GET YOU BACK IN THE AIR--

NO.

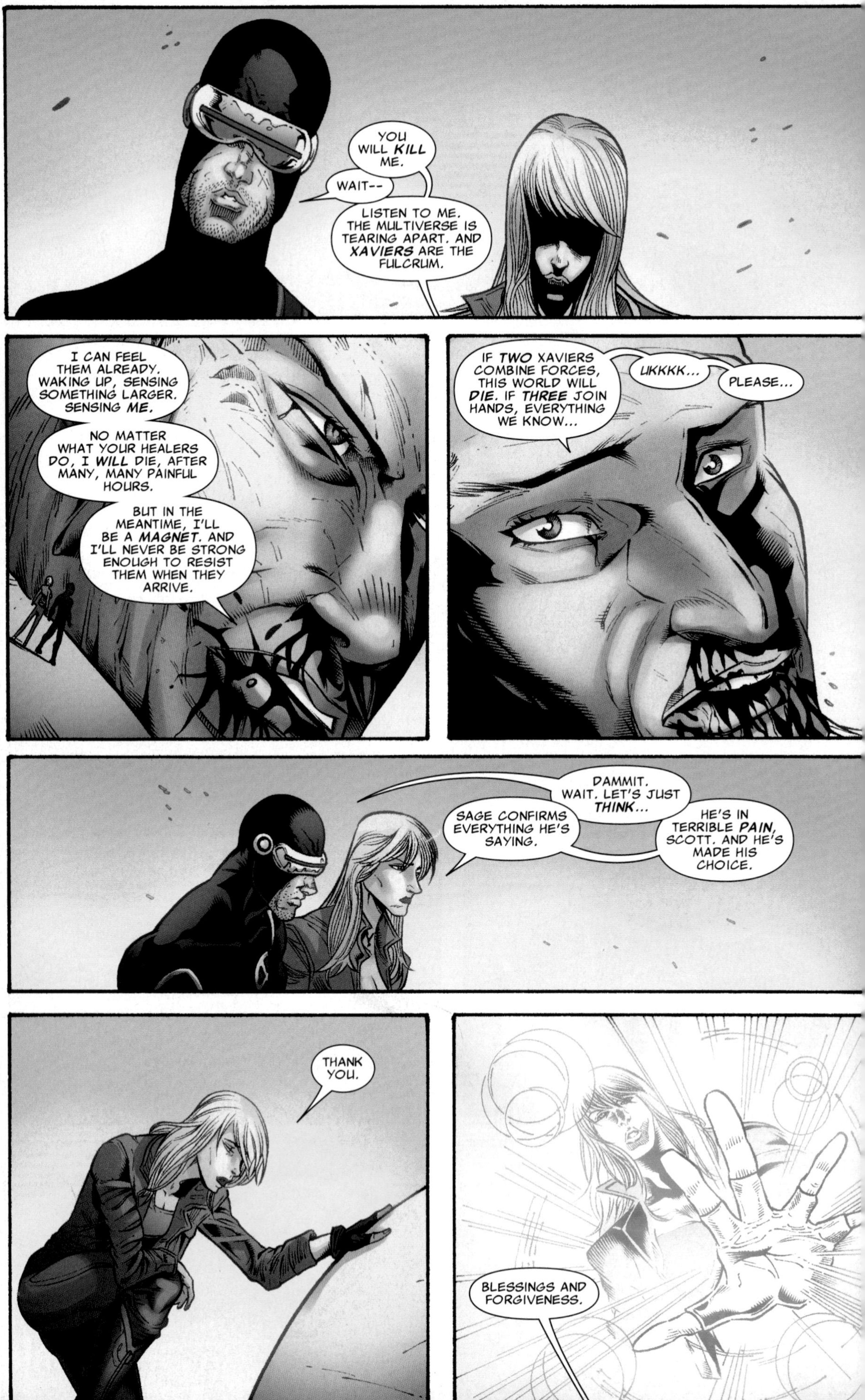

YOU WILL KILL ME.
WAIT--
LISTEN TO ME. THE MULTIVERSE IS TEARING APART. AND XAVIERS ARE THE FULCRUM.
I CAN FEEL THEM ALREADY. WAKING UP, SENSING SOMETHING LARGER. SENSING ME.
NO MATTER WHAT YOUR HEALERS DO, I WILL DIE, AFTER MANY, MANY PAINFUL HOURS.
BUT IN THE MEANTIME, I'LL BE A MAGNET. AND I'LL NEVER BE STRONG ENOUGH TO RESIST THEM WHEN THEY ARRIVE.
IF TWO XAVIERS COMBINE FORCES, THIS WORLD WILL DIE. IF THREE JOIN HANDS, EVERYTHING WE KNOW...
UKKKK...
PLEASE...
DAMMIT. WAIT. LET'S JUST THINK...
SAGE CONFIRMS EVERYTHING HE'S SAYING.
HE'S IN TERRIBLE PAIN, SCOTT. AND HE'S MADE HIS CHOICE.
THANK YOU.
BLESSINGS AND FORGIVENESS.

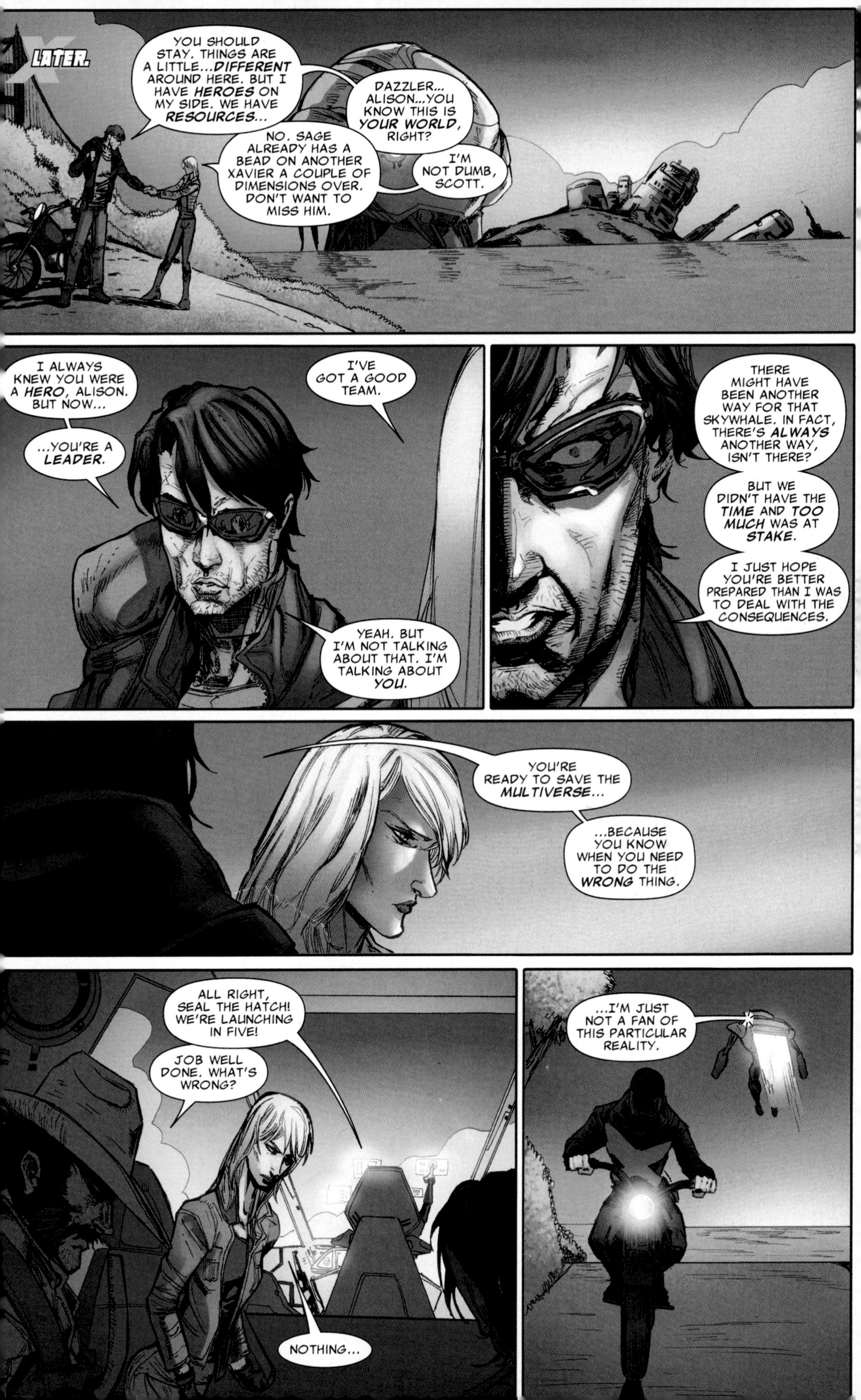
LATER.
YOU SHOULD STAY. THINGS ARE A LITTLE...DIFFERENT AROUND HERE. BUT I HAVE HEROES ON MY SIDE. WE HAVE RESOURCES...
NO. SAGE ALREADY HAS A BEAD ON ANOTHER XAVIER A COUPLE OF DIMENSIONS OVER. DON'T WANT TO MISS HIM.
DAZZLER... ALISON...YOU KNOW THIS IS YOUR WORLD, RIGHT?
I'M NOT DUMB, SCOTT.
I ALWAYS KNEW YOU WERE A HERO, ALISON. BUT NOW...
...YOU'RE A LEADER.
I'VE GOT A GOOD TEAM.
YEAH. BUT I'M NOT TALKING ABOUT THAT. I'M TALKING ABOUT YOU.
THERE MIGHT HAVE BEEN ANOTHER WAY FOR THAT SKYWHALE. IN FACT, THERE'S ALWAYS ANOTHER WAY, ISN'T THERE?
BUT WE DIDN'T HAVE THE TIME AND TOO MUCH WAS AT STAKE.
I JUST HOPE YOU'RE BETTER PREPARED THAN I WAS TO DEAL WITH THE CONSEQUENCES.
YOU'RE READY TO SAVE THE MULTIVERSE...
...BECAUSE YOU KNOW WHEN YOU NEED TO DO THE WRONG THING.
ALL RIGHT, SEAL THE HATCH! WE'RE LAUNCHING IN FIVE!
JOB WELL DONE. WHAT'S WRONG?
NOTHING...
...I'M JUST NOT A FAN OF THIS PARTICULAR REALITY.

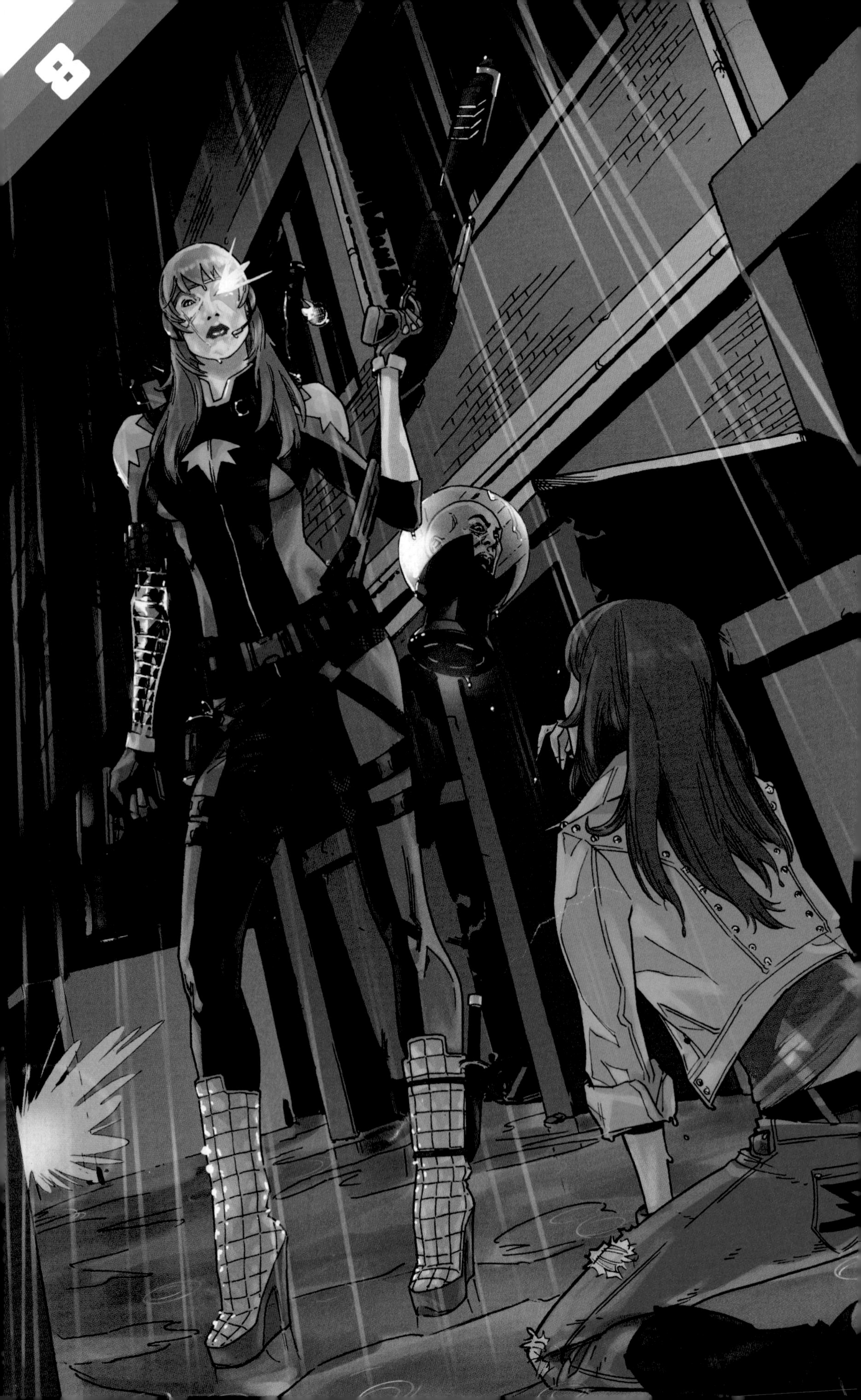
8

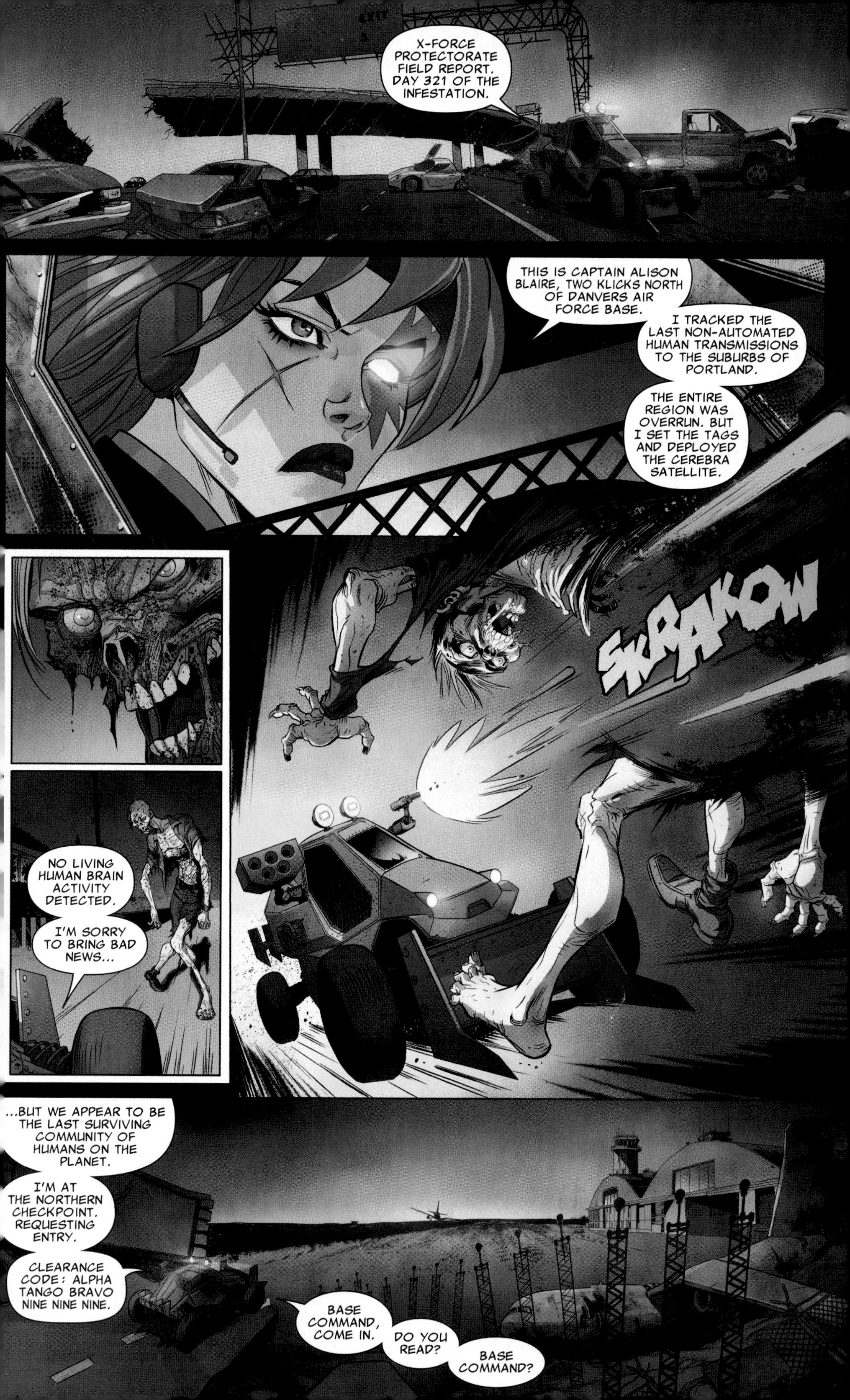

EXIT
X-FORCE PROTECTORATE FIELD REPORT. DAY 321 OF THE INFESTATION.
THIS IS CAPTAIN ALISON BLAIRE, TWO KLICKS NORTH OF DANVERS AIR FORCE BASE.
I TRACKED THE LAST NON-AUTOMATED HUMAN TRANSMISSIONS TO THE SUBURBS OF PORTLAND.
THE ENTIRE REGION WAS OVERRUN. BUT I SET THE TAGS AND DEPLOYED THE CEREBRA SATELLITE.
NO LIVING HUMAN BRAIN ACTIVITY DETECTED.
I'M SORRY TO BRING BAD NEWS...
SKRAKOW
...BUT WE APPEAR TO BE THE LAST SURVIVING COMMUNITY OF HUMANS ON THE PLANET.
I'M AT THE NORTHERN CHECKPOINT. REQUESTING ENTRY.
CLEARANCE CODE: ALPHA TANGO BRAVO NINE NINE NINE.
BASE COMMAND, COME IN.
DO YOU READ?
BASE COMMAND?

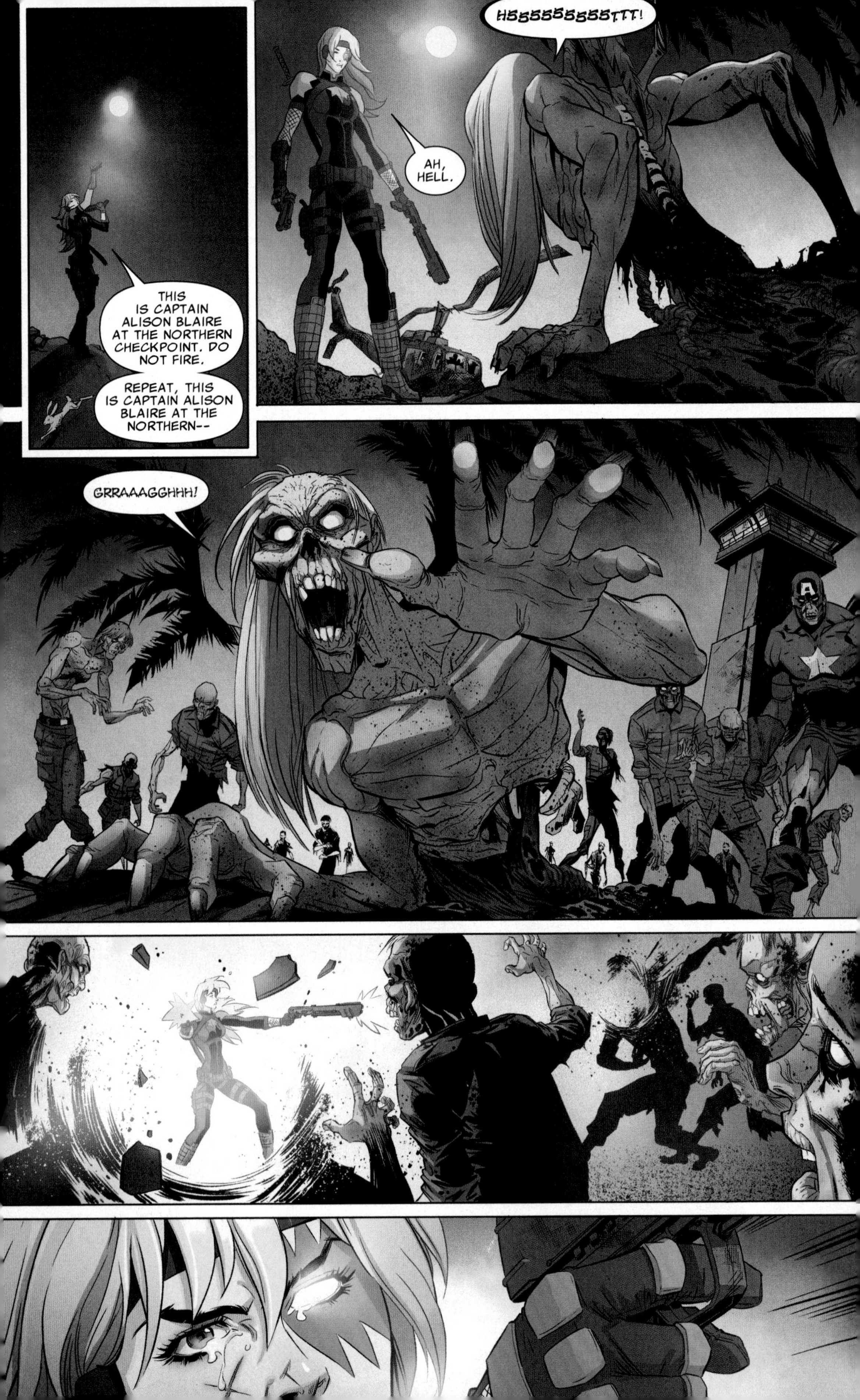
THIS IS CAPTAIN ALISON BLAIRE AT THE NORTHERN CHECKPOINT. DO NOT FIRE.
REPEAT, THIS IS CAPTAIN ALISON BLAIRE AT THE NORTHERN--
AH, HELL.
HSSSSSSSSSTTT!
GRRAAAGGHHH!

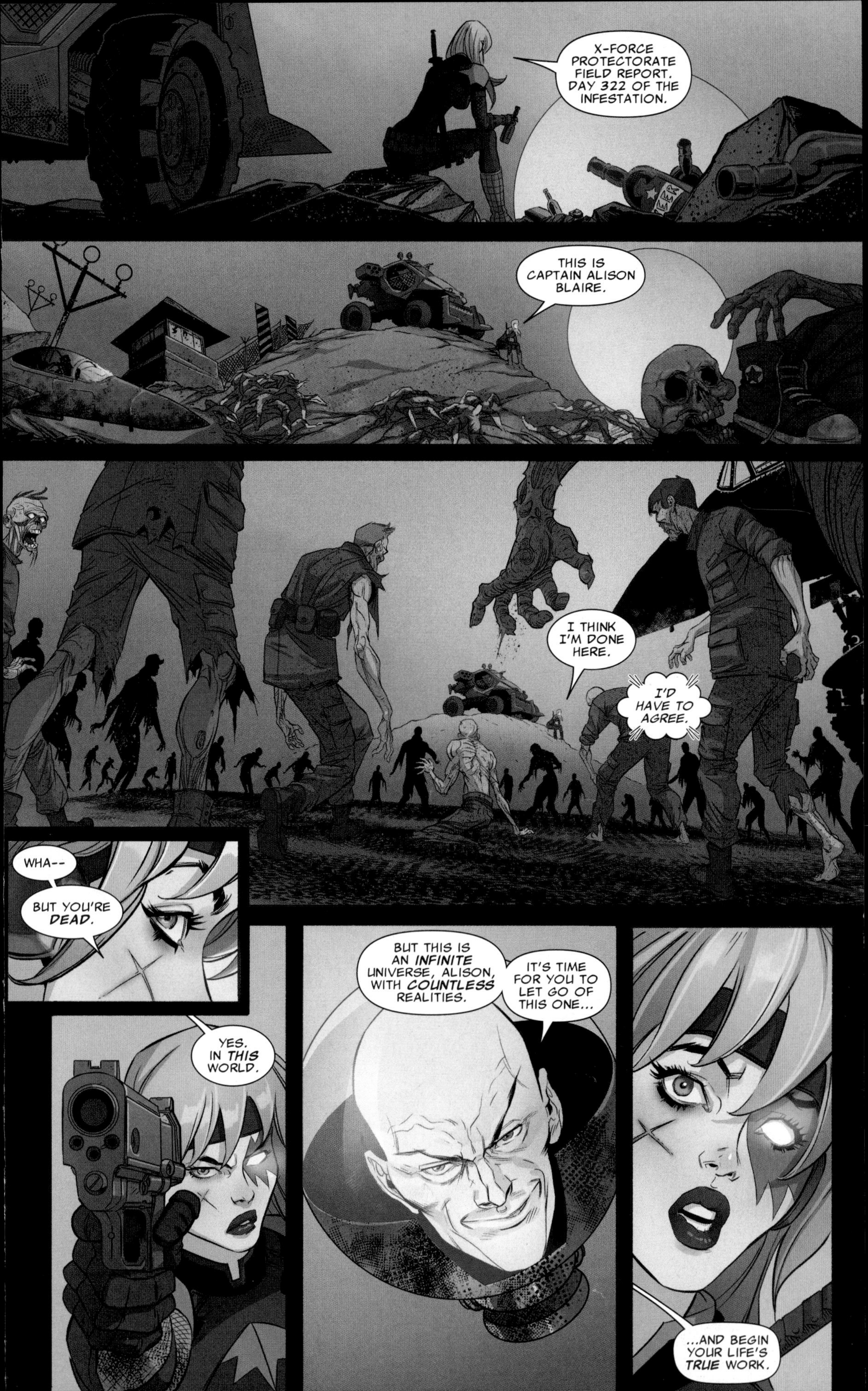
X-FORCE PROTECTORATE FIELD REPORT. DAY 322 OF THE INFESTATION.
THIS IS CAPTAIN ALISON BLAIRE.
I THINK I'M DONE HERE.
I'D HAVE TO AGREE.
WHA--
BUT YOU'RE DEAD.
YES. IN THIS WORLD.
BUT THIS IS AN INFINITE UNIVERSE, ALISON, WITH COUNTLESS REALITIES.
IT'S TIME FOR YOU TO LET GO OF THIS ONE...
...AND BEGIN YOUR LIFE'S TRUE WORK.

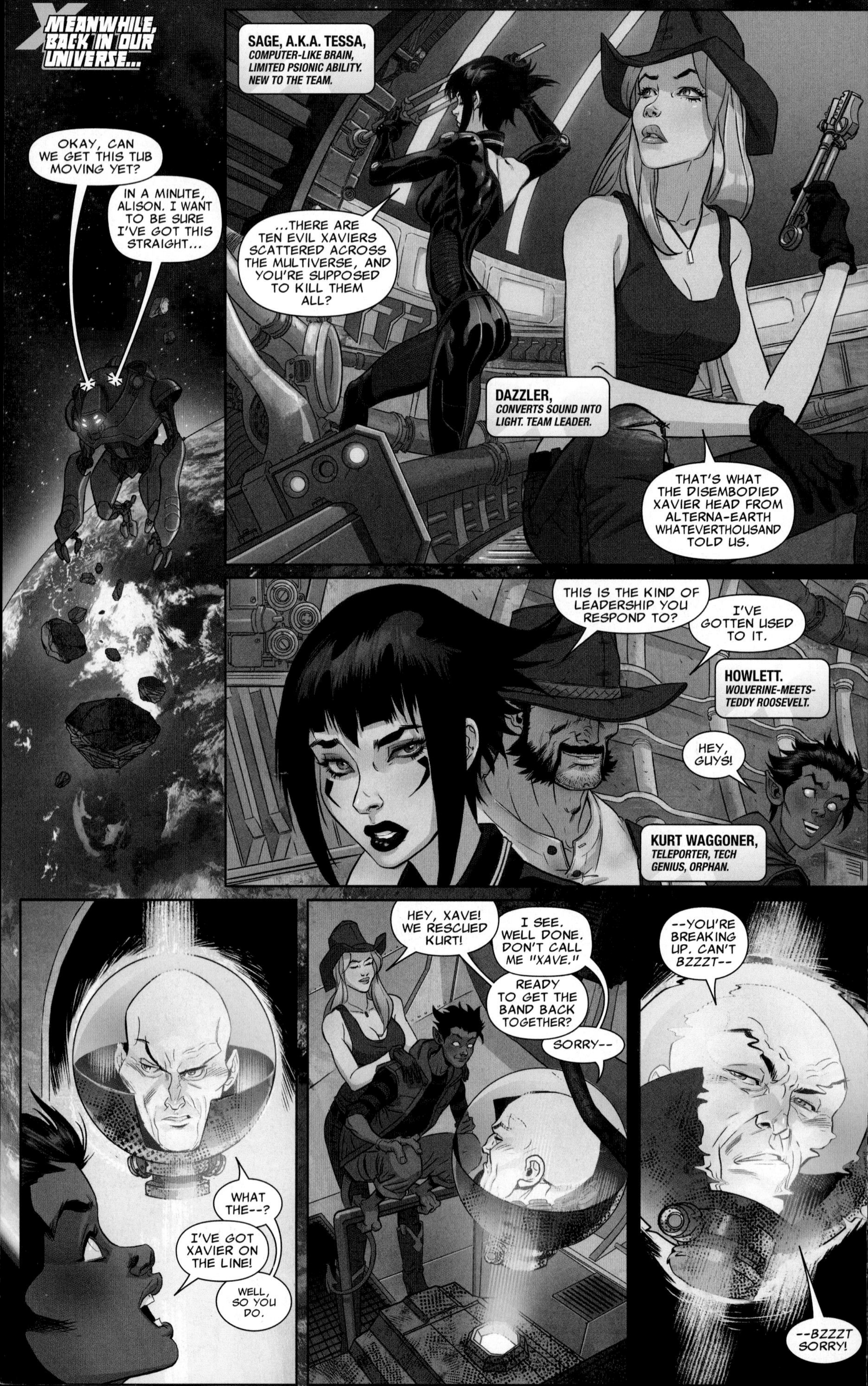
MEANWHILE, BACK IN OUR UNIVERSE...
OKAY, CAN WE GET THIS TUB MOVING YET?
IN A MINUTE, ALISON. I WANT TO BE SURE I'VE GOT THIS STRAIGHT...
SAGE, A.K.A. TESSA, COMPUTER-LIKE BRAIN, LIMITED PSIONIC ABILITY. NEW TO THE TEAM.
...THERE ARE TEN EVIL XAVIERS SCATTERED ACROSS THE MULTIVERSE, AND YOU'RE SUPPOSED TO KILL THEM ALL?
DAZZLER, CONVERTS SOUND INTO LIGHT. TEAM LEADER.
THAT'S WHAT THE DISEMBODIED XAVIER HEAD FROM ALTERNA-EARTH WHATEVERTHOUSAND TOLD US.
THIS IS THE KIND OF LEADERSHIP YOU RESPOND TO?
I'VE GOTTEN USED TO IT.
HOWLETT. WOLVERINE-MEETS-TEDDY ROOSEVELT.
HEY, GUYS!
KURT WAGGONER, TELEPORTER, TECH GENIUS, ORPHAN.
WHAT THE--?
I'VE GOT XAVIER ON THE LINE!
WELL, SO YOU DO.
HEY, XAVE! WE RESCUED KURT!
I SEE. WELL DONE. DON'T CALL ME "XAVE."
READY TO GET THE BAND BACK TOGETHER?
SORRY--
--YOU'RE BREAKING UP. CAN'T BZZZT--
--BZZZT SORRY!

THAT WAS... STRANGE.

DID HE MAKE THAT BZZZT BZZZZT SOUND WITH HIS MOUTH?

AND THAT'S THE PERSON YOU'VE ENTRUSTED YOUR LIVES WITH?

WHO EVER SAID I TRUST HIM? WHAT ARE YOU HIDING, GIRL?

TWO WORLDS AGO, THE XAVIER HEAD TOLD ME THAT EVIL OLD WEST XAVIER HAD FIGURED OUT HIS "SECRET."

SECRET?

"HE KNOWS WHAT I'M CAPABLE OF." THAT'S WHAT THE HEAD SAID.

WE HAVE TO TRACK THAT SO-AND-SO DOWN AND FIND OUT WHAT THE HELL HE'S GOING TO DO.

NOW HOW LONG 'TIL WE FIGURE OUT HOW TO MAKE THIS JUMP WITHOUT XAVIER'S HELP?

WE CRACKED IT HALF AN HOUR AGO.

JUST WANTED TO MAKE SURE WE WERE ALL ON THE SAME PAGE.

HA.

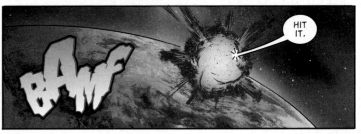

BAMF

HIT IT.

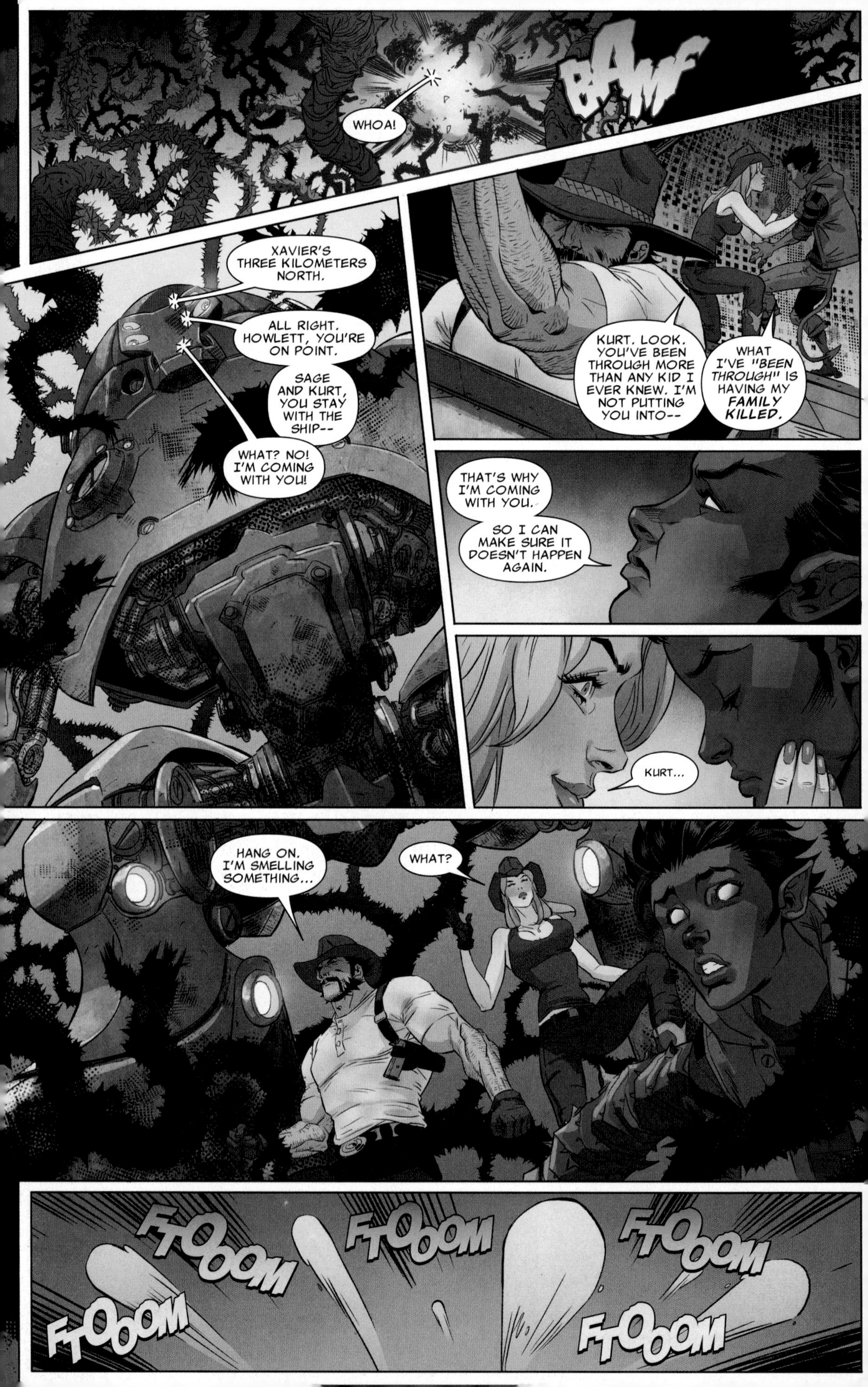
WHOA!
BAMF
XAVIER'S THREE KILOMETERS NORTH.
ALL RIGHT. HOWLETT, YOU'RE ON POINT.
SAGE AND KURT, YOU STAY WITH THE SHIP--
WHAT? NO! I'M COMING WITH YOU!
KURT. LOOK. YOU'VE BEEN THROUGH MORE THAN ANY KID I EVER KNEW. I'M NOT PUTTING YOU INTO--
WHAT I'VE "BEEN THROUGH" IS HAVING MY FAMILY KILLED.
THAT'S WHY I'M COMING WITH YOU.
SO I CAN MAKE SURE IT DOESN'T HAPPEN AGAIN.
KURT...
HANG ON. I'M SMELLING SOMETHING...
WHAT?
FTOOOM
FTOOOM
FTOOOM
FTOOOM
FTOOOM

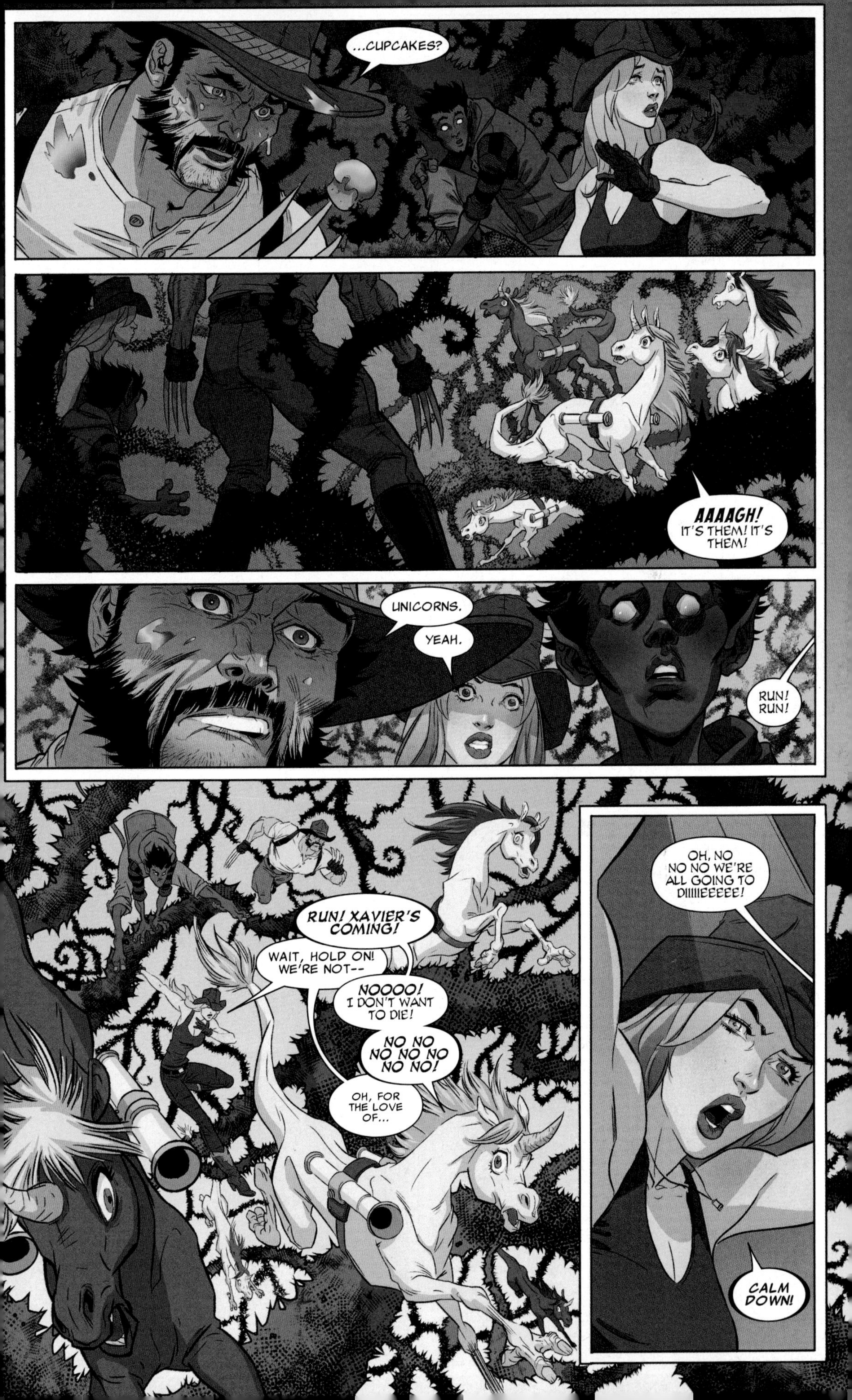
...CUPCAKES?
AAAAGH! IT'S THEM! IT'S THEM!
UNICORNS.
YEAH.
RUN! RUN!
RUN! XAVIER'S COMING!
WAIT, HOLD ON! WE'RE NOT--
NOOOO! I DON'T WANT TO DIE!
NO NO NO NO NO NO NO!
OH, FOR THE LOVE OF...
OH, NO NO NO NO WE'RE ALL GOING TO DIIIIEEEEE!
CALM DOWN!

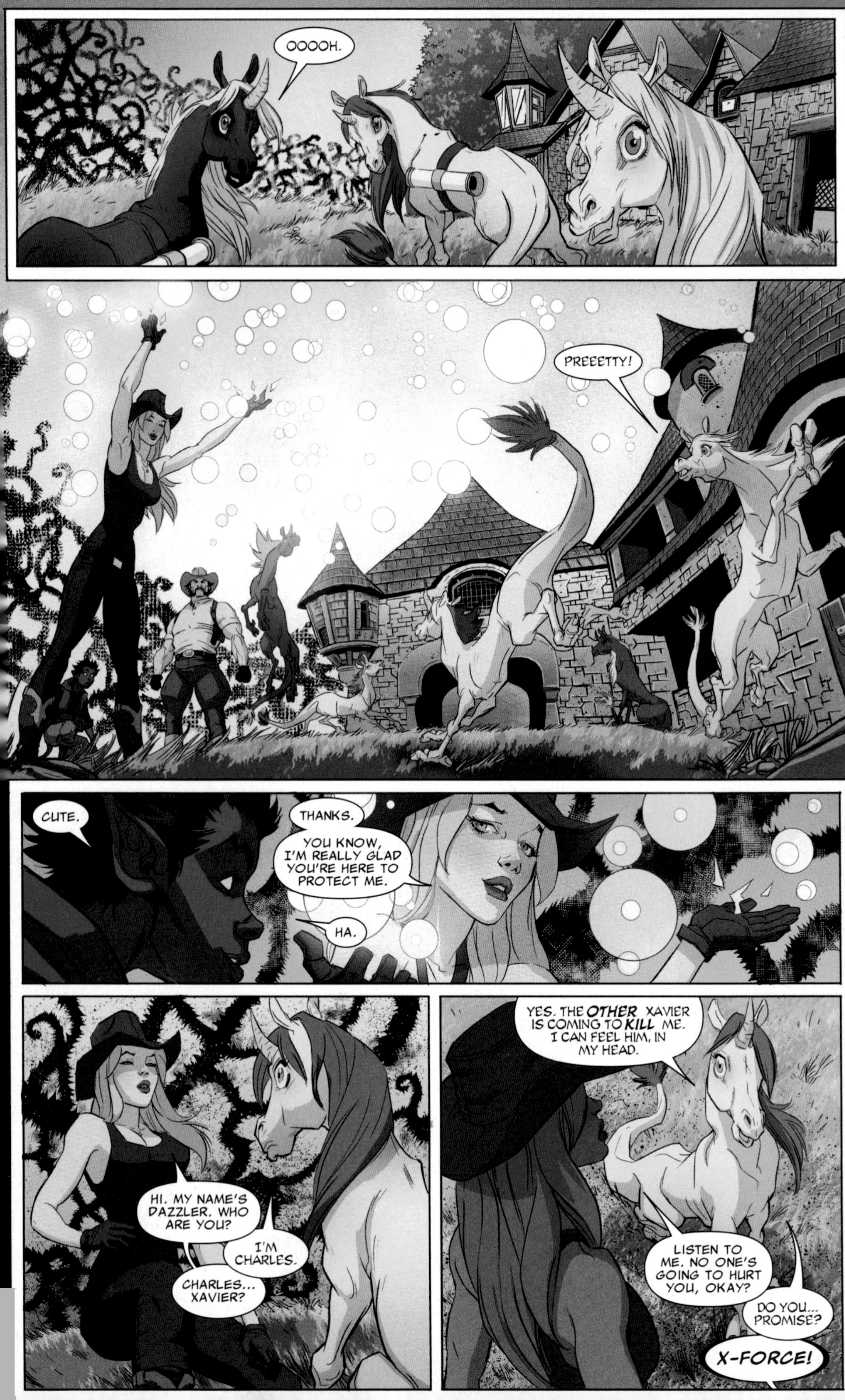
OOOOH.
PREEETTY!
CUTE.
THANKS.
YOU KNOW, I'M REALLY GLAD YOU'RE HERE TO PROTECT ME.
HA.
HI. MY NAME'S DAZZLER. WHO ARE YOU?
I'M CHARLES.
CHARLES... XAVIER?
YES. THE OTHER XAVIER IS COMING TO KILL ME. I CAN FEEL HIM, IN MY HEAD.
LISTEN TO ME. NO ONE'S GOING TO HURT YOU, OKAY?
DO YOU... PROMISE?
X-FORCE!

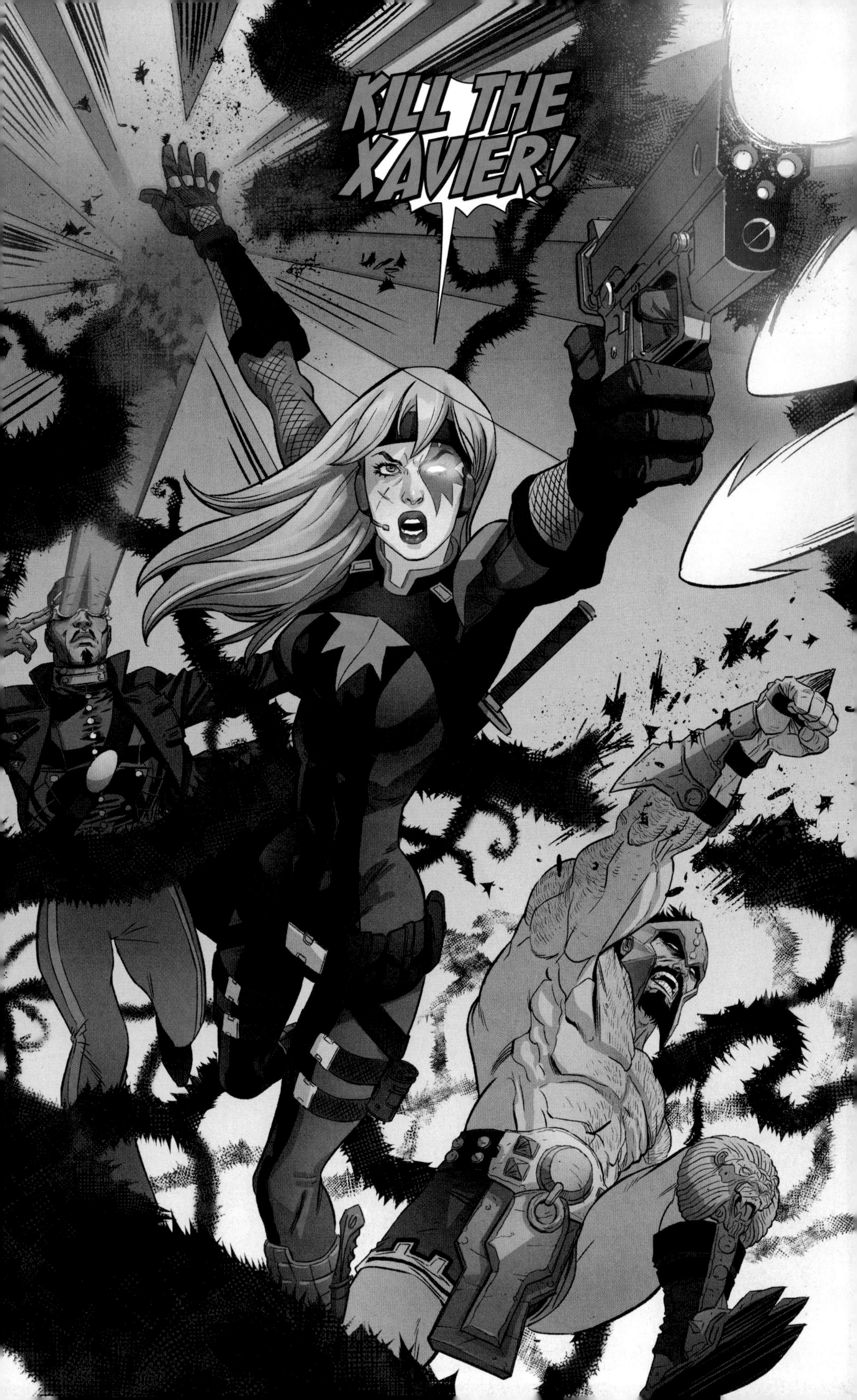
KILL THE XAVIER!

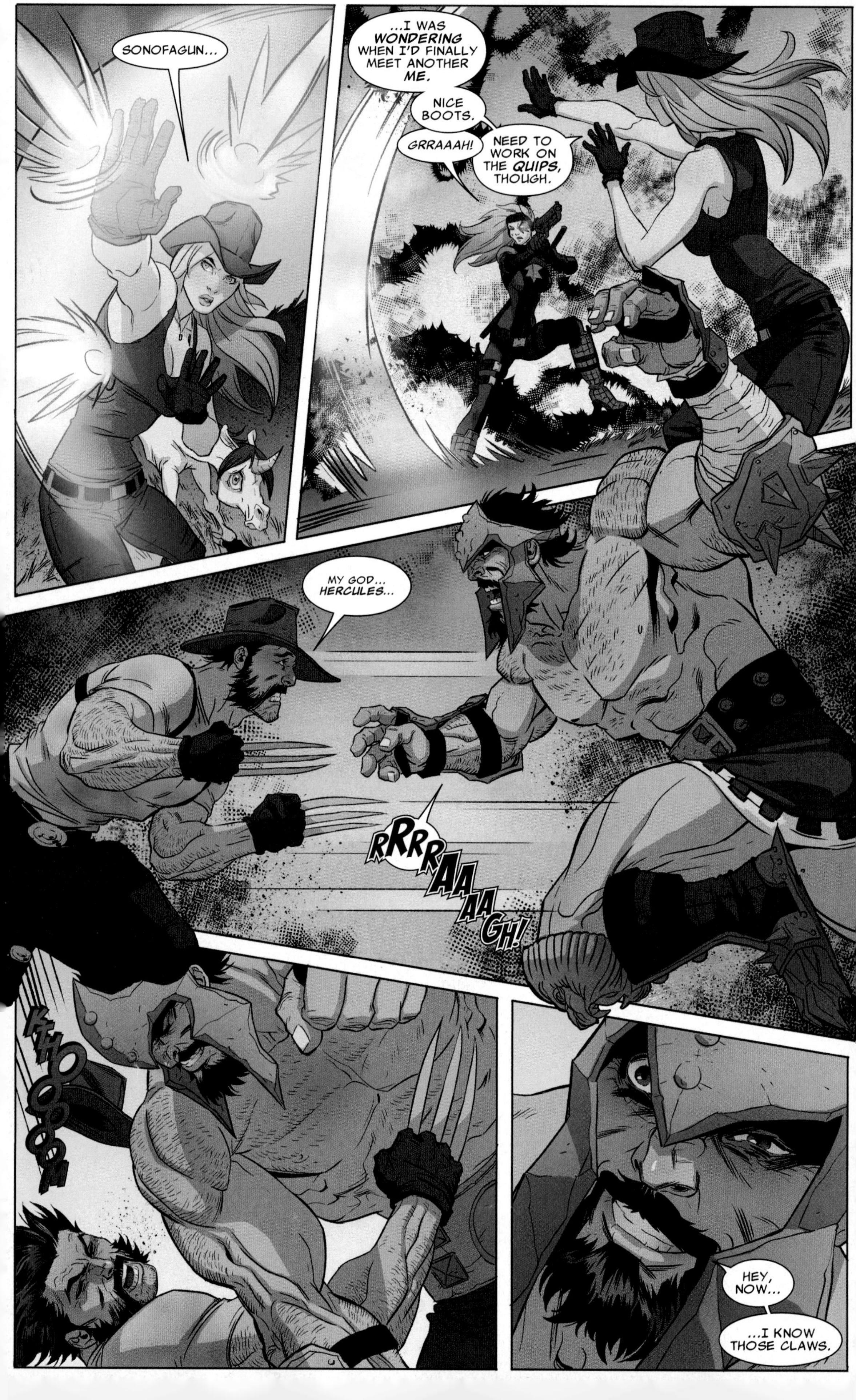
SONOFAGUN...
...I WAS WONDERING WHEN I'D FINALLY MEET ANOTHER ME.
NICE BOOTS.
GRRAAAH!
NEED TO WORK ON THE QUIPS, THOUGH.
MY GOD... HERCULES...
RRRRAAAAGH!
KTHOOOOM
HEY, NOW...
...I KNOW THOSE CLAWS.

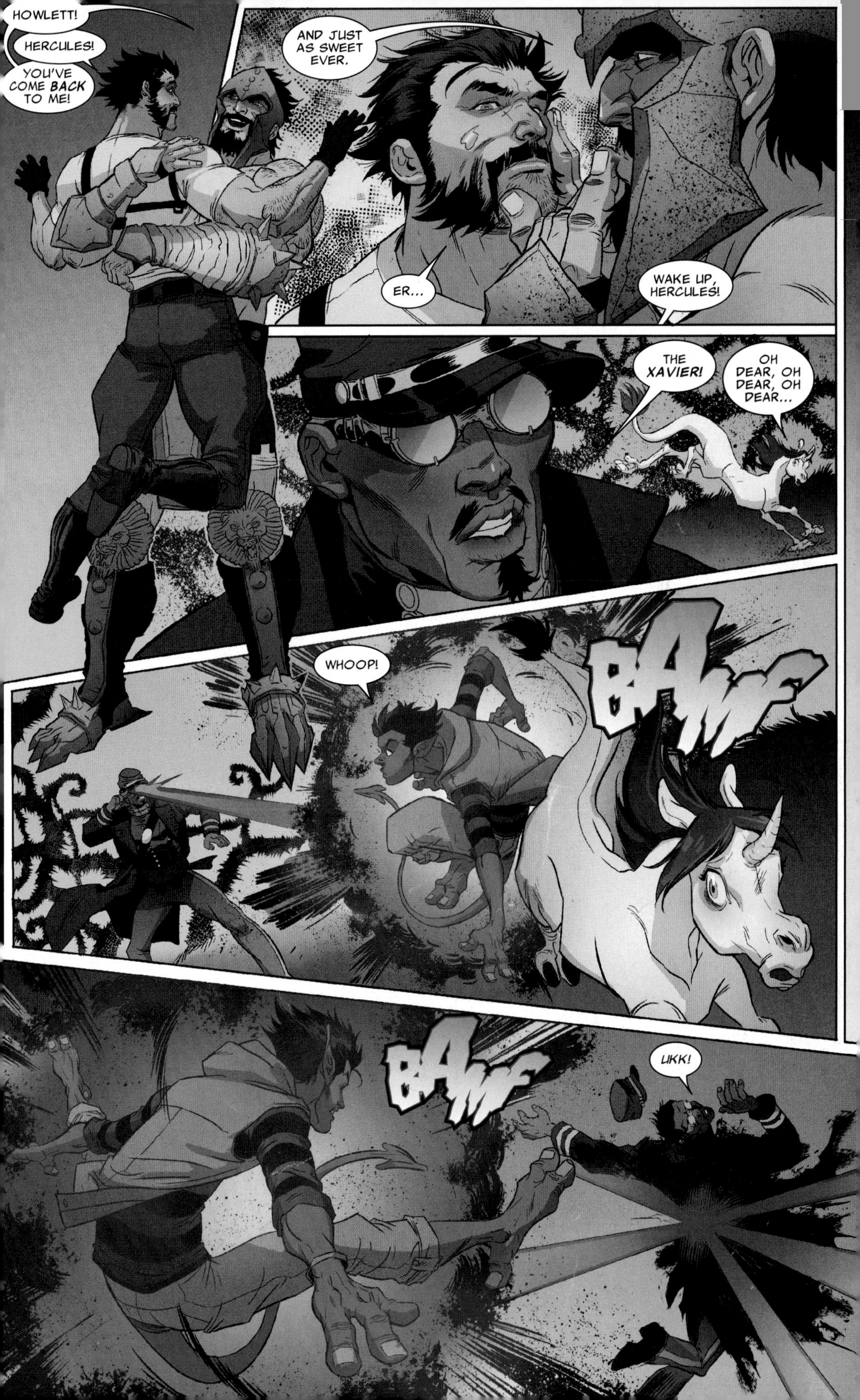
HOWLETT!
HERCULES!
YOU'VE COME BACK TO ME!
AND JUST AS SWEET EVER.
ER...
WAKE UP, HERCULES!
THE XAVIER!
OH DEAR, OH DEAR, OH DEAR...
WHOOP!
BAMF
BAMF
UKK!

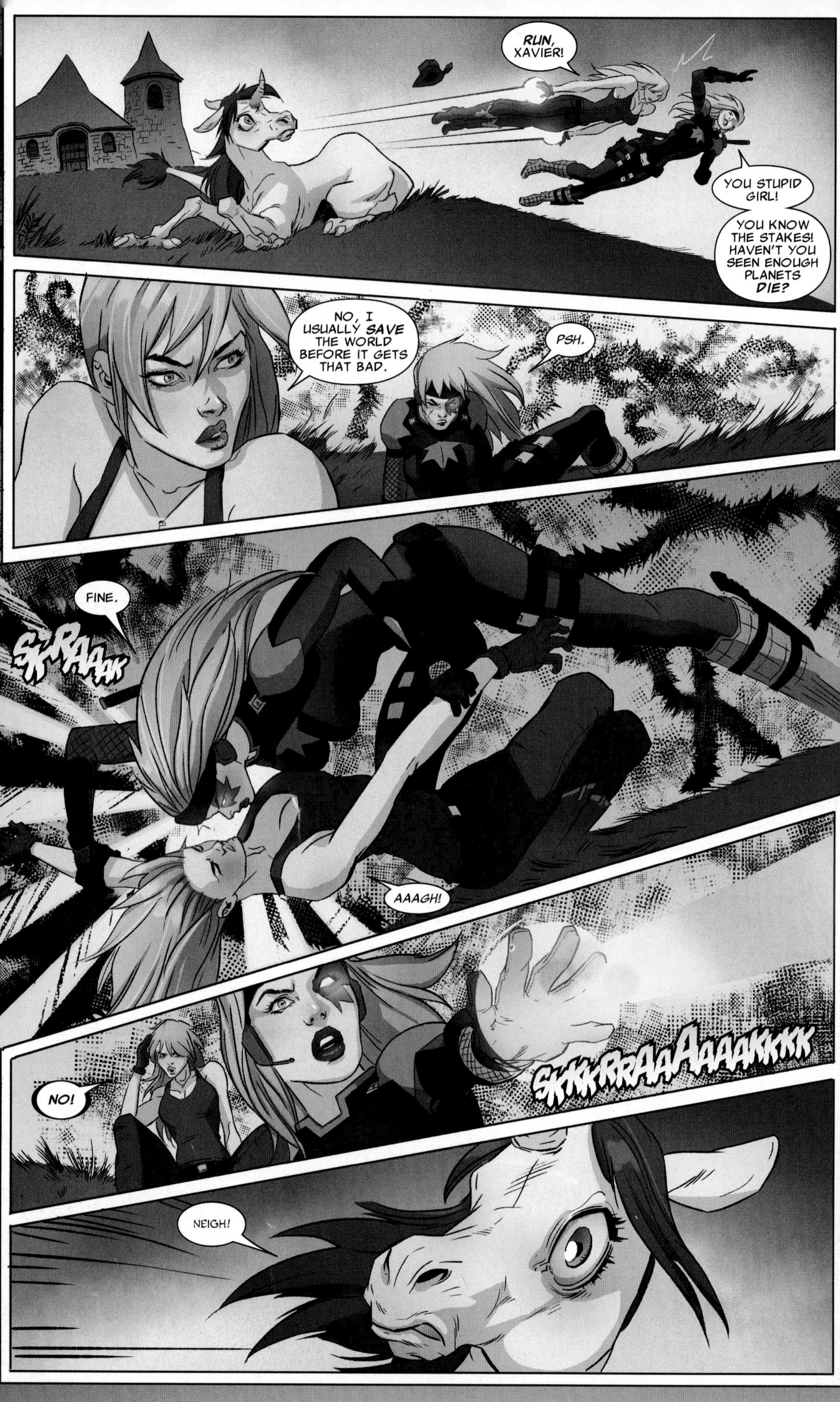
RUN, XAVIER!
YOU STUPID GIRL!
YOU KNOW THE STAKES! HAVEN'T YOU SEEN ENOUGH PLANETS DIE?
NO, I USUALLY SAVE THE WORLD BEFORE IT GETS THAT BAD.
PSH.
FINE.
SKRAAAK
AAAGH!
SKKKRRAAAAAAKKKK
NO!
NEIGH!

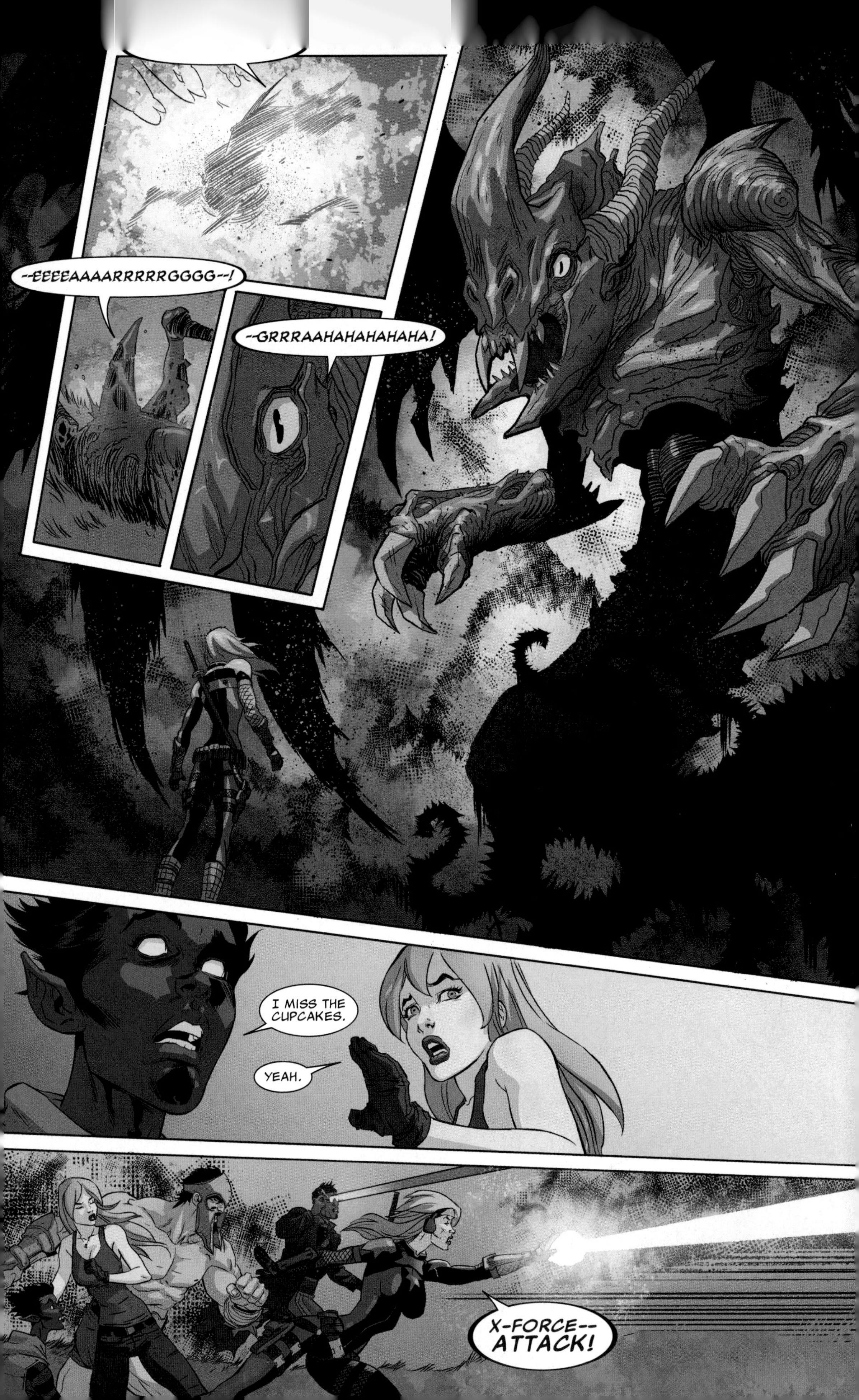
--EEEEAAAARRRRRGGGG--!
--GRRRAAHAHAHAHAHA!
I MISS THE CUPCAKES.
YEAH.
X-FORCE--
ATTACK!

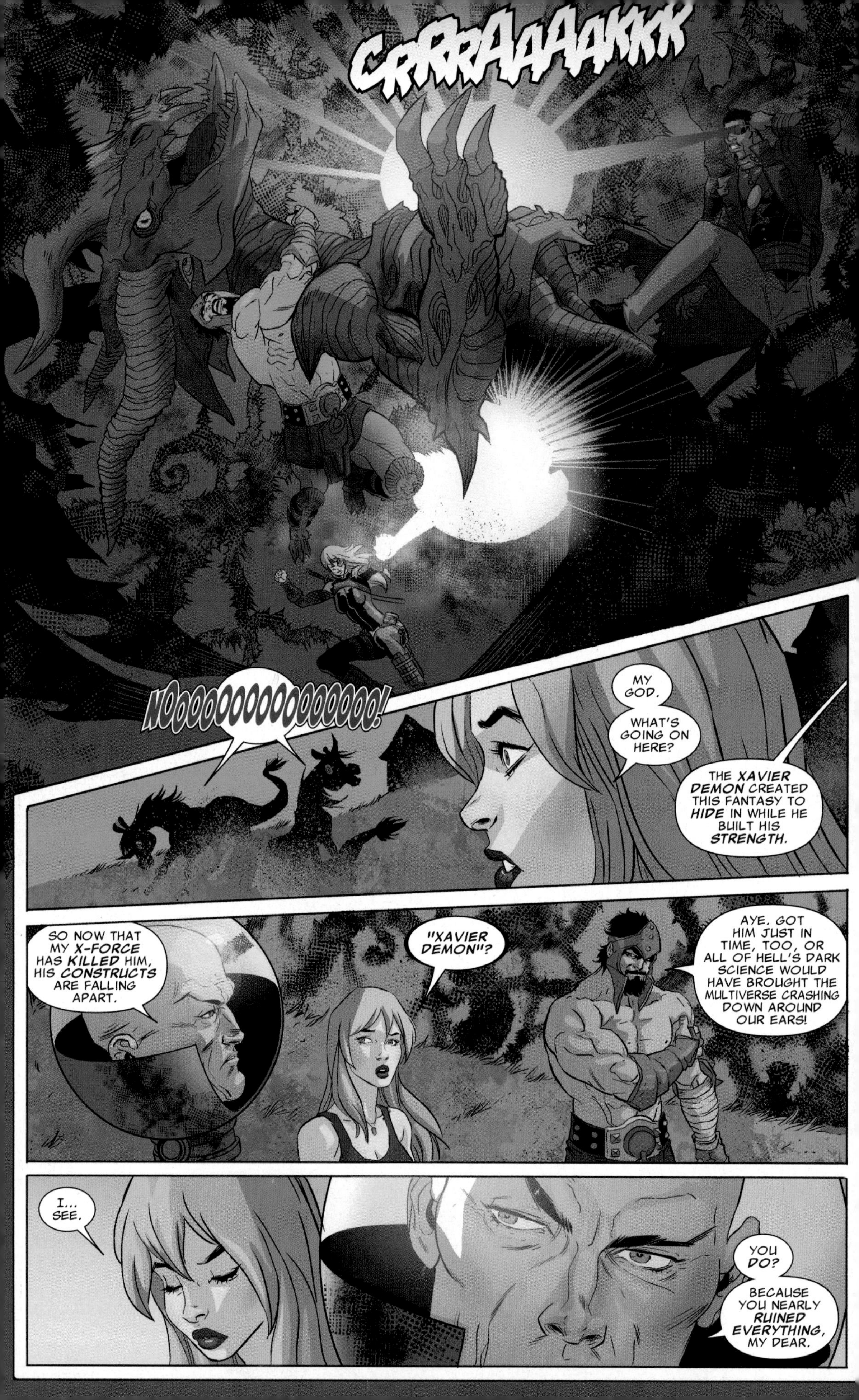
CRRRAAAAKKK
NOOOOOOOOOOOOOOO!
MY GOD.
WHAT'S GOING ON HERE?
THE XAVIER DEMON CREATED THIS FANTASY TO HIDE IN WHILE HE BUILT HIS STRENGTH.
SO NOW THAT MY X-FORCE HAS KILLED HIM, HIS CONSTRUCTS ARE FALLING APART.
"XAVIER DEMON"?
AYE. GOT HIM JUST IN TIME, TOO, OR ALL OF HELL'S DARK SCIENCE WOULD HAVE BROUGHT THE MULTIVERSE CRASHING DOWN AROUND OUR EARS!
I... SEE.
YOU DO?
BECAUSE YOU NEARLY RUINED EVERYTHING, MY DEAR.

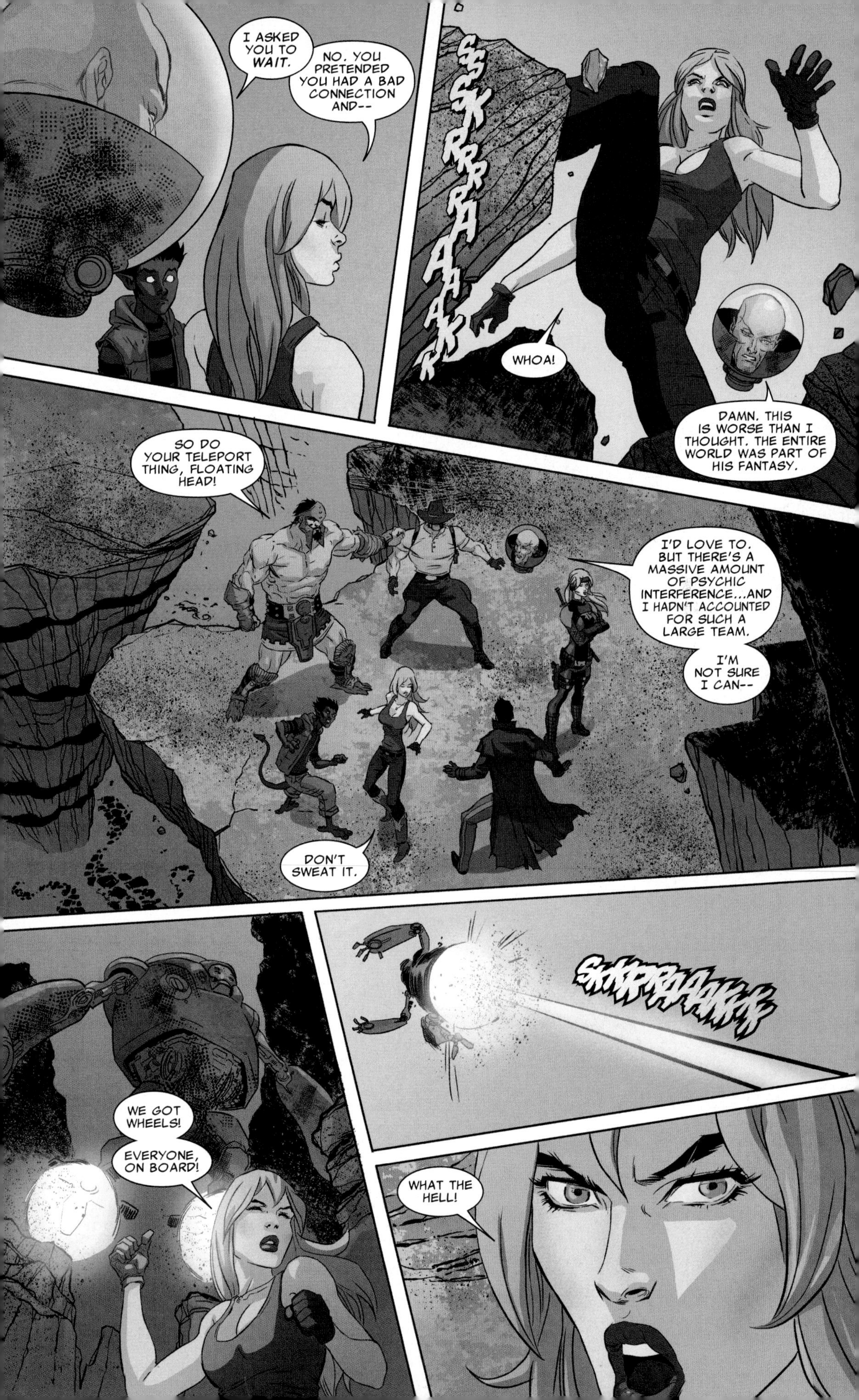

I ASKED YOU TO WAIT.
NO. YOU PRETENDED YOU HAD A BAD CONNECTION AND--
SSSKRRRRAAAAKK
WHOA!
DAMN. THIS IS WORSE THAN I THOUGHT. THE ENTIRE WORLD WAS PART OF HIS FANTASY.
SO DO YOUR TELEPORT THING, FLOATING HEAD!
I'D LOVE TO. BUT THERE'S A MASSIVE AMOUNT OF PSYCHIC INTERFERENCE...AND I HADN'T ACCOUNTED FOR SUCH A LARGE TEAM.
I'M NOT SURE I CAN--
DON'T SWEAT IT.
WE GOT WHEELS!
EVERYONE, ON BOARD!
SKRRRAAKK
WHAT THE HELL!

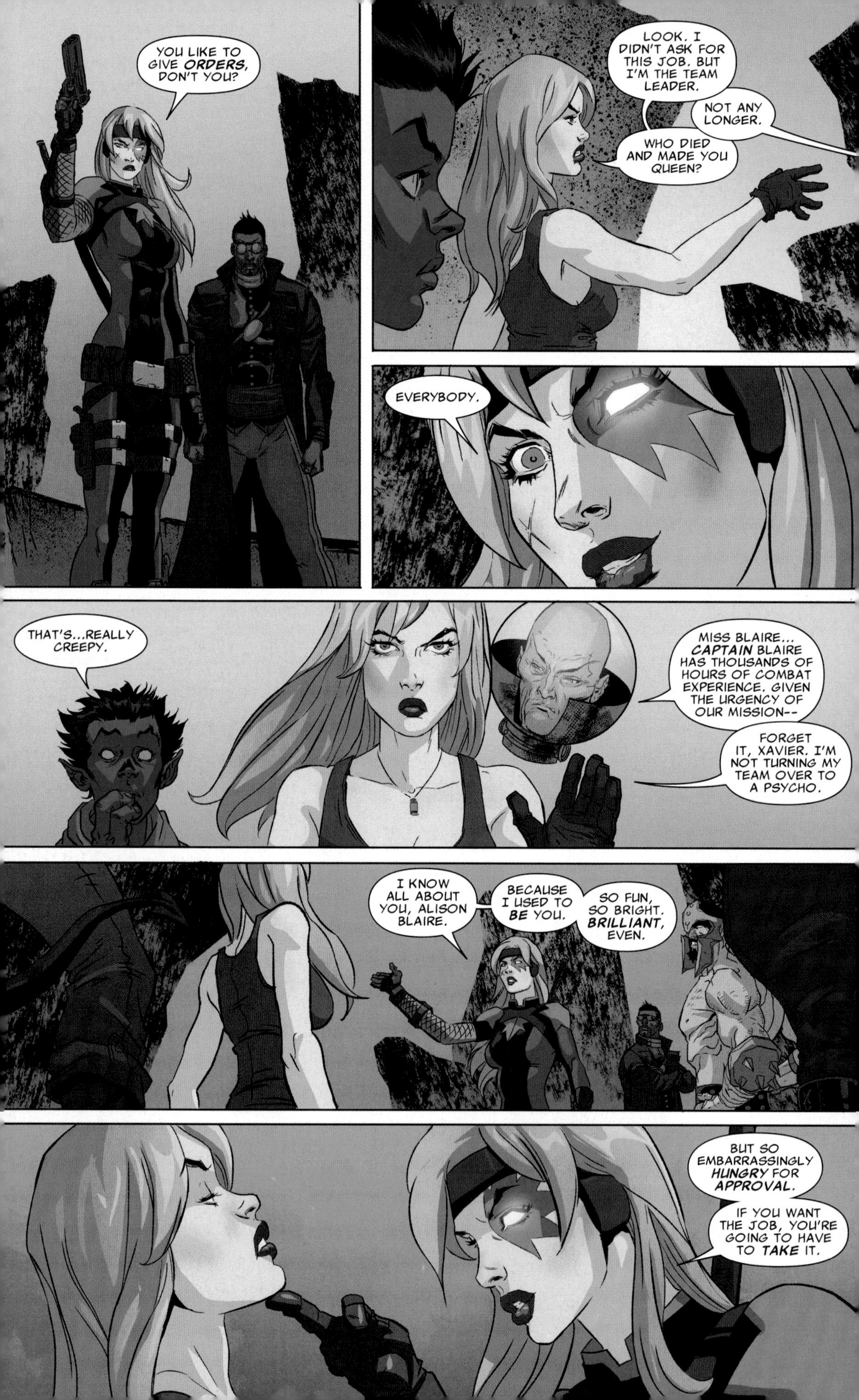
YOU LIKE TO GIVE ORDERS, DON'T YOU?
LOOK. I DIDN'T ASK FOR THIS JOB. BUT I'M THE TEAM LEADER.
NOT ANY LONGER.
WHO DIED AND MADE YOU QUEEN?
EVERYBODY.
THAT'S...REALLY CREEPY.
MISS BLAIRE... CAPTAIN BLAIRE HAS THOUSANDS OF HOURS OF COMBAT EXPERIENCE. GIVEN THE URGENCY OF OUR MISSION--
FORGET IT, XAVIER. I'M NOT TURNING MY TEAM OVER TO A PSYCHO.
I KNOW ALL ABOUT YOU, ALISON BLAIRE.
BECAUSE I USED TO BE YOU.
SO FUN, SO BRIGHT. BRILLIANT, EVEN.
BUT SO EMBARRASSINGLY HUNGRY FOR APPROVAL.
IF YOU WANT THE JOB, YOU'RE GOING TO HAVE TO TAKE IT.

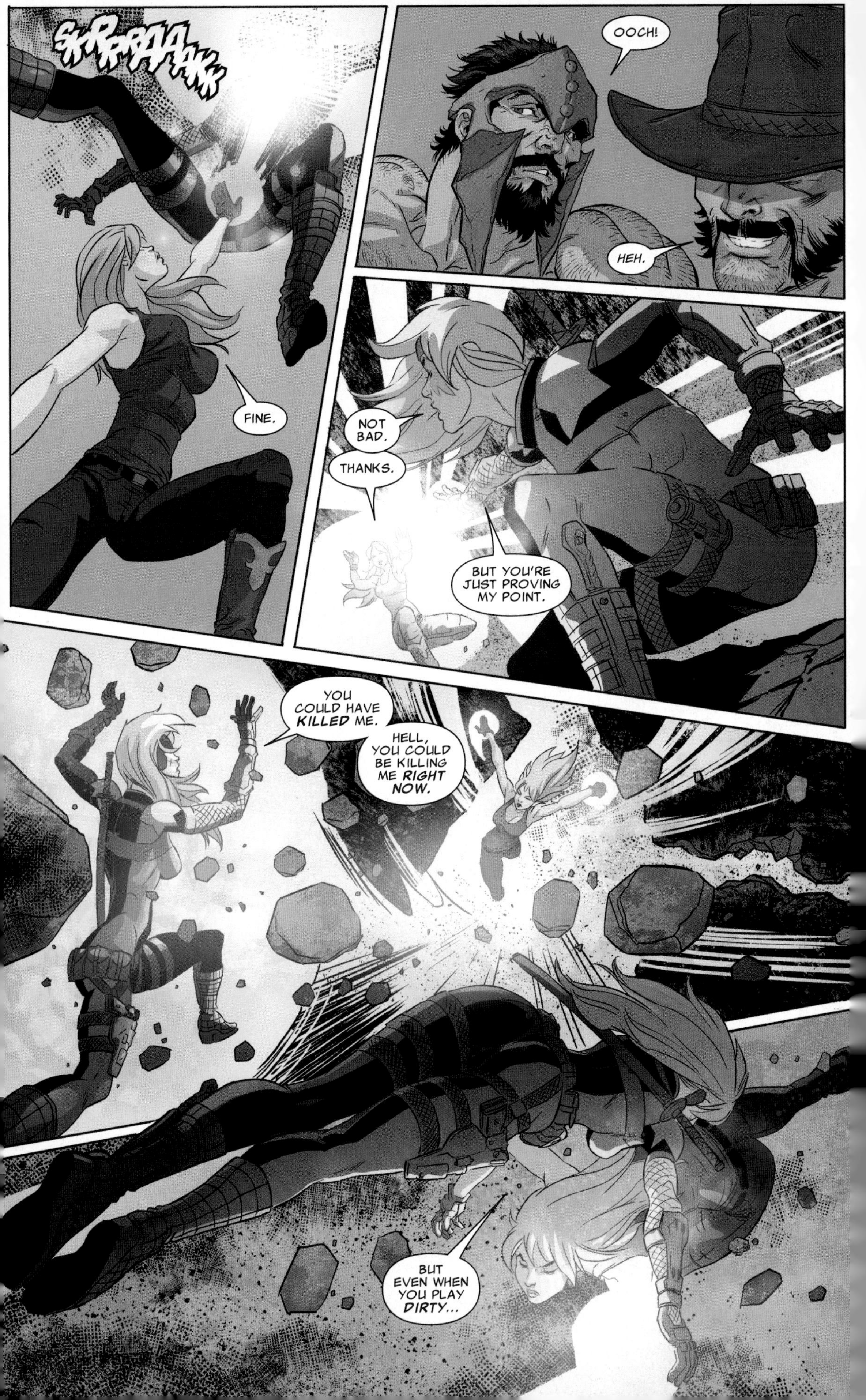
SKRRBLAAAK
OOCH!
HEH.
FINE.
NOT BAD.
THANKS.
BUT YOU'RE JUST PROVING MY POINT.
YOU COULD HAVE *KILLED* ME.
HELL, YOU COULD BE KILLING ME *RIGHT NOW.*
BUT EVEN WHEN YOU PLAY *DIRTY...*

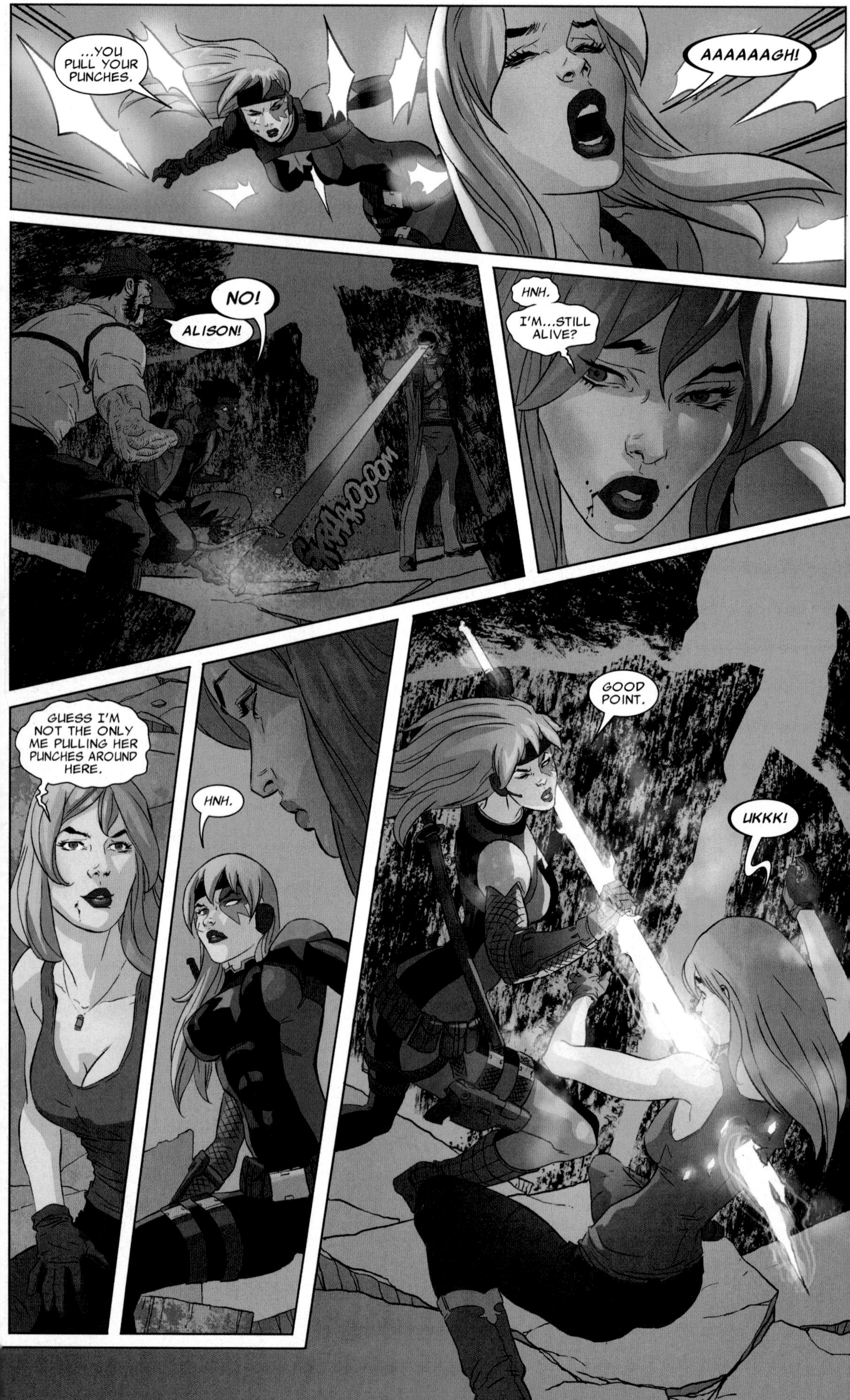
...YOU PULL YOUR PUNCHES.
AAAAAAGH!
NO!
ALISON!
HNH.
I'M...STILL ALIVE?
GUESS I'M NOT THE ONLY ME PULLING HER PUNCHES AROUND HERE.
HNH.
GOOD POINT.
UKKK!

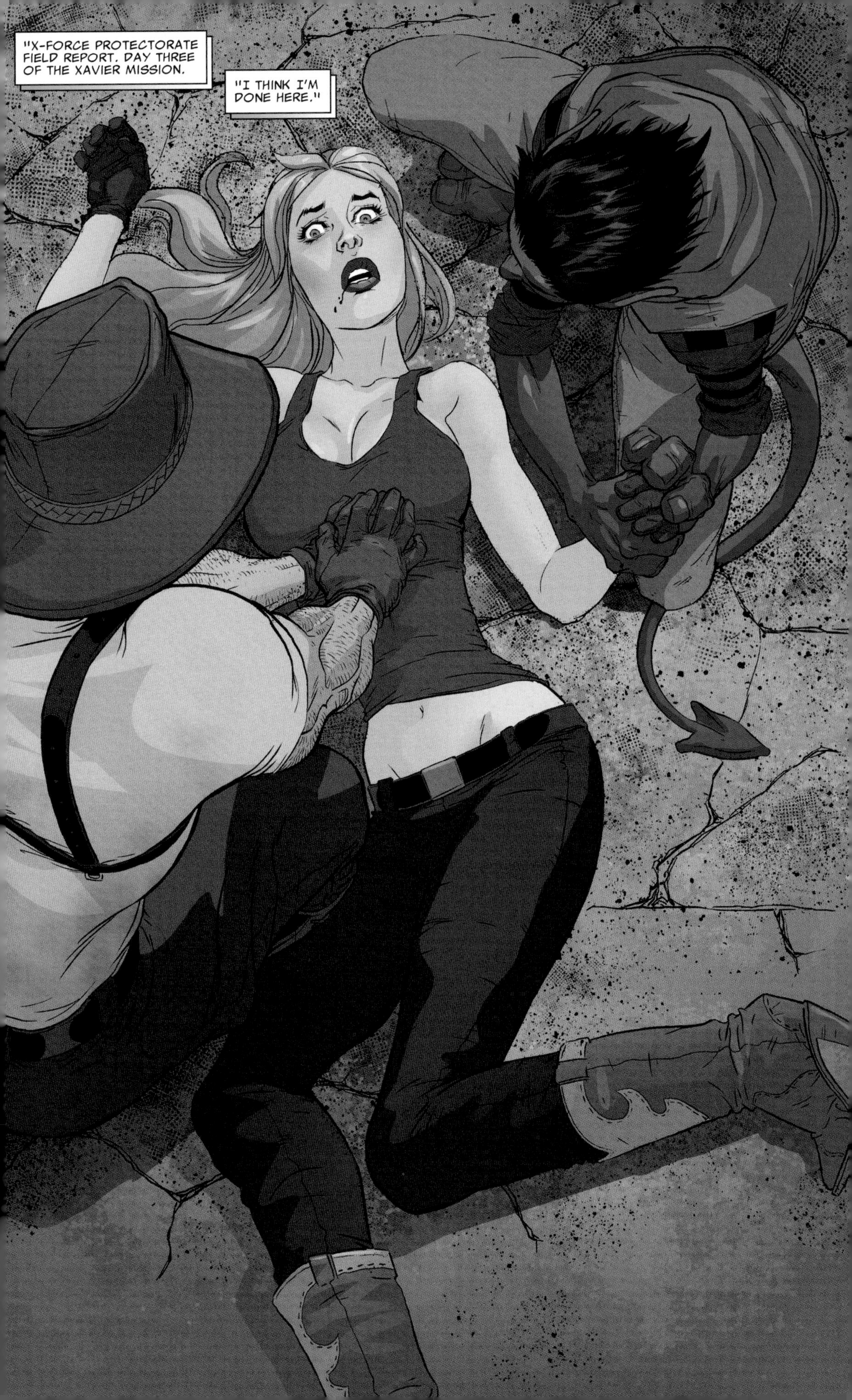
"X-FORCE PROTECTORATE FIELD REPORT. DAY THREE OF THE XAVIER MISSION.
"I THINK I'M DONE HERE."

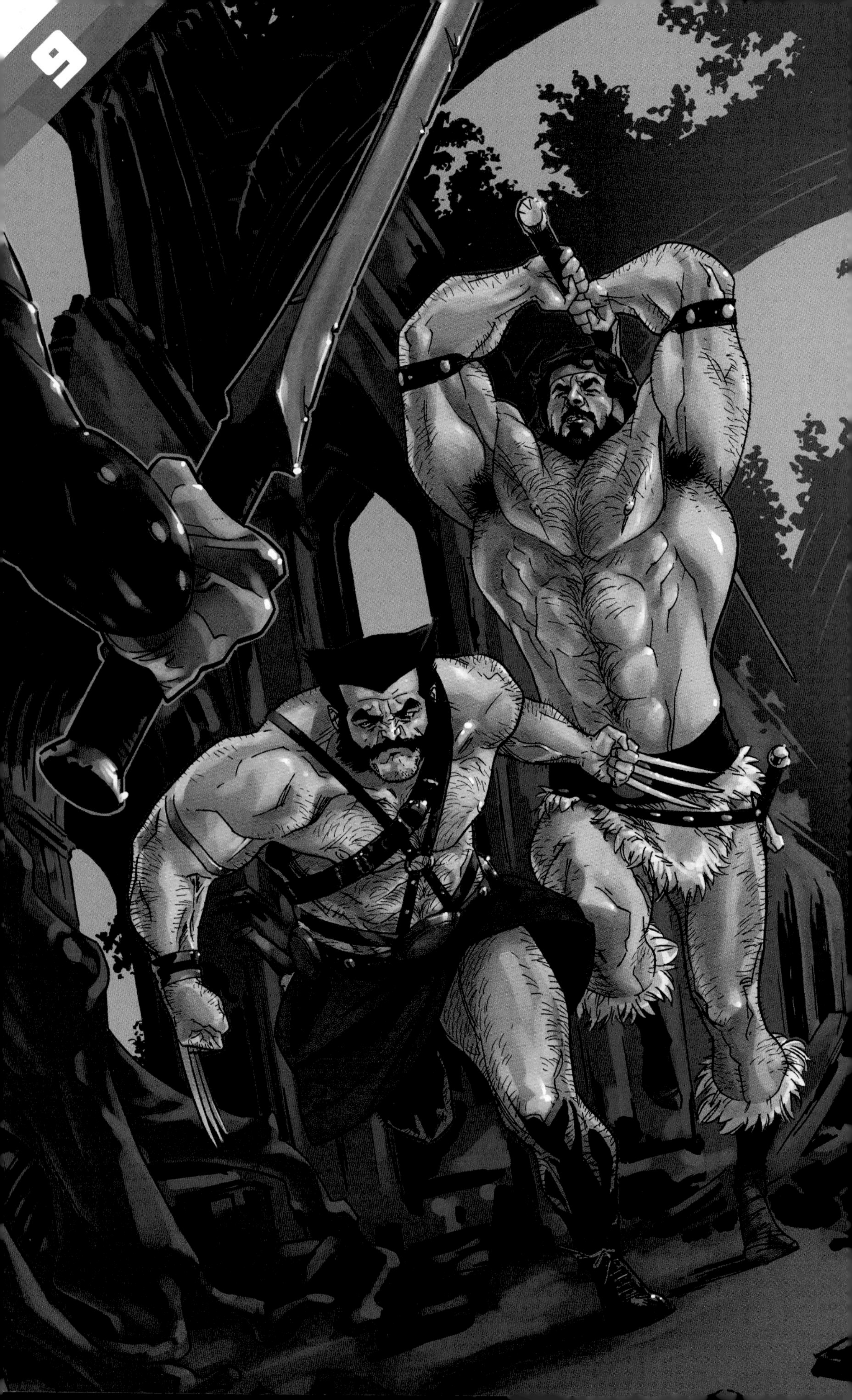
9

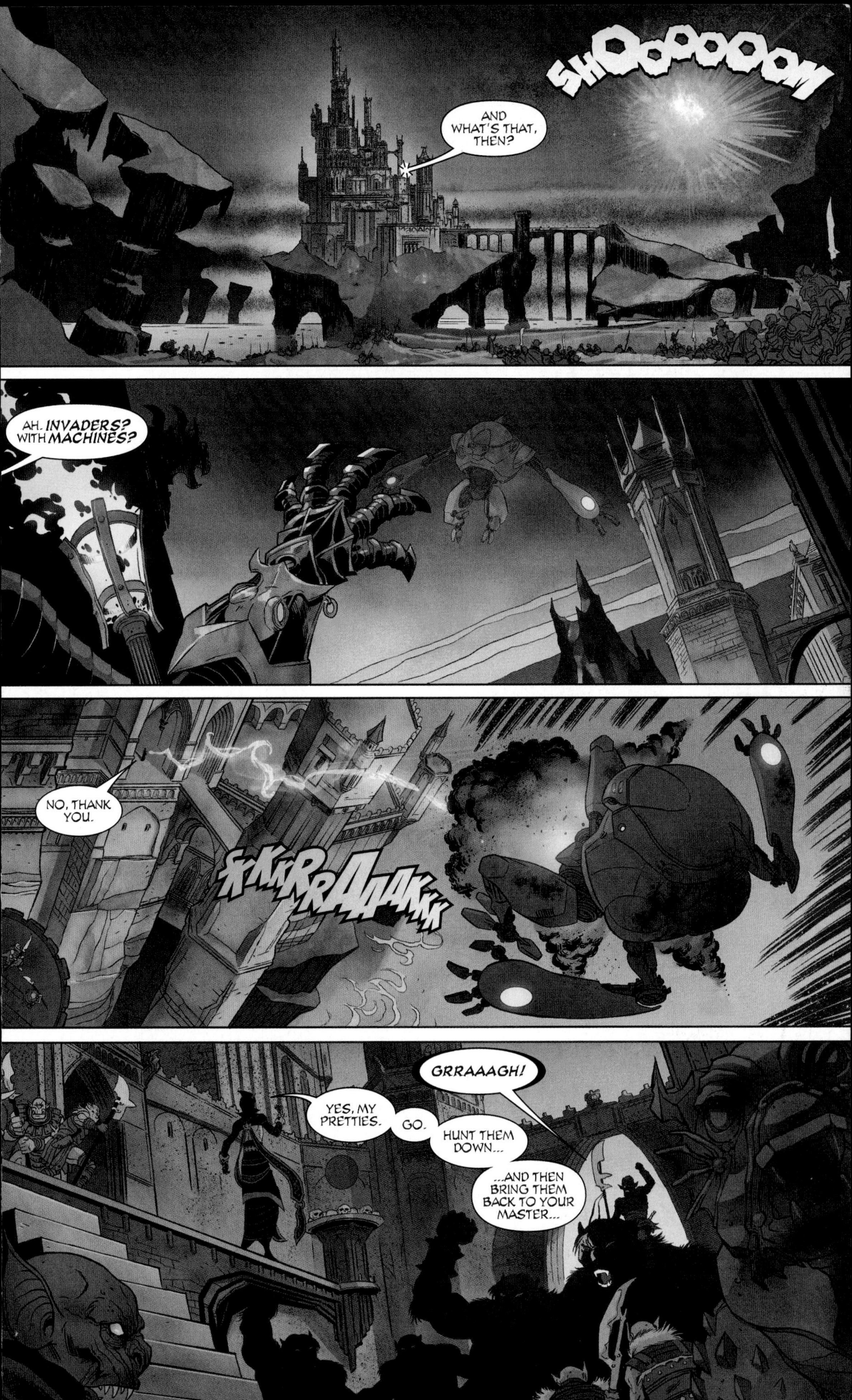
SHOOOOOOM
AND WHAT'S THAT, THEN?
AH. INVADERS? WITH MACHINES?
NO, THANK YOU.
SKKKRRAAAKKK
GRRAAAGH!
YES, MY PRETTIES.
GO.
HUNT THEM DOWN...
...AND THEN BRING THEM BACK TO YOUR MASTER...

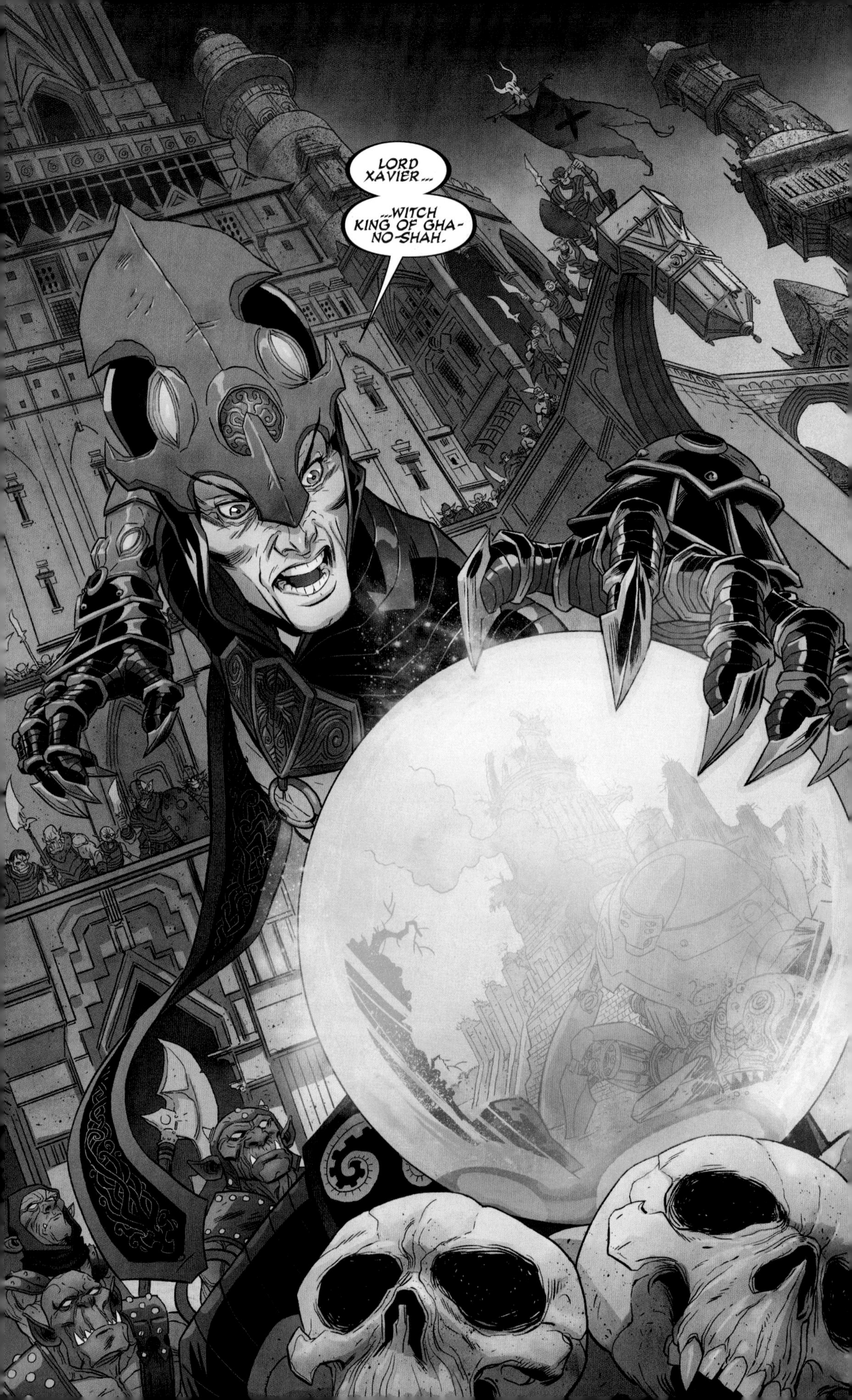
LORD XAVIER...
...WITCH KING OF GHA-NO-SHAH.

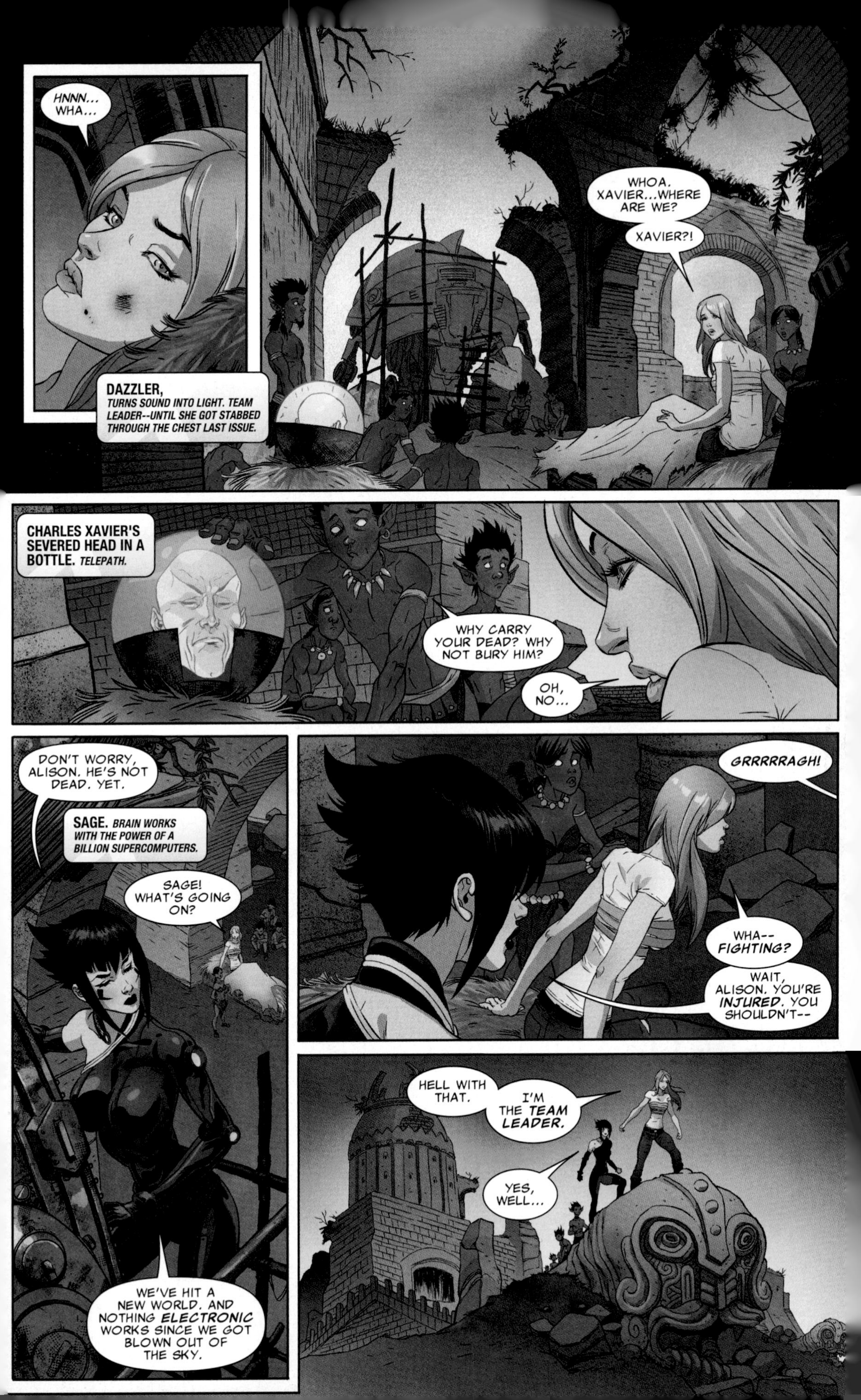

HNNN... WHA...
DAZZLER, TURNS SOUND INTO LIGHT. TEAM LEADER--UNTIL SHE GOT STABBED THROUGH THE CHEST LAST ISSUE.
WHOA, XAVIER...WHERE ARE WE?
XAVIER?!
CHARLES XAVIER'S SEVERED HEAD IN A BOTTLE. TELEPATH.
WHY CARRY YOUR DEAD? WHY NOT BURY HIM?
OH, NO...
DON'T WORRY, ALISON. HE'S NOT DEAD. YET.
SAGE. BRAIN WORKS WITH THE POWER OF A BILLION SUPERCOMPUTERS.
SAGE! WHAT'S GOING ON?
WE'VE HIT A NEW WORLD. AND NOTHING ELECTRONIC WORKS SINCE WE GOT BLOWN OUT OF THE SKY.
GRRRRRAGH!
WHA-- FIGHTING?
WAIT, ALISON. YOU'RE INJURED. YOU SHOULDN'T--
HELL WITH THAT.
I'M THE TEAM LEADER.
YES, WELL...

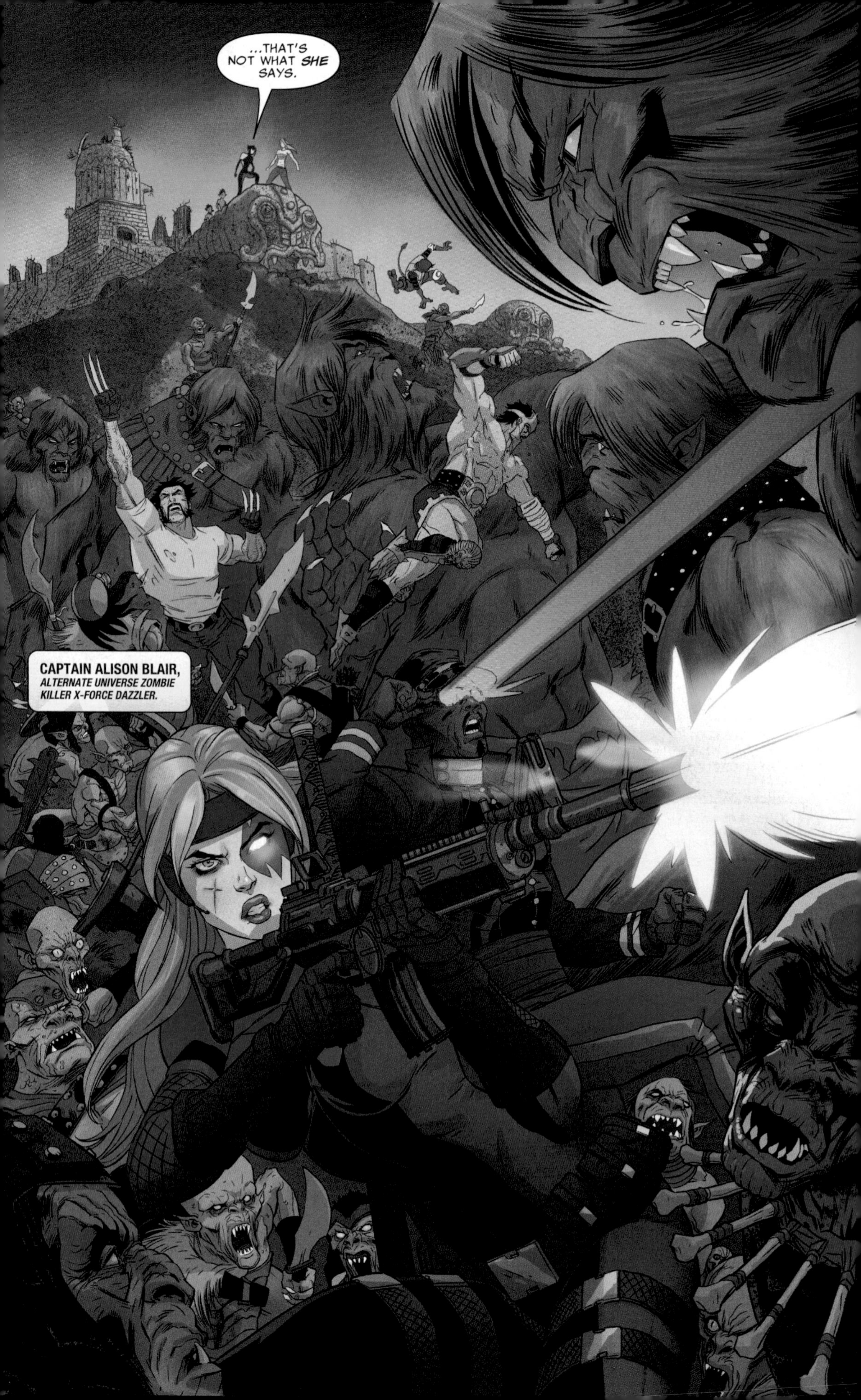
...THAT'S NOT WHAT SHE SAYS.
CAPTAIN ALISON BLAIR,
ALTERNATE UNIVERSE ZOMBIE KILLER X-FORCE DAZZLER.

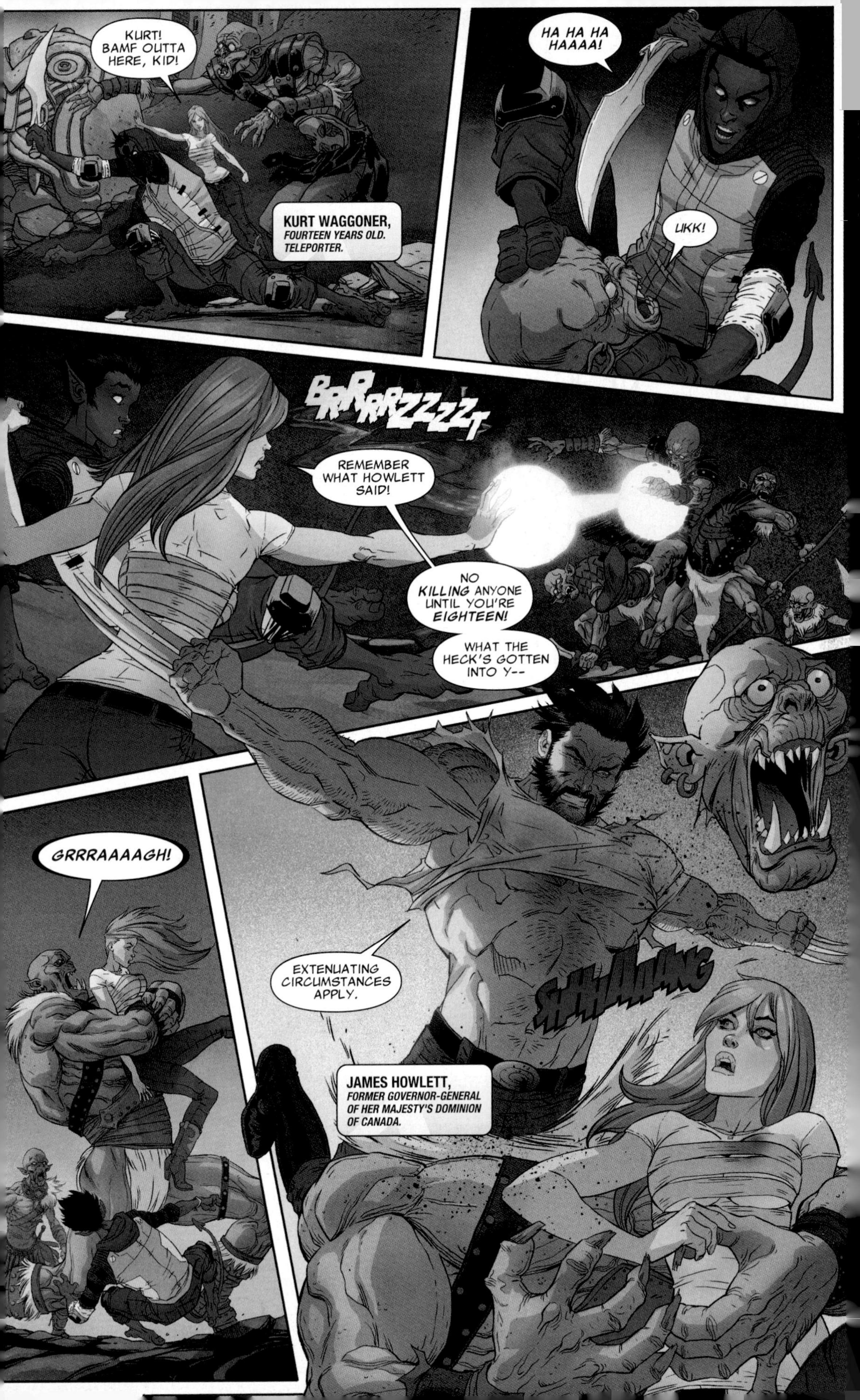
KURT! BAMF OUTTA HERE, KID!
KURT WAGGONER, FOURTEEN YEARS OLD. TELEPORTER.
HA HA HA HAAAA!
UKK!
BRRRRRZZZZZT
REMEMBER WHAT HOWLETT SAID!
NO KILLING ANYONE UNTIL YOU'RE EIGHTEEN!
WHAT THE HECK'S GOTTEN INTO Y--
GRRRAAAAGH!
EXTENUATING CIRCUMSTANCES APPLY.
SHHHAAAANG
JAMES HOWLETT, FORMER GOVERNOR-GENERAL OF HER MAJESTY'S DOMINION OF CANADA.

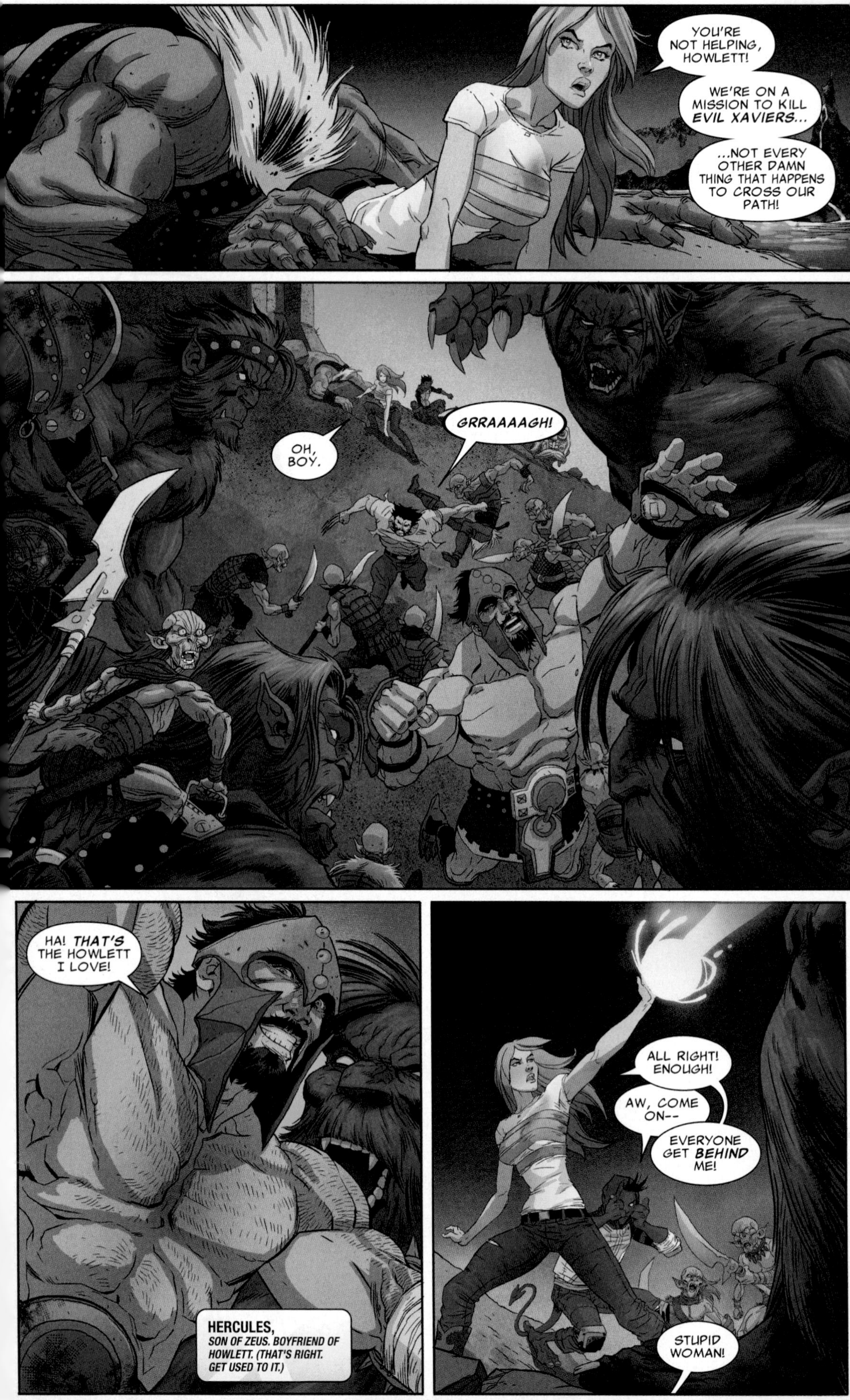
YOU'RE NOT HELPING, HOWLETT!
WE'RE ON A MISSION TO KILL EVIL XAVIERS...
...NOT EVERY OTHER DAMN THING THAT HAPPENS TO CROSS OUR PATH!
OH, BOY.
GRRAAAAGH!
HA! THAT'S THE HOWLETT I LOVE!
HERCULES, SON OF ZEUS. BOYFRIEND OF HOWLETT. (THAT'S RIGHT. GET USED TO IT.)
ALL RIGHT! ENOUGH!
AW, COME ON--
EVERYONE GET BEHIND ME!
STUPID WOMAN!

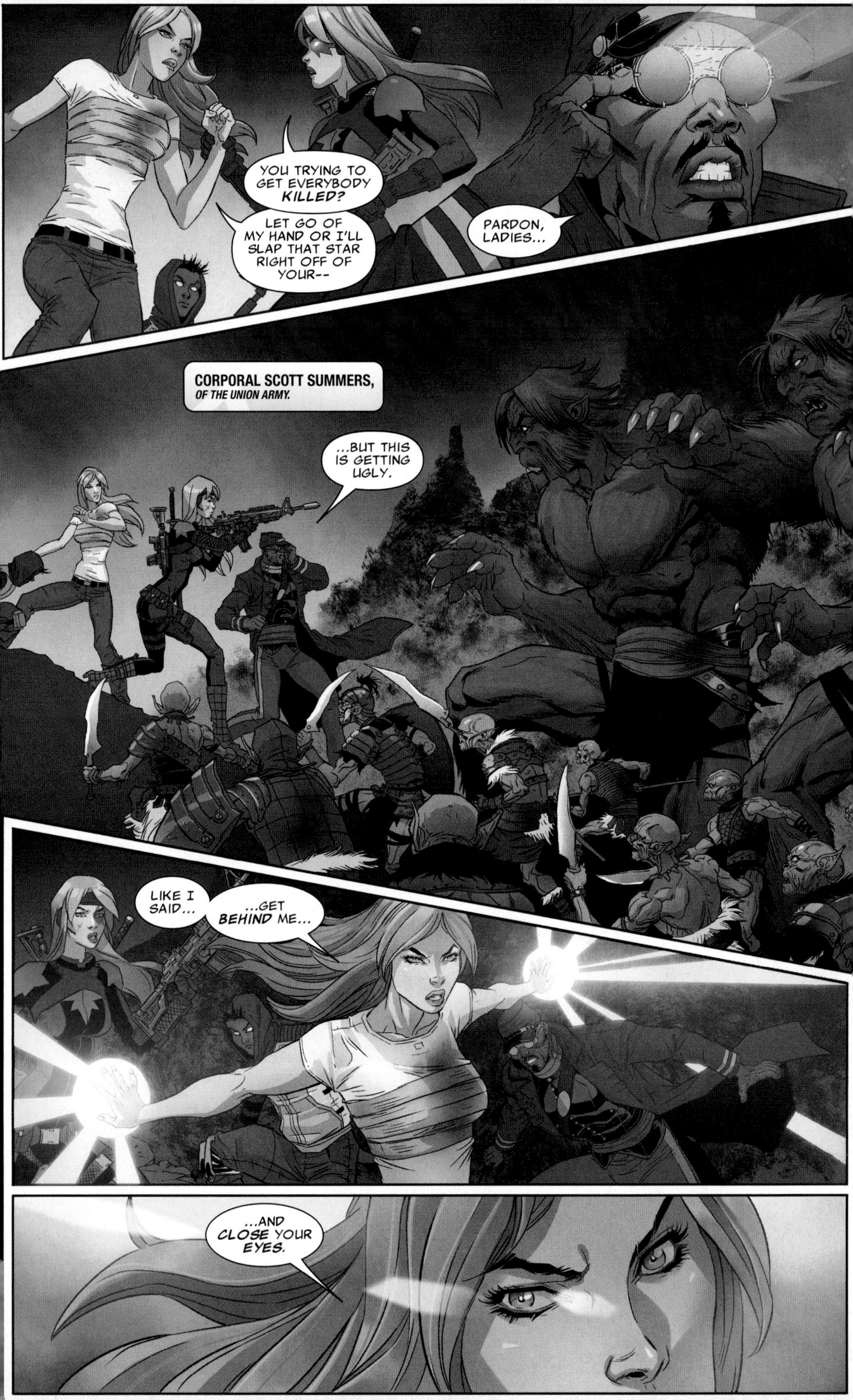
YOU TRYING TO GET EVERYBODY KILLED?
LET GO OF MY HAND OR I'LL SLAP THAT STAR RIGHT OFF OF YOUR--
PARDON, LADIES...
CORPORAL SCOTT SUMMERS, OF THE UNION ARMY.
...BUT THIS IS GETTING UGLY.
LIKE I SAID...
...GET BEHIND ME...
...AND CLOSE YOUR EYES.

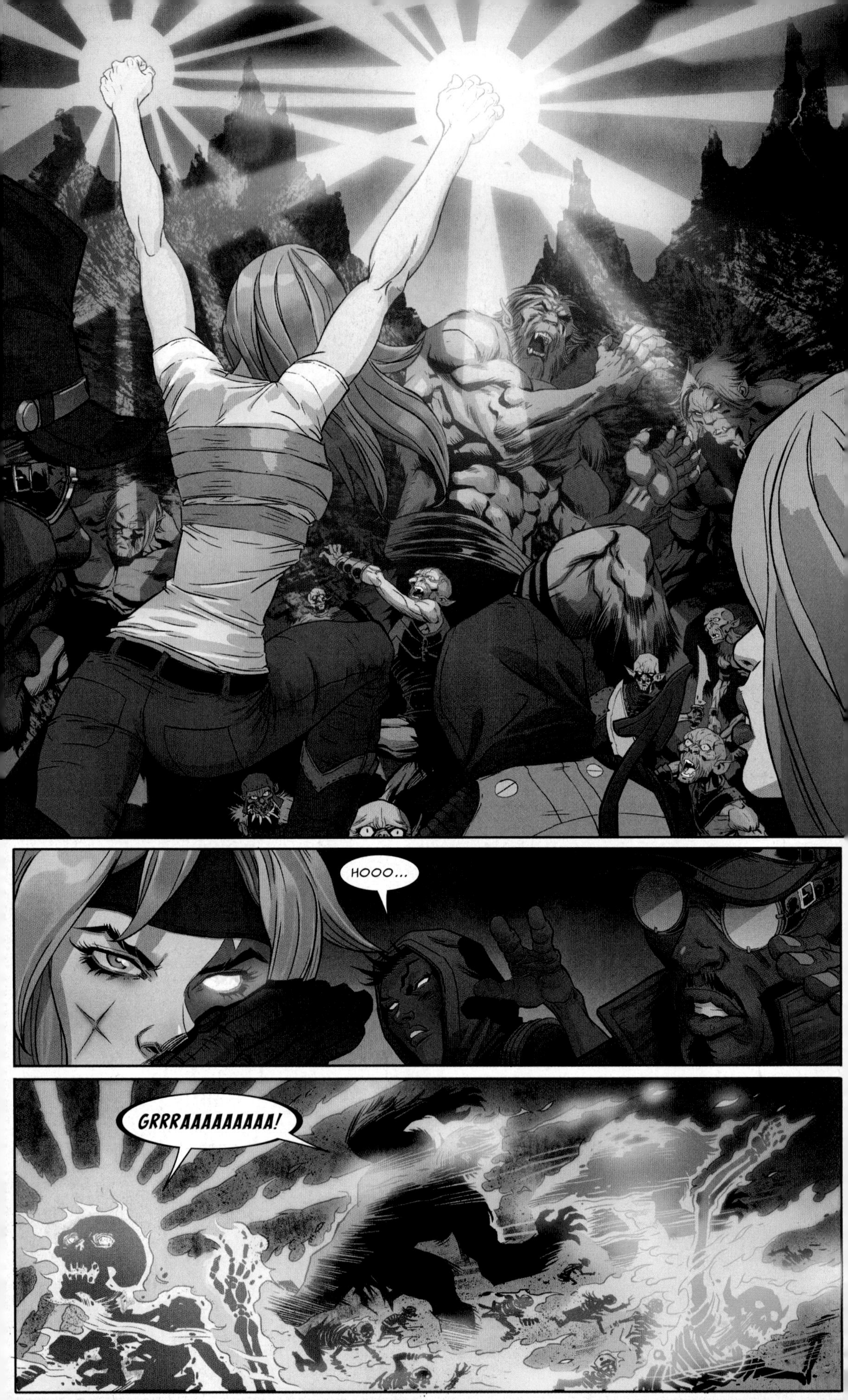
HOOO...
GRRRAAAAAAAAA!

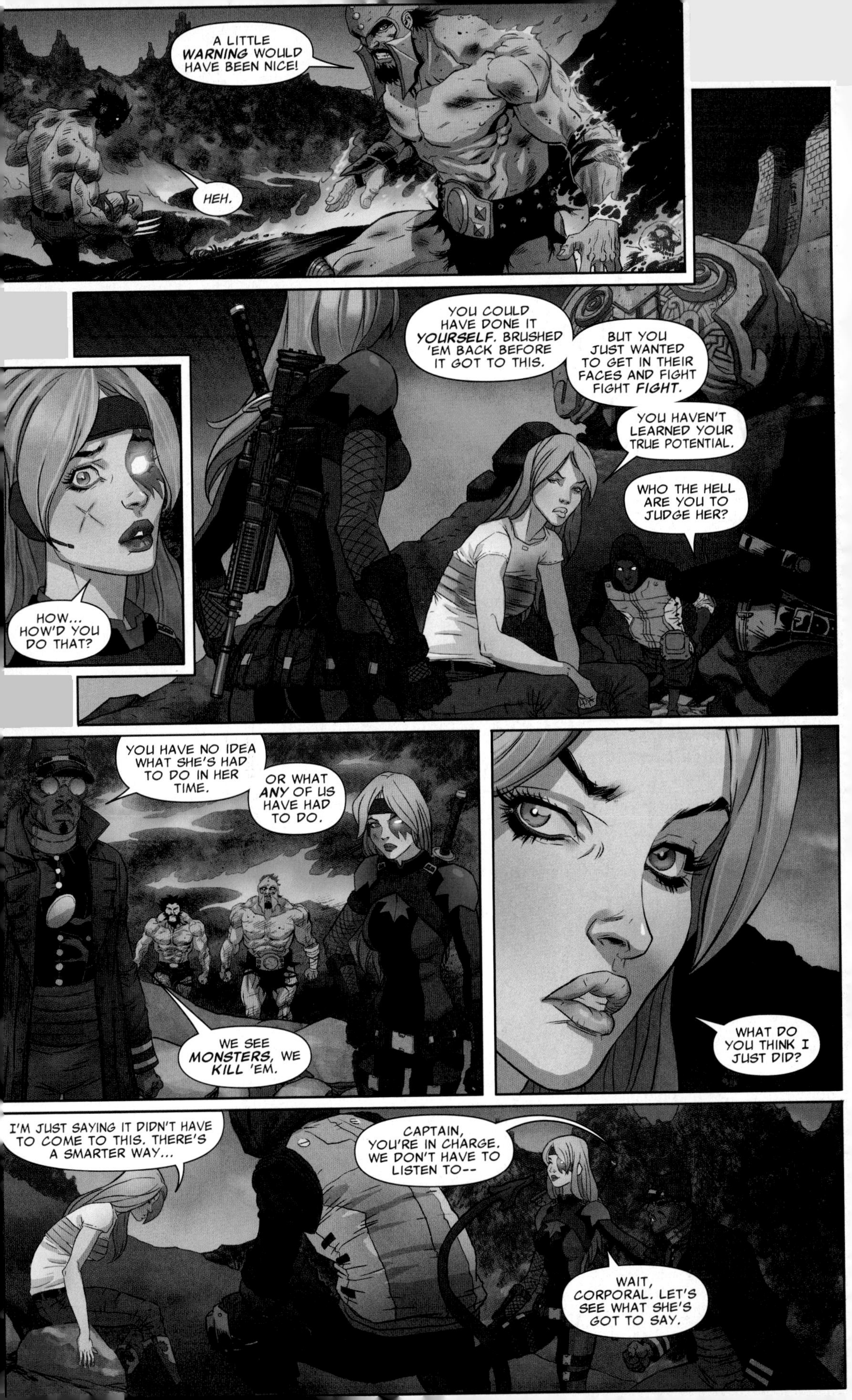
A LITTLE WARNING WOULD HAVE BEEN NICE!
HEH.
YOU COULD HAVE DONE IT YOURSELF. BRUSHED 'EM BACK BEFORE IT GOT TO THIS.
BUT YOU JUST WANTED TO GET IN THEIR FACES AND FIGHT FIGHT FIGHT.
YOU HAVEN'T LEARNED YOUR TRUE POTENTIAL.
WHO THE HELL ARE YOU TO JUDGE HER?
HOW... HOW'D YOU DO THAT?
YOU HAVE NO IDEA WHAT SHE'S HAD TO DO IN HER TIME.
OR WHAT ANY OF US HAVE HAD TO DO.
WE SEE MONSTERS, WE KILL 'EM.
WHAT DO YOU THINK I JUST DID?
I'M JUST SAYING IT DIDN'T HAVE TO COME TO THIS. THERE'S A SMARTER WAY...
CAPTAIN, YOU'RE IN CHARGE. WE DON'T HAVE TO LISTEN TO--
WAIT, CORPORAL. LET'S SEE WHAT SHE'S GOT TO SAY.

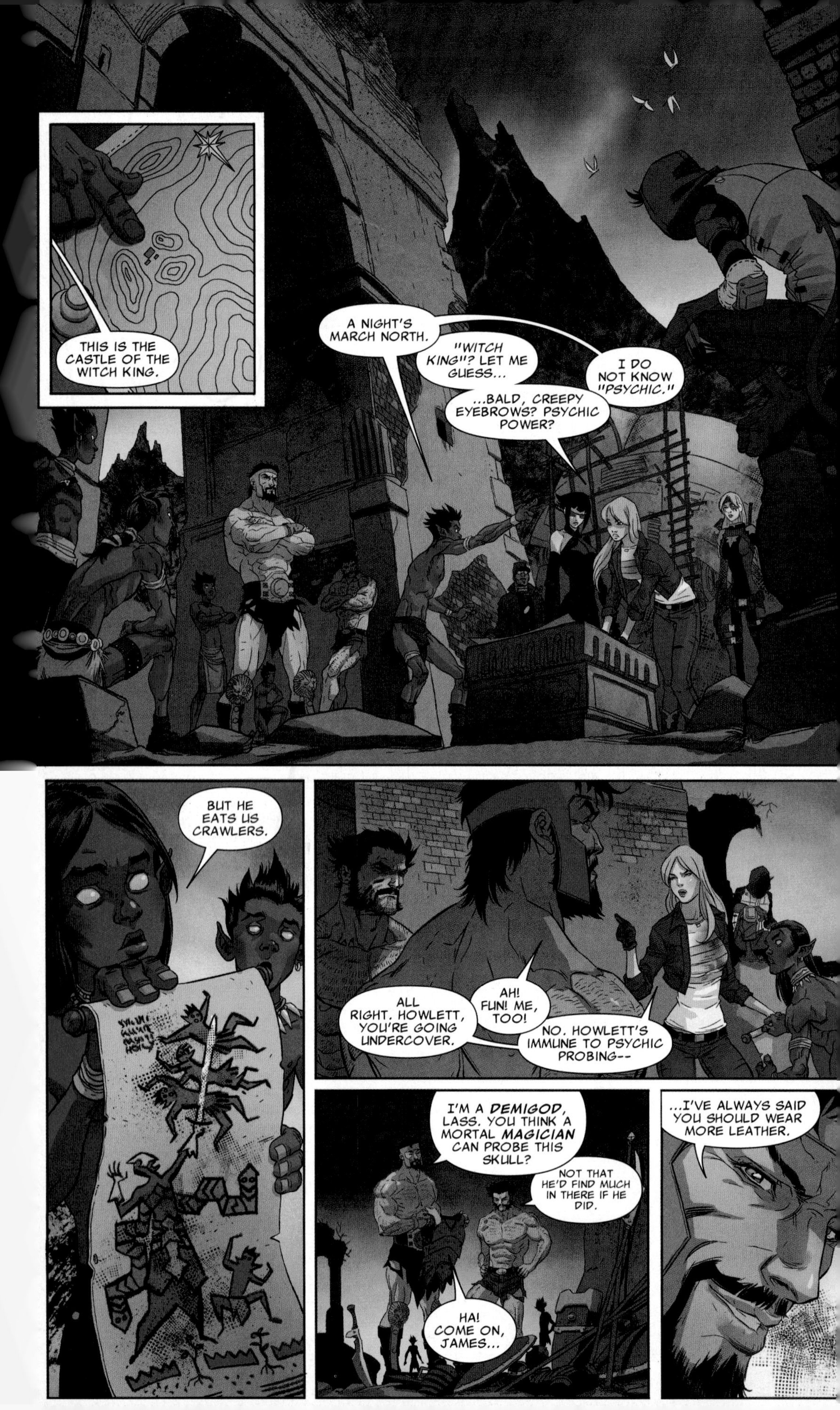
THIS IS THE CASTLE OF THE WITCH KING.
A NIGHT'S MARCH NORTH.
"WITCH KING"? LET ME GUESS...
...BALD, CREEPY EYEBROWS? PSYCHIC POWER?
I DO NOT KNOW "PSYCHIC."
BUT HE EATS US CRAWLERS.
ALL RIGHT. HOWLETT, YOU'RE GOING UNDERCOVER.
AH! FUN! ME, TOO!
NO. HOWLETT'S IMMUNE TO PSYCHIC PROBING--
I'M A DEMIGOD, LASS. YOU THINK A MORTAL MAGICIAN CAN PROBE THIS SKULL?
NOT THAT HE'D FIND MUCH IN THERE IF HE DID.
HA! COME ON, JAMES...
...I'VE ALWAYS SAID YOU SHOULD WEAR MORE LEATHER.

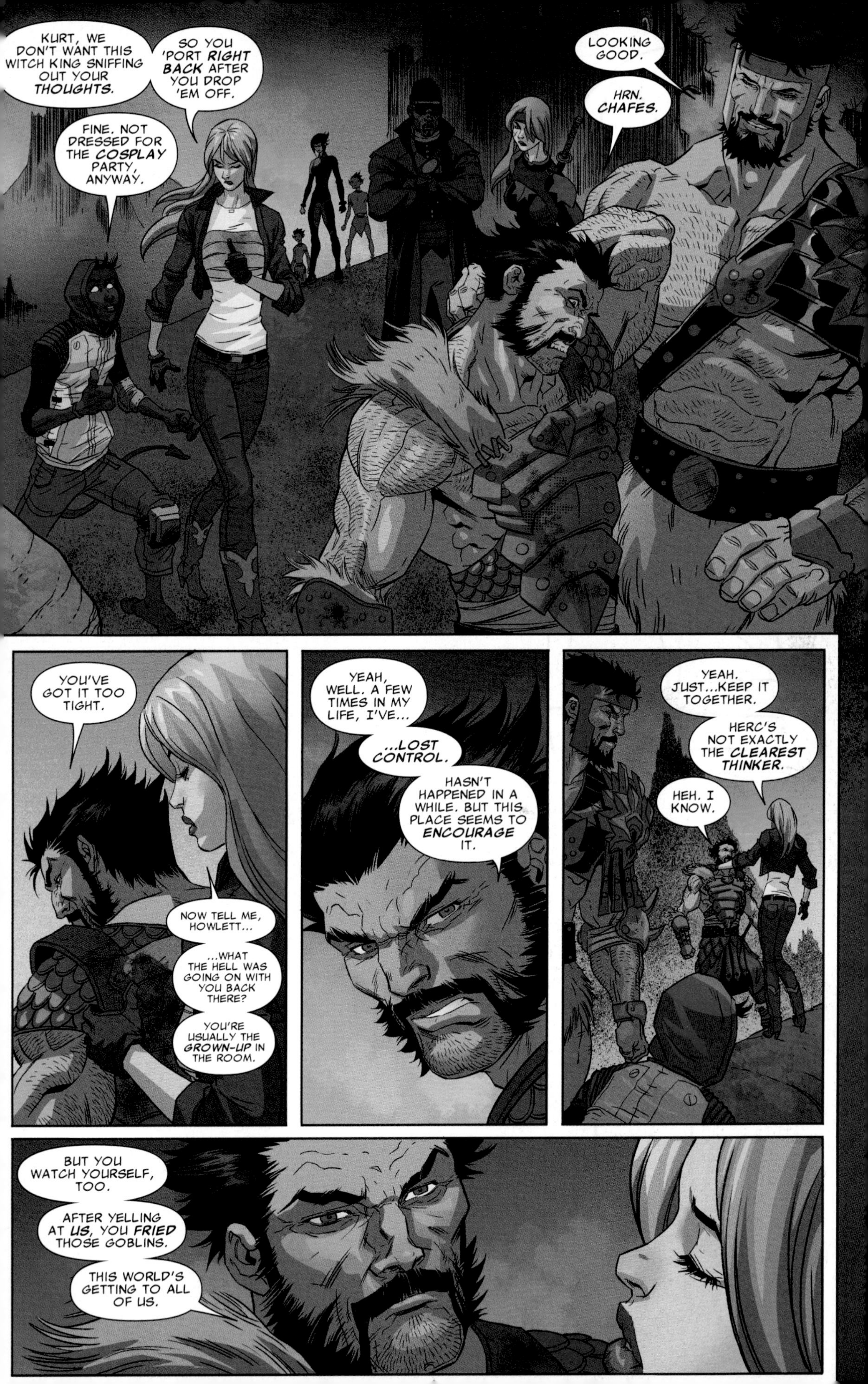
KURT, WE DON'T WANT THIS WITCH KING SNIFFING OUT YOUR THOUGHTS.
SO YOU 'PORT RIGHT BACK AFTER YOU DROP 'EM OFF.
FINE. NOT DRESSED FOR THE COSPLAY PARTY, ANYWAY.
LOOKING GOOD.
HRN. CHAFES.
YOU'VE GOT IT TOO TIGHT.
NOW TELL ME, HOWLETT...
...WHAT THE HELL WAS GOING ON WITH YOU BACK THERE?
YOU'RE USUALLY THE GROWN-UP IN THE ROOM.
YEAH, WELL. A FEW TIMES IN MY LIFE, I'VE...
...LOST CONTROL.
HASN'T HAPPENED IN A WHILE. BUT THIS PLACE SEEMS TO ENCOURAGE IT.
YEAH. JUST...KEEP IT TOGETHER.
HERC'S NOT EXACTLY THE CLEAREST THINKER.
HEH. I KNOW.
BUT YOU WATCH YOURSELF, TOO.
AFTER YELLING AT US, YOU FRIED THOSE GOBLINS.
THIS WORLD'S GETTING TO ALL OF US.

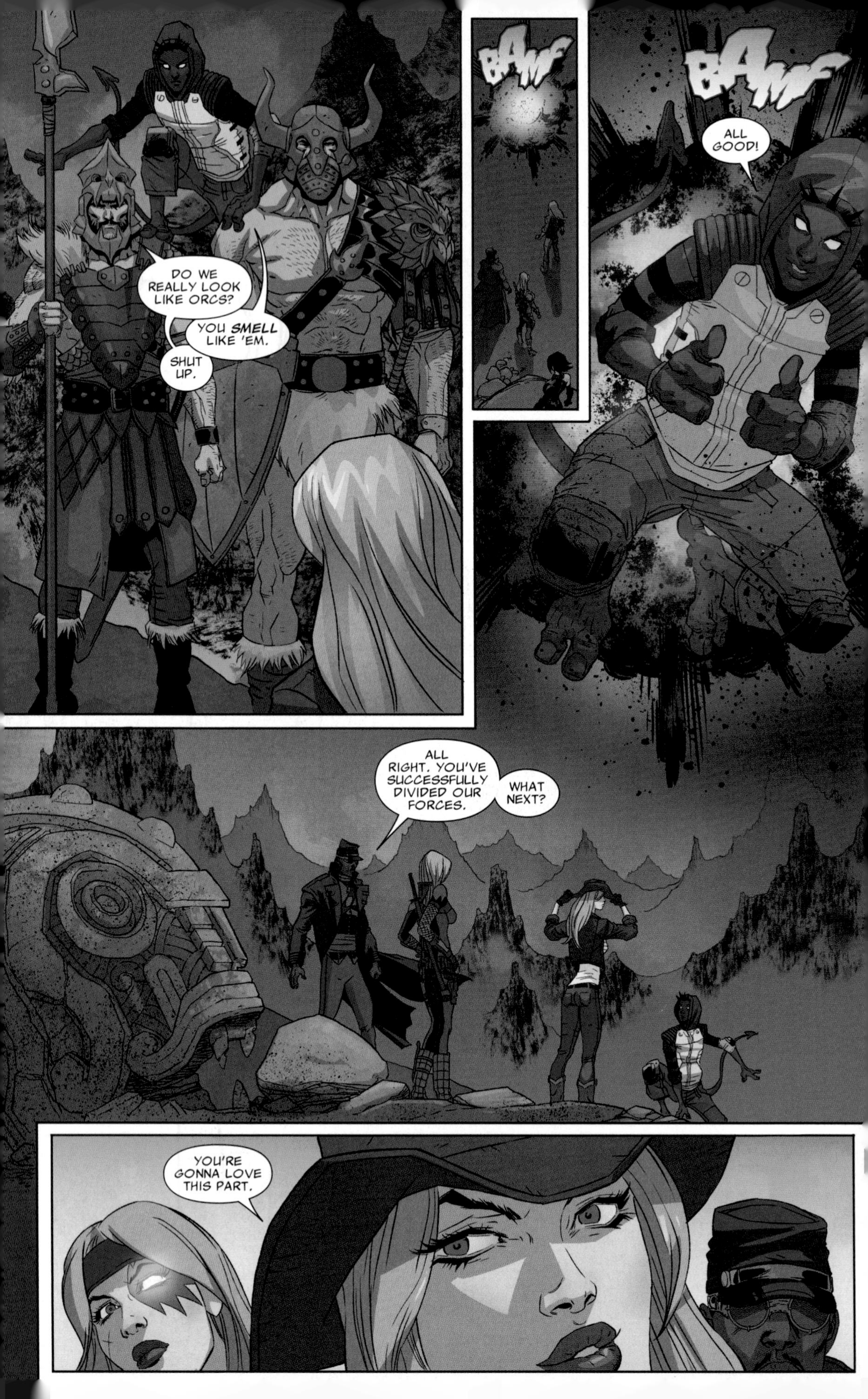
DO WE REALLY LOOK LIKE ORCS?
YOU SMELL LIKE 'EM.
SHUT UP.
BAMF
BAMF
ALL GOOD!
ALL RIGHT. YOU'VE SUCCESSFULLY DIVIDED OUR FORCES.
WHAT NEXT?
YOU'RE GONNA LOVE THIS PART.

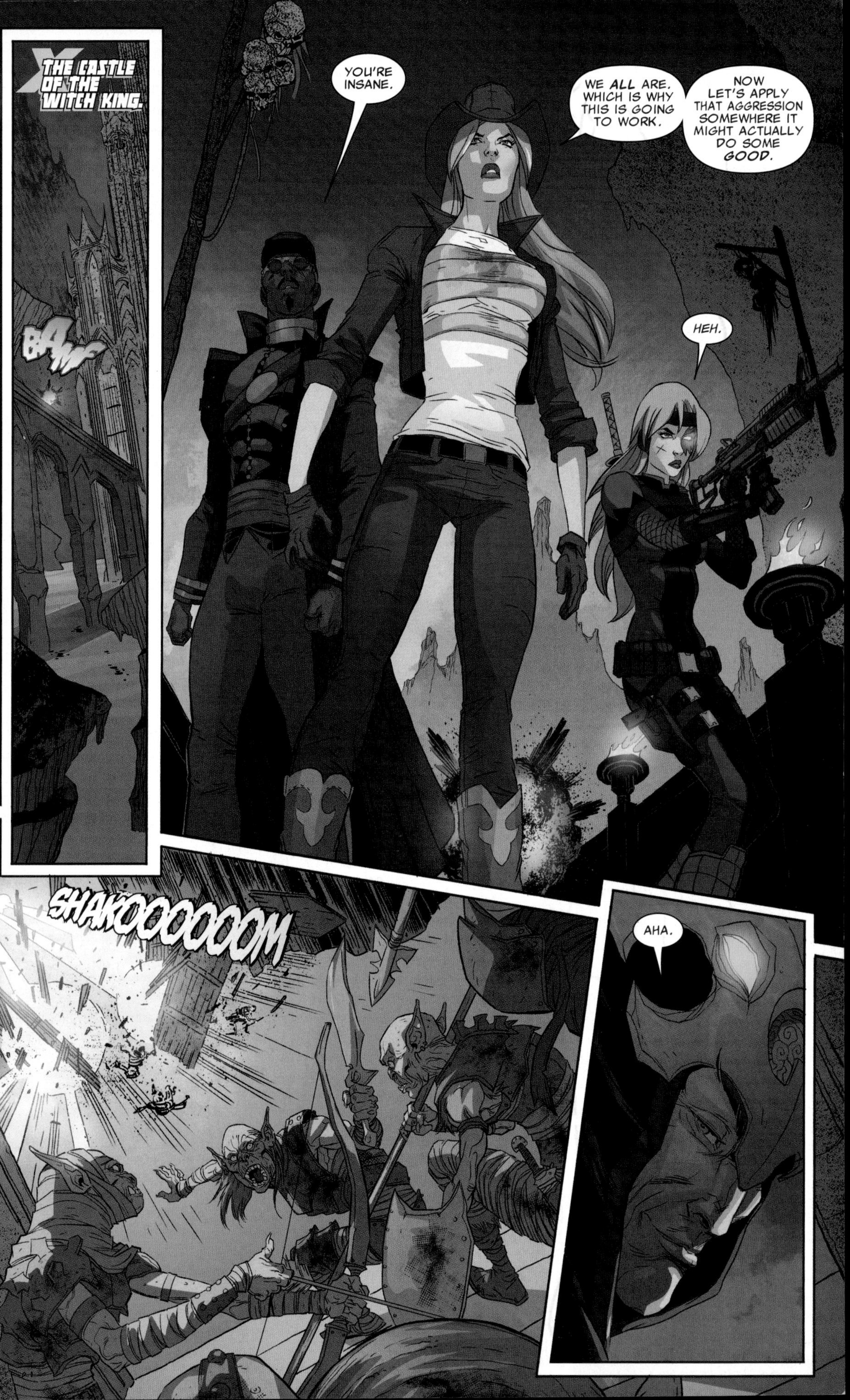
THE CASTLE OF THE WITCH KING.
YOU'RE INSANE.
WE ALL ARE. WHICH IS WHY THIS IS GOING TO WORK.
NOW LET'S APPLY THAT AGGRESSION SOMEWHERE IT MIGHT ACTUALLY DO SOME GOOD.
BAMF
HEH.
SHAKOOOOOOOM
AHA.

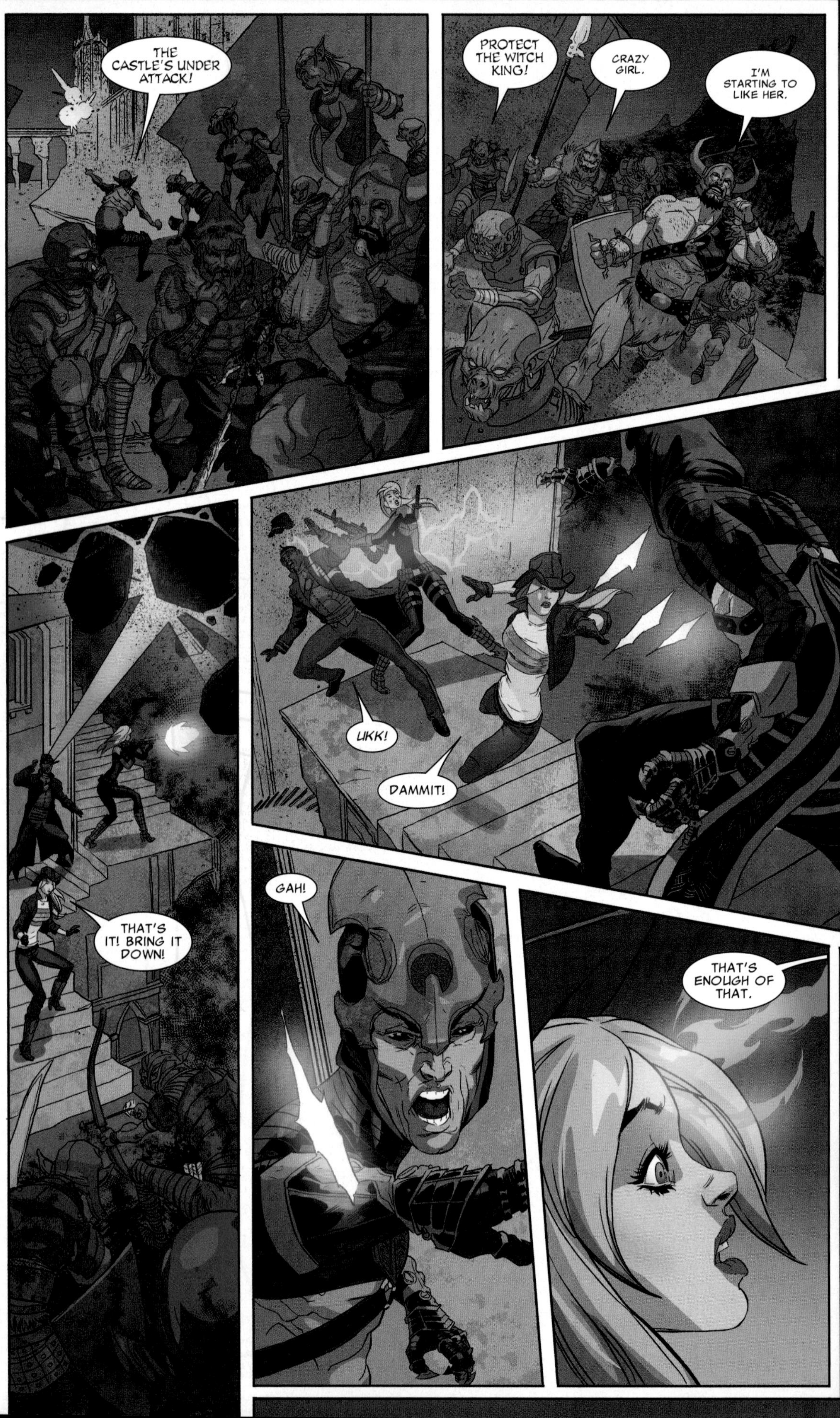
THE CASTLE'S UNDER ATTACK!
PROTECT THE WITCH KING!
CRAZY GIRL.
I'M STARTING TO LIKE HER.
UKK!
DAMMIT!
THAT'S IT! BRING IT DOWN!
GAH!
THAT'S ENOUGH OF THAT.

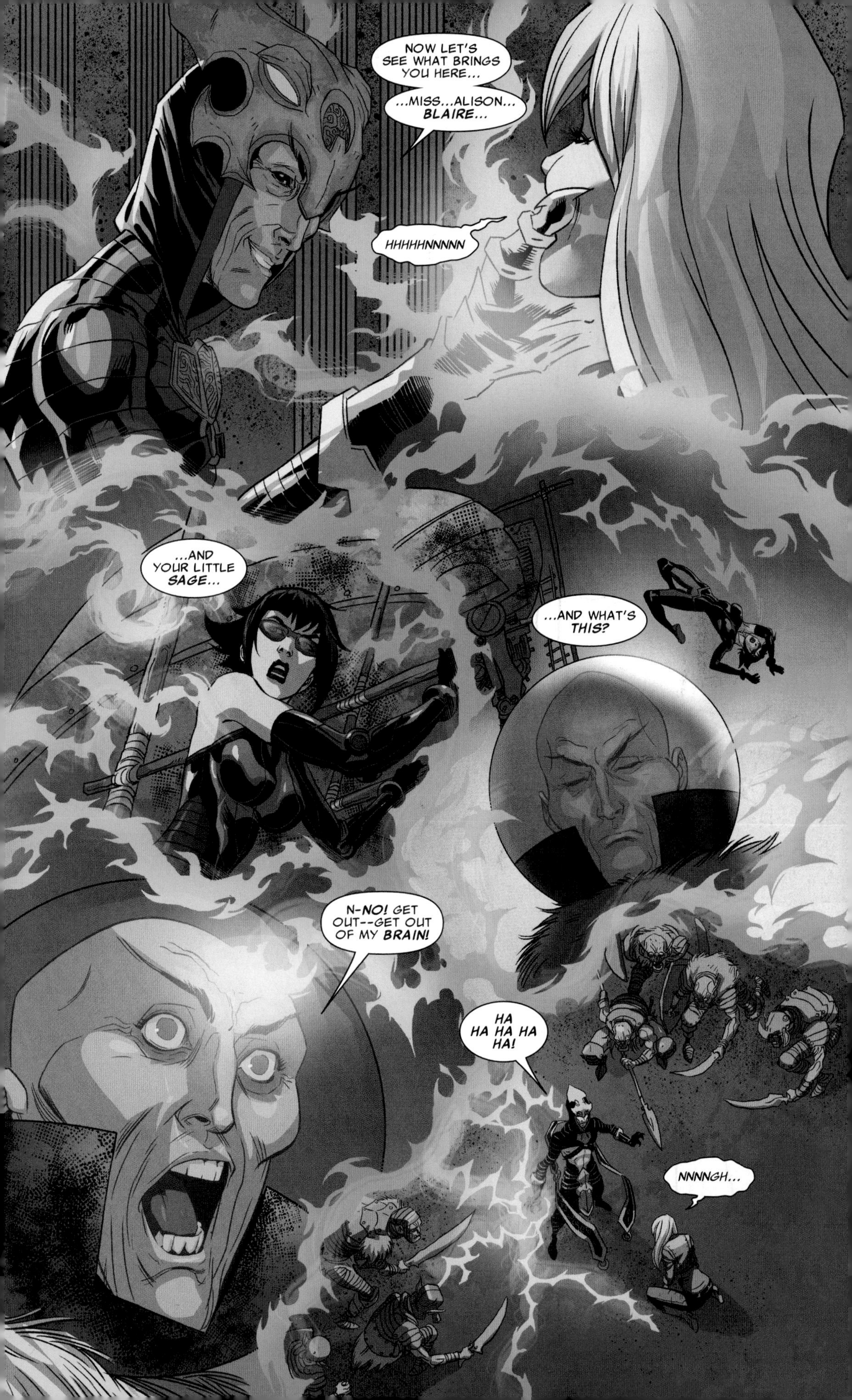
NOW LET'S SEE WHAT BRINGS YOU HERE...
...MISS...ALISON... BLAIRE...
HHHHHNNNNN
...AND YOUR LITTLE SAGE...
...AND WHAT'S THIS?
N-NO! GET OUT--GET OUT OF MY BRAIN!
HA HA HA HA HA!
NNNNGH...

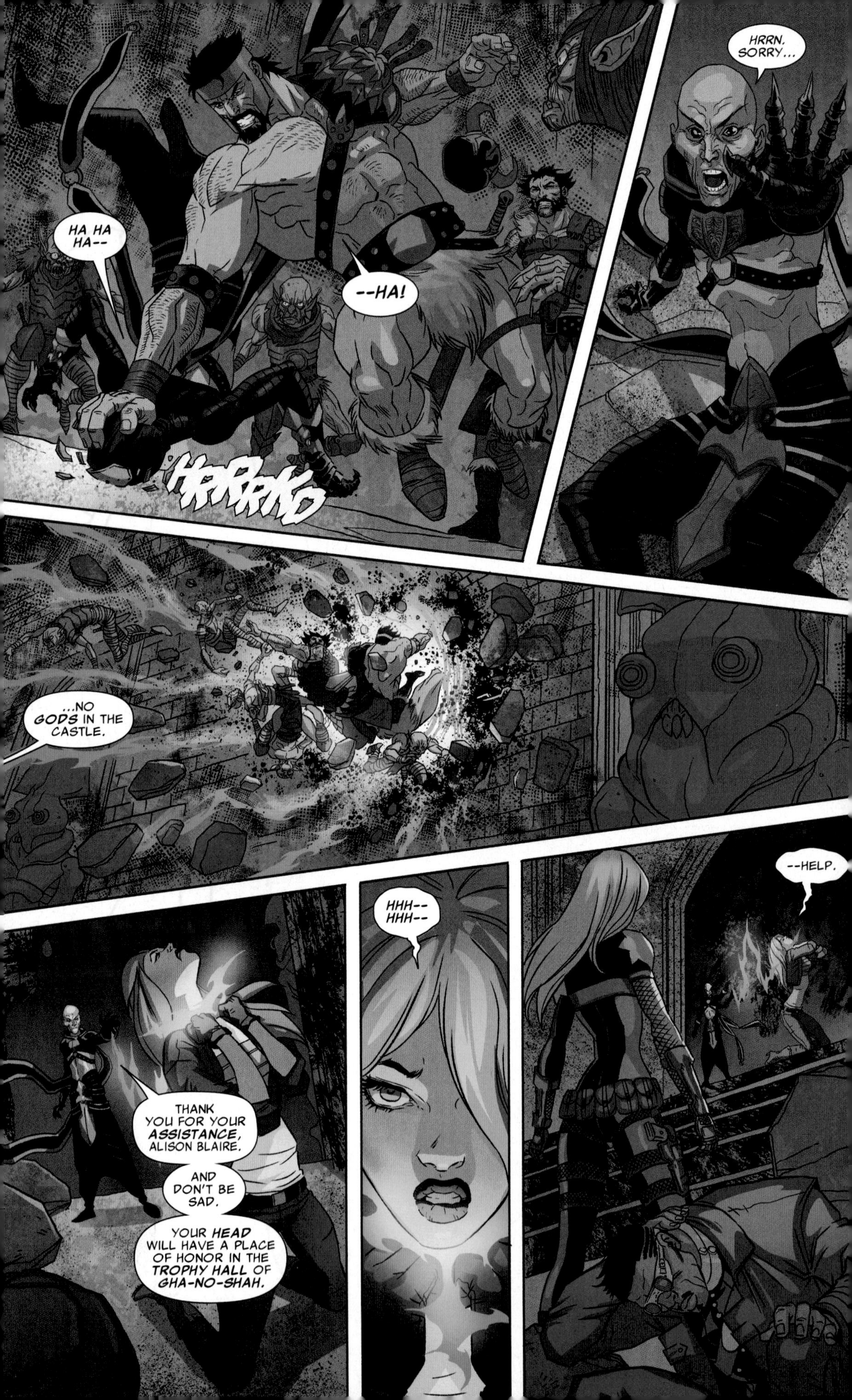
HA HA HA--
--HA!
HRRRKO
HRRN, SORRY...
...NO GODS IN THE CASTLE.
THANK YOU FOR YOUR ASSISTANCE, ALISON BLAIRE.
AND DON'T BE SAD.
YOUR HEAD WILL HAVE A PLACE OF HONOR IN THE TROPHY HALL OF GHA-NO-SHAH.
HHH-- HHH--
--HELP.

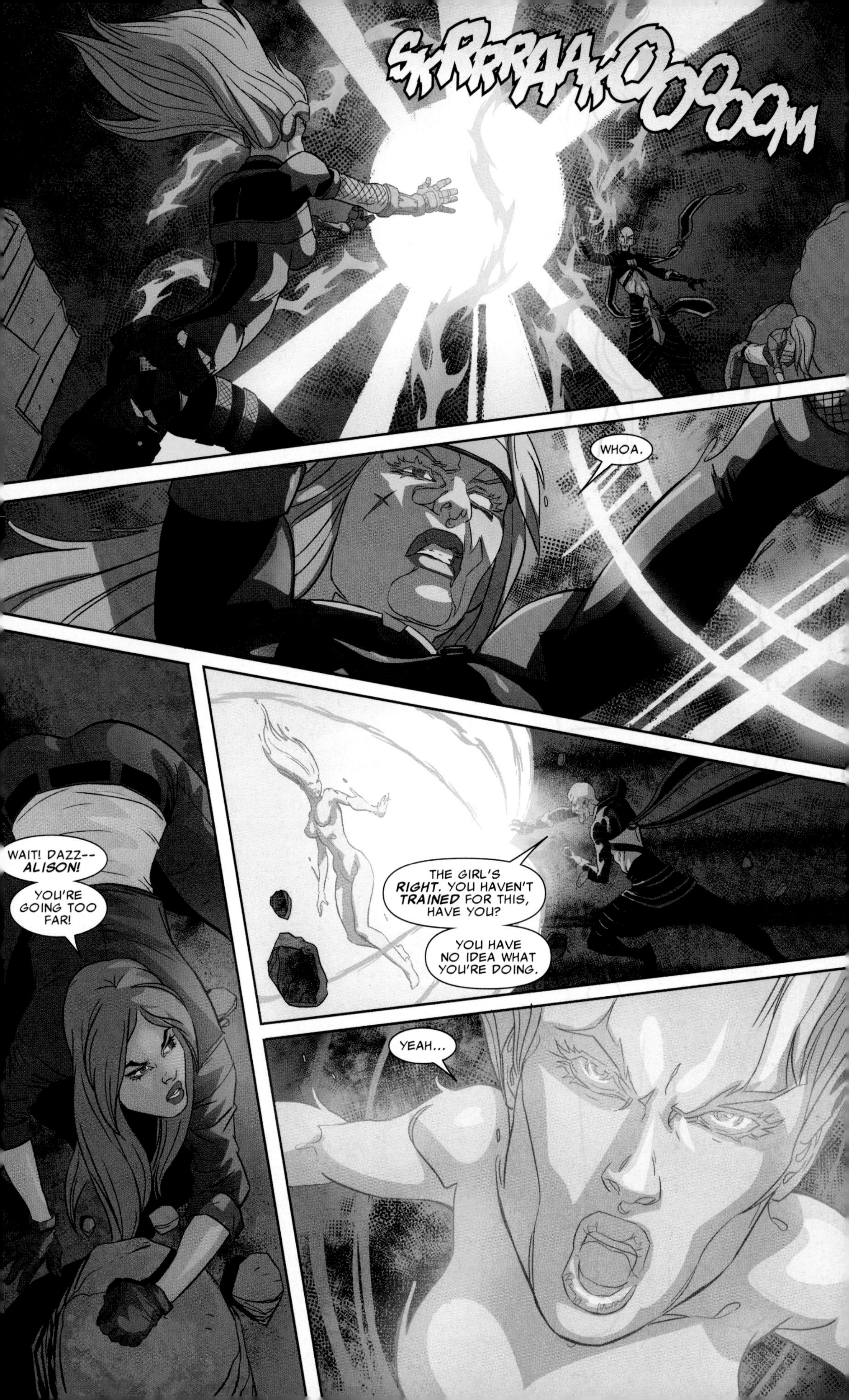
SKRRRAAKOOOOOOM
WHOA.
THE GIRL'S RIGHT. YOU HAVEN'T TRAINED FOR THIS, HAVE YOU?
YOU HAVE NO IDEA WHAT YOU'RE DOING.
WAIT! DAZZ-- ALISON!
YOU'RE GOING TOO FAR!
YEAH...

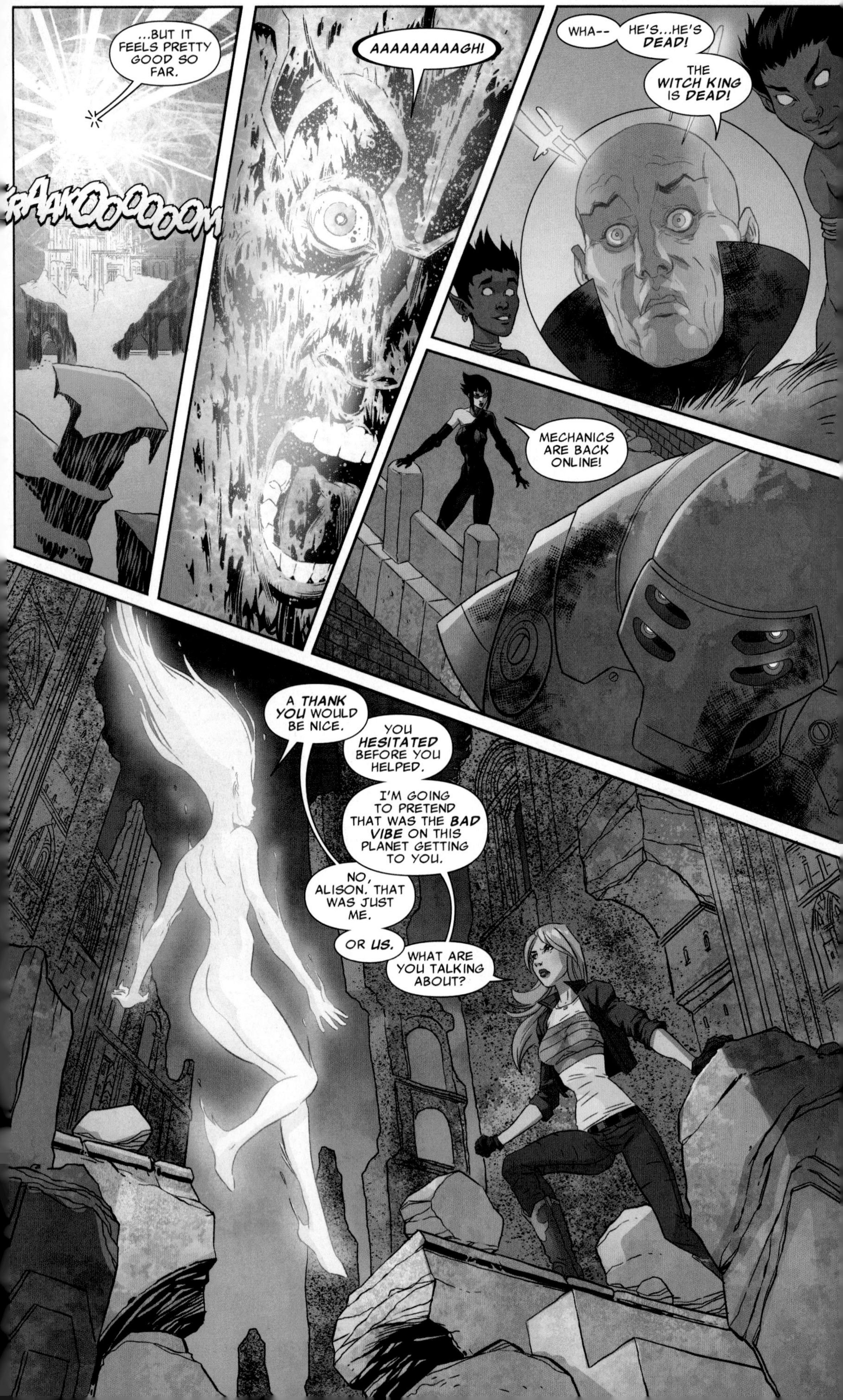
...BUT IT FEELS PRETTY GOOD SO FAR.
KRAAKOOOOOOOM
AAAAAAAAAGH!
WHA--
HE'S...HE'S DEAD!
THE WITCH KING IS DEAD!
MECHANICS ARE BACK ONLINE!
A THANK YOU WOULD BE NICE.
YOU HESITATED BEFORE YOU HELPED.
I'M GOING TO PRETEND THAT WAS THE BAD VIBE ON THIS PLANET GETTING TO YOU.
NO, ALISON. THAT WAS JUST ME.
OR US.
WHAT ARE YOU TALKING ABOUT?

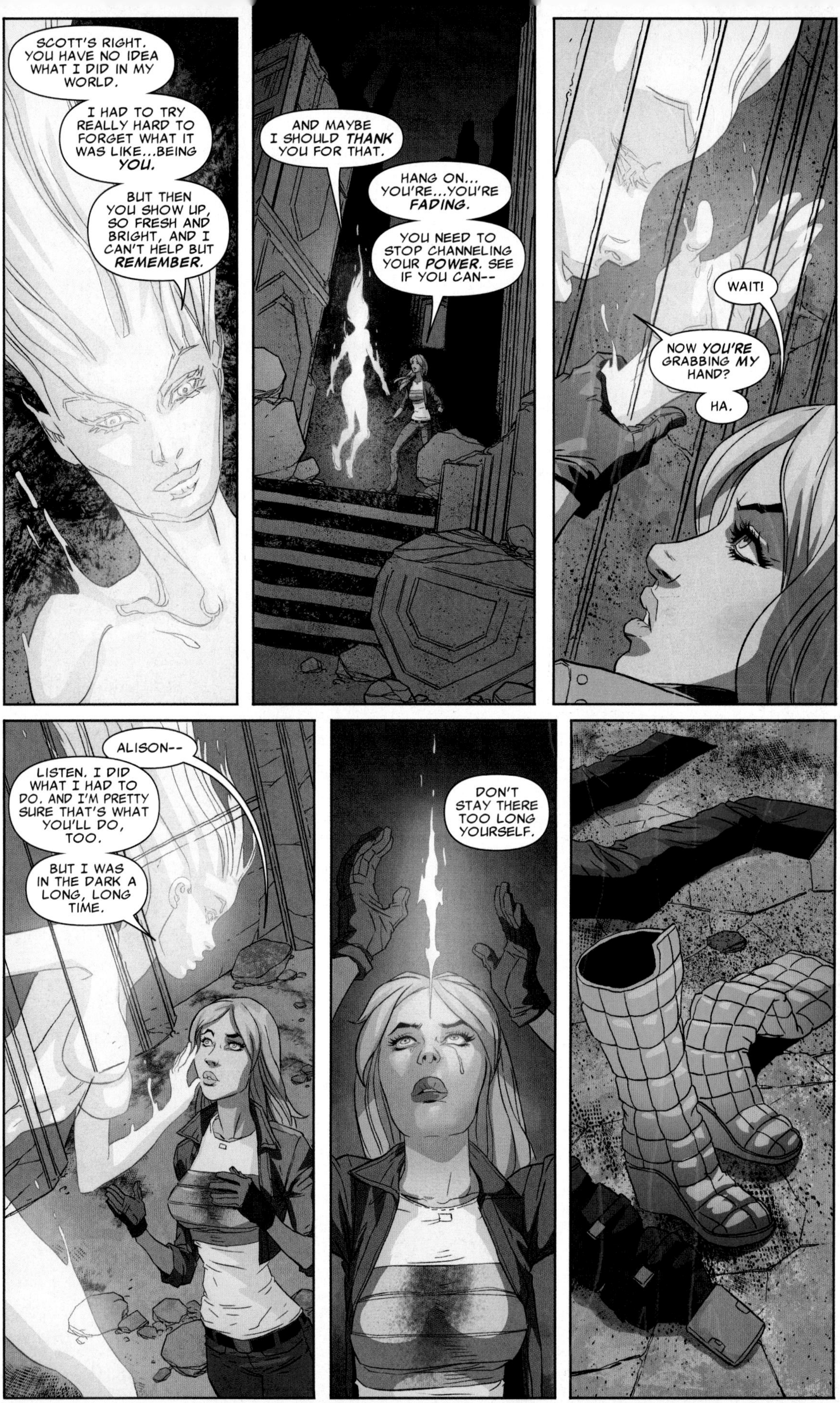
SCOTT'S RIGHT. YOU HAVE NO IDEA WHAT I DID IN MY WORLD.
I HAD TO TRY REALLY HARD TO FORGET WHAT IT WAS LIKE...BEING *YOU.*
BUT THEN YOU SHOW UP, SO FRESH AND BRIGHT, AND I CAN'T HELP BUT *REMEMBER.*
AND MAYBE I SHOULD *THANK* YOU FOR THAT.
HANG ON... YOU'RE...YOU'RE *FADING.*
YOU NEED TO STOP CHANNELING YOUR *POWER.* SEE IF YOU CAN--
WAIT!
NOW *YOU'RE* GRABBING *MY* HAND?
HA.
ALISON--
LISTEN. I DID WHAT I HAD TO DO. AND I'M PRETTY SURE THAT'S WHAT YOU'LL DO, TOO.
BUT I WAS IN THE DARK A LONG, LONG TIME.
DON'T STAY THERE TOO LONG YOURSELF.

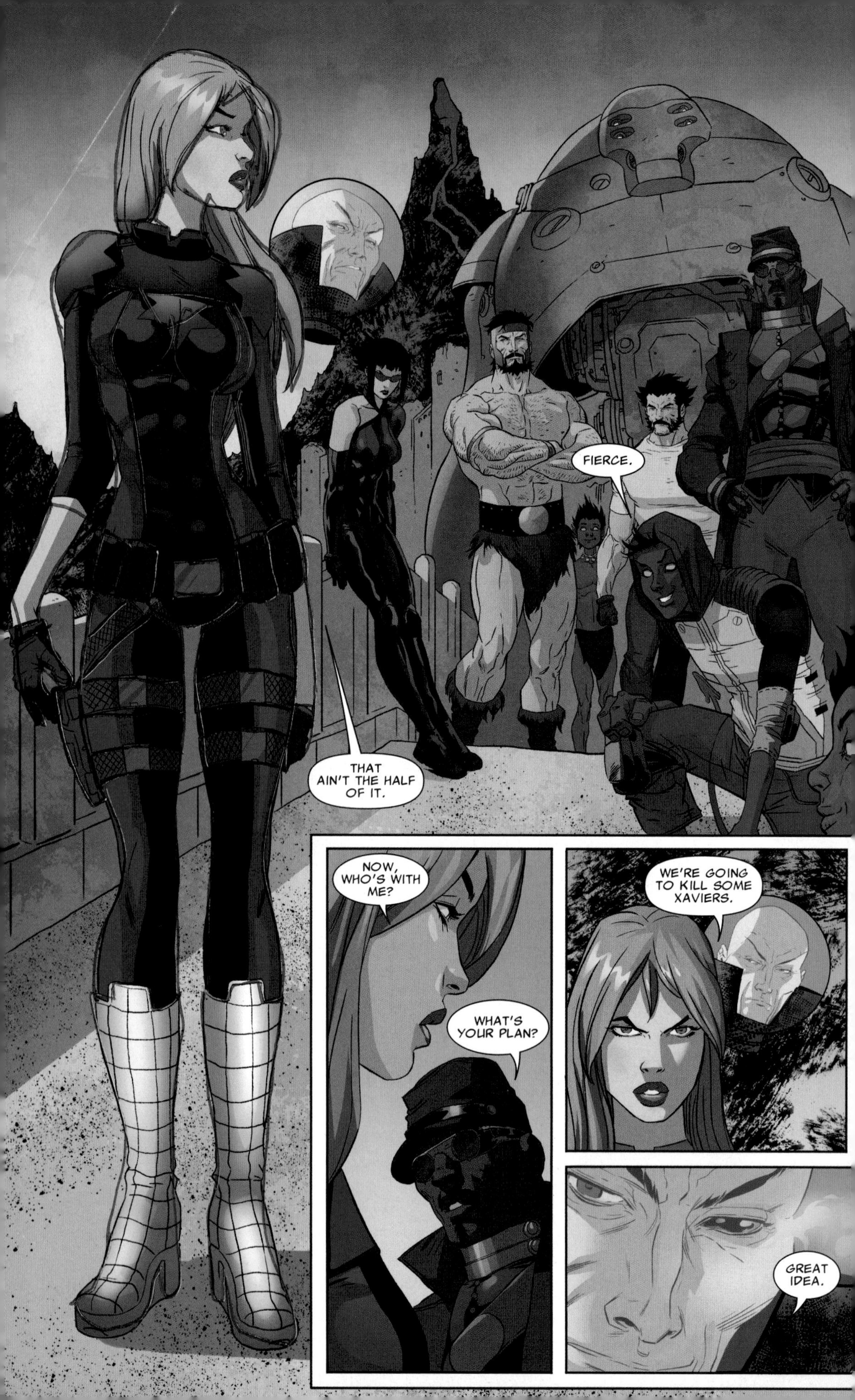
FIERCE.
THAT AIN'T THE HALF OF IT.
NOW, WHO'S WITH ME?
WHAT'S YOUR PLAN?
WE'RE GOING TO KILL SOME XAVIERS.
GREAT IDEA.

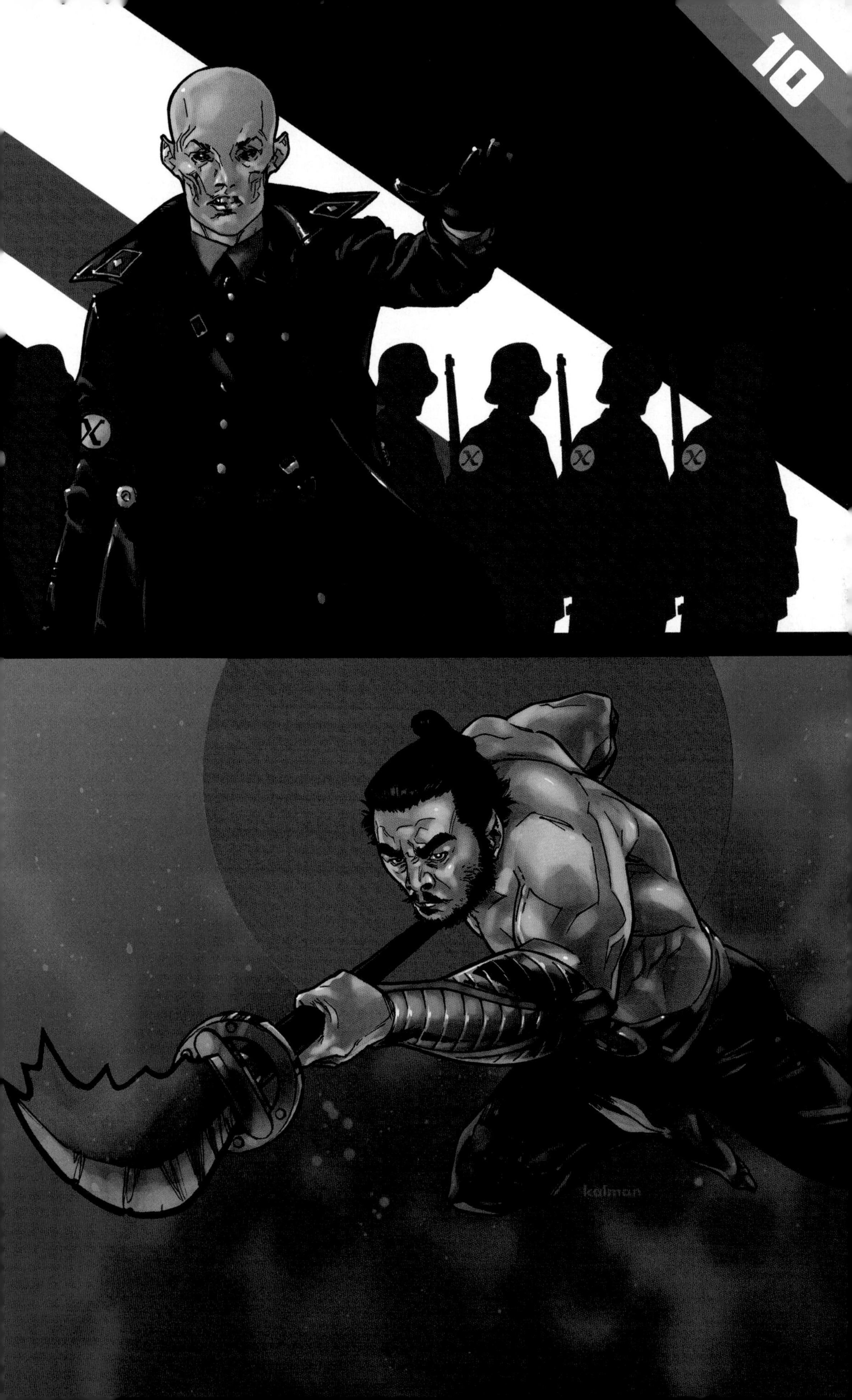
10
kalman

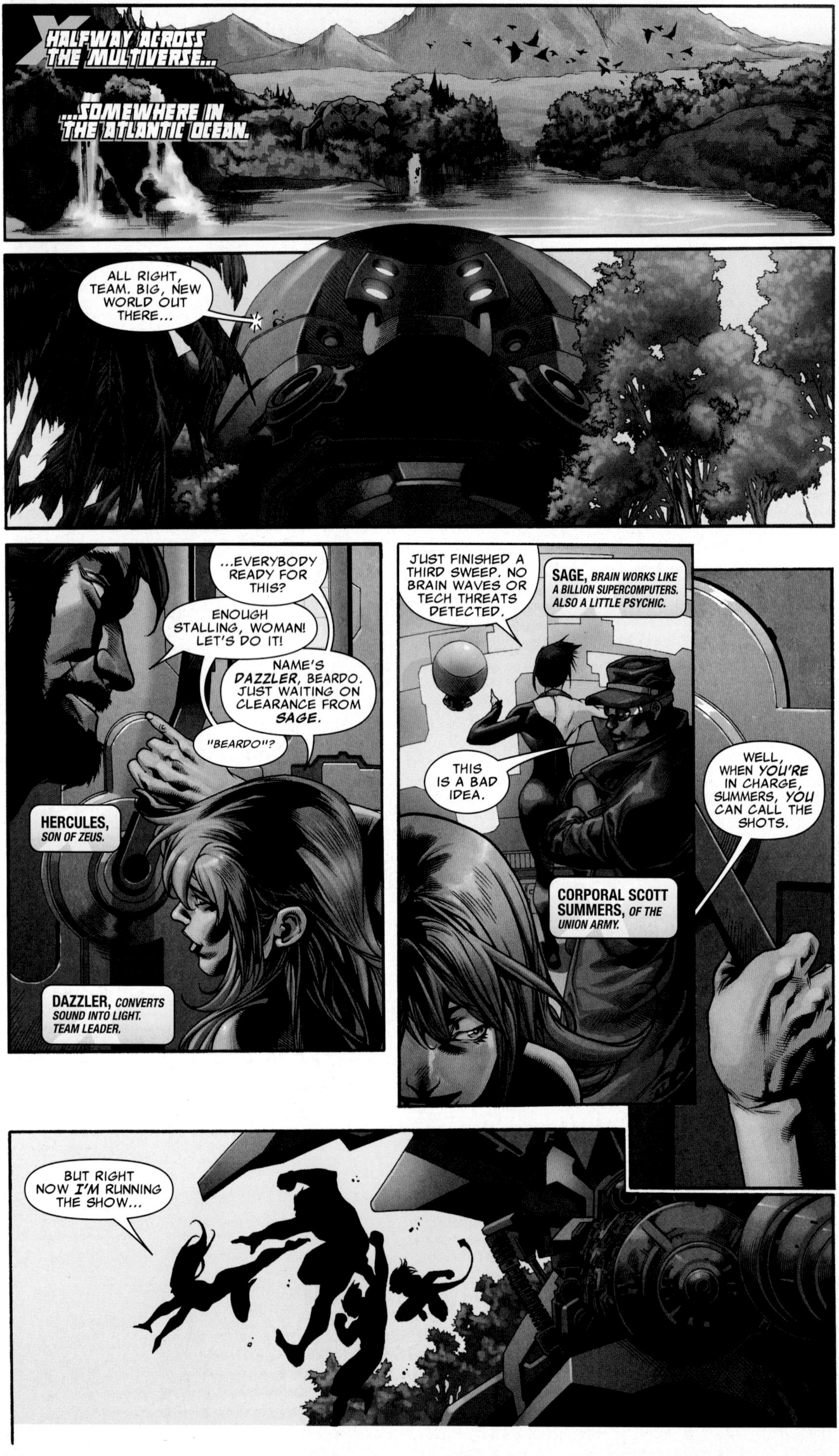
HALFWAY ACROSS THE MULTIVERSE...
...SOMEWHERE IN THE ATLANTIC OCEAN.
ALL RIGHT, TEAM. BIG, NEW WORLD OUT THERE...
...EVERYBODY READY FOR THIS?
ENOUGH STALLING, WOMAN! LET'S DO IT!
NAME'S DAZZLER, BEARDO. JUST WAITING ON CLEARANCE FROM SAGE.
"BEARDO"?
HERCULES, SON OF ZEUS.
DAZZLER, CONVERTS SOUND INTO LIGHT. TEAM LEADER.
JUST FINISHED A THIRD SWEEP. NO BRAIN WAVES OR TECH THREATS DETECTED.
SAGE, BRAIN WORKS LIKE A BILLION SUPERCOMPUTERS. ALSO A LITTLE PSYCHIC.
THIS IS A BAD IDEA.
CORPORAL SCOTT SUMMERS, OF THE UNION ARMY.
WELL, WHEN YOU'RE IN CHARGE, SUMMERS, YOU CAN CALL THE SHOTS.
BUT RIGHT NOW I'M RUNNING THE SHOW...

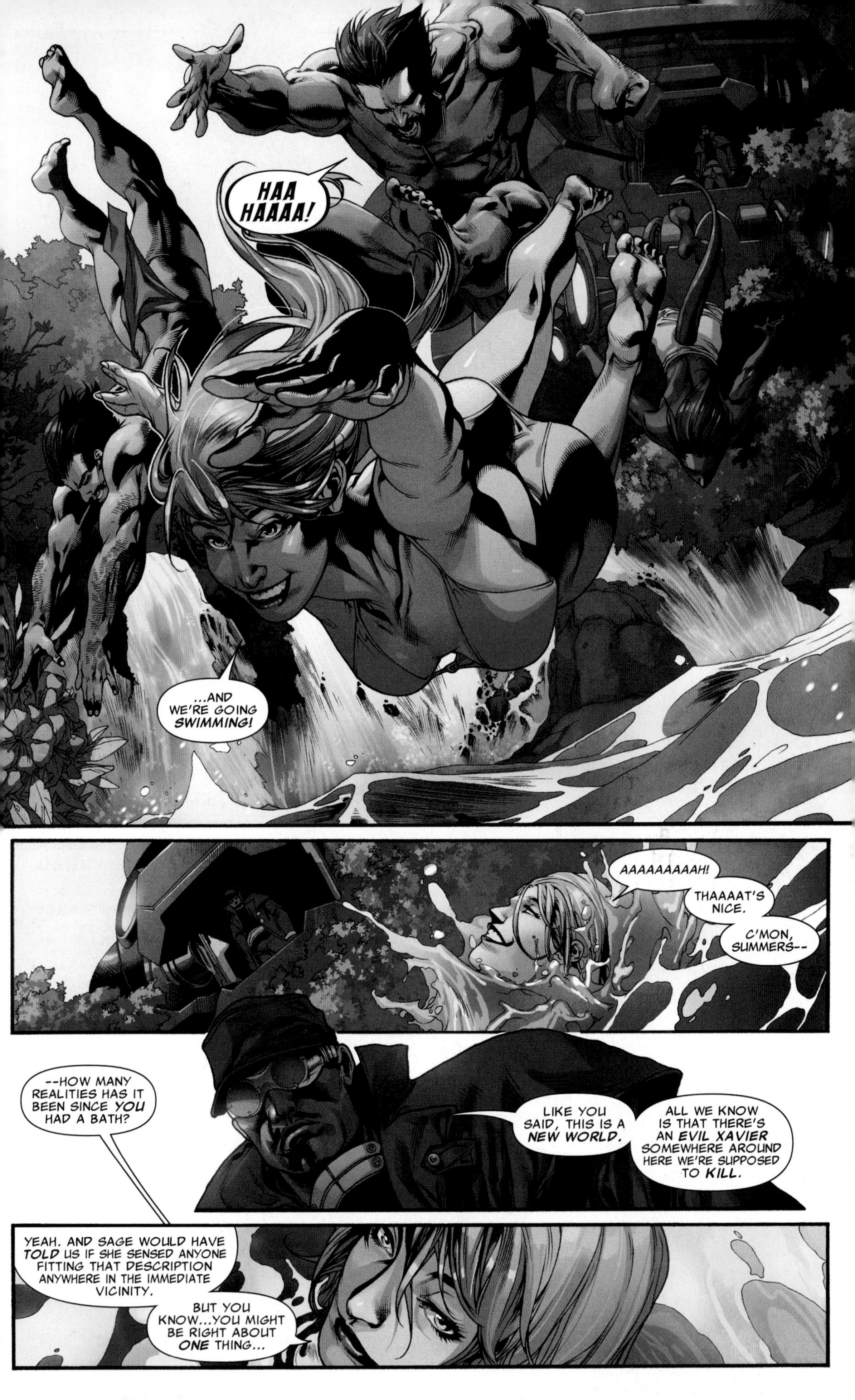
HAA HAAAA!
...AND WE'RE GOING SWIMMING!
AAAAAAAAAH!
THAAAAT'S NICE.
C'MON, SUMMERS--
--HOW MANY REALITIES HAS IT BEEN SINCE YOU HAD A BATH?
LIKE YOU SAID, THIS IS A NEW WORLD.
ALL WE KNOW IS THAT THERE'S AN EVIL XAVIER SOMEWHERE AROUND HERE WE'RE SUPPOSED TO KILL.
YEAH. AND SAGE WOULD HAVE TOLD US IF SHE SENSED ANYONE FITTING THAT DESCRIPTION ANYWHERE IN THE IMMEDIATE VICINITY.
BUT YOU KNOW...YOU MIGHT BE RIGHT ABOUT ONE THING...

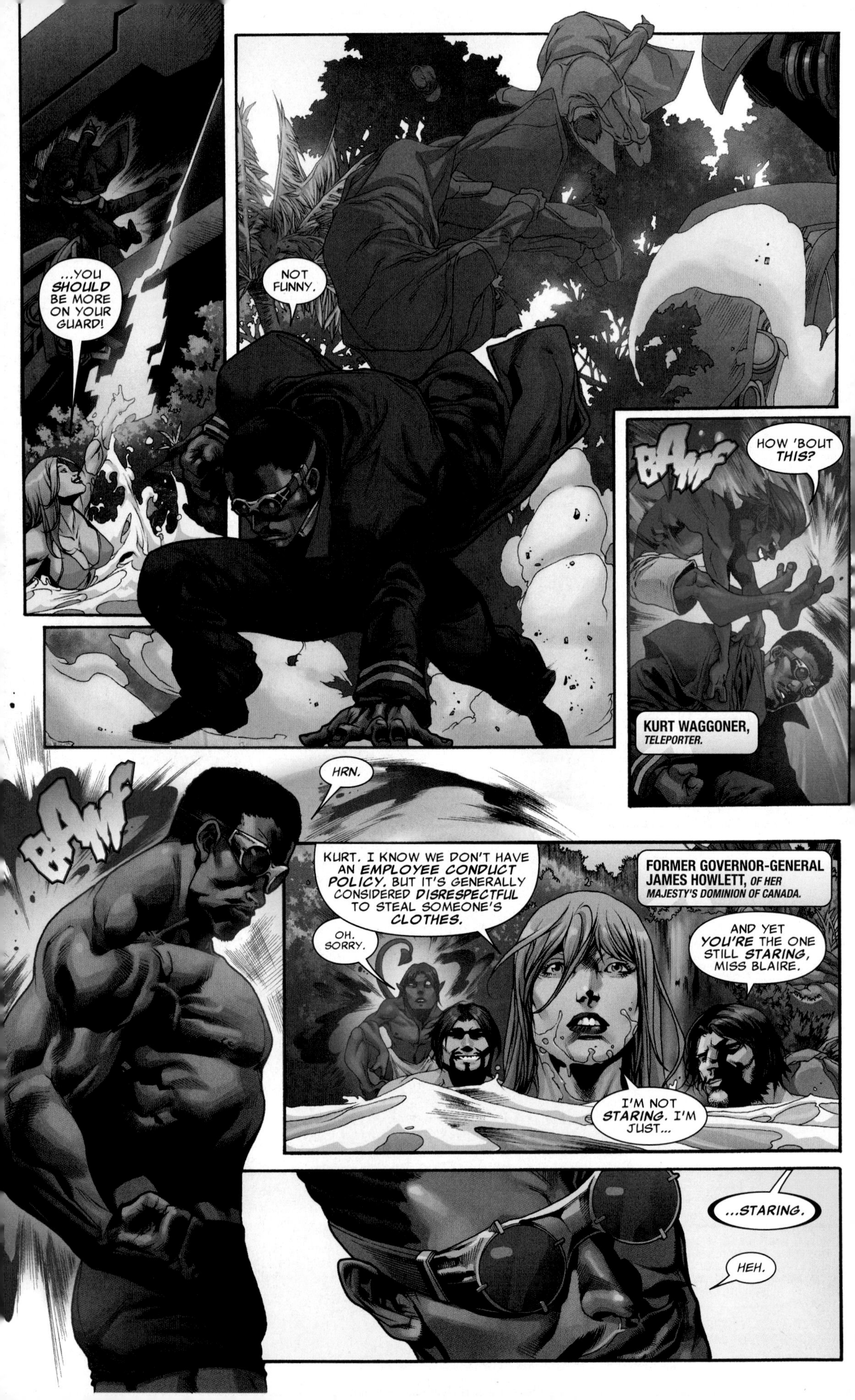
...YOU SHOULD BE MORE ON YOUR GUARD!
NOT FUNNY.
BAMF
HOW 'BOUT THIS?
KURT WAGGONER, TELEPORTER.
BAMF
HRN.
KURT. I KNOW WE DON'T HAVE AN EMPLOYEE CONDUCT POLICY. BUT IT'S GENERALLY CONSIDERED DISRESPECTFUL TO STEAL SOMEONE'S CLOTHES.
FORMER GOVERNOR-GENERAL JAMES HOWLETT, OF HER MAJESTY'S DOMINION OF CANADA.
OH. SORRY.
AND YET YOU'RE THE ONE STILL STARING, MISS BLAIRE.
I'M NOT STARING. I'M JUST...
...STARING.
HEH.

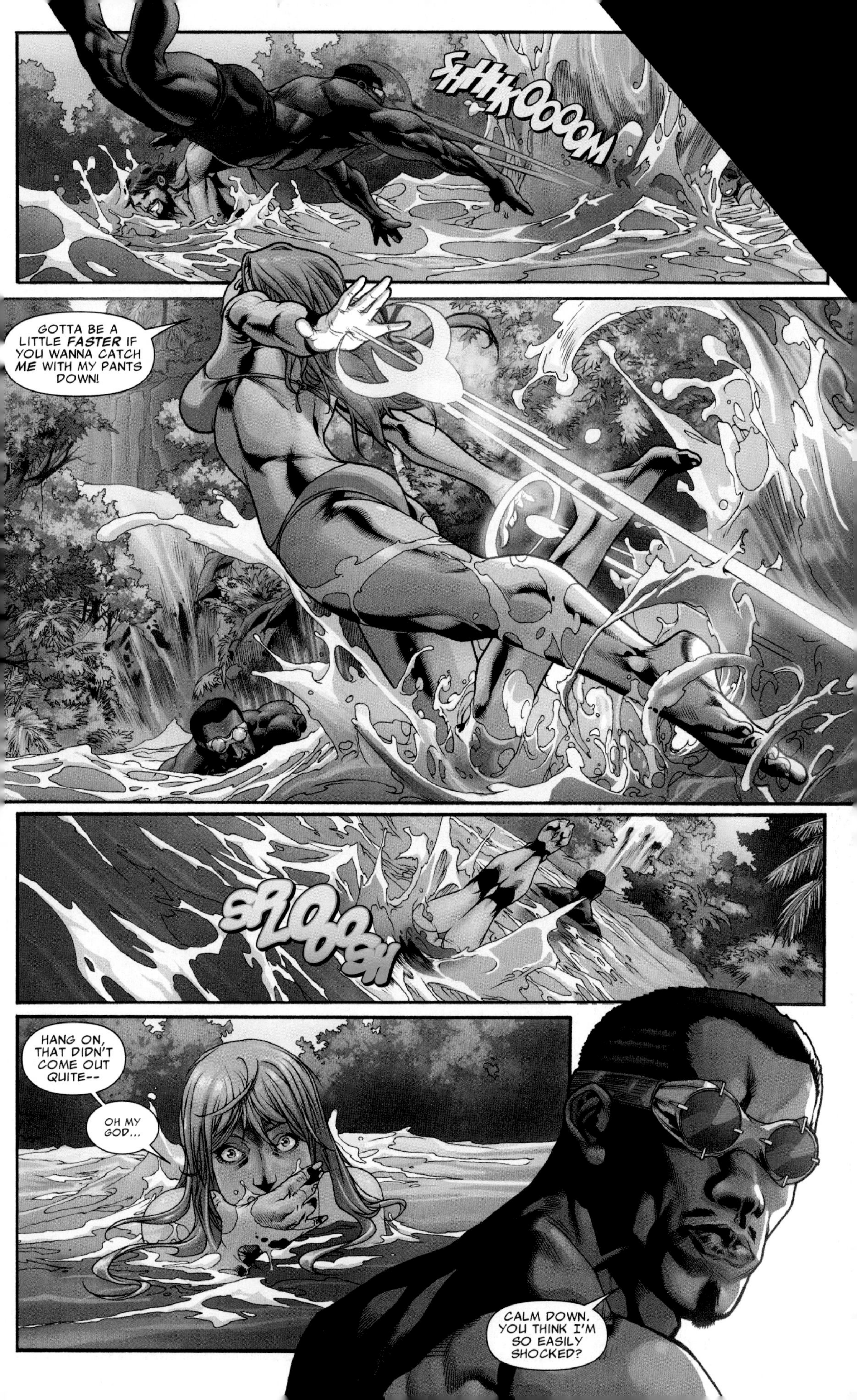
SHHKOOOOM
GOTTA BE A LITTLE FASTER IF YOU WANNA CATCH ME WITH MY PANTS DOWN!
SPLOOOSH
HANG ON, THAT DIDN'T COME OUT QUITE--
OH MY GOD...
CALM DOWN. YOU THINK I'M SO EASILY SHOCKED?

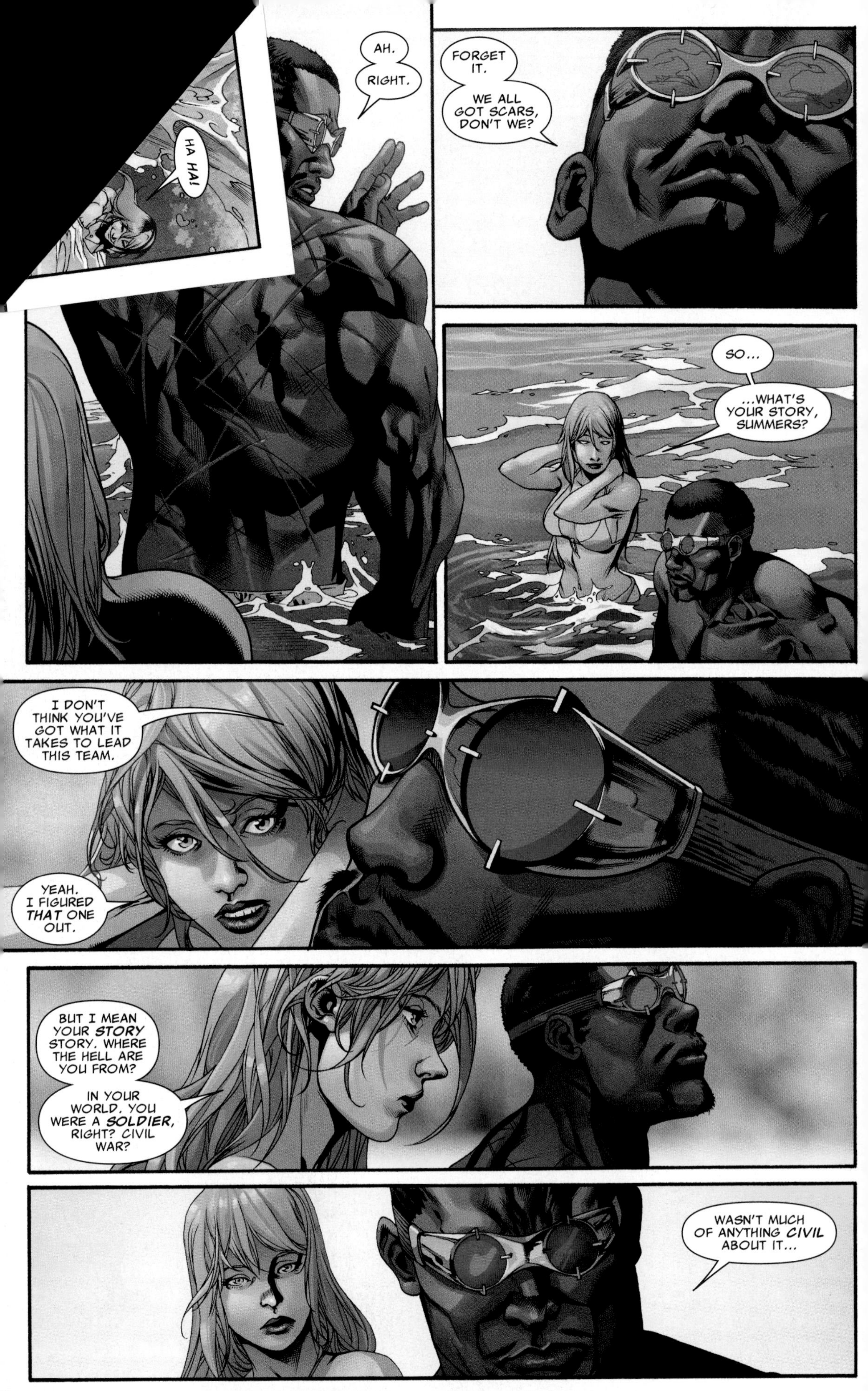
HA HA!
AH.
RIGHT.
FORGET IT.
WE ALL GOT SCARS, DON'T WE?
SO...
...WHAT'S YOUR STORY, SUMMERS?
I DON'T THINK YOU'VE GOT WHAT IT TAKES TO LEAD THIS TEAM.
YEAH. I FIGURED *THAT* ONE OUT.
BUT I MEAN YOUR *STORY* STORY. WHERE THE HELL ARE YOU FROM?
IN YOUR WORLD. YOU WERE A *SOLDIER*, RIGHT? CIVIL WAR?
WASN'T MUCH OF ANYTHING *CIVIL* ABOUT IT...

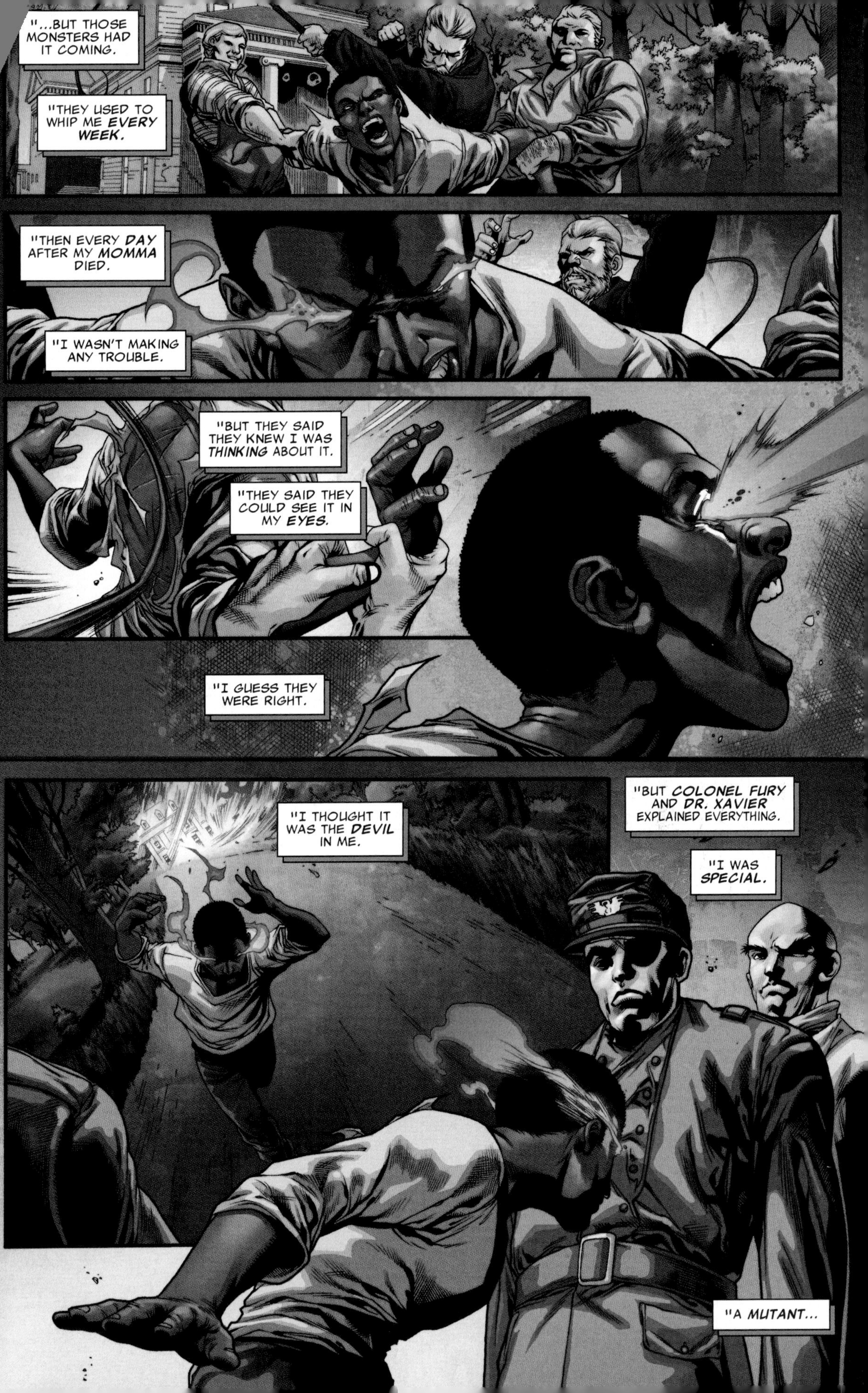
"...BUT THOSE MONSTERS HAD IT COMING.
"THEY USED TO WHIP ME EVERY WEEK.
"THEN EVERY DAY AFTER MY MOMMA DIED.
"I WASN'T MAKING ANY TROUBLE.
"BUT THEY SAID THEY KNEW I WAS THINKING ABOUT IT.
"THEY SAID THEY COULD SEE IT IN MY EYES.
"I GUESS THEY WERE RIGHT.
"I THOUGHT IT WAS THE DEVIL IN ME.
"BUT COLONEL FURY AND DR. XAVIER EXPLAINED EVERYTHING.
"I WAS SPECIAL.
"A MUTANT...

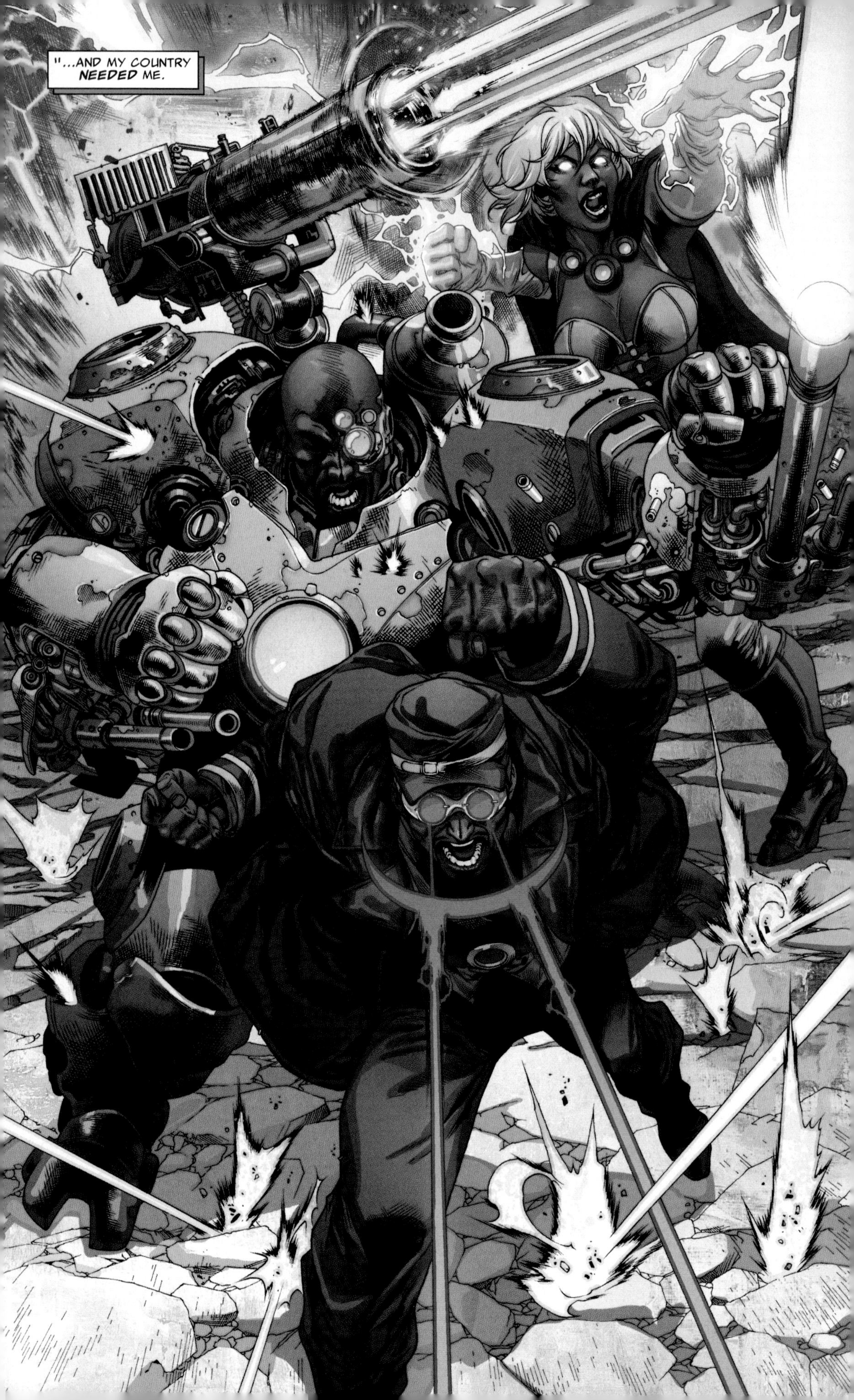
"...AND MY COUNTRY NEEDED ME.

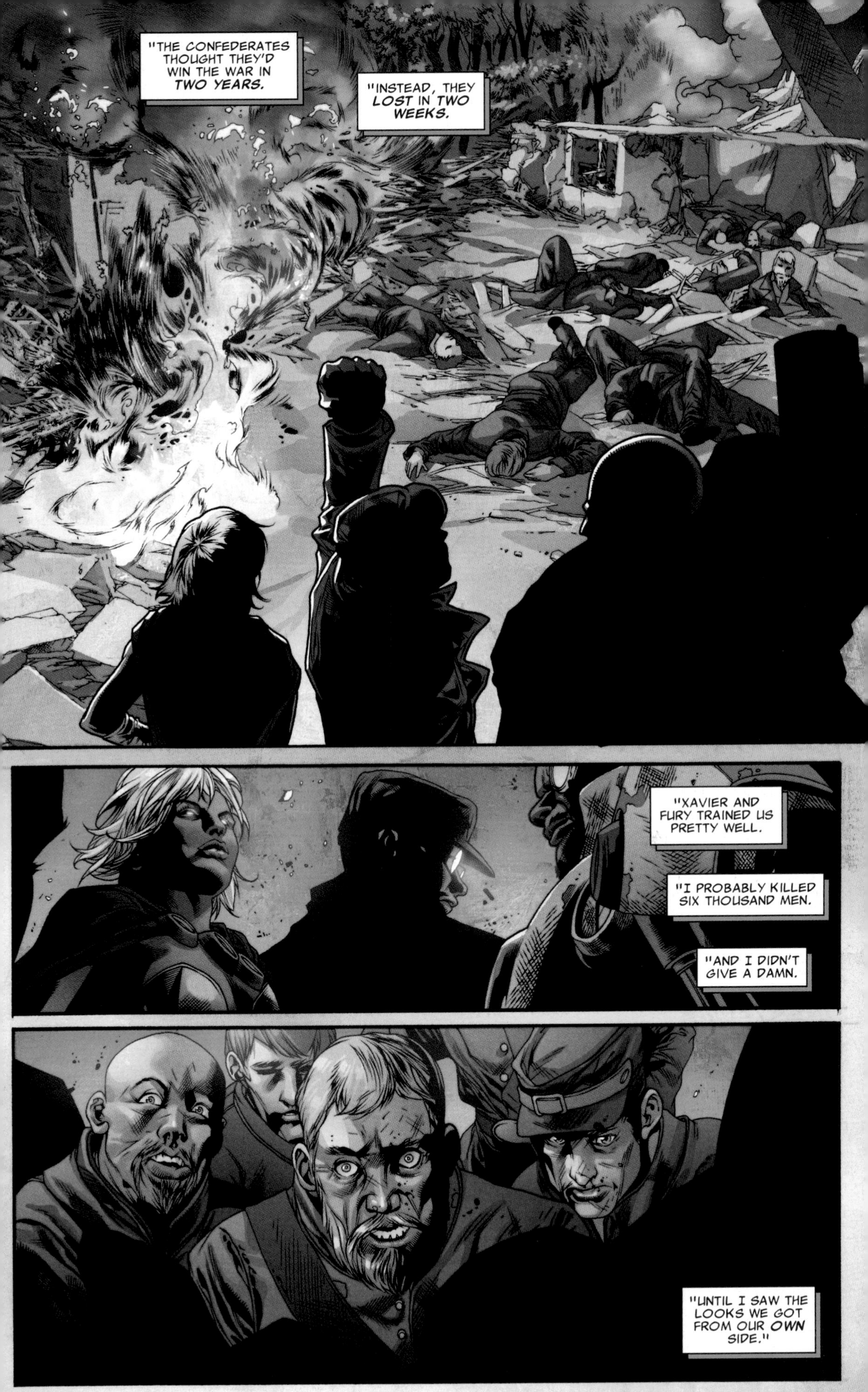
"THE CONFEDERATES THOUGHT THEY'D WIN THE WAR IN TWO YEARS.
"INSTEAD, THEY LOST IN TWO WEEKS.
"XAVIER AND FURY TRAINED US PRETTY WELL.
"I PROBABLY KILLED SIX THOUSAND MEN.
"AND I DIDN'T GIVE A DAMN.
"UNTIL I SAW THE LOOKS WE GOT FROM OUR OWN SIDE."

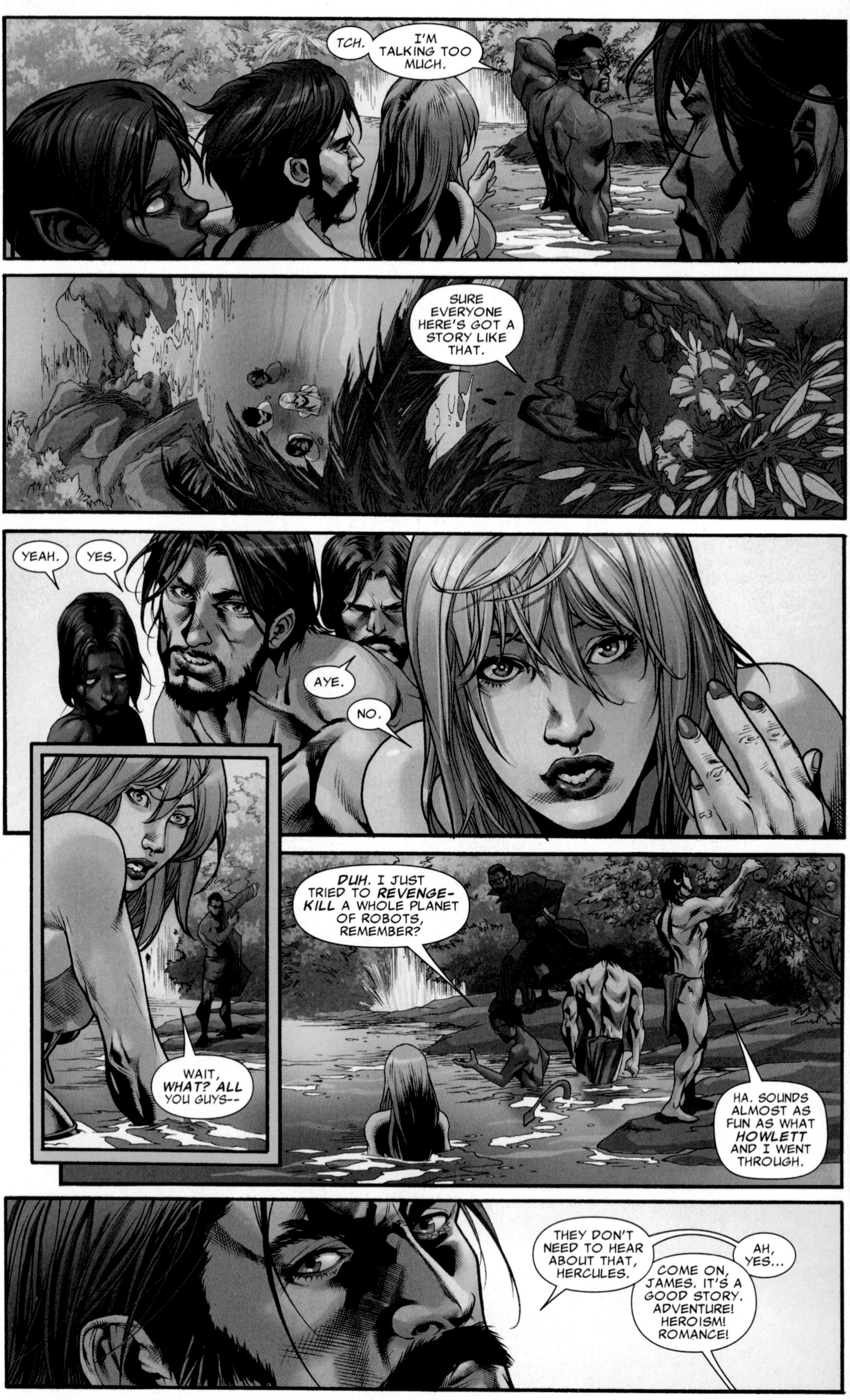
TCH.
I'M TALKING TOO MUCH.
SURE EVERYONE HERE'S GOT A STORY LIKE THAT.
YEAH.
YES.
AYE.
NO.
WAIT, WHAT? ALL YOU GUYS--
DUH. I JUST TRIED TO REVENGE-KILL A WHOLE PLANET OF ROBOTS, REMEMBER?
HA. SOUNDS ALMOST AS FUN AS WHAT HOWLETT AND I WENT THROUGH.
THEY DON'T NEED TO HEAR ABOUT THAT, HERCULES.
AH, YES...
COME ON, JAMES. IT'S A GOOD STORY. ADVENTURE! HEROISM! ROMANCE!

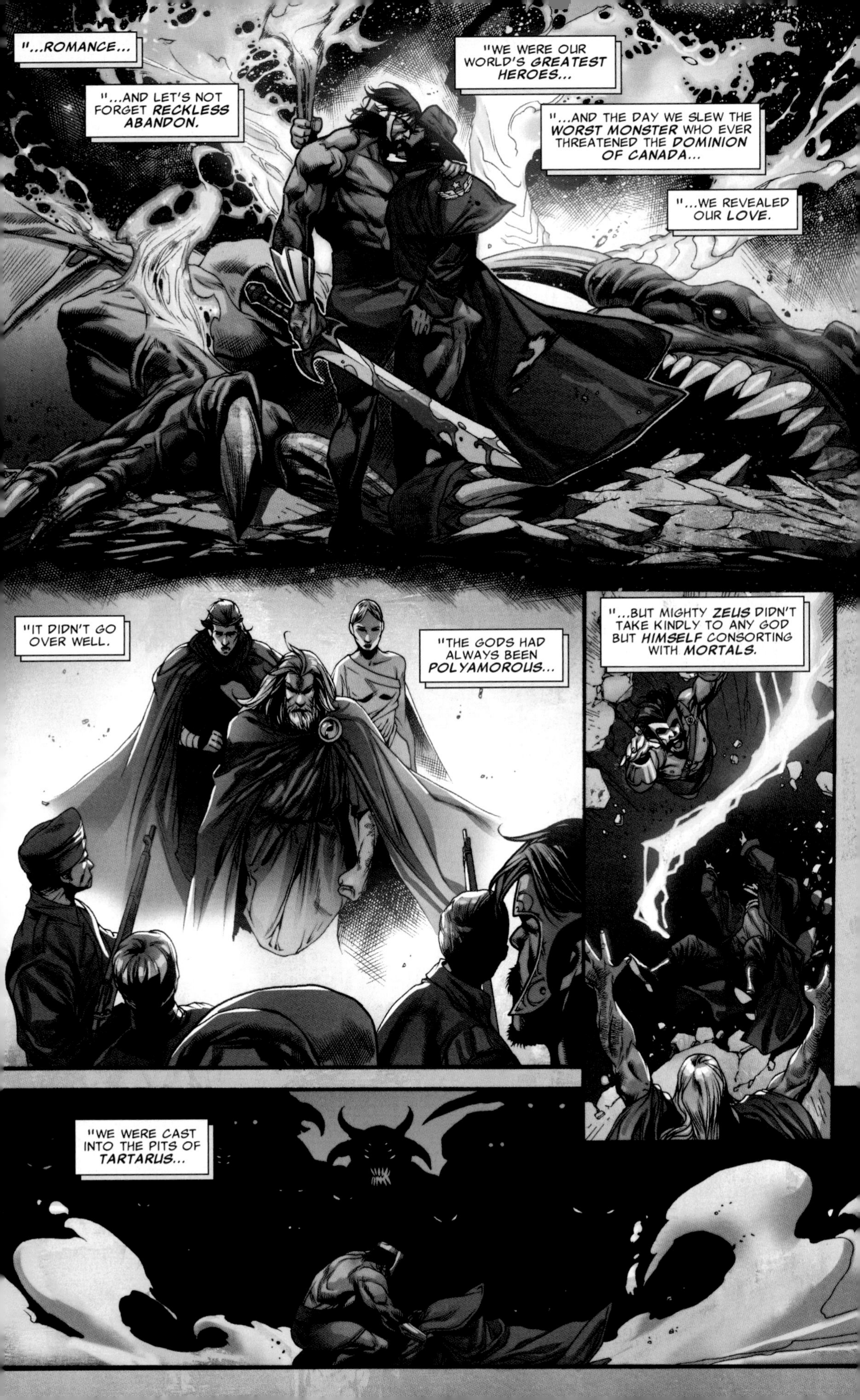
"...ROMANCE...
"...AND LET'S NOT FORGET RECKLESS ABANDON.
"WE WERE OUR WORLD'S GREATEST HEROES...
"...AND THE DAY WE SLEW THE WORST MONSTER WHO EVER THREATENED THE DOMINION OF CANADA...
"...WE REVEALED OUR LOVE.
"IT DIDN'T GO OVER WELL.
"THE GODS HAD ALWAYS BEEN POLYAMOROUS...
"...BUT MIGHTY ZEUS DIDN'T TAKE KINDLY TO ANY GOD BUT HIMSELF CONSORTING WITH MORTALS.
"WE WERE CAST INTO THE PITS OF TARTARUS...

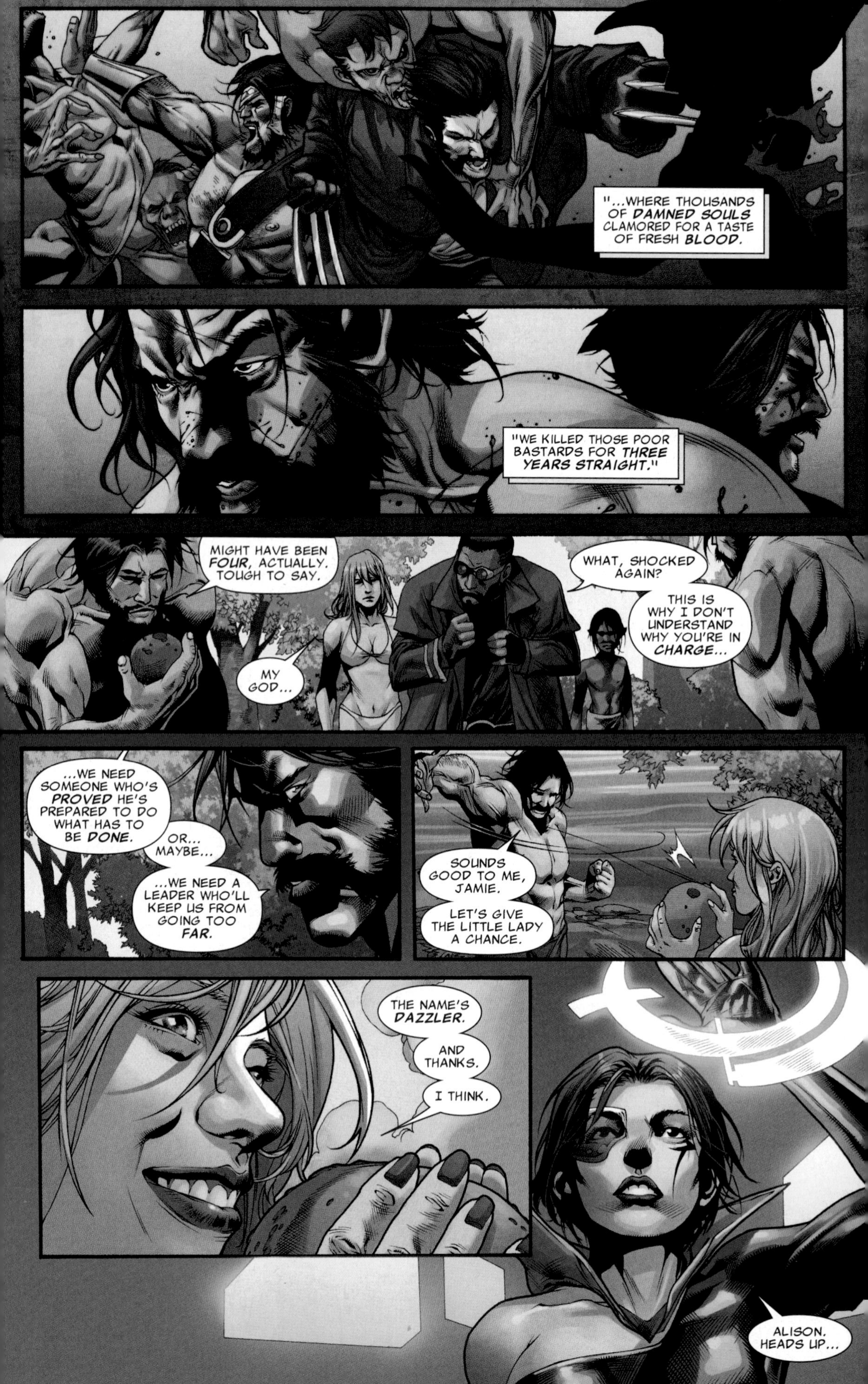
"...WHERE THOUSANDS OF DAMNED SOULS CLAMORED FOR A TASTE OF FRESH BLOOD.
"WE KILLED THOSE POOR BASTARDS FOR THREE YEARS STRAIGHT."
MIGHT HAVE BEEN FOUR, ACTUALLY. TOUGH TO SAY.
MY GOD...
WHAT, SHOCKED AGAIN?
THIS IS WHY I DON'T UNDERSTAND WHY YOU'RE IN CHARGE...
...WE NEED SOMEONE WHO'S PROVED HE'S PREPARED TO DO WHAT HAS TO BE DONE.
OR... MAYBE...
...WE NEED A LEADER WHO'LL KEEP US FROM GOING TOO FAR.
SOUNDS GOOD TO ME, JAMIE.
LET'S GIVE THE LITTLE LADY A CHANCE.
THE NAME'S DAZZLER.
AND THANKS.
I THINK.
ALISON. HEADS UP...

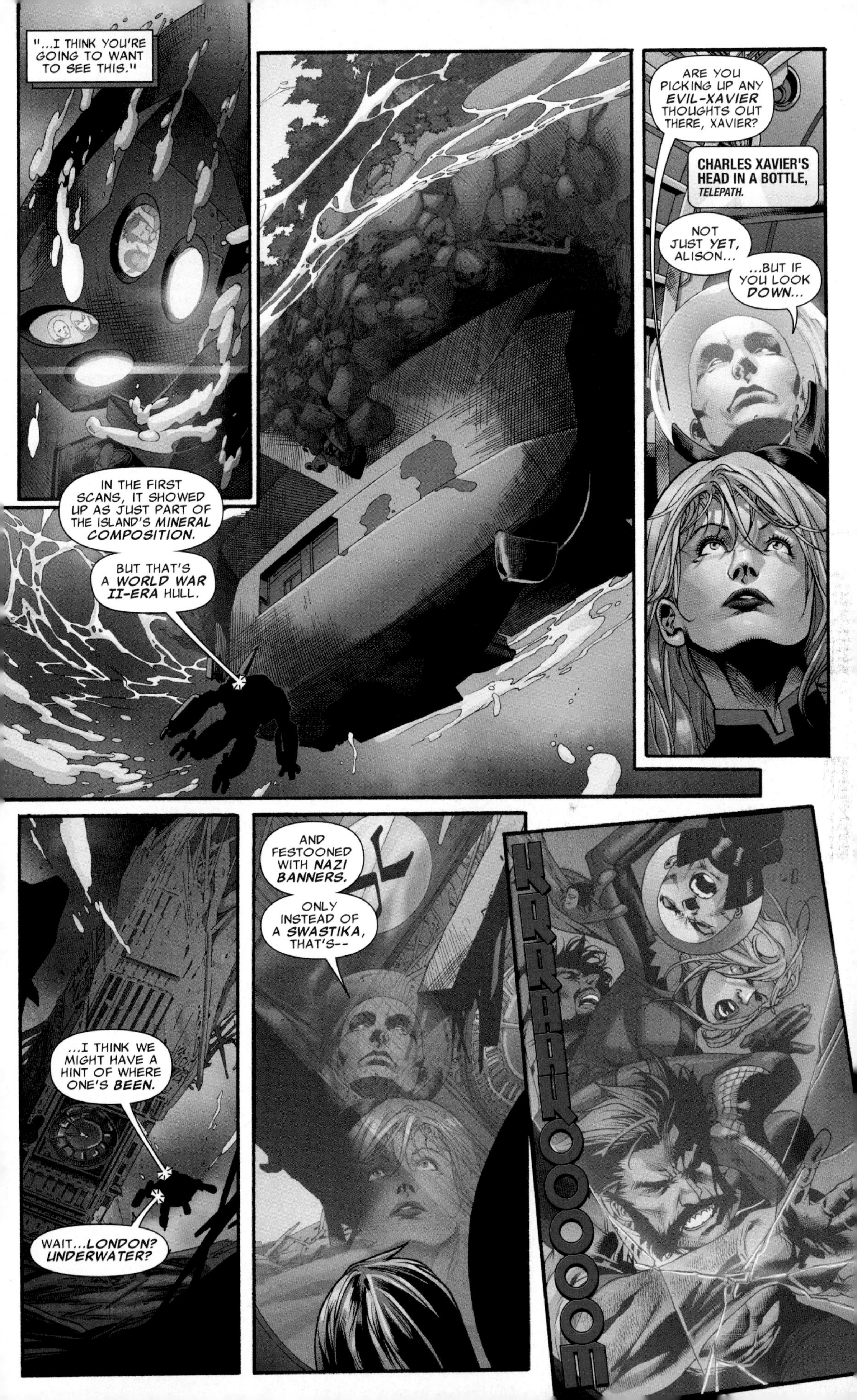
"...I THINK YOU'RE GOING TO WANT TO SEE THIS."
ARE YOU PICKING UP ANY EVIL-XAVIER THOUGHTS OUT THERE, XAVIER?
CHARLES XAVIER'S HEAD IN A BOTTLE, TELEPATH.
NOT JUST YET, ALISON...
...BUT IF YOU LOOK DOWN...
IN THE FIRST SCANS, IT SHOWED UP AS JUST PART OF THE ISLAND'S MINERAL COMPOSITION.
BUT THAT'S A WORLD WAR II-ERA HULL.
...I THINK WE MIGHT HAVE A HINT OF WHERE ONE'S BEEN.
WAIT...LONDON? UNDERWATER?
AND FESTOONED WITH NAZI BANNERS.
ONLY INSTEAD OF A SWASTIKA, THAT'S--
KRRAAKOOOOOOM

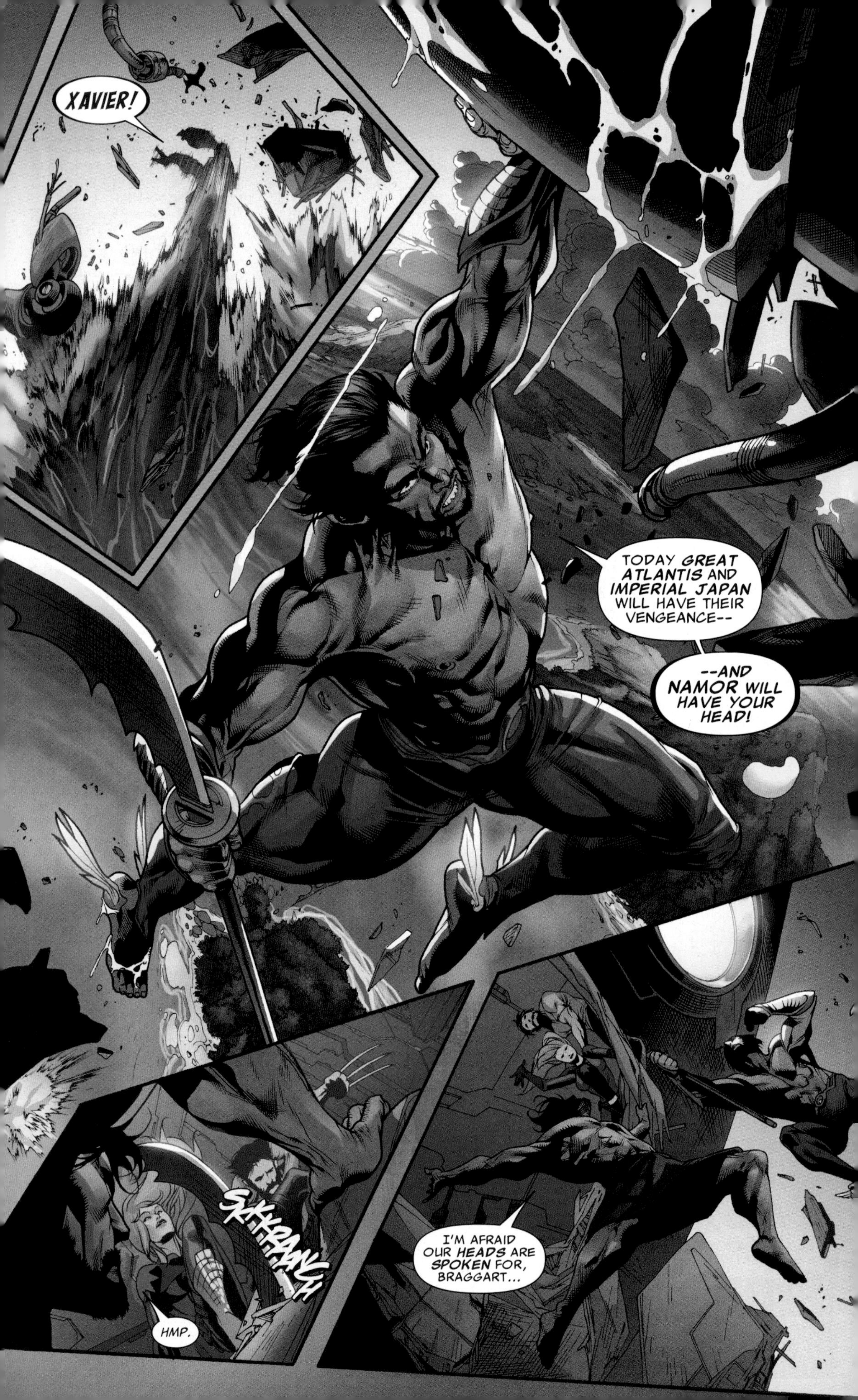
XAVIER!
TODAY GREAT ATLANTIS AND IMPERIAL JAPAN WILL HAVE THEIR VENGEANCE--
--AND NAMOR WILL HAVE YOUR HEAD!
SKKRANCH
HMP.
I'M AFRAID OUR HEADS ARE SPOKEN FOR, BRAGGART...

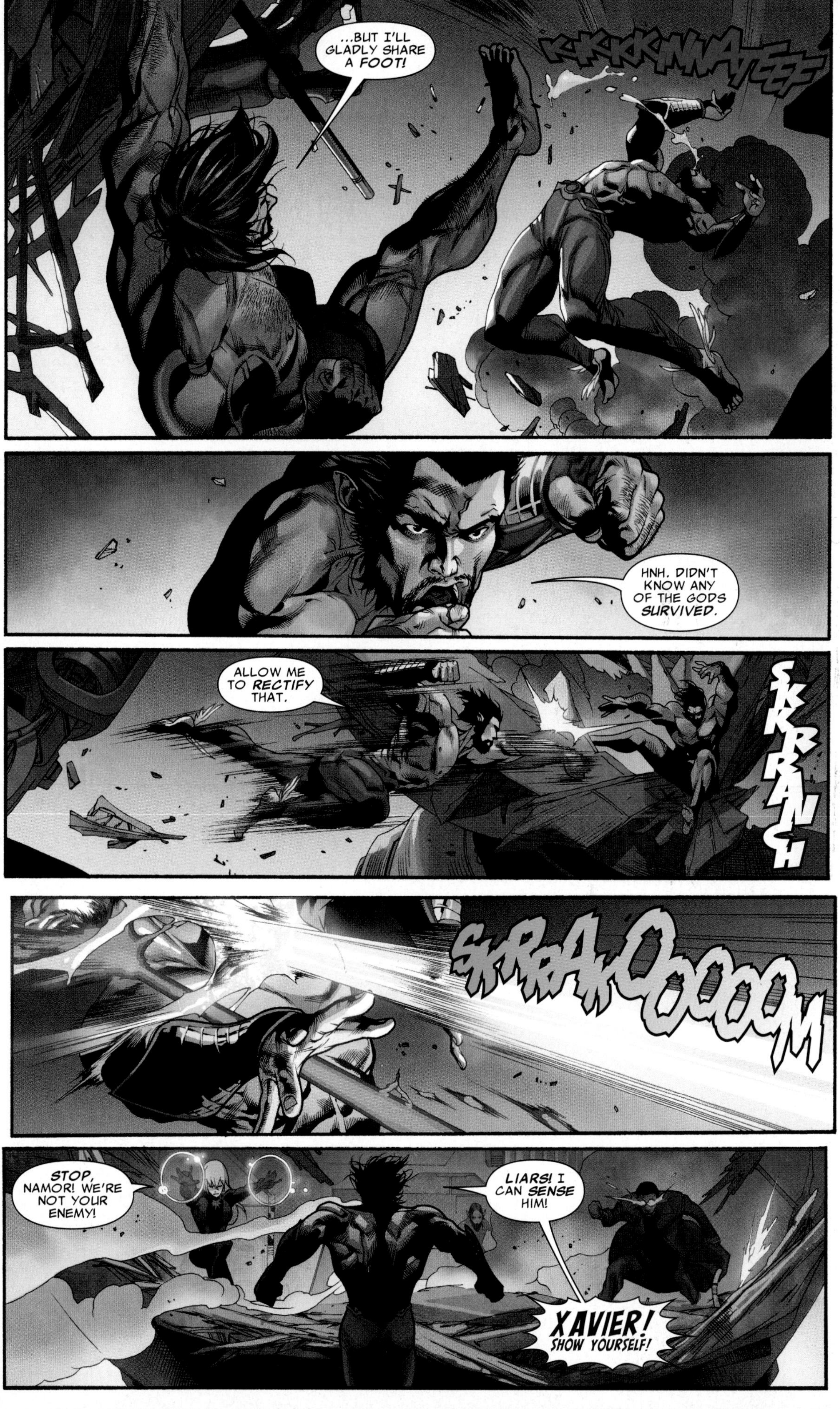
...BUT I'LL GLADLY SHARE A FOOT!
KKKKNNATEEF
HNH. DIDN'T KNOW ANY OF THE GODS SURVIVED.
ALLOW ME TO RECTIFY THAT.
SKRANCH
SKRAKOOOOOM
STOP, NAMOR! WE'RE NOT YOUR ENEMY!
LIARS! I CAN SENSE HIM!
XAVIER! SHOW YOURSELF!

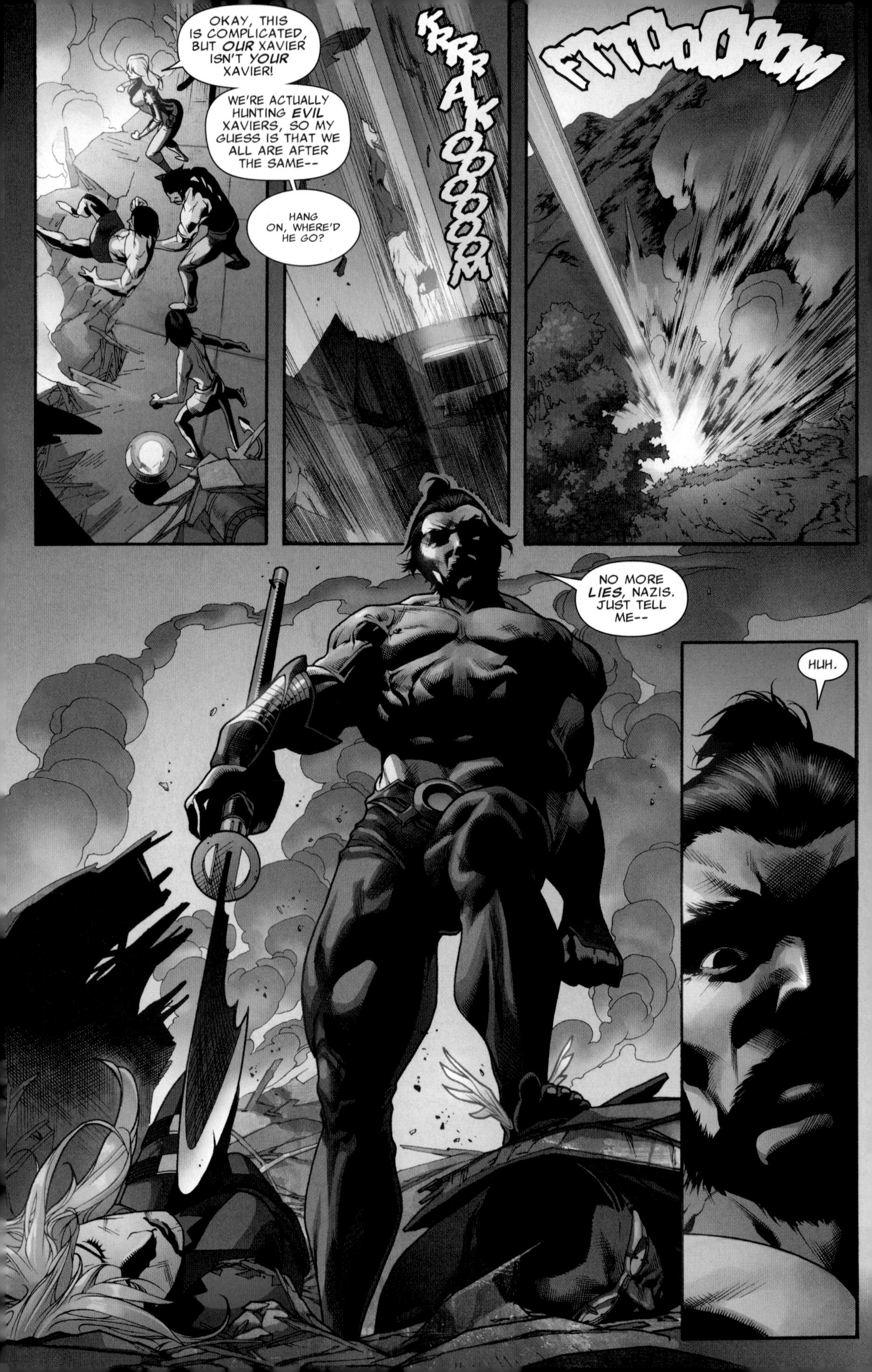
OKAY, THIS IS COMPLICATED, BUT OUR XAVIER ISN'T YOUR XAVIER!
WE'RE ACTUALLY HUNTING EVIL XAVIERS, SO MY GUESS IS THAT WE ALL ARE AFTER THE SAME--
HANG ON, WHERE'D HE GO?
KRRRAKOOOOOOOM
FTTOOOOOOM
NO MORE LIES, NAZIS. JUST TELL ME--
HUH.

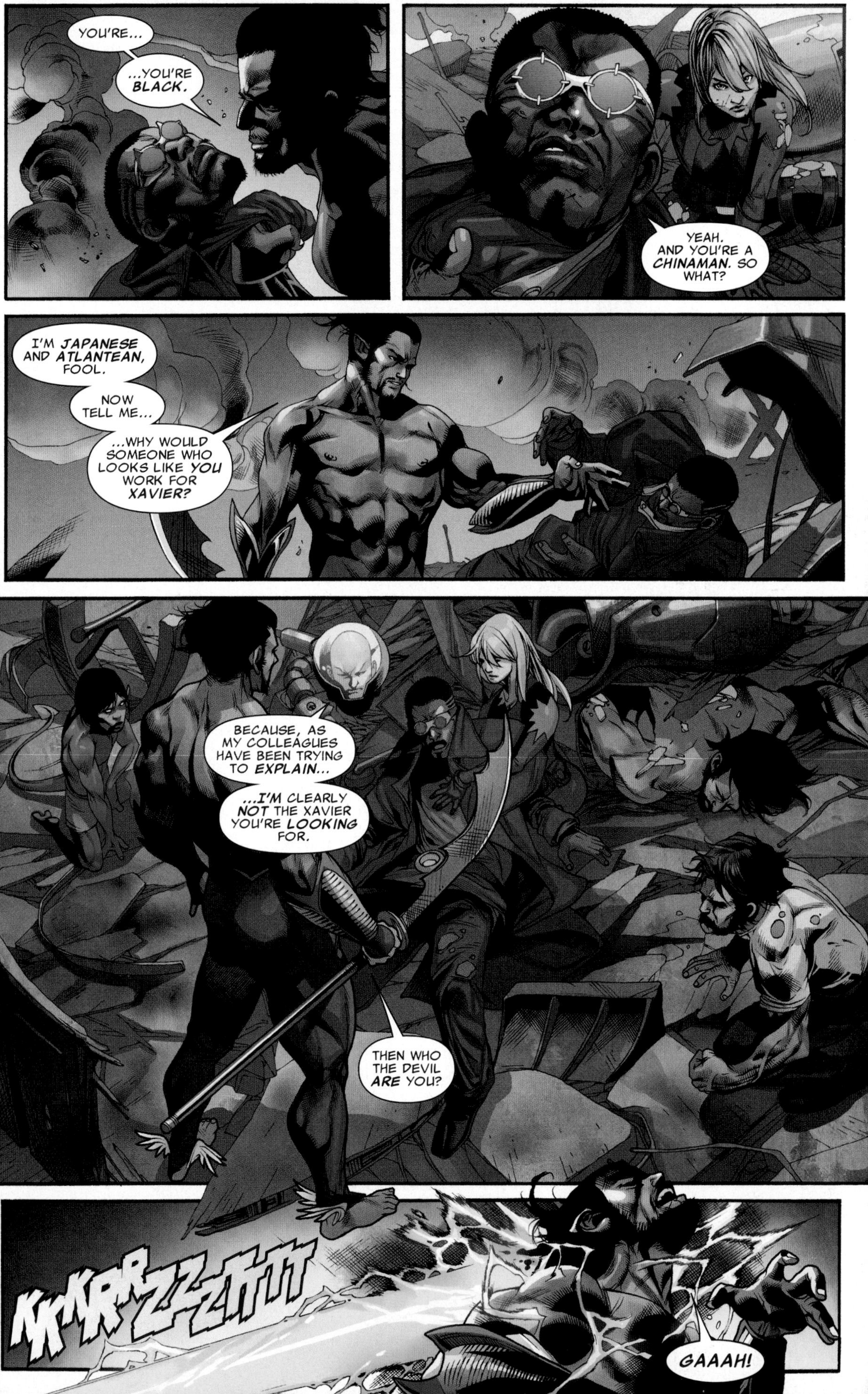
YOU'RE...
...YOU'RE BLACK.
YEAH. AND YOU'RE A CHINAMAN. SO WHAT?
I'M JAPANESE AND ATLANTEAN, FOOL.
NOW TELL ME...
...WHY WOULD SOMEONE WHO LOOKS LIKE YOU WORK FOR XAVIER?
BECAUSE, AS MY COLLEAGUES HAVE BEEN TRYING TO EXPLAIN...
...I'M CLEARLY NOT THE XAVIER YOU'RE LOOKING FOR.
THEN WHO THE DEVIL ARE YOU?
KKKRRZZZZTTTT
GAAAH!

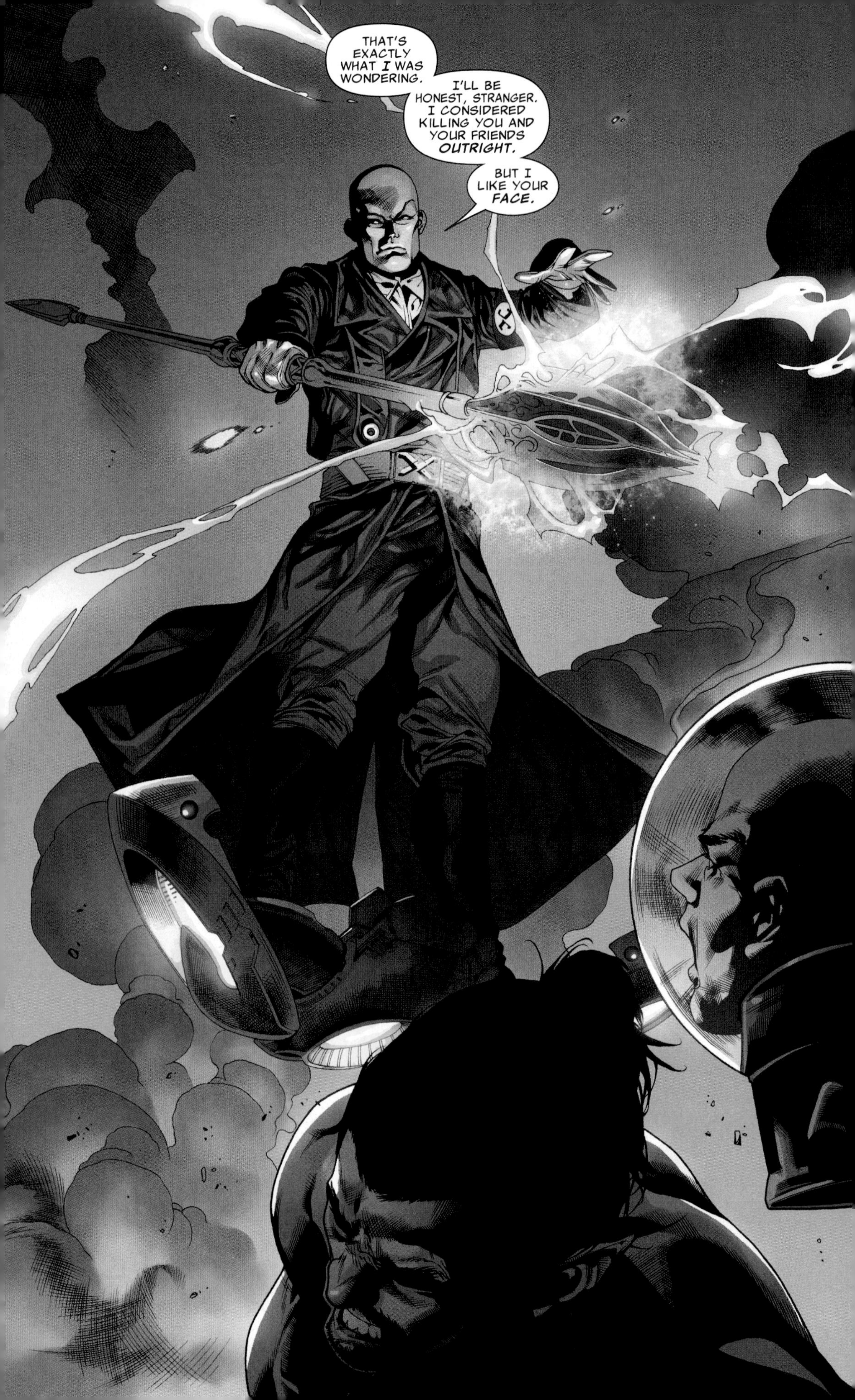
THAT'S EXACTLY WHAT I WAS WONDERING.
I'LL BE HONEST, STRANGER. I CONSIDERED KILLING YOU AND YOUR FRIENDS OUTRIGHT.
BUT I LIKE YOUR FACE.

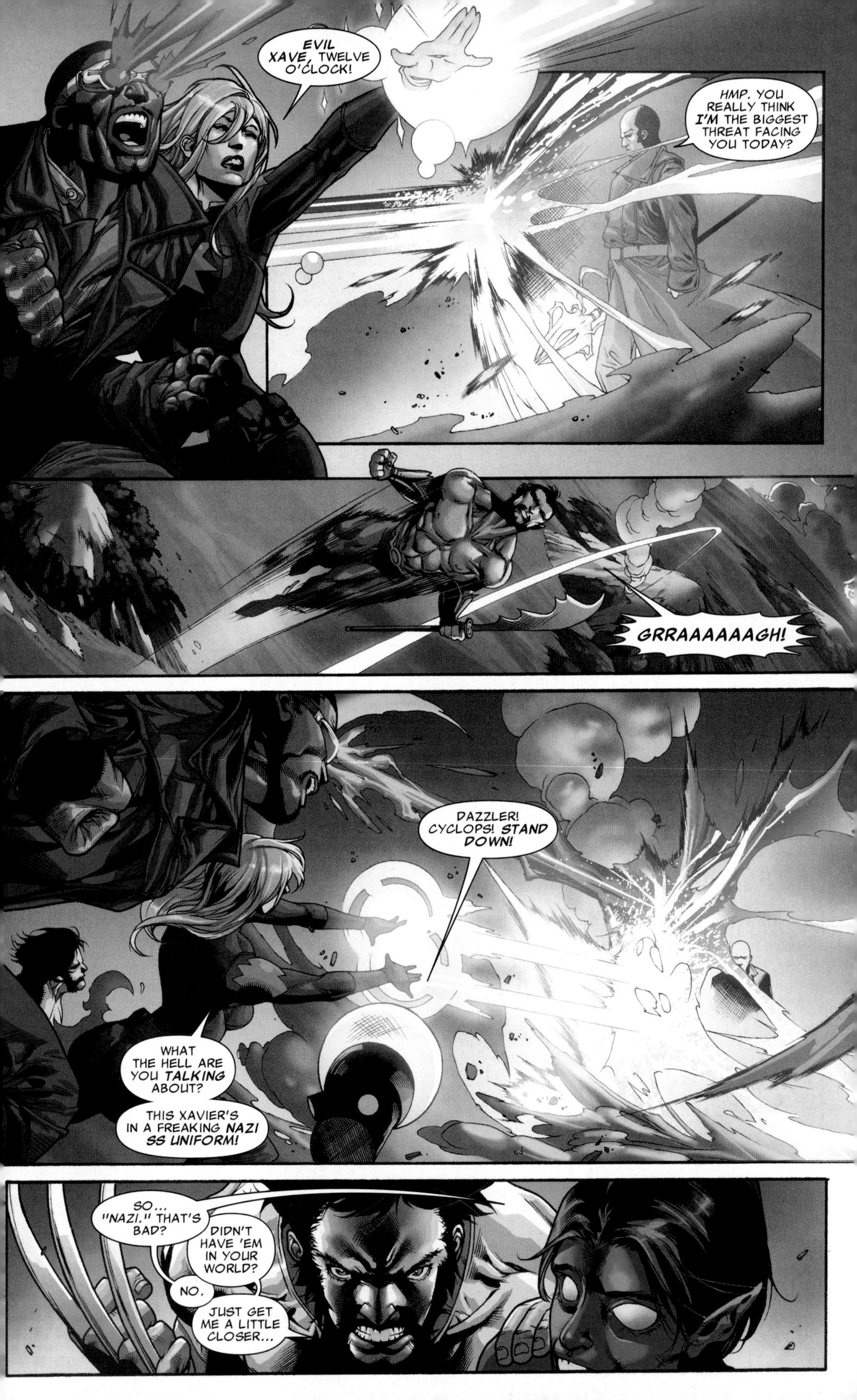
EVIL XAVE, TWELVE O'CLOCK!
HMP. YOU REALLY THINK I'M THE BIGGEST THREAT FACING YOU TODAY?
GRRAAAAAAGH!
DAZZLER! CYCLOPS! STAND DOWN!
WHAT THE HELL ARE YOU TALKING ABOUT?
THIS XAVIER'S IN A FREAKING NAZI SS UNIFORM!
SO... "NAZI," THAT'S BAD?
DIDN'T HAVE 'EM IN YOUR WORLD?
NO.
JUST GET ME A LITTLE CLOSER...

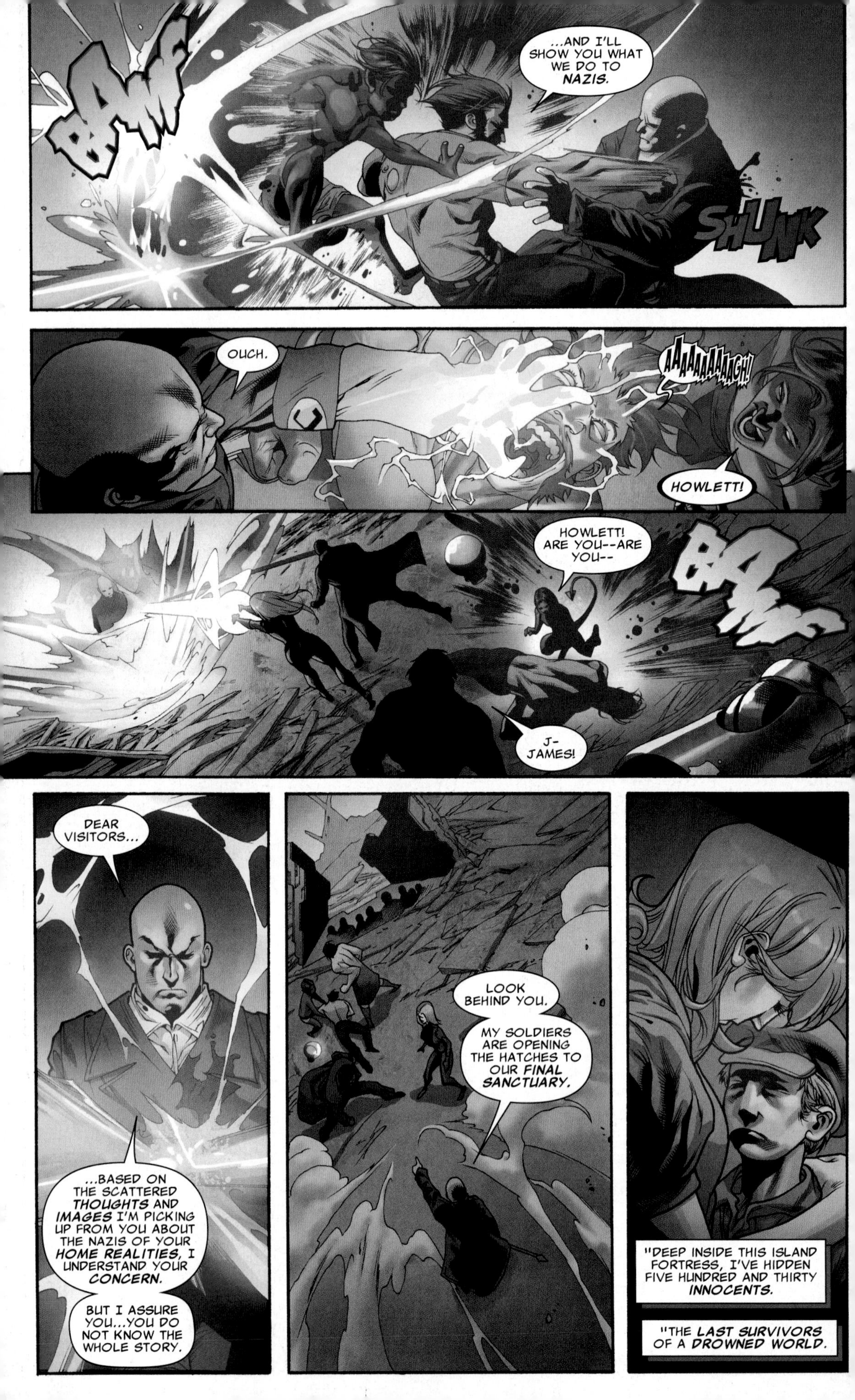
BAMF
...AND I'LL SHOW YOU WHAT WE DO TO NAZIS.
SHUNK
OUCH.
AAAAAAAAAGH!
HOWLETT!
HOWLETT! ARE YOU--ARE YOU--
BAMF
J-JAMES!
DEAR VISITORS...
...BASED ON THE SCATTERED THOUGHTS AND IMAGES I'M PICKING UP FROM YOU ABOUT THE NAZIS OF YOUR HOME REALITIES, I UNDERSTAND YOUR CONCERN.
BUT I ASSURE YOU...YOU DO NOT KNOW THE WHOLE STORY.
LOOK BEHIND YOU.
MY SOLDIERS ARE OPENING THE HATCHES TO OUR FINAL SANCTUARY.
"DEEP INSIDE THIS ISLAND FORTRESS, I'VE HIDDEN FIVE HUNDRED AND THIRTY INNOCENTS.
"THE LAST SURVIVORS OF A DROWNED WORLD.

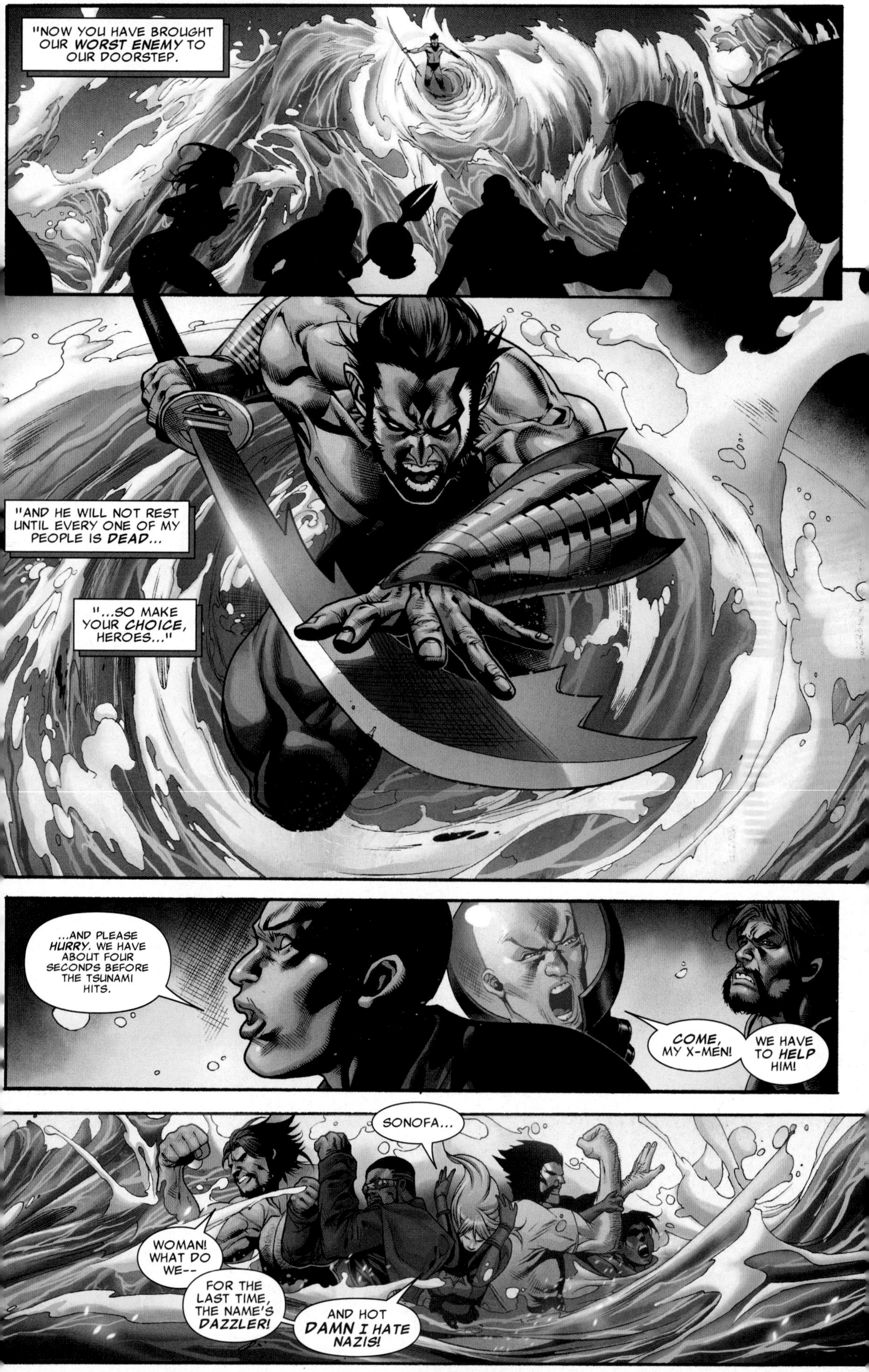
"NOW YOU HAVE BROUGHT OUR WORST ENEMY TO OUR DOORSTEP.
"AND HE WILL NOT REST UNTIL EVERY ONE OF MY PEOPLE IS DEAD...
"...SO MAKE YOUR CHOICE, HEROES..."
...AND PLEASE HURRY. WE HAVE ABOUT FOUR SECONDS BEFORE THE TSUNAMI HITS.
COME, MY X-MEN!
WE HAVE TO HELP HIM!
SONOFA...
WOMAN! WHAT DO WE--
FOR THE LAST TIME, THE NAME'S DAZZLER!
AND HOT DAMN I HATE NAZIS!

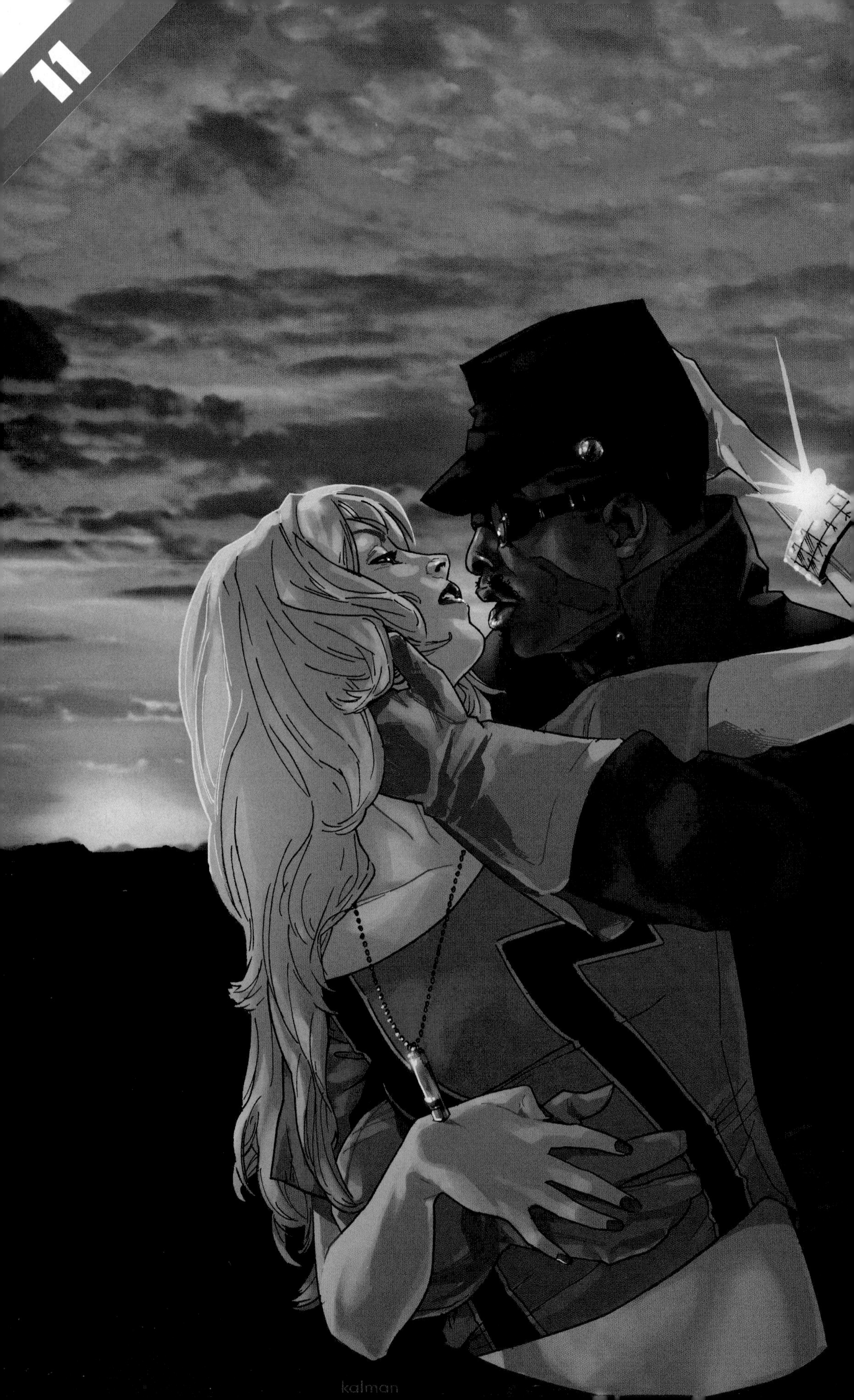
11
kalman

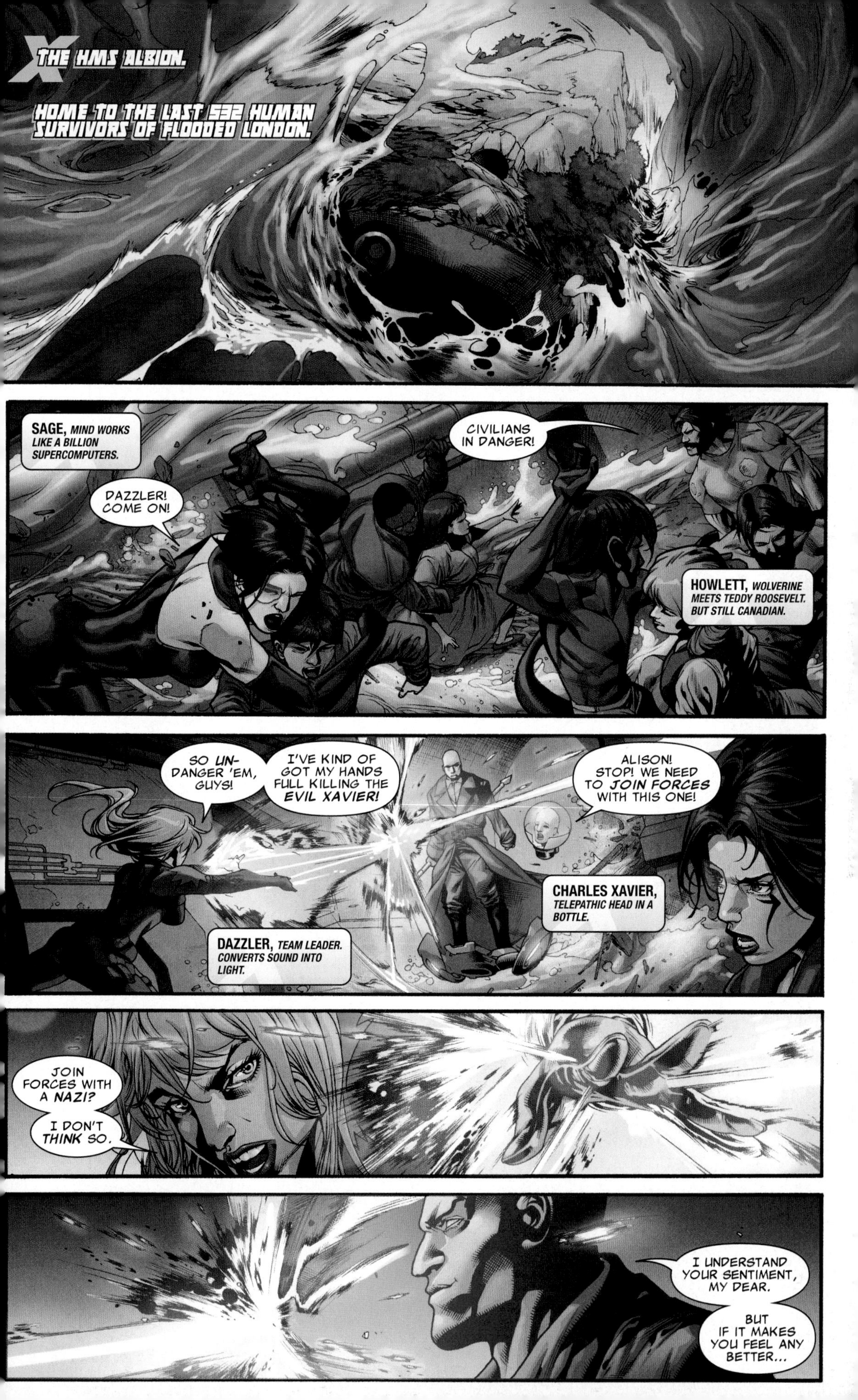
THE HMS ALBION.
HOME TO THE LAST 532 HUMAN SURVIVORS OF FLOODED LONDON.
SAGE, MIND WORKS LIKE A BILLION SUPERCOMPUTERS.
DAZZLER! COME ON!
CIVILIANS IN DANGER!
HOWLETT, WOLVERINE MEETS TEDDY ROOSEVELT. BUT STILL CANADIAN.
SO UN-DANGER 'EM, GUYS!
I'VE KIND OF GOT MY HANDS FULL KILLING THE EVIL XAVIER!
ALISON! STOP! WE NEED TO JOIN FORCES WITH THIS ONE!
CHARLES XAVIER, TELEPATHIC HEAD IN A BOTTLE.
DAZZLER, TEAM LEADER. CONVERTS SOUND INTO LIGHT.
JOIN FORCES WITH A NAZI?
I DON'T THINK SO.
I UNDERSTAND YOUR SENTIMENT, MY DEAR.
BUT IF IT MAKES YOU FEEL ANY BETTER...

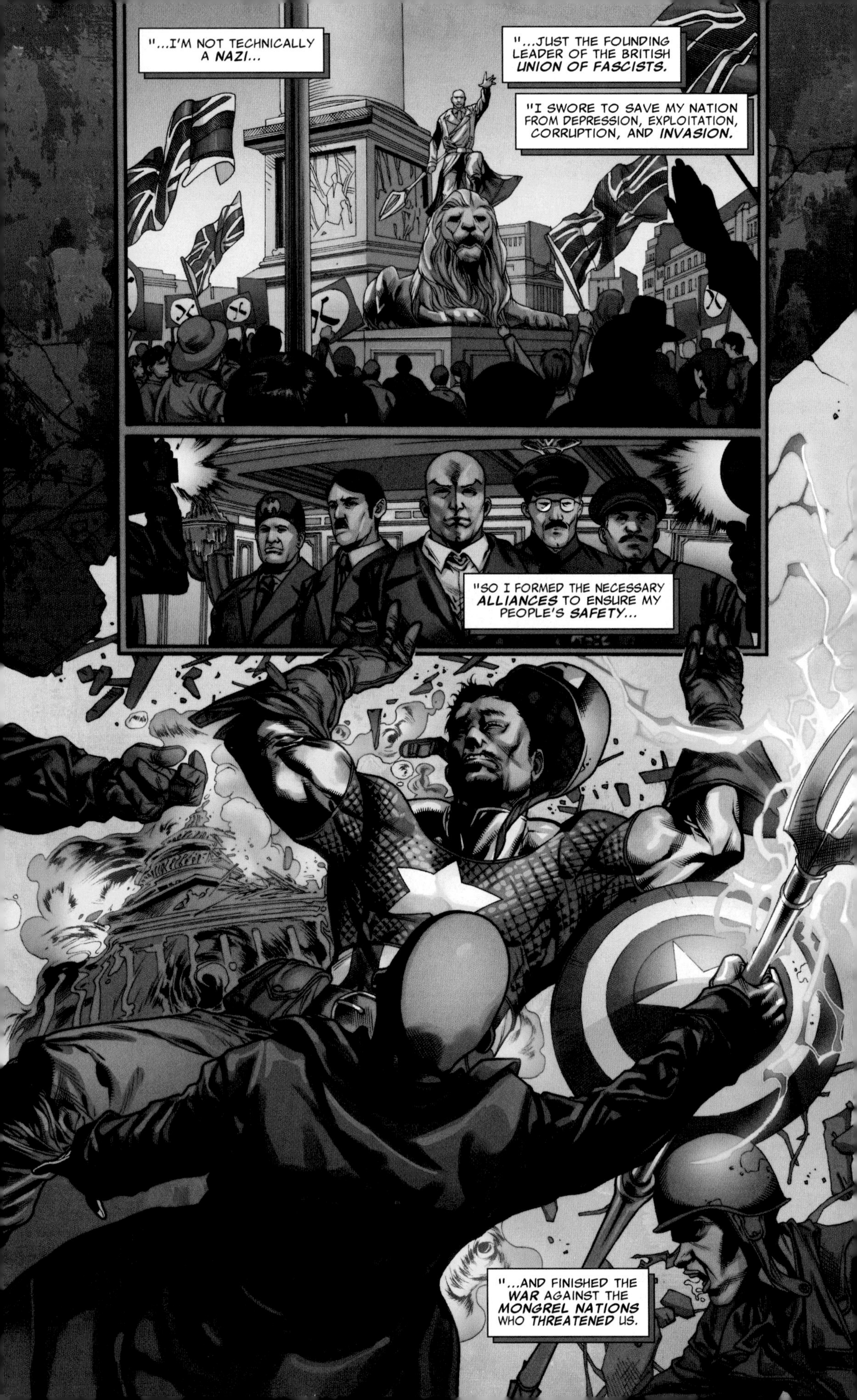
"...I'M NOT TECHNICALLY A NAZI...
"...JUST THE FOUNDING LEADER OF THE BRITISH UNION OF FASCISTS.
"I SWORE TO SAVE MY NATION FROM DEPRESSION, EXPLOITATION, CORRUPTION, AND INVASION.
"SO I FORMED THE NECESSARY ALLIANCES TO ENSURE MY PEOPLE'S SAFETY...
"...AND FINISHED THE WAR AGAINST THE MONGREL NATIONS WHO THREATENED US.

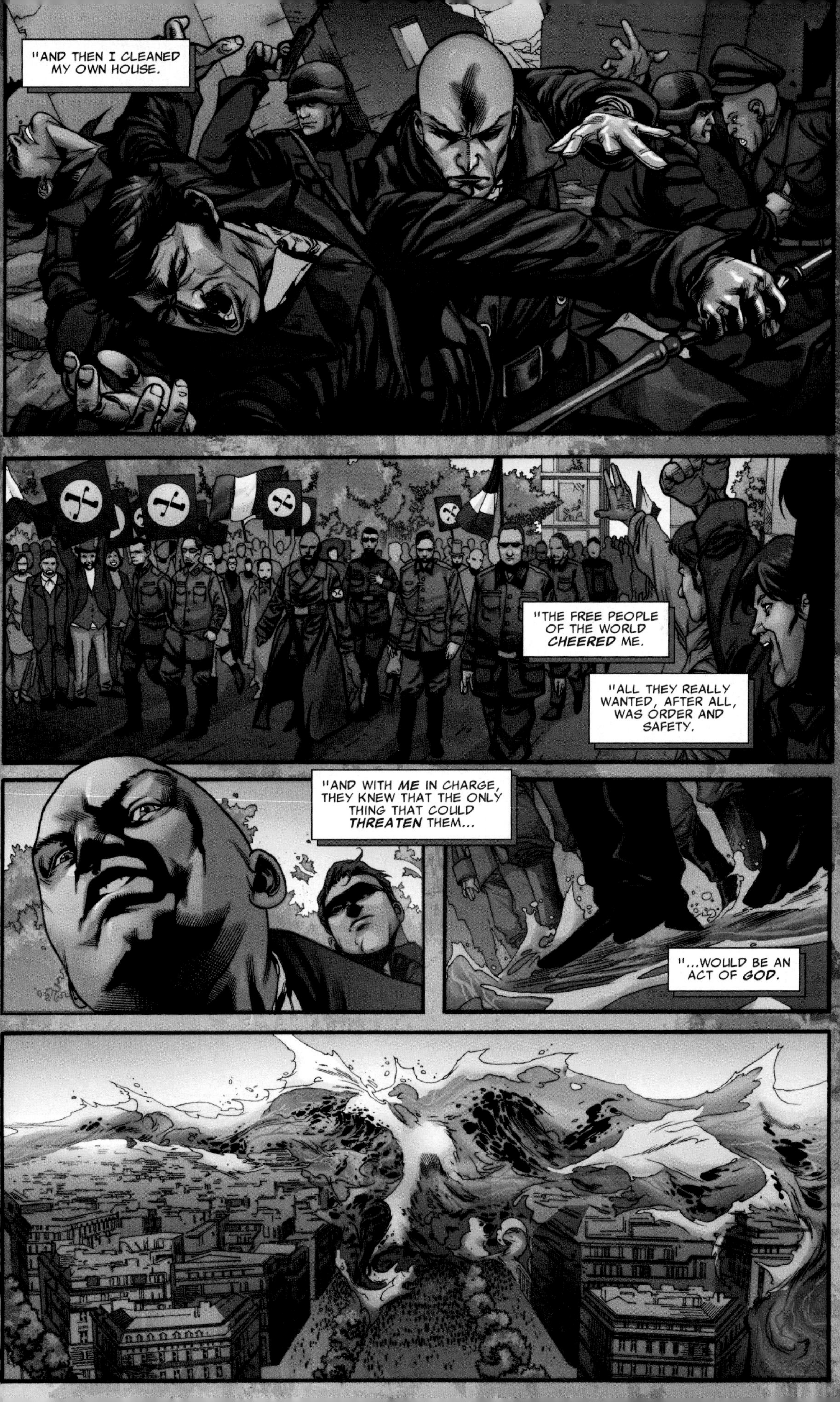
"AND THEN I CLEANED MY OWN HOUSE.
"THE FREE PEOPLE OF THE WORLD CHEERED ME.
"ALL THEY REALLY WANTED, AFTER ALL, WAS ORDER AND SAFETY.
"AND WITH ME IN CHARGE, THEY KNEW THAT THE ONLY THING THAT COULD THREATEN THEM...
"...WOULD BE AN ACT OF GOD.

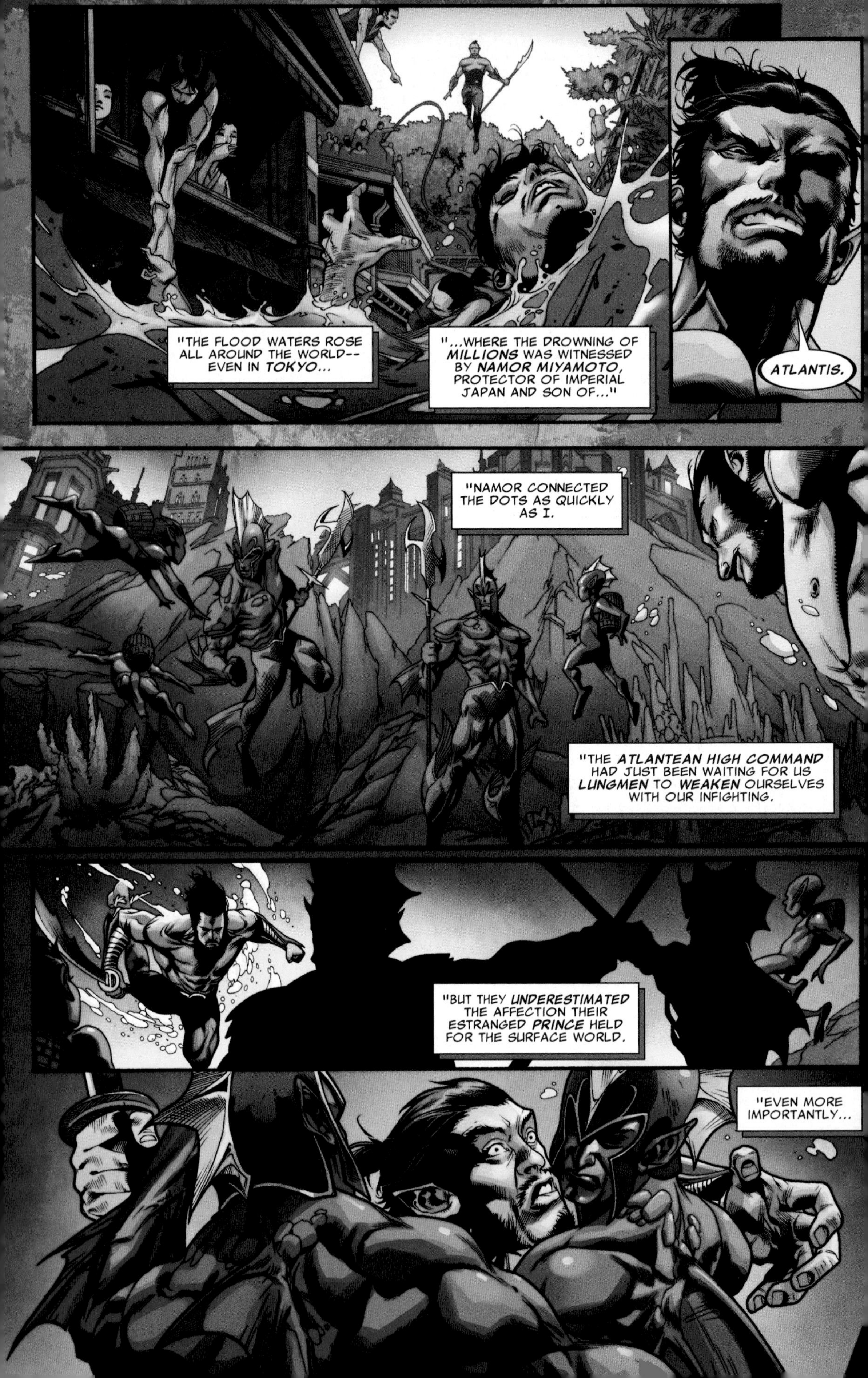

"THE FLOOD WATERS ROSE ALL AROUND THE WORLD-- EVEN IN TOKYO...
"...WHERE THE DROWNING OF MILLIONS WAS WITNESSED BY NAMOR MIYAMOTO, PROTECTOR OF IMPERIAL JAPAN AND SON OF..."
ATLANTIS.
"NAMOR CONNECTED THE DOTS AS QUICKLY AS I.
"THE ATLANTEAN HIGH COMMAND HAD JUST BEEN WAITING FOR US LUNGMEN TO WEAKEN OURSELVES WITH OUR INFIGHTING.
"BUT THEY UNDERESTIMATED THE AFFECTION THEIR ESTRANGED PRINCE HELD FOR THE SURFACE WORLD.
"EVEN MORE IMPORTANTLY...

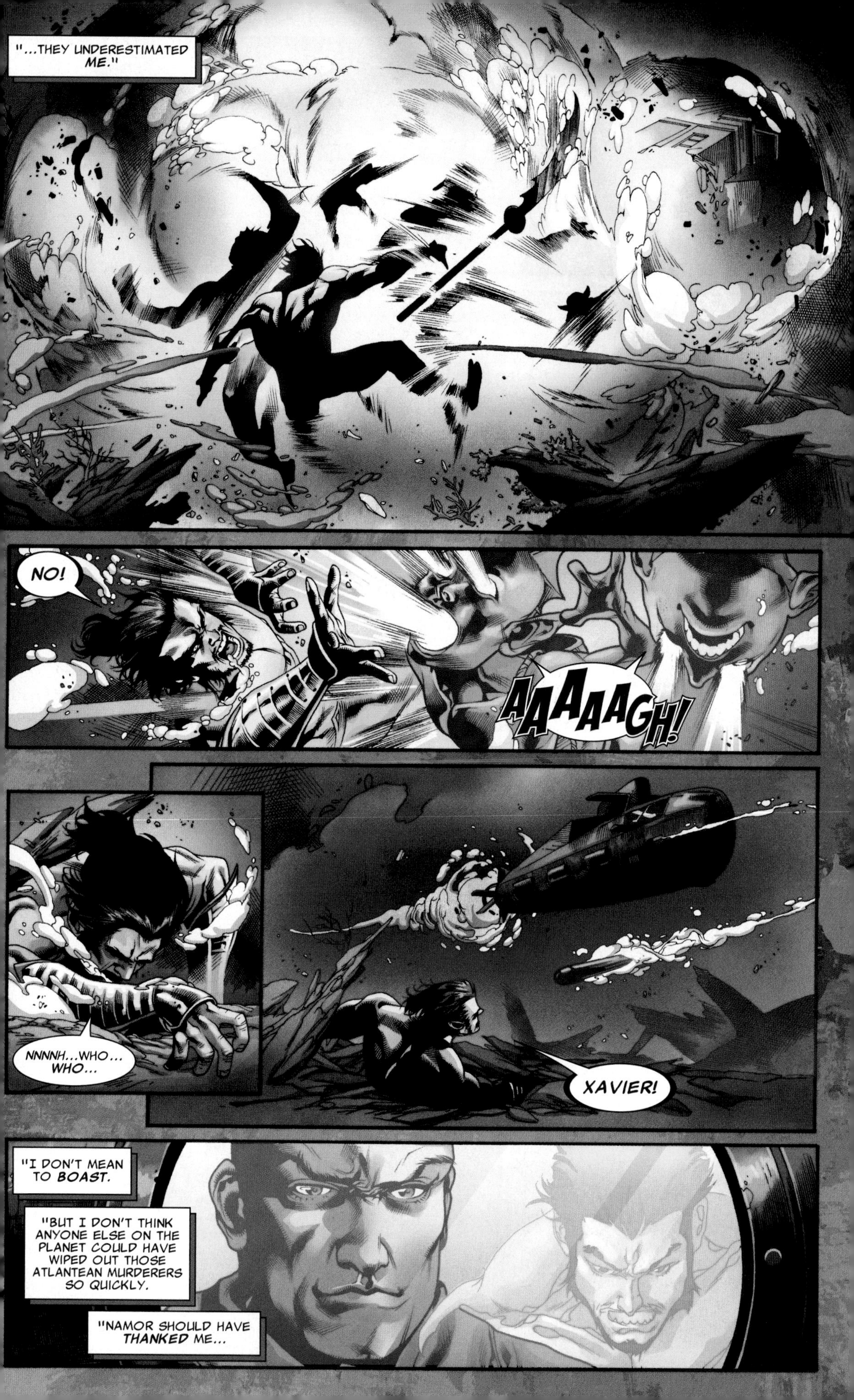
"...THEY UNDERESTIMATED ME."
NO!
AAAAAGH!
NNNNH...WHO... WHO...
XAVIER!
"I DON'T MEAN TO BOAST.
"BUT I DON'T THINK ANYONE ELSE ON THE PLANET COULD HAVE WIPED OUT THOSE ATLANTEAN MURDERERS SO QUICKLY.
"NAMOR SHOULD HAVE THANKED ME...

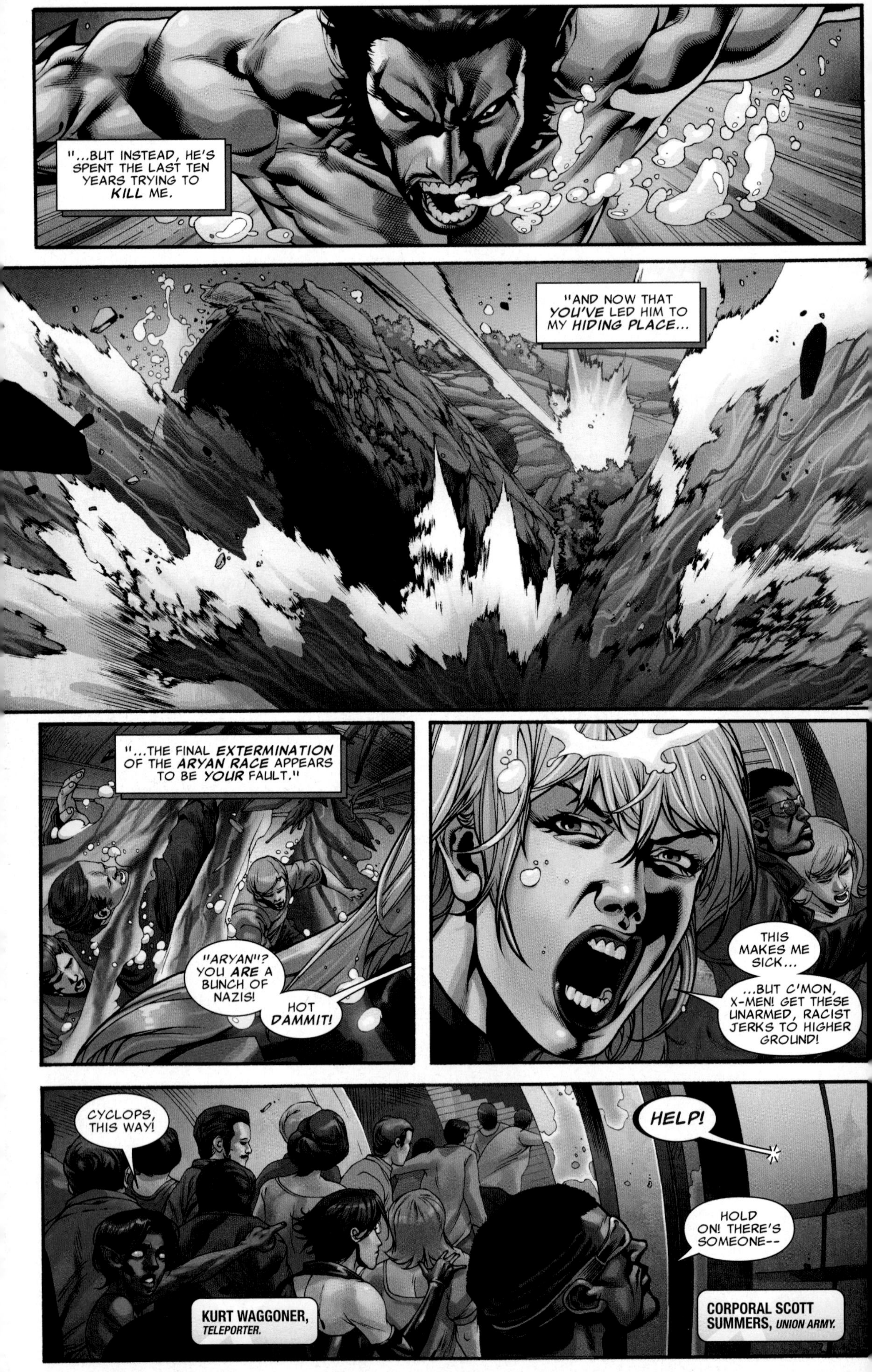
"...BUT INSTEAD, HE'S SPENT THE LAST TEN YEARS TRYING TO KILL ME.
"AND NOW THAT YOU'VE LED HIM TO MY HIDING PLACE...
"...THE FINAL EXTERMINATION OF THE ARYAN RACE APPEARS TO BE YOUR FAULT."
"ARYAN"? YOU ARE A BUNCH OF NAZIS!
HOT DAMMIT!
THIS MAKES ME SICK...
...BUT C'MON, X-MEN! GET THESE UNARMED, RACIST JERKS TO HIGHER GROUND!
CYCLOPS, THIS WAY!
HELP!
HOLD ON! THERE'S SOMEONE--
KURT WAGGONER, TELEPORTER.
CORPORAL SCOTT SUMMERS, UNION ARMY.

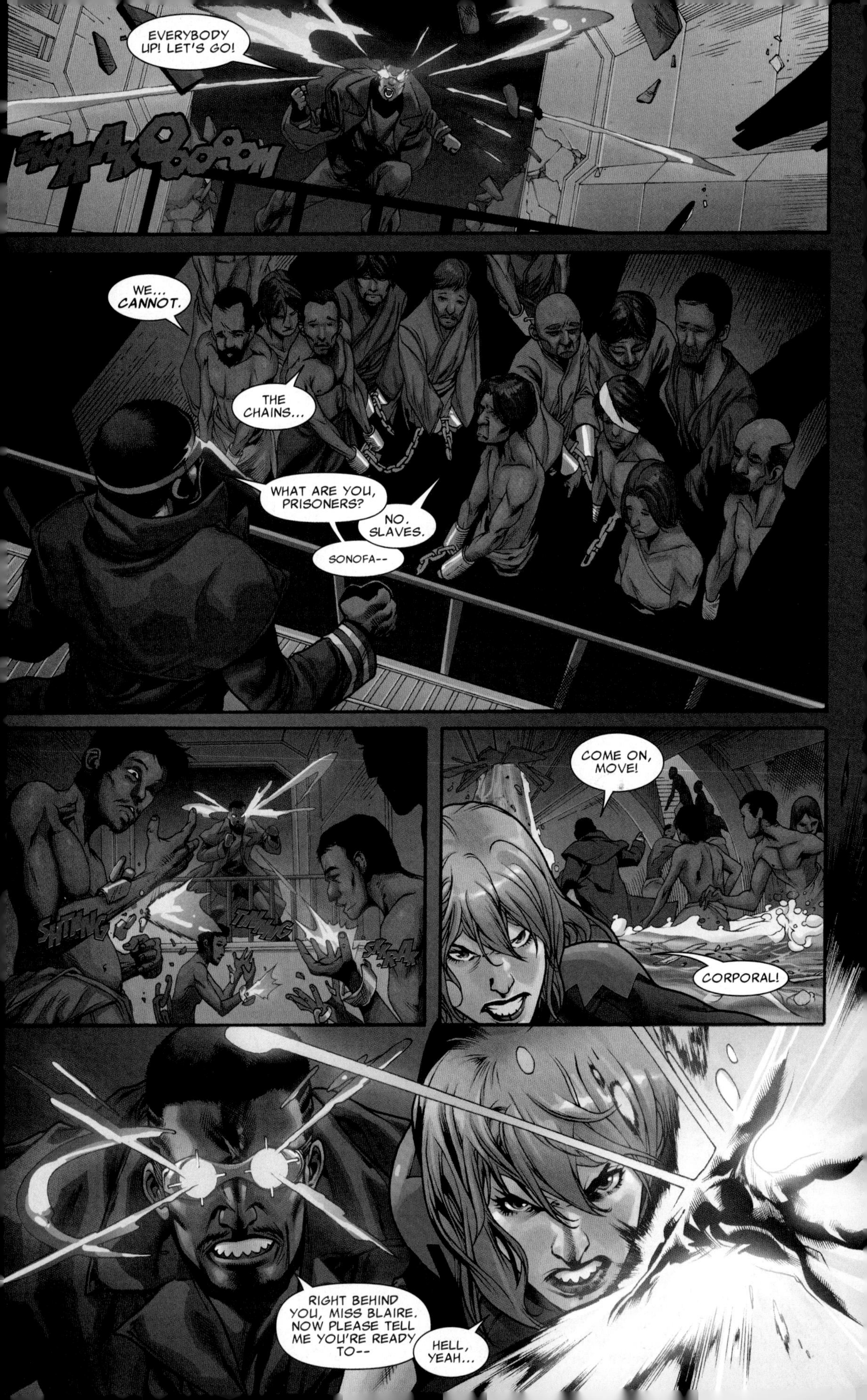
EVERYBODY UP! LET'S GO!
SKRAKAKOOOOOM
WE... CANNOT.
THE CHAINS...
WHAT ARE YOU, PRISONERS?
NO. SLAVES.
SONOFA--
SHTING
TANNG
SKRAK
COME ON, MOVE!
CORPORAL!
RIGHT BEHIND YOU, MISS BLAIRE. NOW PLEASE TELL ME YOU'RE READY TO--
HELL, YEAH...

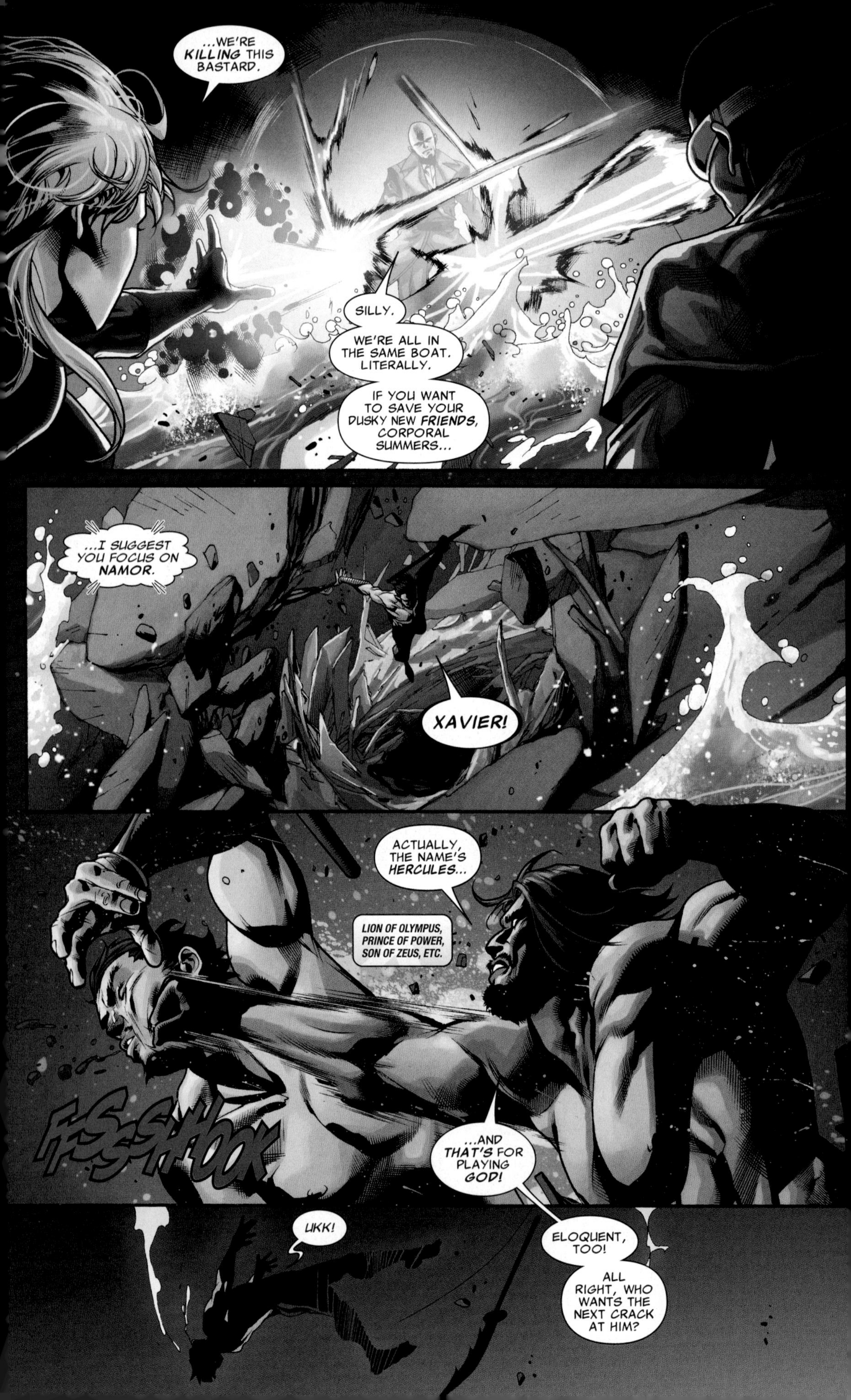
...WE'RE KILLING THIS BASTARD.
SILLY.
WE'RE ALL IN THE SAME BOAT. LITERALLY.
IF YOU WANT TO SAVE YOUR DUSKY NEW FRIENDS, CORPORAL SUMMERS...
...I SUGGEST YOU FOCUS ON NAMOR.
XAVIER!
ACTUALLY, THE NAME'S HERCULES...
LION OF OLYMPUS, PRINCE OF POWER, SON OF ZEUS, ETC.
...AND THAT'S FOR PLAYING GOD!
FSSHOOK
UKK!
ELOQUENT, TOO!
ALL RIGHT, WHO WANTS THE NEXT CRACK AT HIM?

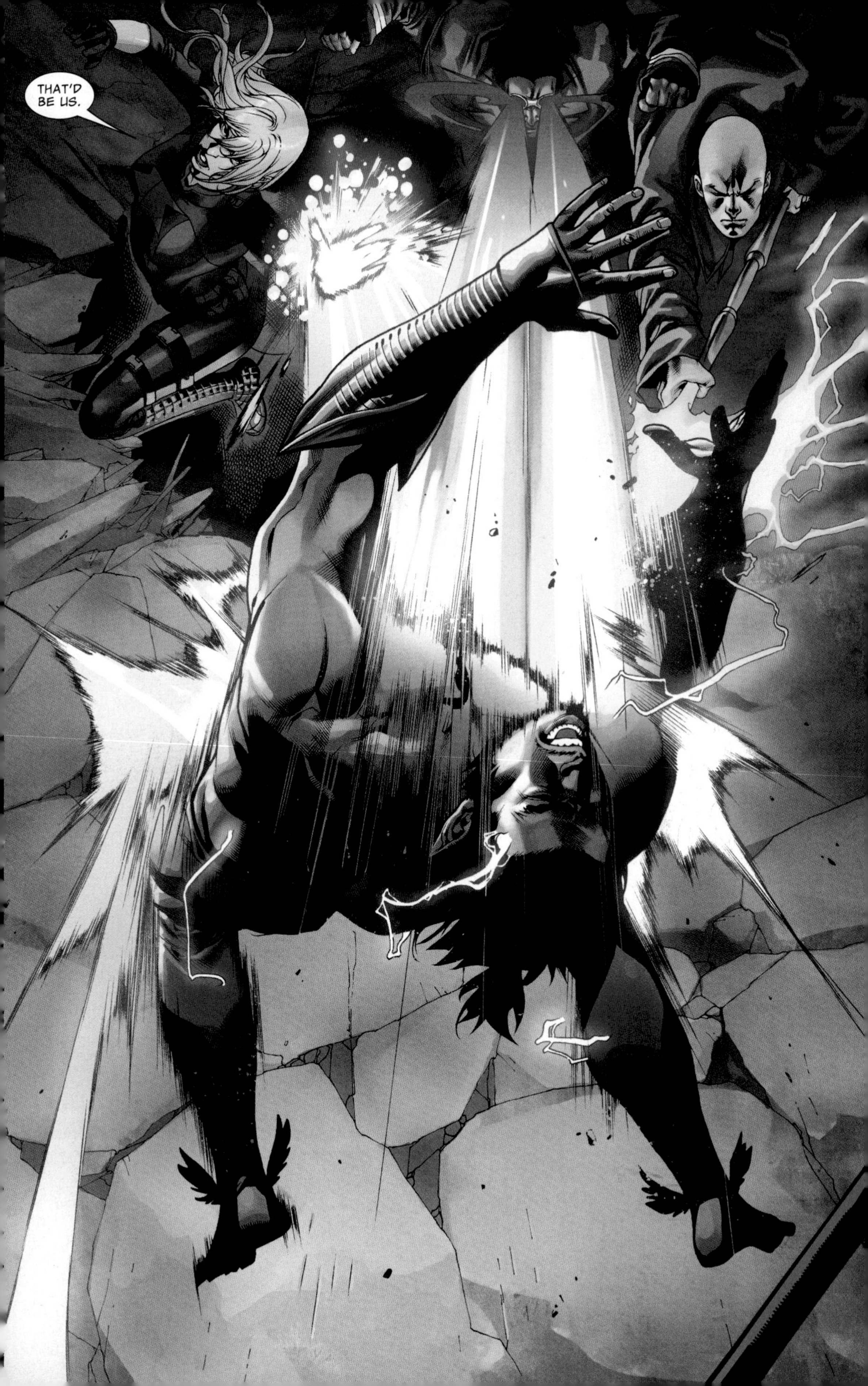
THAT'D BE US.

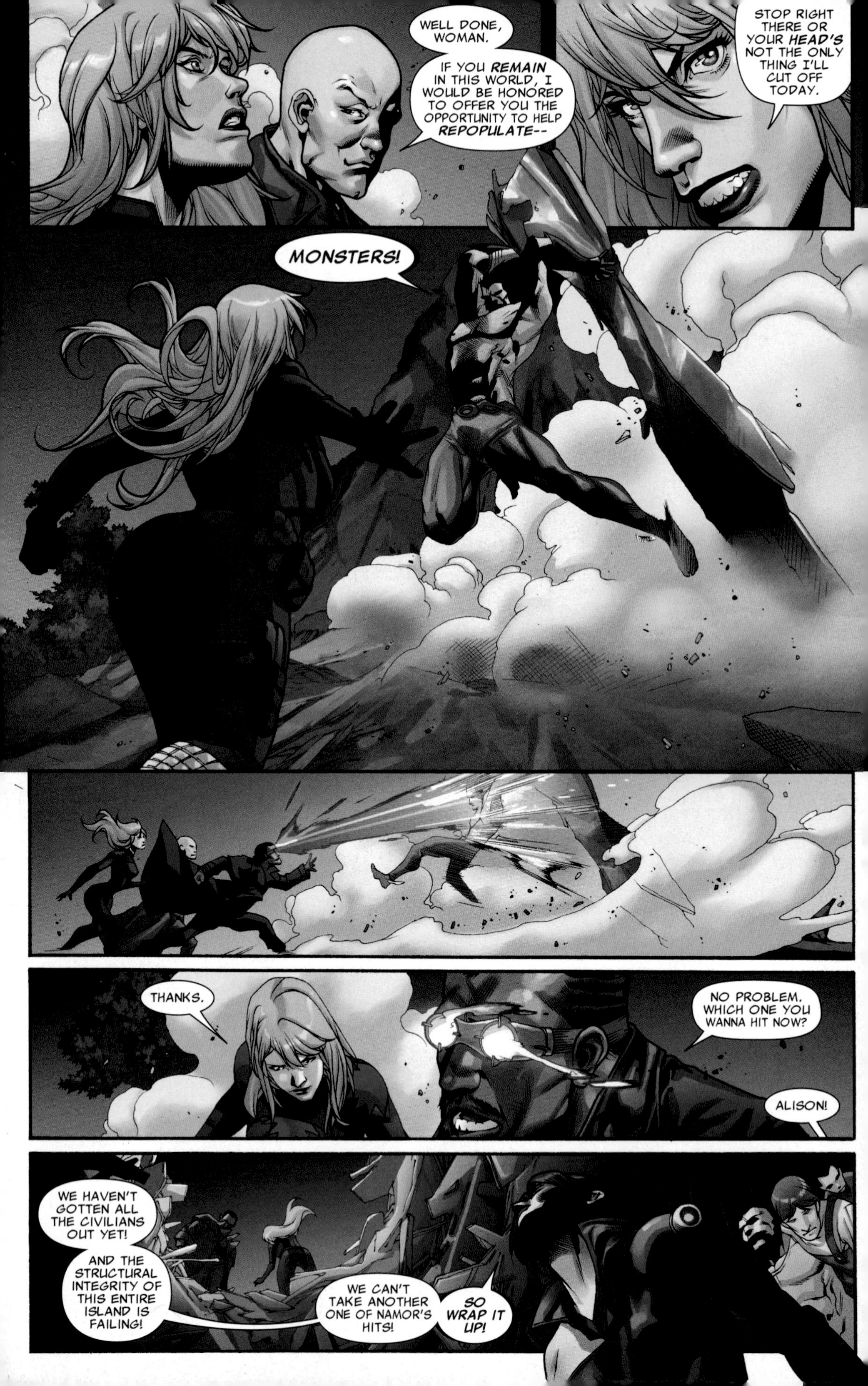
WELL DONE, WOMAN.
IF YOU REMAIN IN THIS WORLD, I WOULD BE HONORED TO OFFER YOU THE OPPORTUNITY TO HELP REPOPULATE--
STOP RIGHT THERE OR YOUR HEAD'S NOT THE ONLY THING I'LL CUT OFF TODAY.
MONSTERS!
THANKS.
NO PROBLEM. WHICH ONE YOU WANNA HIT NOW?
ALISON!
WE HAVEN'T GOTTEN ALL THE CIVILIANS OUT YET!
AND THE STRUCTURAL INTEGRITY OF THIS ENTIRE ISLAND IS FAILING!
WE CAN'T TAKE ANOTHER ONE OF NAMOR'S HITS!
SO WRAP IT UP!

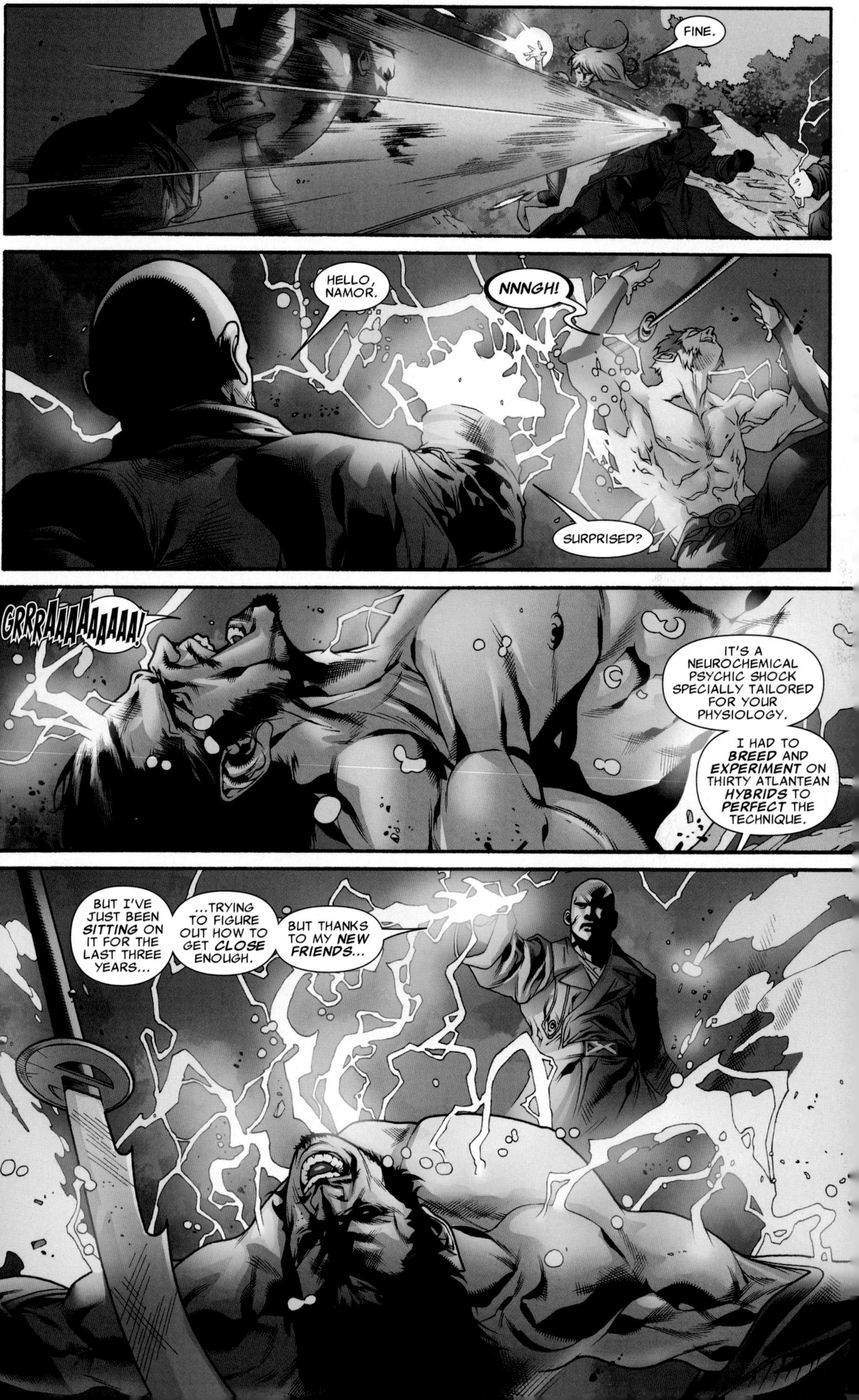
FINE.
HELLO, NAMOR.
NNNGH!
SURPRISED?
GRRRAAAAAAAAA!
IT'S A NEUROCHEMICAL PSYCHIC SHOCK SPECIALLY TAILORED FOR YOUR PHYSIOLOGY.
I HAD TO BREED AND EXPERIMENT ON THIRTY ATLANTEAN HYBRIDS TO PERFECT THE TECHNIQUE.
BUT I'VE JUST BEEN SITTING ON IT FOR THE LAST THREE YEARS...
...TRYING TO FIGURE OUT HOW TO GET CLOSE ENOUGH.
BUT THANKS TO MY NEW FRIENDS...

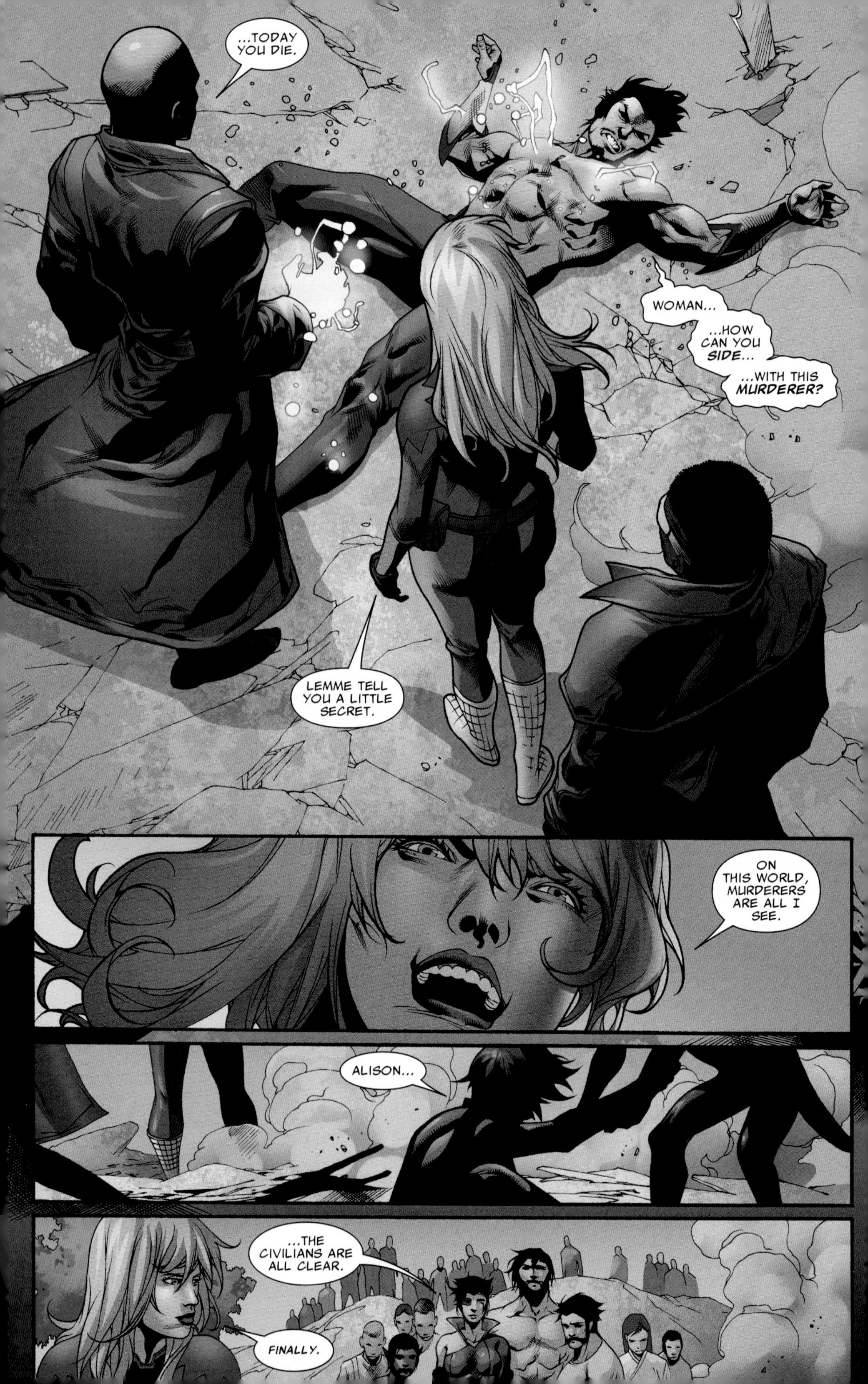
...TODAY YOU DIE.
WOMAN...
...HOW CAN YOU SIDE...
...WITH THIS MURDERER?
LEMME TELL YOU A LITTLE SECRET.
ON THIS WORLD, MURDERERS ARE ALL I SEE.
ALISON...
...THE CIVILIANS ARE ALL CLEAR.
FINALLY.

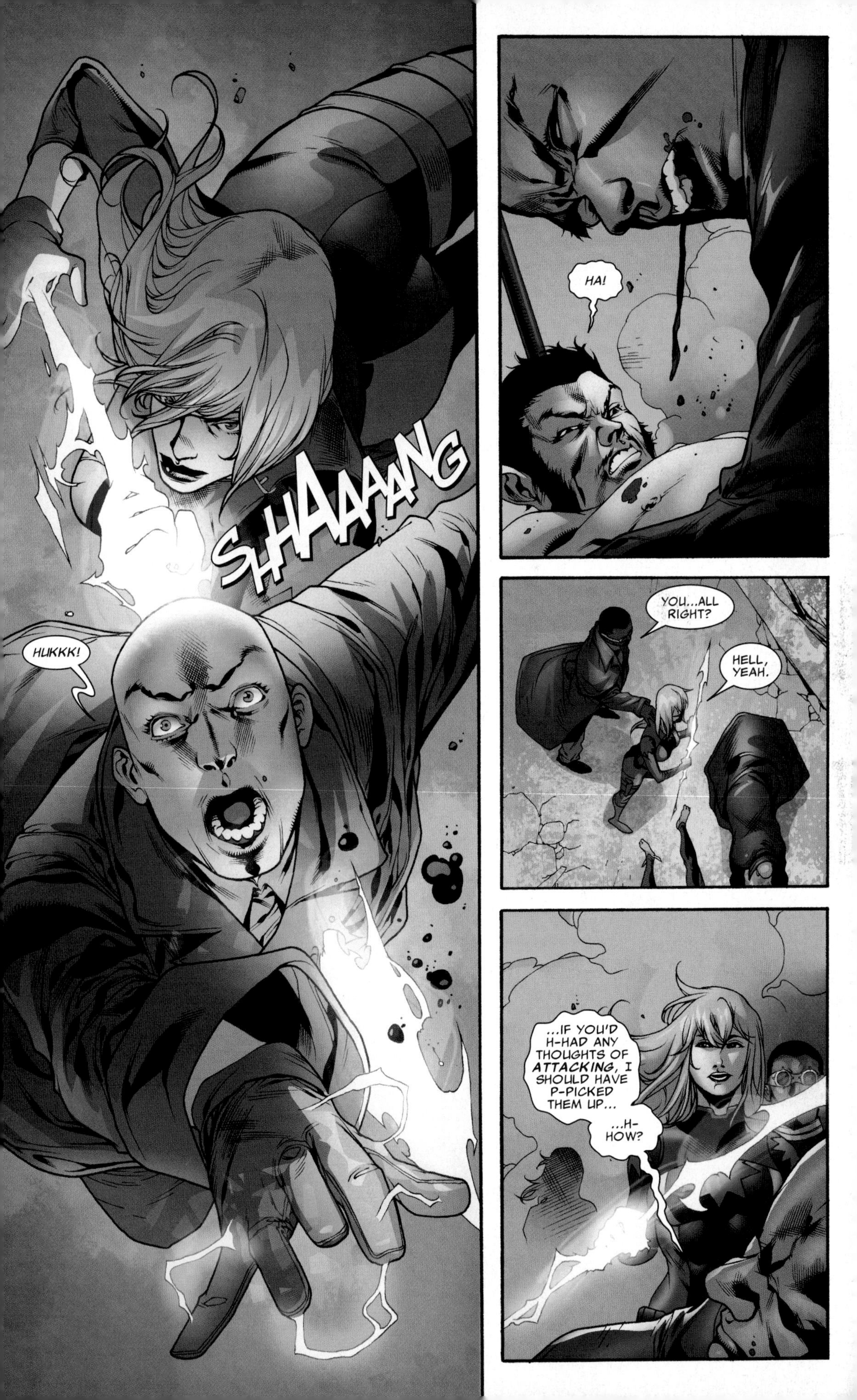
SHHAAAAANG
HUKKK!
HA!
YOU...ALL RIGHT?
HELL, YEAH.
...IF YOU'D H-HAD ANY THOUGHTS OF **ATTACKING**, I SHOULD HAVE P-PICKED THEM UP...
...H-HOW?

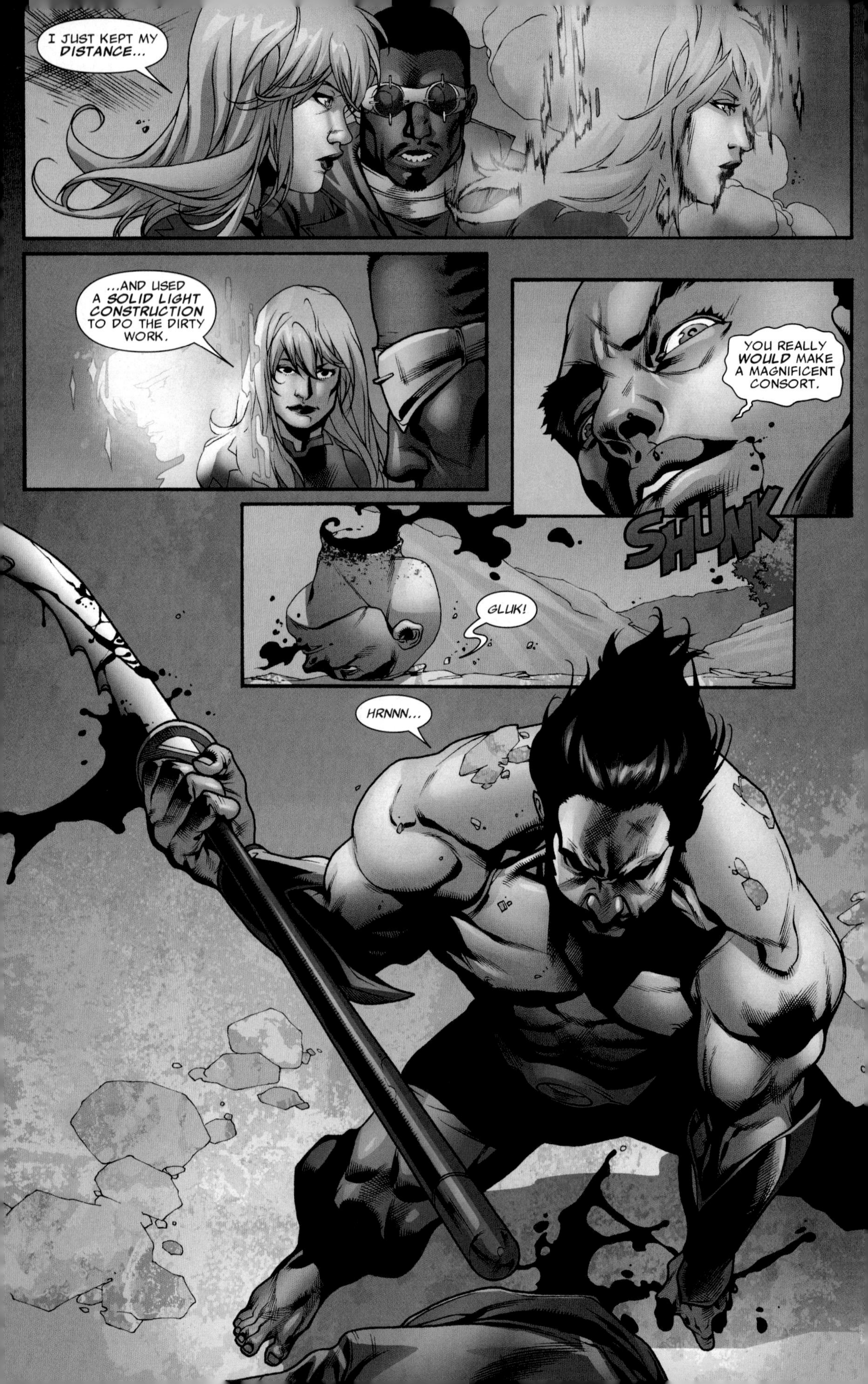
I JUST KEPT MY DISTANCE...
...AND USED A SOLID LIGHT CONSTRUCTION TO DO THE DIRTY WORK.
YOU REALLY WOULD MAKE A MAGNIFICENT CONSORT.
SHUNK
GLUK!
HRNNN...

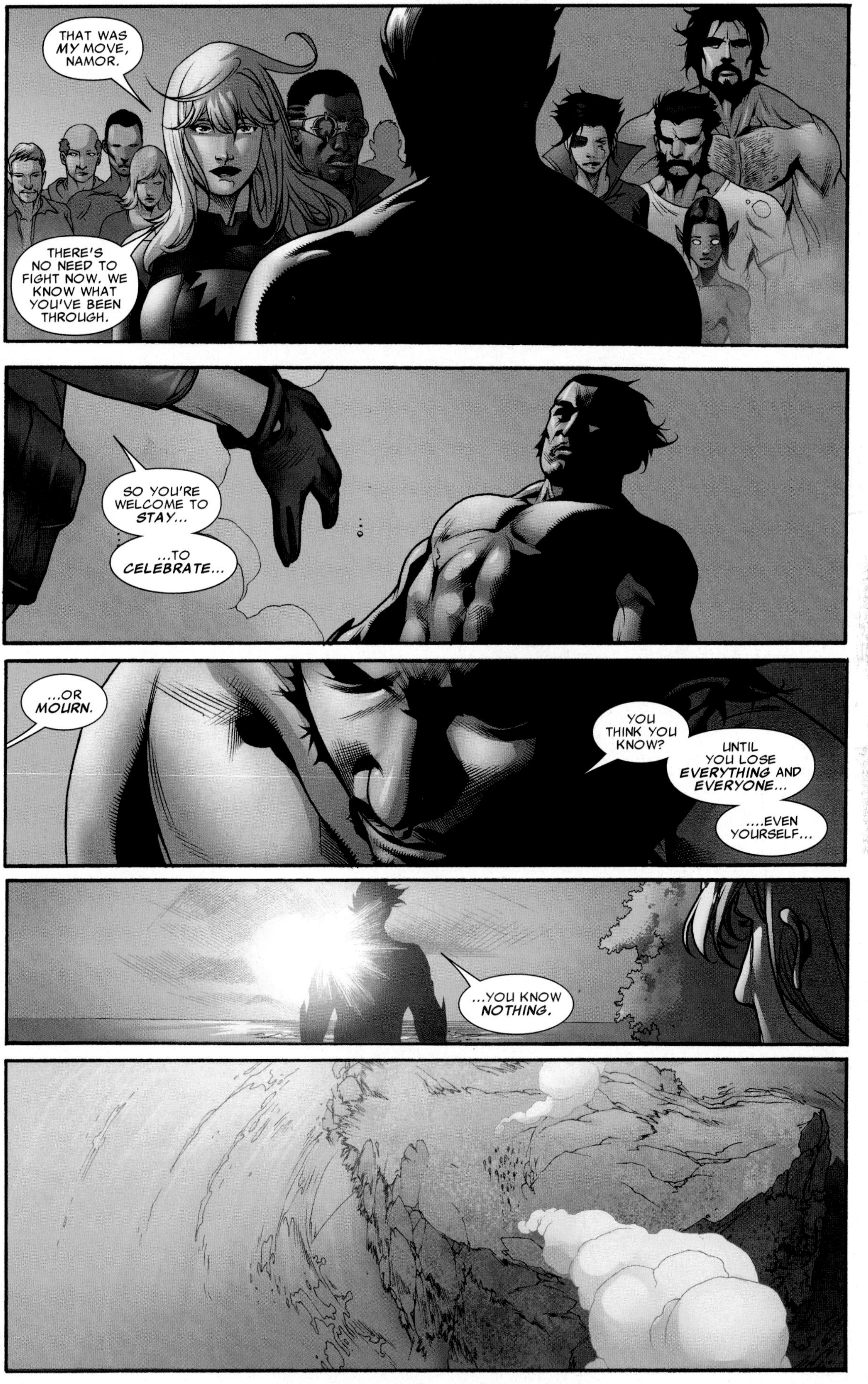
THAT WAS MY MOVE, NAMOR.
THERE'S NO NEED TO FIGHT NOW. WE KNOW WHAT YOU'VE BEEN THROUGH.
SO YOU'RE WELCOME TO STAY...
...TO CELEBRATE...
...OR MOURN.
YOU THINK YOU KNOW?
UNTIL YOU LOSE EVERYTHING AND EVERYONE...
....EVEN YOURSELF...
...YOU KNOW NOTHING.

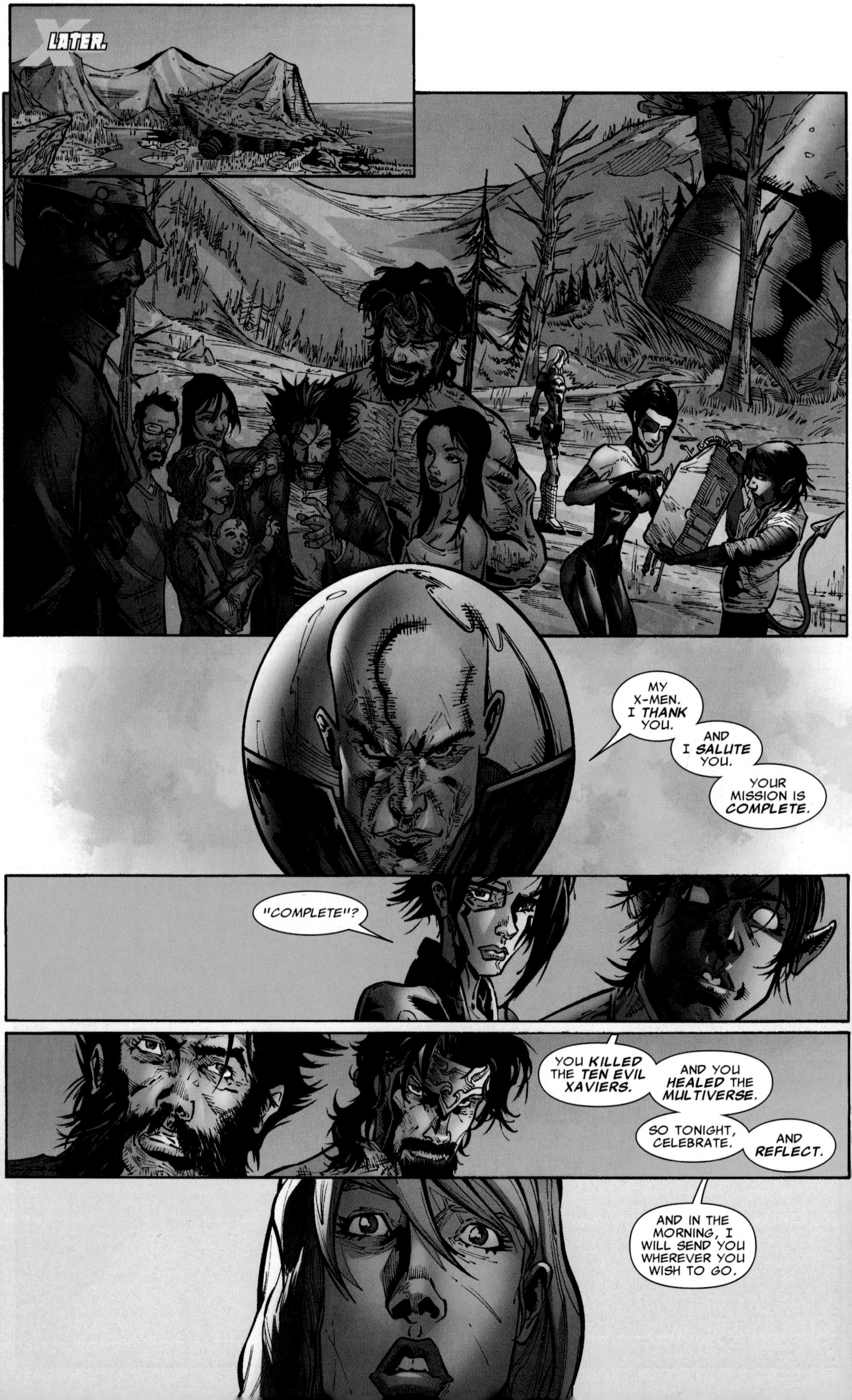
LATER.
MY X-MEN. I THANK YOU.
AND I SALUTE YOU.
YOUR MISSION IS COMPLETE.
"COMPLETE"?
YOU KILLED THE TEN EVIL XAVIERS.
AND YOU HEALED THE MULTIVERSE.
SO TONIGHT, CELEBRATE.
AND REFLECT.
AND IN THE MORNING, I WILL SEND YOU WHEREVER YOU WISH TO GO.

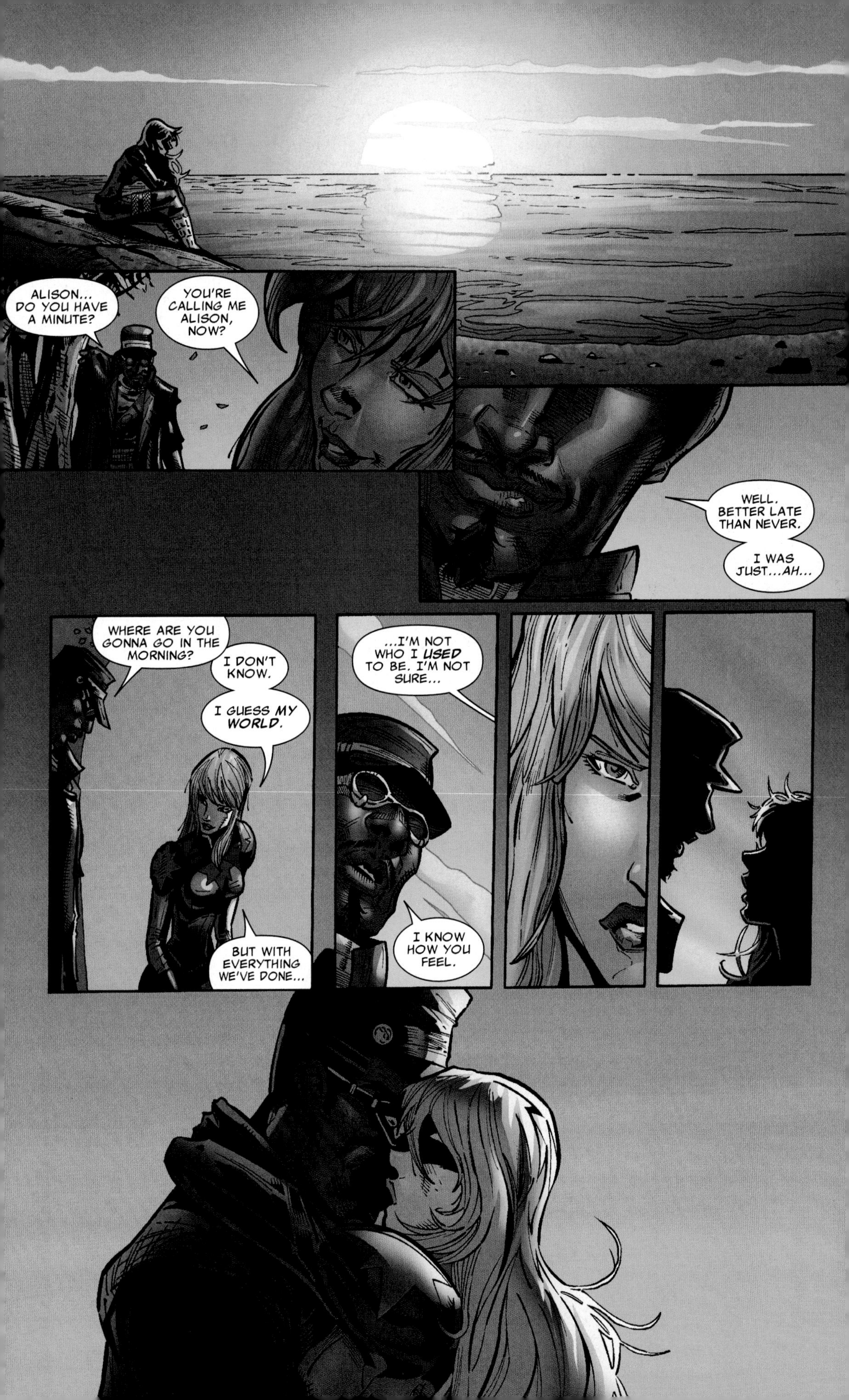

ALISON... DO YOU HAVE A MINUTE?
YOU'RE CALLING ME ALISON, NOW?
WELL. BETTER LATE THAN NEVER.
I WAS JUST...AH...
WHERE ARE YOU GONNA GO IN THE MORNING?
I DON'T KNOW.
I GUESS MY WORLD.
BUT WITH EVERYTHING WE'VE DONE...
...I'M NOT WHO I USED TO BE. I'M NOT SURE...
I KNOW HOW YOU FEEL.

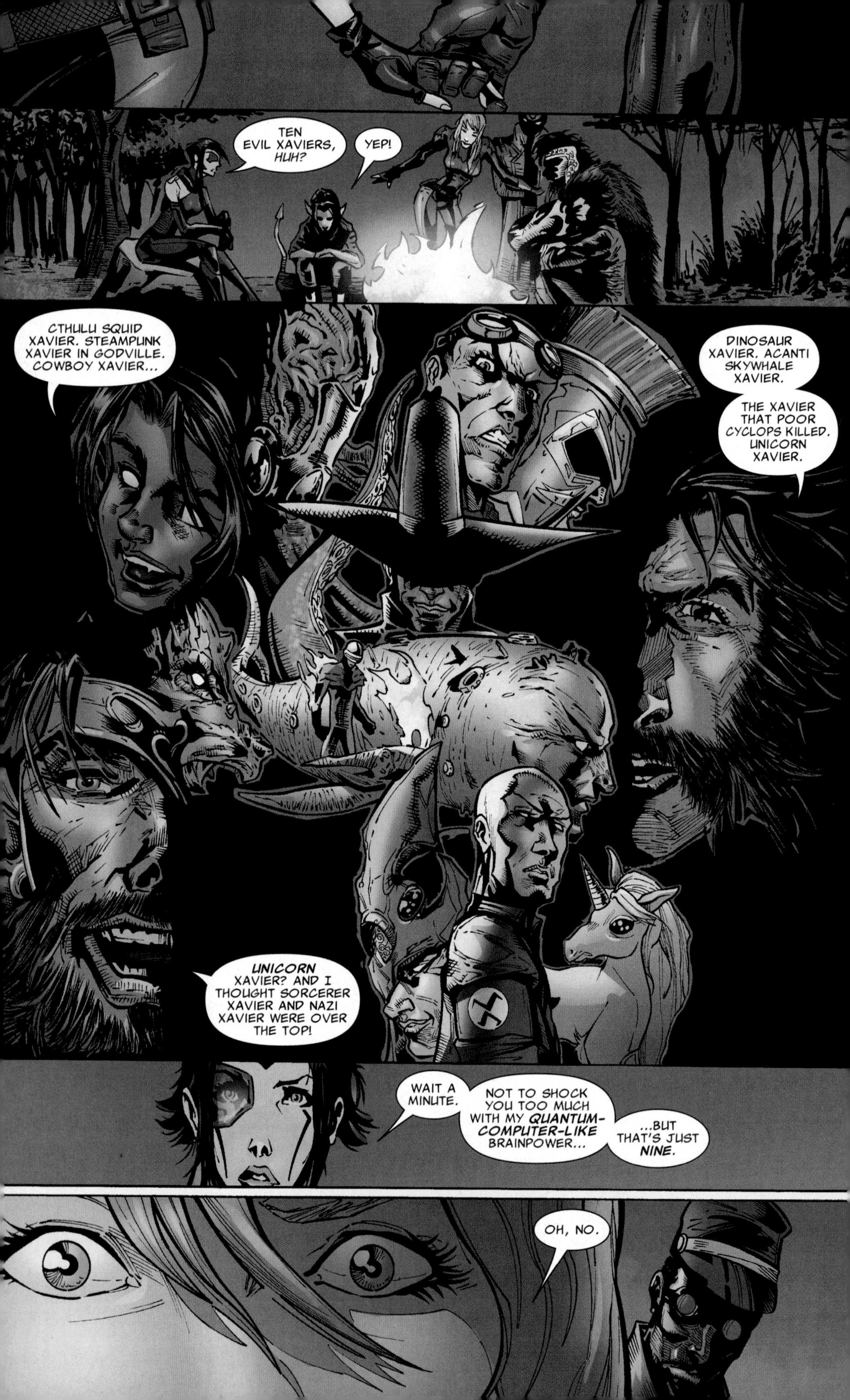

TEN EVIL XAVIERS, HUH?
YEP!
CTHULU SQUID XAVIER. STEAMPUNK XAVIER IN GODVILLE. COWBOY XAVIER...
DINOSAUR XAVIER. ACANTI SKYWHALE XAVIER.
THE XAVIER THAT POOR CYCLOPS KILLED. UNICORN XAVIER.
UNICORN XAVIER? AND I THOUGHT SORCERER XAVIER AND NAZI XAVIER WERE OVER THE TOP!
WAIT A MINUTE.
NOT TO SHOCK YOU TOO MUCH WITH MY *QUANTUM-COMPUTER-LIKE* BRAINPOWER...
...BUT THAT'S JUST *NINE*.
OH, NO.

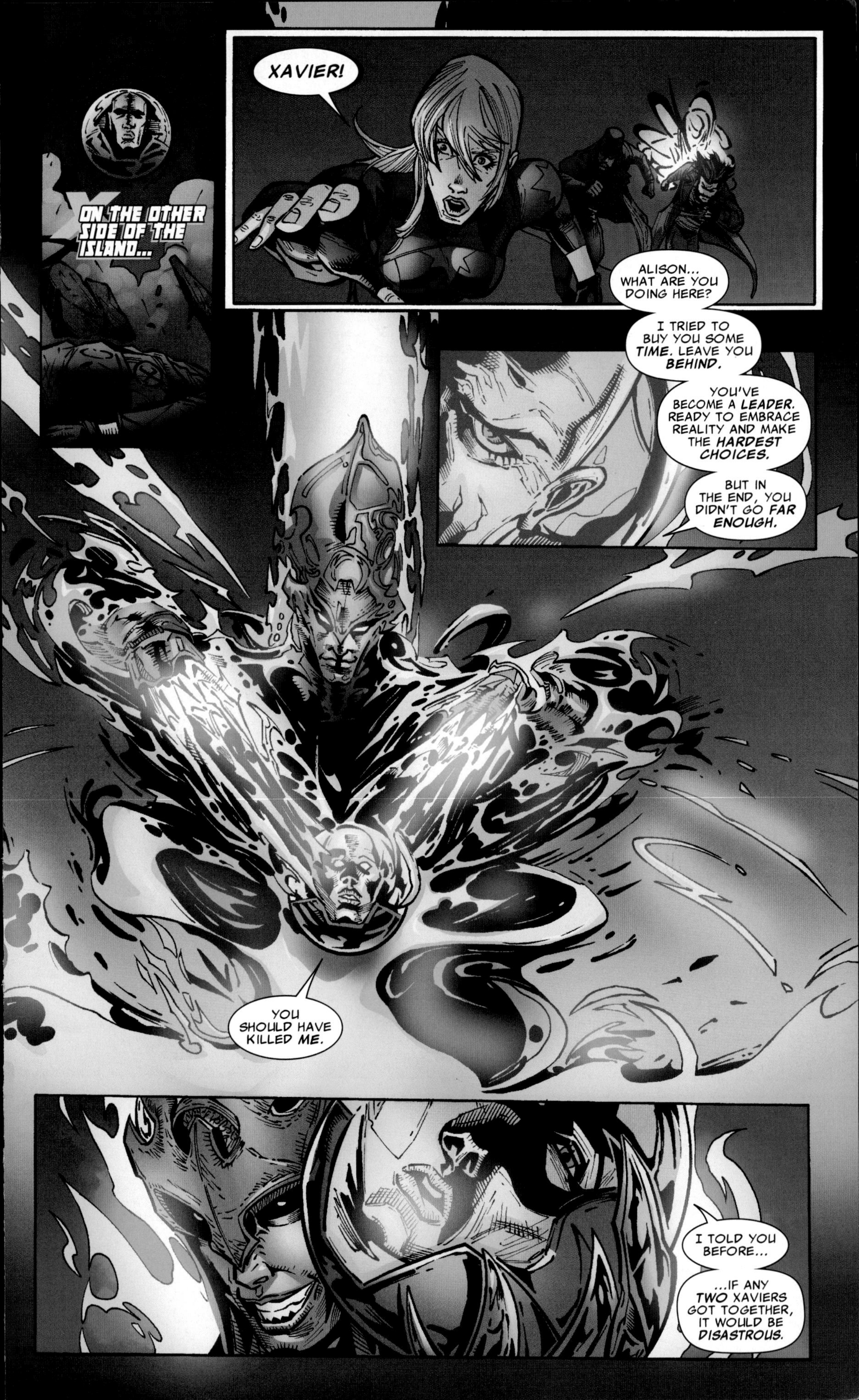

ON THE OTHER SIDE OF THE ISLAND...
XAVIER!
ALISON... WHAT ARE YOU DOING HERE?
I TRIED TO BUY YOU SOME TIME. LEAVE YOU BEHIND.
YOU'VE BECOME A LEADER. READY TO EMBRACE REALITY AND MAKE THE HARDEST CHOICES.
BUT IN THE END, YOU DIDN'T GO FAR ENOUGH.
YOU SHOULD HAVE KILLED ME.
I TOLD YOU BEFORE...
...IF ANY TWO XAVIERS GOT TOGETHER, IT WOULD BE DISASTROUS.

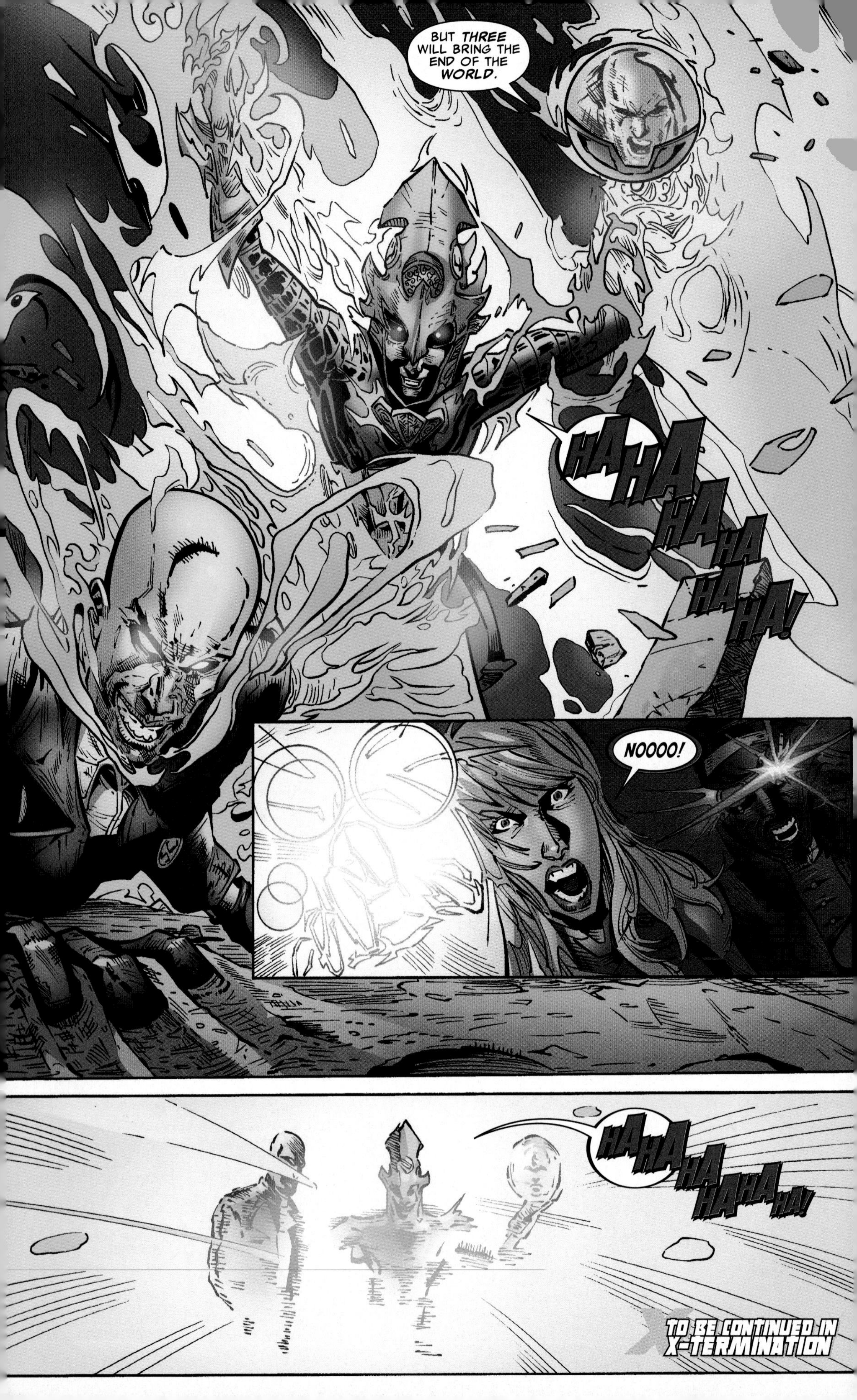

BUT THREE WILL BRING THE END OF THE WORLD.
HAHAHAHAHAHAHAHA!
NOOOO!
HAHAHAHAHAHAHAHA!
TO BE CONTINUED IN X-TERMINATION

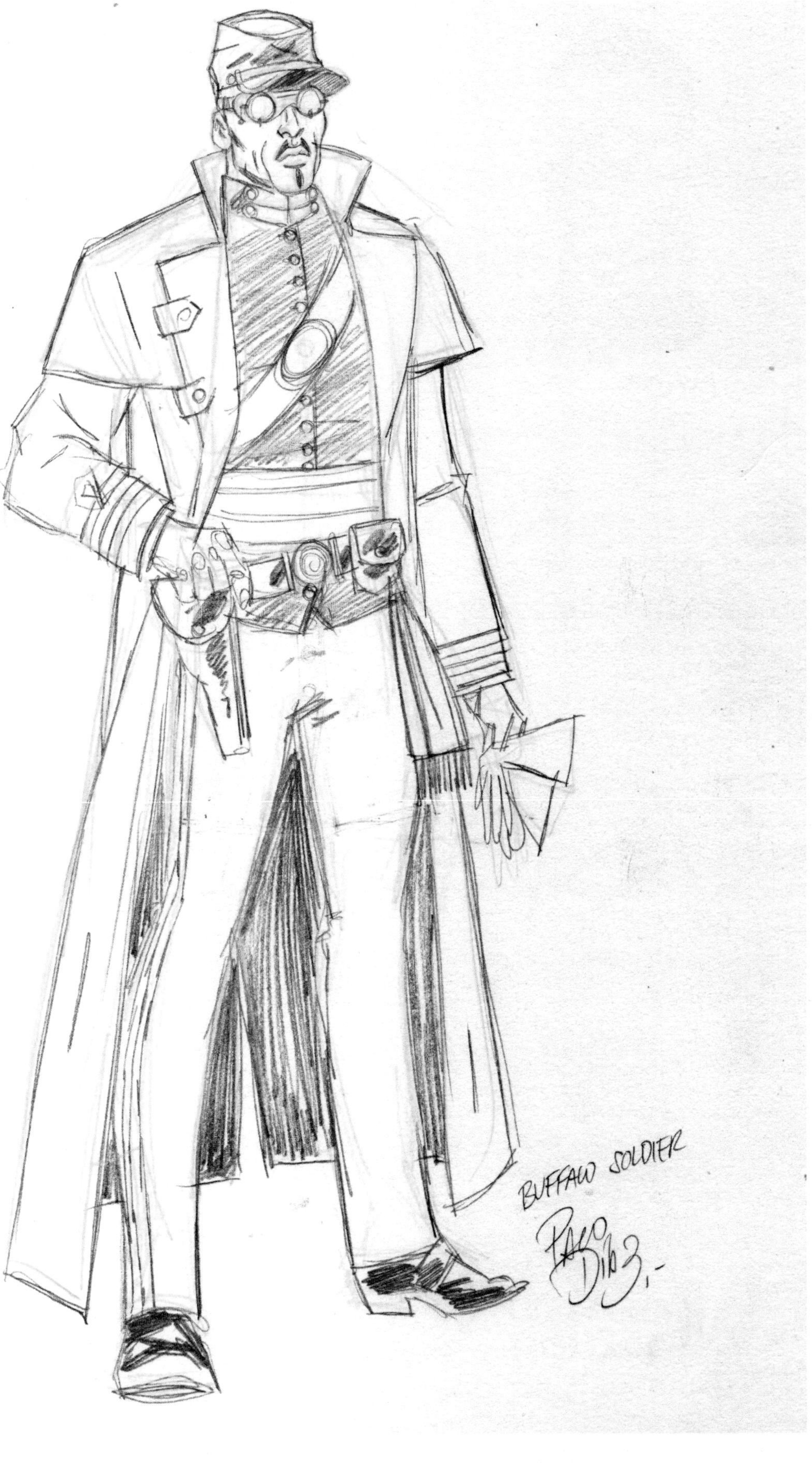
BUFFALO SOLDIER
PACO DIAZ

CYCLOPS & SAGE COSTUME BY PACO DIAZ

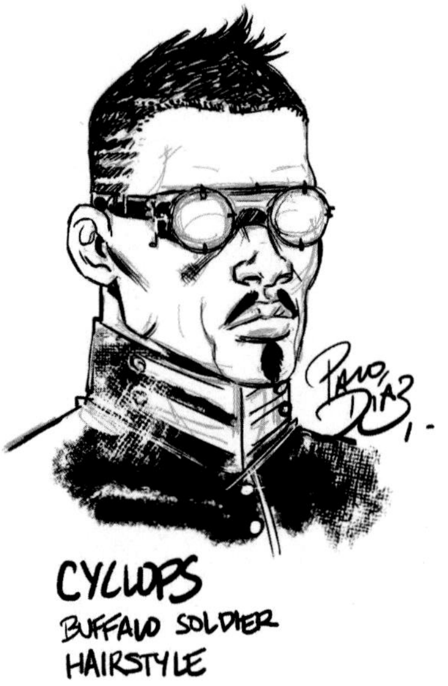
PACO DIAZ
CYCLOPS
BUFFALO SOLDIER
HAIRSTYLE

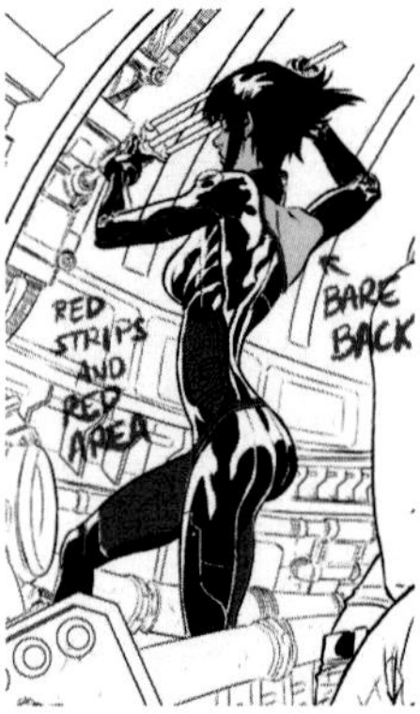
RED STRIPS AND RED AREA
BARE BACK

CYCLOPS & SAGE BY ANDRÉ ARAÚJO

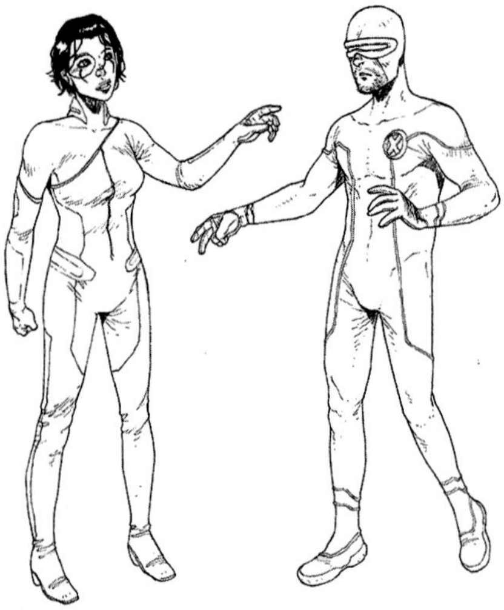

SAGE ROBOT BY RAUL VALDES

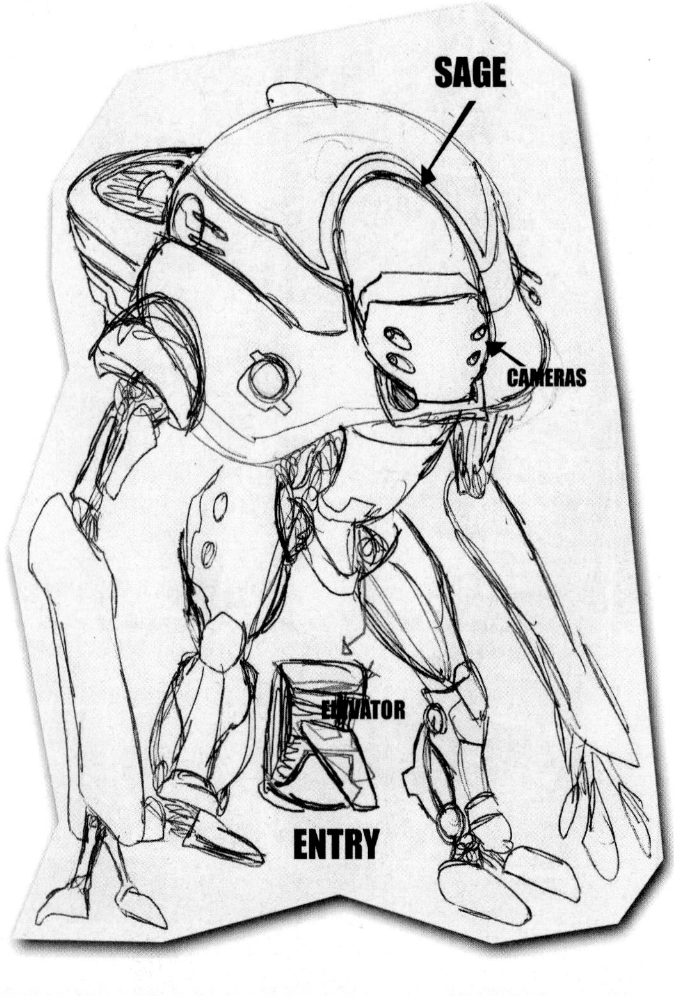
SAGE
CAMERAS
ELEVATOR
ENTRY

#6, PAGE 17 PENCILS & INKS

BY RAUL VALDES & LORENZO RUGGIERO

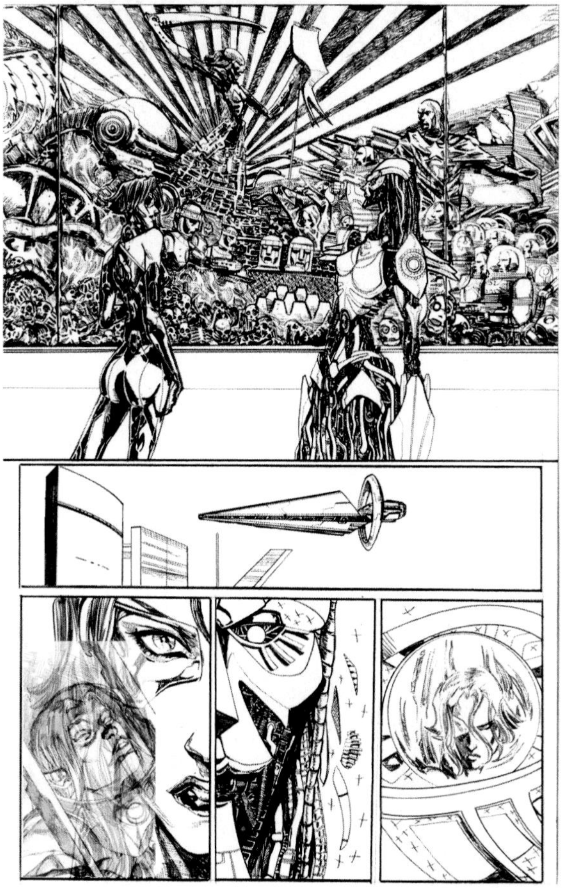

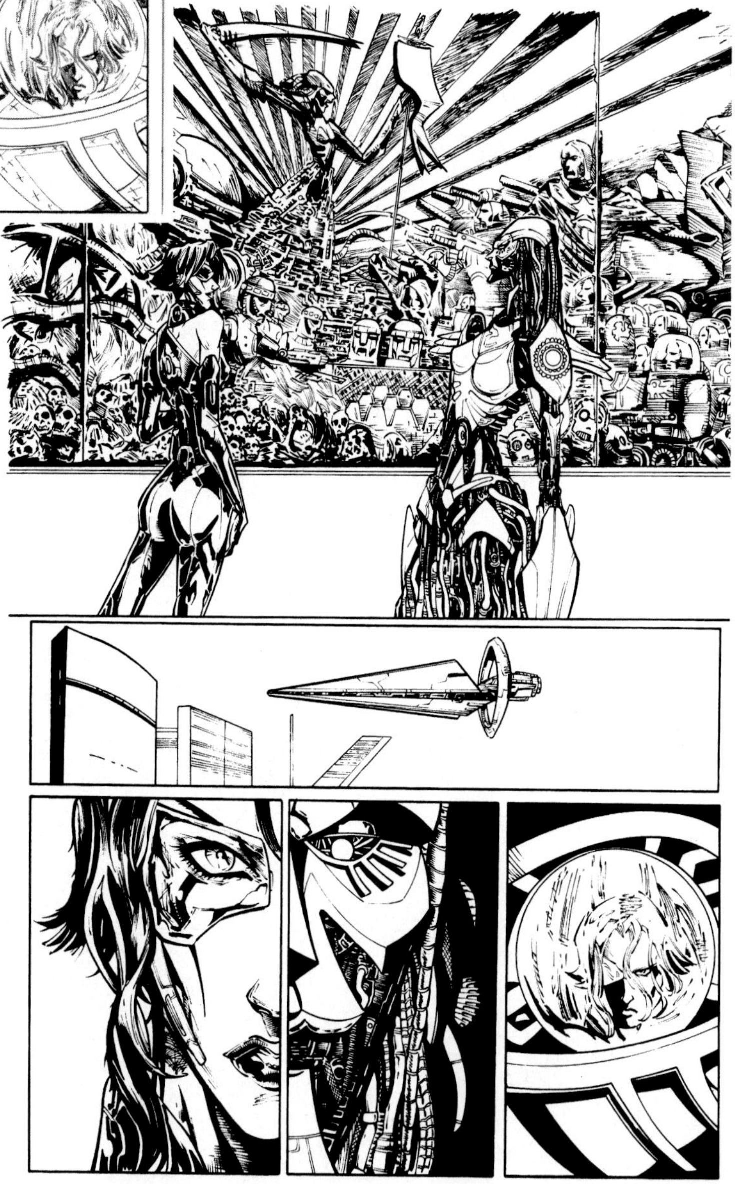

#6, PAGE 20 PENCILS & INKS
BY RAUL VALDES & LORENZO RUGGIERO

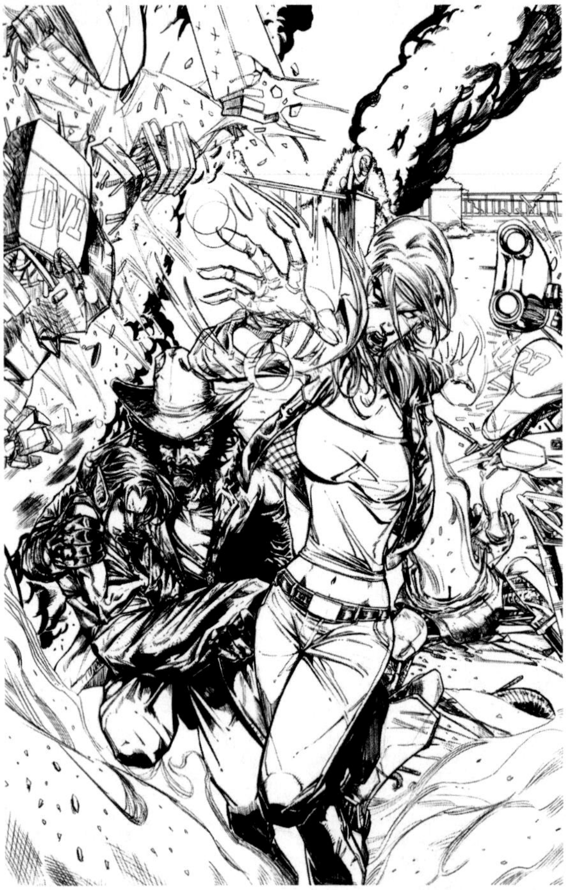
DV1

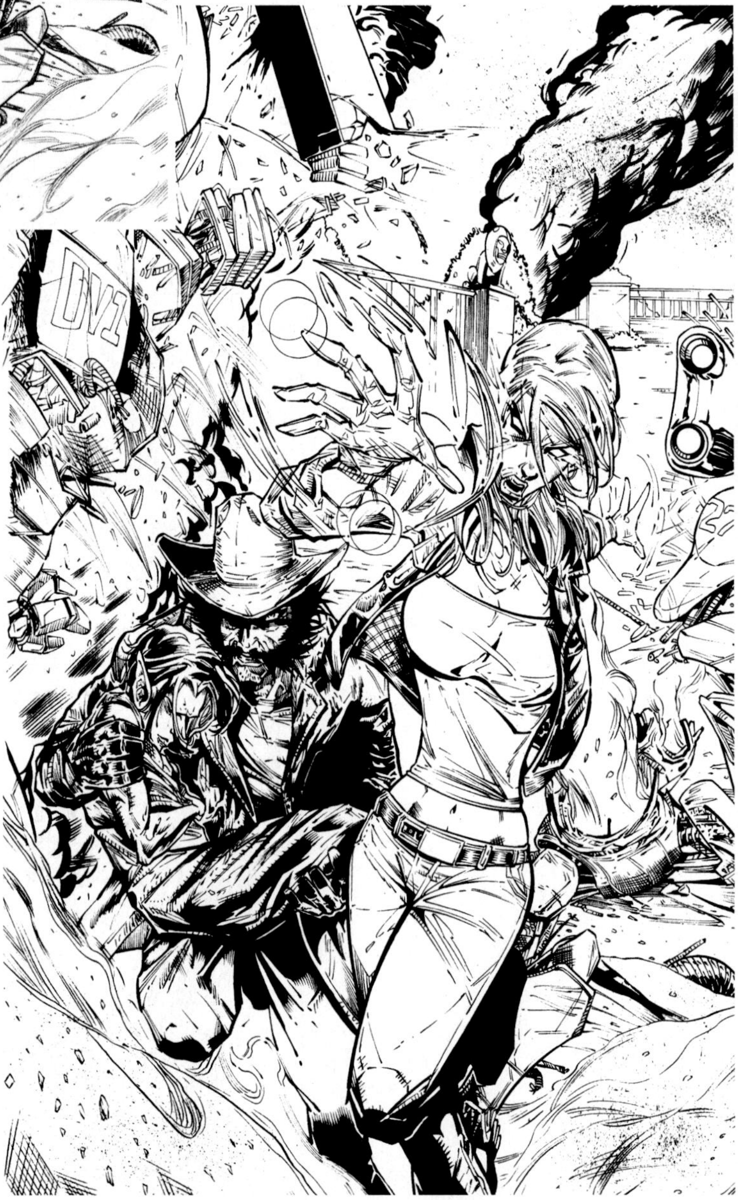
DV1

#8, PAGE 15 PENCILS & INKS

BY PACO DIAZ

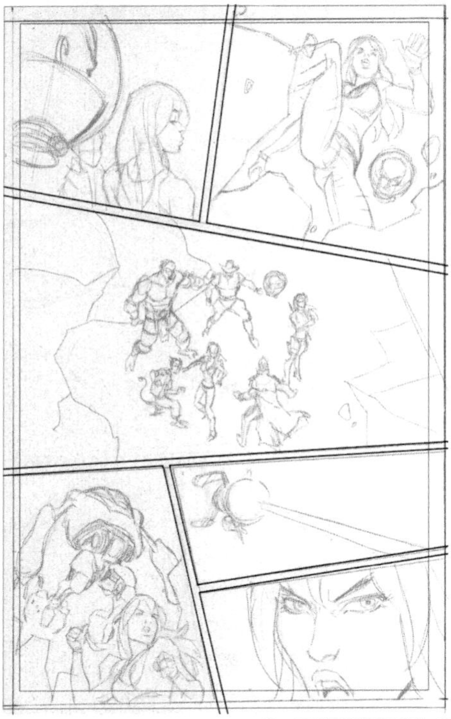

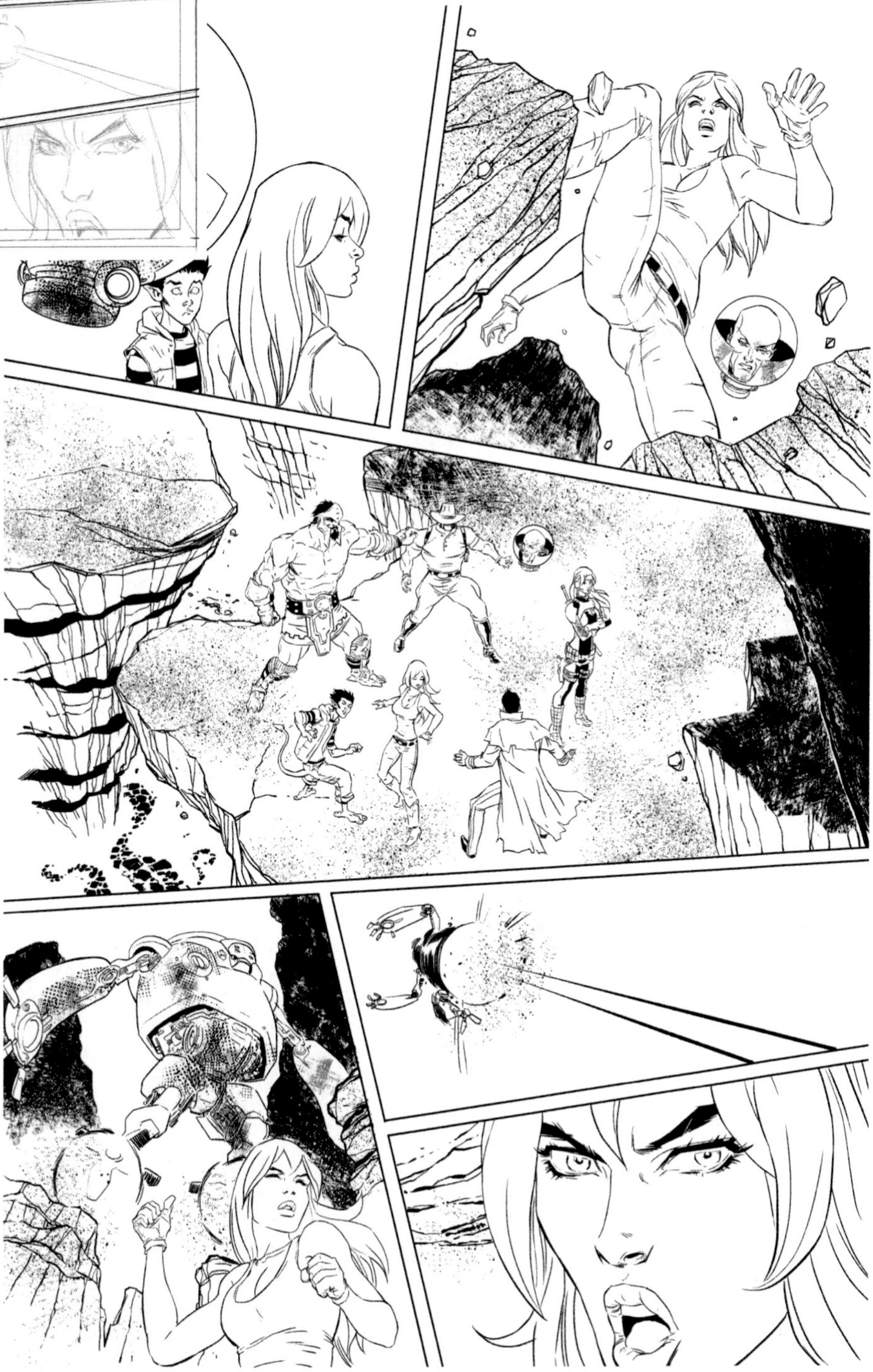

#10, PAGE 20 LAYOUT & PENCILS
BY STEPHEN SEGOVIA

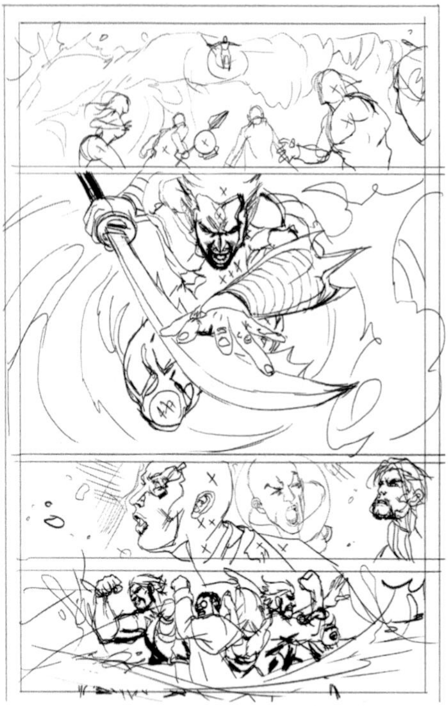

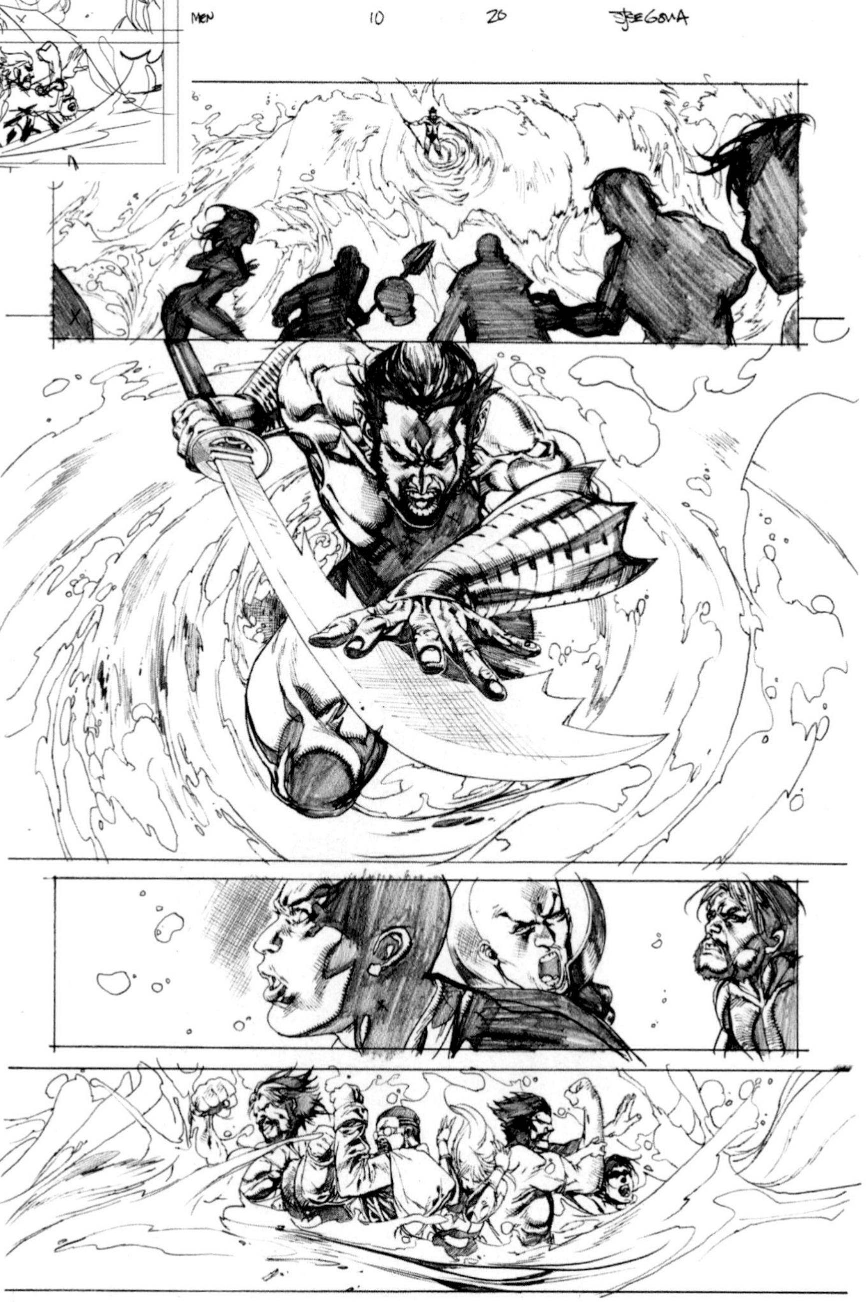

MEN
10
20

#10, PAGE 20 INKS BY DENNIS CRISOSTOMO

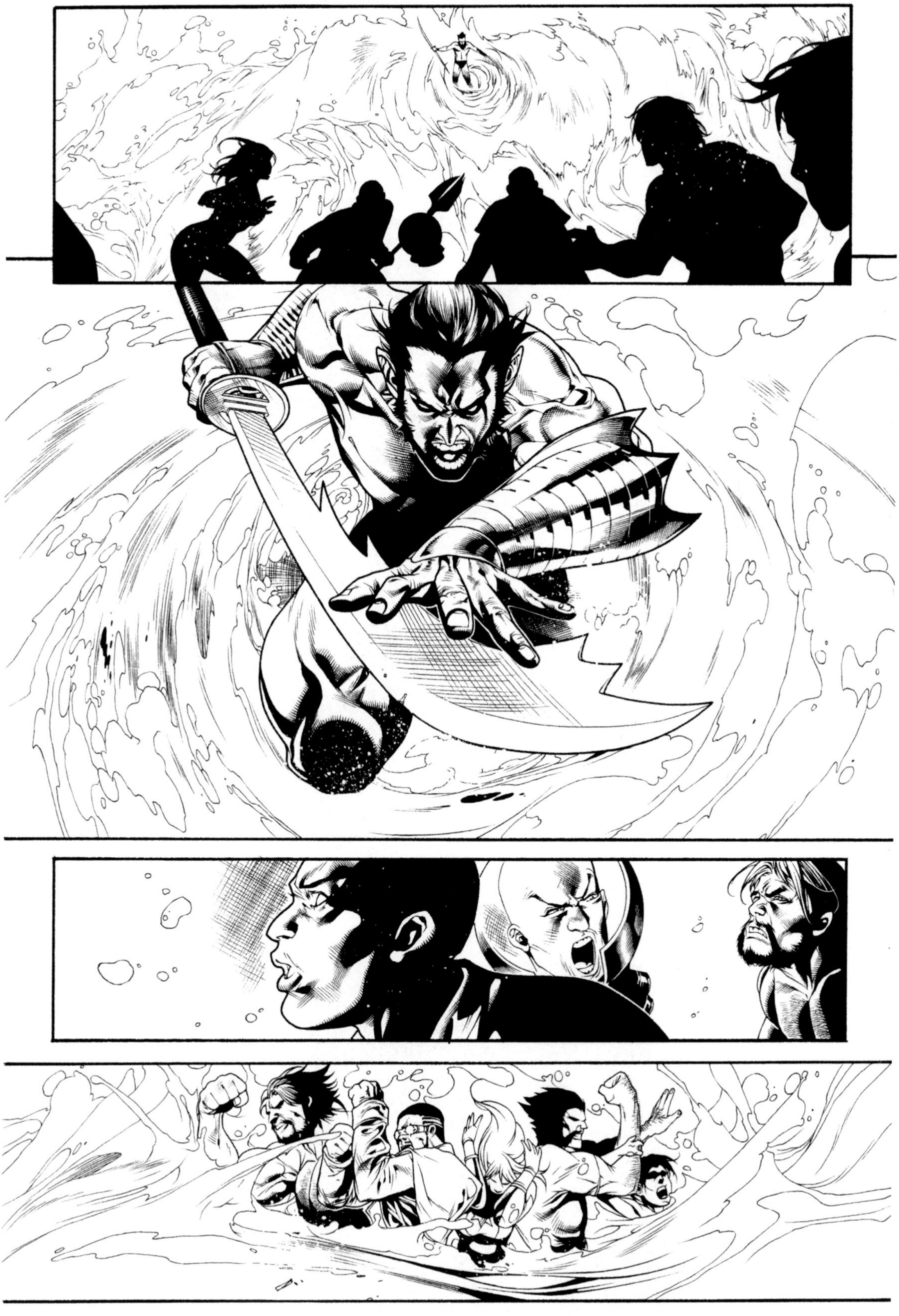

#7.1, PAGE 2 LAYOUT & PENCILS
BY ANDRÉ ARAÚJO

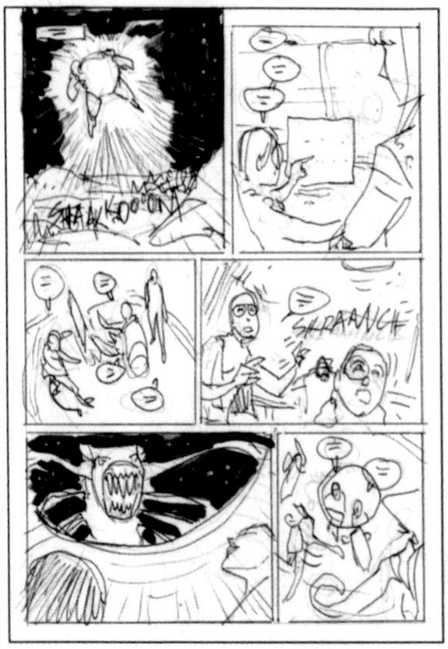
SKRAANCH

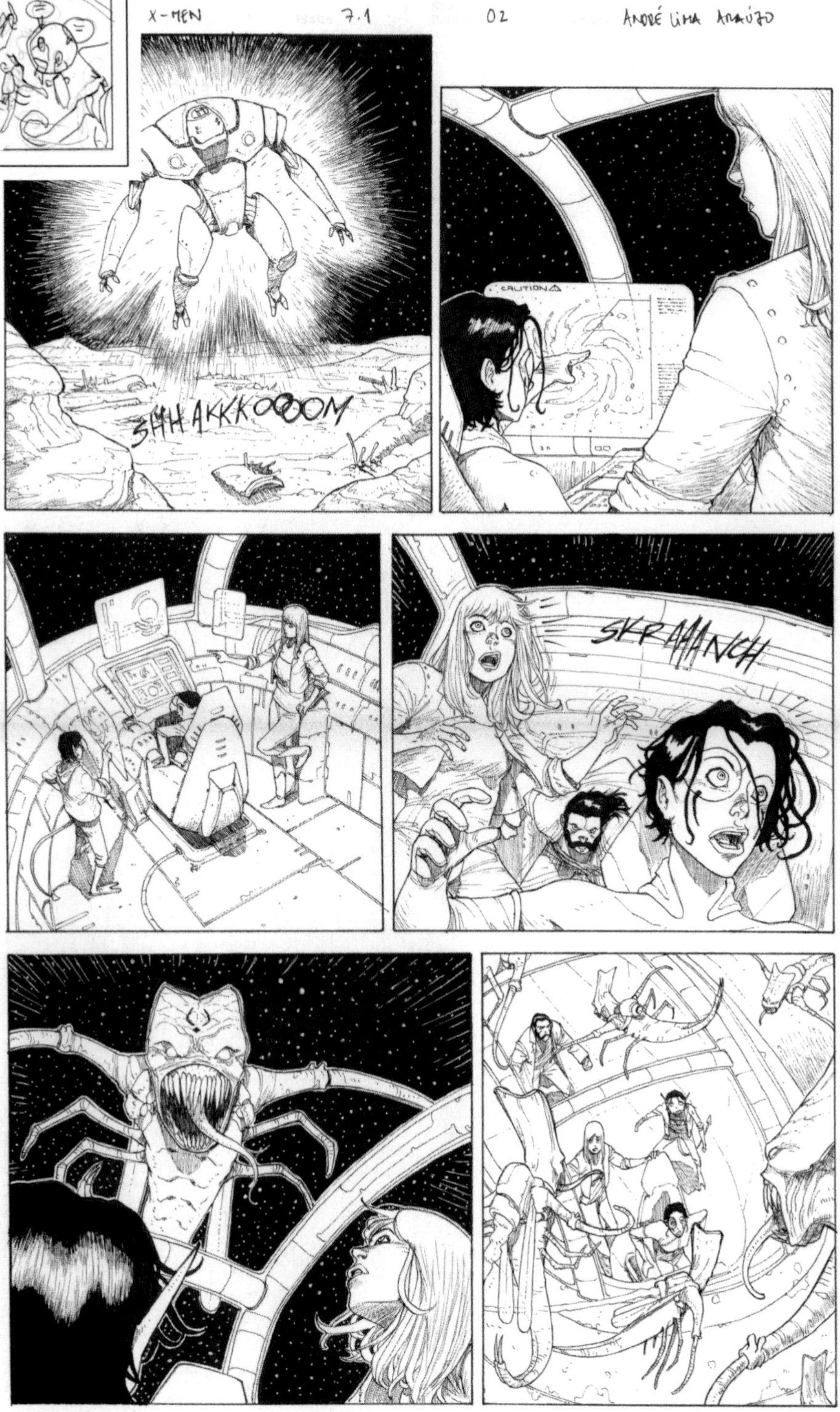
X-MEN
7.1
02
ANDRÉ LIMA ARAÚJO
CAUTION
SHHAKKOOOOM
SKRAAANCH